Cooperating out of poverty
The renaissance of the African cooperative movement

Patrick Develtere, Ignace Pollet & Fredrick Wanyama (eds.)

2008

International Labour Office
World Bank Institute

Acknowledgements and disclaimer

This book is the result of a study programme undertaken in 2006 funded by the UK Department for International Development (DFID) for the benefit of the African countries. The study programme Essential Research for a Cooperative Facility for Africa was initiated by the Cooperative Department of the International Labour Office and was coordinated by HIVA (Katholieke Universiteit Leuven, Belgium). The research team is grateful for the support it received for its work. We wish to thank J. Schwettmann, Guy Tchami and their colleagues at the ILO Cooperative Department for the tremendous effort in bringing together all parties concerned with this research. Much time has been devoted to this programme by hundreds of cooperative leaders and members, support agency personnel, government officials and staff of donor agencies. We wish to express our particular appreciation for the help, suggestions and reflections from the International Cooperative Alliance and its African offices. We would also like to thank Frannie Leautier at the World Bank Institute and Jose Manuel Salazar-Xirinachs at the ILO for prefacing this book. Finally, Joan Macdonald in Geneva and Gillian Lonergan and the UK Co-operative College in Manchester spent much time helping with the editorial work, for which we are very grateful.

The views expressed in this book, however, are the sole responsibility of the authors of respective chapters and do not necessarily represent or correspond with those of DFID, the ILO and its COOPAfrica programme or HIVA.

Cover pictures: © ILO - COOPAfrica

ILO/Patrick Develtere, Ignace Pollet, and Fredrick O. Wanyama
Cooperating out of Poverty
(Geneva), International Labour Office, 2008
ISBN 978-92-2-120722-1

Contents

Contents continued

Acronyms

This is a general list of acronyms and abbreviations. For country-specific acronyms, please see the relevant country studies in the book.

ACDI/VOCA .... Agricultural Cooperative Development International/ Volunteers in Overseas Cooperative Assistance

CBO .... Community Based Organization

CCA .... Canadian Cooperative Association

CGAP .... Consultative Group to Assist the Poor

DANIDA .... Danish International Development Agency

DGRV .... Deutschen Genossenschafts- und Raiffeisenverband

DFID .... Department for International Development

EU .... European Union

FAO .... United Nations Food and Agriculture Organization

GDP .... Gross Domestic Product

GNP .... Gross National Product

GTZ .... German Technical Co-operation

HIVA .... Higher Institute for Labour Studies (University of Leuven, Belgium)

ICA .... International Cooperative Alliance

ILO .... International Labour Office

LDC .... Least Developed Country

Acronyms continued

NGO . . . . Non-governmental organization

PRSP . . . . Poverty Reduction Strategic Paper

SACCO . . . . . . Saving and credit cooperative

SAP . . . . Structural Adjustment Programme

SCC . . . . Swedish Cooperative Centre

STEP . . . . Strategies and Tools against Social Exclusion and Poverty

SWOT . . . . (analysis) strengths, weaknesses, opportunities, threats

UNDP . . . . . . United Nations Development Programme

USAID . . . . . . United States Agency for International Development

WB . . . . World Bank

WOCCU . . . . . World Council of Credit Unions

Cooperative meeting, Côte d'Ivorie. © ILO: J. Maillard

Members of the Bukoba Women's Savings
and Credit Co-operative, Tanzania.
© Co-operative College: Cilla Ross

Member of the Kampala shoe shiners'
cooperative, Uganda.
© Stirling Smith

Participants at a student cooperative forum at the Lesotho Co-operative College.
© Co-operative College: Mervyn Wilson

Learners in a cooperative class at Wazalendo Secondary School, Moshi, Tanzania, a school started and supported by the local savings and credit cooperative.
© Co-operative College: Cilla Ross/Catherine Hughes

Foreword

Eradicating poverty in Sub-Saharan Africa continues to be the biggest challenge for the global community today. During the last 25 years, the number of poor has doubled from 150 million to 300 million, half the population surviving on $1 a day or less. According to the report of the Commission for Africa, "the continent needs successful African entrepreneurs and a strong and vibrant small enterprise sector to provide the innovation and productivity growth necessary for long-term poverty reduction".

Cooperatives are omnipresent on the African continent and represent a significant part of the private sector in most African countries. In a context of global effort led by the United Nations to reduce poverty the question is then to find out what potential does the cooperative form have in practice to contribute to the development process[1] and then to the set objective? In 1993, the World Bank acknowledged the development potential of cooperatives, provided they were restructured and disentangled from the state and run on business principles in line with the market economy[2]. Reports on their failure were abundant at that time especially because cooperatives were introduced in Africa as a foreign model specifically designed for colonial purposes. During that period, cooperatives in Africa were used by the colonial powers as a strategic tool to group rural producers into clusters, so that essential export commodities such as coffee, cocoa and cotton, could be collected more cost-effectively. After independence, the governments of the now sovereign States accorded an essential role to cooperatives, in particular for the development of rural areas. Cooperatives enjoyed preferential treatment and were granted supply and marketing monopolies which protected them from competition. They paid for these privileges with the total loss of autonomy, democratic control and business efficiency. Cooperatives degenerated into tools of government, or mass organizations of the ruling party. This was the situation in many African countries, when the era of structural adjustment began in the late 1980s. Structural adjustment resulted in the withdrawal of the State from economic and development functions, and the sudden liberalization of state-controlled cooperatives. The great majority of development partners promoted the concepts of liberalization, deregulation and privatization – in this context, cooperatives were considered an obsolete model. The disintegration of many state-controlled cooperative movements in the 1990s seemed to confirm this observation. But it was then that a *third* generation of African cooperatives appeared: authentic self-help organizations began emerging from the grassroots, being rooted in local communities, giving voice to local producers, and building strength in local economies.

This book contains many examples of successful, genuine and economically viable African cooperatives which create economic opportunities, provide a basic level of social protection and security, and provide their members with voice and representation. Commissioned by the Cooperative Branch of the International Labour Office, the Higher Institute for Labour Studies coordinated in 2005 a one-year research project funded by the UK Department for International Development. This project aimed at assessing the contribution and potential of cooperatives and group-based enterprises to create decent employment, economic activities, basic social protection and voice and representation in African economies including rural and informal sector.

In the first part, the book gives an overview of cooperative development in Africa up to the 1990s with the five different "traditions" that appeared under the various colonial administrations: a unified cooperative model, a social economy model, a social movement model, a producers' model and an indigenous model. Based on field research, this first part also offers the reader insights proving that cooperatives continue to play an important role in African economies. To illustrate this "Renaissance of African cooperatives", the second part provides the reader with eleven in-depth country studies carried out by academically qualified local researchers. Besides theses in-depth studies, the field research consisted of a rapid appraisal by "cooperative insiders" carried out by either the apex body or the government department in charge of cooperatives in sixteen African countries.

The task entrusted to the authors was not an easy one especially with the lack of recent literature and data surrounding this particular form of organization. This deficiency is one of the reasons explaining that the contribution of the cooperative model to poverty alleviation continues to go unrecognised by development policy makers. The case of Mwalimu Savings and Credit Cooperative Society of Kenya with accumulated savings of close to one hundred million US-$; the example of Mooriben in Niger which provides 25 000 households with affordable, nutritious food; and the UNICOOP cooperative in Cape Verde, the country's largest supplier of consumer goods, provide concrete evidence that demonstrate the potential of cooperatives in Africa. 150 000 collective socio-economic undertakings have been listed in the eleven-country sample, most of them registered as cooperatives. The study tells us that out of one hundred African households, seven belong to a cooperative-type organization. Many Africans are convinced that *cooperating out of poverty* is possible.

The book does not conceal the weaknesses and deficiencies of cooperatives in certain countries or sectors. Most notably is the insufficient capacity of cooperatives to defend the interests of their members vis-à-vis governments, donors and other social and political actors. This calls for greater horizontal and vertical integration of primary cooperatives.

We are convinced that this book will contribute to boosting the "Renaissance of the African Cooperatives", thus supporting the global fight against poverty. The World Bank Institute and the International Labour Office are grateful to the authors for having taken up this challenge.

Jose M. Salazar-Xirinachs
Executive Director
Employment Sector
International Labour Office

Frannie A. Léautier
Vice President
World Bank Institute
The World Bank

---

[1] Birchall J. (2003), Rediscovering the cooperative advantage, Geneva, ILO.

[2] Hussi, P., Murphy, J., Lindberg, O. and Brenneman, L. (1993), *The Development of Cooperatives and Other Rural Organizations: The Role of the World Bank*, The World Bank, Washington, D.C.; Porvali, H. ed. (1993), *The Development Of Cooperatives*, Agriculture and Rural Development Series No. 8, The World Bank, Washington, D.C.

A market in Dar-es-Salaam, Tanzania. Loans from a savings and credit cooperative help women to develop viable businesses including cooking for market traders and selling vegetables.
© Stirling Smith

Introduction

Patrick Develtere[1], Ignace Pollet[2] & Fredrick Wanyama[3]

The history of cooperative development in Africa has resulted into two popular, but very contradictory conclusions. On the one hand, there is the view that cooperatives in Africa have failed to live up to the challenges of developing the continent. That they ceased to be development agents when they were hijacked by governments and other state agencies. As government instruments, they do not resonate with the local culture and have subsequently performed poorly as evidenced by the many malfunctioning cooperatives. On the other hand, there is the opinion that cooperative entrepreneurship is the way forward for African development. Those who hold this view have maintained that cooperatives as private enterprises do also fit very well with communal cultures in Africa. That this combination of business enterprises (for the mobilization of resources) with the concern for communal welfare has seen many cooperatives help poor people out of poverty and create wealth in their communities.

This research project was set up to help disentangle these contradictory perceptions that have continuously preoccupied many people, including cooperative members and leaders as well as government and donor agencies. The central objective of the study was thus to make an objective analysis of the state of affairs of the cooperative sector in Africa since the liberalization of the economy in the early 1990s. We know that the cooperative sector is very heterogeneous, that the continent is vast and that the problem is extremely complex. We also know that very little is known about the cooperative sector, particularly in the said period; that it is very data-deficient and that not much scientific research has been done before. We therefore had to make a number of critical choices on how to proceed with this delicate exercise.

We decided that we did not want to lose a historical perspective in favour of a more prospective one. Cooperatives in every African country were introduced many decades ago. The colonial and post-colonial phases they went through have definitely left their mark on the way people look at cooperatives, the way cooperatives operate, and the way external patrons such as governments and the donor community relate with them. This is what economists and other social scientists call "path dependency". To get a grasp of this historical burden, we first studied the cooperative traditions on the continent from the existing literature. We discovered indeed a unified cooperative tradition, a social movement tradition, a social economy tradition and an indigenous model. These traditions cut across countries and linguistic frontiers, but are to some extent related to the colonial roots of cooperative development in Africa. Five researchers who are very familiar with these traditions, therefore, produced background papers on them. They have been extremely useful for the writing of the first chapter in this book.

Secondly, we decided to take a birds' eye view of the cooperative panorama in Africa using the rapid appraisal methodology. To get as many perspectives as possible, we worked with 16 cooperative experts in 16 African countries who did an appraisal of the cooperative sector in their respective countries. These experts, in most cases, are themselves involved in cooperative institutions such as government departments for cooperatives, cooperative apex bodies or cooperative colleges. Through their lenses, we learned that the cooperative sector is still very much alive and kicking, fraught with many problems and obstacles, but showing signs of rejuvenation and rapid expansion in some fields.

With these insights, we sought to have more assurance on the reliability of the available data and documentation, knowing that many registered cooperatives are dormant and realizing that many cooperatives do not seek registration or seek refuge in other legal or *de facto* forms of organizations. Amongst others, we discovered that the social economy tradition, which has its roots in Francophone countries with its many pre-cooperative, mutual help and mutual support organizations other than cooperatives, was making inroads in other countries as well. We thus chose to have in-depth studies executed in 11 countries by professional researchers in the latter part of 2005. The studies helped to grasp more precisely the extent of the cooperative sector, but also to understand the way it was integrated and structured. In addition, the studies shed light on the major strengths and weaknesses of the cooperative sector and its many constituent parts. Intrigued by the reasons for the vibrancy or failure of cooperative undertakings, each national study also looked more closely at the operations of a selected number of relatively more successful and the less successful cooperative ventures. A total of 27 case studies were generated through this exercise.

As already noted above, the cooperative movement in Africa is heterogeneous and complex, such that a single study may not be able to cover all its activities. This is particularly the case because all genuine cooperatives have their own agenda and also write their own scripts. In addition to this, we also know that cooperatives, just like other popular institutions operating in a development context, are continuously bombarded with new challenges, fashions and programme objectives that originate from governmental and donor arenas. Ultimately, there can be so much to cover that a single study may not execute effectively. We, therefore, had to draw some limitations. We selected four themes that are at present (among many others) high on the development agenda for Africa, namely employment creation, poverty reduction, social protection and voice and representation. For practical, of course not ideological, reasons other topical subjects such as environmental protection and gender were not retained. For each of the selected themes we wanted to know how cooperatives were contributing and performing in the eleven selected countries, as well as to understand the extent to which these concerns are also shared and perceived by the cooperative members and leaders. So in each national study contained in the subsequent chapters of this book, a more general picture of the cooperative sector will be followed by a look at these four issues.

Whereas part one of the book discusses the various traditions of the African cooperative movement and gives an overall view of the findings of the study, the second part of the book presents the findings of the eleven country studies. Taking the historical perspective as well as the overall analysis of the state of affairs of cooperatives in the 16 countries from which data were gathered, the researchers concluded during a three-day workshop in Addis Ababa, Ethiopia that we are witnessing a renaissance of the cooperative sector in Africa. Cooperatives can work in Africa and work for Africa. Cooperatives have gone through a lot of upheavals in the past; but at present they represent a significant number of people, of which the majority is poor. Their cooperative, however strong or weak it might be, is more often than not the only institution they can rely on to protect themselves against the hard conditions of the market and society. Cooperating out of poverty is the only perspective they see. Nevertheless, the movement is currently very fragmented and dispersed. Its visibility is very low and the voices of this silent group are not heard very much by the national and international élite. We hope that this book can somehow remedy this.

---

[1] Patrick Develtere holds a PhD from the Katholieke University of Leuven, Belgium. He has been studying cooperatives and other civil society organizations in Europe, Africa, Asia and Latin America for more than 20 years. He is the director of the Research Group on Sustainable Development and Development Cooperation as well as of the Research Group on Civil Society and Social Economy of the Higher Institute for Labour Studies (HIVA) at the Katholieke University of Leuven. He has published several books and articles on cooperatives, the social economy and development.

[2] Ignace Pollet is a senior researcher of the Higher Institute for Labour Studies at the Katholieke University of Leuven. As an organization specialist, he has a track record in research on different types of popular organizations as well as enterprises in both Belgium and developing countries.

[3] Fredrick O. Wanyama holds a PhD in Political Science from Maseno University, Kenya and is a Senior Lecturer in the School of Development and Strategic Studies at the same university. Specializing in local organizations and politics in the African development process, he has contributed many chapters and articles to academic edited books and refereed journals. He is a recipient of fellowships from distinguished bodies like CODESRIA, DAAD, the Five College African Scholars Program, Amherst, Massachusetts, USA and HIVA at the Katholieke University of Leuven, Belgium.

Mohair weaving at Lesotho Handicrafts Co-operative headquarters in Maseru.
© Co-operative College: Mervyn Wilson

Members of the Amizero Women's Association in Kigali, Rwanda, are making their living out of recycling household waste. © Stirling Smith

Celebrations at a savings and credit cooperative in Eastern Uganda.
© Stirling Smith

Members of a worker co-operative caring for HIV/AIDS sufferers in South Africa.
© Canadian Co-operative Association: Peter Wilson

Executive Summary

Though cooperatives in Africa have their origins in foreign models that were largely designed to achieve exterior motives, they have become one of the main forms of popular economic and social organization for the alleviation of poverty. Their functioning over the decades has, however, been influenced by at least five different models that are mainly, but not exclusively, traced to the colonial traditions on the continent. These are a unified cooperative model; a social economy model; a social movement model; a producers' model; and an indigenous model. Regardless of their different orientations, all these models had, by the early 1990s, conditioned virtually all cooperatives to emerge as dependent agents or clients of the state and other semi-public agencies in many countries. They hardly operated as private business enterprises that are primarily driven by the interests of their members. Most of the studies on African cooperatives up to the 1990s subsequently concluded that they were performing poorly partly due to this dependent relationship with the state that undermined their operation as business enterprises.

The advent of the liberalization of the economy in the early 1990s was, therefore, expected to give co-operators the chance to become the real owners of their cooperative businesses and turnaround the performance of their business enterprises. However, the impact of the liberalization measures on African cooperatives is little known. One hardly comes across comprehensive accounts that inform the current status and functioning of the cooperative movement in any country on the continent since the early 1990s. The main motivation of this study was, therefore, to show the state of affairs of the cooperative sector in Africa in this period by indicating the presence and growth of cooperatives as well as their contribution to employment creation, social protection, voice and representation and, ultimately, poverty reduction.

With field accounts from sixteen African countries, this study demonstrates that cooperatives have not withered away with the liberalization measures, for they continue to play an important role in the economy. Approximately seven per cent of the African population reportedly belongs to a cooperative, though some countries like Egypt, Senegal, Ghana, Kenya and Rwanda report a higher penetration rate of over ten per cent. In some countries, the number and membership of cooperatives have significantly increased since the early 1990s, following the revitalization of the previously underperforming cooperatives and the emergence of new ones. We are confident that there are about 150,000 cooperative or cooperative-type organizations in the countries under review. With regard to size, there are both large and small cooperatives; the former are mainly found in "traditional" cooperative sectors like credit and agriculture while the latter are organized around the relatively new cooperative activities like handicraft, distribution, manufacturing and social services. For instance, one of the largest cooperatives in Africa in terms of membership is Harambee Savings and Credit Cooperative Society in Kenya with 84,920 members, but Mwalimu Savings and Credit Cooperative Society in the same country, with a membership of 44,400, probably has one of the highest annual turnover of Kshs. 711,562,812 (US$. 98,828,816). Small cooperatives can also be viable. A good example is the Rooibos Tea Cooperative in South Africa that has only 36 members, but with an annual turnover of 1,250,000 South African Rands (US$. 198,413).

This era of "cooperative freedom" has also witnessed a renewal in the integration of the sector as the previously state-imposed and non-viable federations as well as apex bodies have been rendered redundant and alternative voluntary, autonomous, strategic and more viable consensual cooperative networks based on members' needs in the unfolding new socio-economic environment are being formed. Indeed, the emerging networks are increasingly eroding the unified cooperative model that was very common in the Anglophone countries. There are indications that the sector is drifting towards the social economy model, which had been well-established in the Francophone countries, that blends cooperatives and other group-based organizations along socio-economic motives. With cooperatives turning away from being used as instruments of the state to their ideal form of being autonomous group-based democratically controlled enterprises, there is a momentum towards the renaissance of cooperatives in Africa.

The loss of the monopoly status, coupled with the business-oriented demands of the market, is increasingly seeing cooperatives redesign their activities competitively. For instance, though agricultural activities remain predominant, those that are no longer profitable are being abandoned in favour of others that are more viable on the market. This partly explains, for example, why the continent is witnessing substantial growth of savings and credit cooperatives. The main reason is the high demand for financial services on the market and the profit that results from such transactions. Furthermore, some cooperatives are steadily shifting from being unifunctional to take on other activities as demanded by the members as well as the market. For instance, hitherto agricultural cooperatives are diversifying their activities by also venturing into the fields of savings and credit as is the case in Ghana, Egypt and Kenya. To this end, cooperative ventures in Africa are increasingly becoming market-driven and responsive to changing circumstances. With a few exceptions resulting from the poor or inadequate preparation of cooperatives for the competitive market, liberalization has served well the interests of cooperative development on the continent. This is evidenced by the fact that those cooperatives that have adapted to the new environment have come out stronger than they were before the liberalization of the sector.

Whereas past studies correctly indicated that excessive donor funding of activities that had been imposed on cooperatives had significantly contributed to the poor performance of these organizations, the evidence in this study is that successful cooperatives in the new era have enjoyed some structured collaboration and partnership with external actors. Such partners have collaborated with cooperatives in the provision of low-interest credit for capital-intensive investments; marketing of cooperative produce, particularly through fair trade arrangements; facilitating the creation of suitable legal and policy environment for cooperative enterprises; and facilitating educational and training programmes in cooperatives, among others. It is thus apparent that donor support to cooperatives is positive particularly when cooperators are involved in making the decision on what kind of support they require before it is provided. Indeed, the evidence from some countries suggests that lack of such structured support had adversely affected the ability of cooperatives to effectively compete with private enterprises that are financially stronger on the market. The success of African cooperatives, therefore, requires both local and international consultative networking to provide supplementary support services that would enable them to even out with the relatively stronger private competitors.

The study shows that the success of cooperative enterprises in Africa can significantly contribute to poverty alleviation in a number of ways. For instance, it has been demonstrated that cooperatives create employment and income-earning opportunities that enable members to pay school fees, build houses, invest in business and farming, and meet other family expenses. They also create solidarity mechanisms to re-enforce the traditional social security system, which is largely undeveloped, by setting up schemes to cater for expenses related to education, illness, death and other unexpected socio-economic problems. And by integrating the poor and the relatively well-off in the same income-generating opportunities, cooperatives also make a contribution to the reduction of exclusion and inequality. This study has, therefore, succeeded in unveiling the African cooperative sector since the liberalization of the economy in the early 1990s. It is apparent that the cooperative sector is present, but relatively silent and, to a certain extent, timid due to the absence of vertical structures to articulate its interests and show its presence. Perhaps it is this lack of a voice that has seen governments, donors and even researchers by-pass the sector; thereby denying it the very much needed visibility on the development scene. We hope that this study makes a case for the visibility of the cooperative movement on the continent.

Stone breaking was the principal activity for women in the quarries of Mtongani, Tanzania before the establishment of the mushroom and hen house cooperative © ILO: M. Crozet

Wamumo Enterprises & Commercial Services worker cooperative, near Nairobi, Kenya.
© Stirling Smith

Kuapa Kokoo meeting at a village near Kumasi in Ghana. © Stirling Smith

Chapter One – Cooperative Development in Africa up to the 1990s

by Patrick Develtere

The dictum goes that there is never a fresh start for anything. This is certainly true for the cooperative sector in Africa. With a resurgence of interest in cooperative enterprises among grassroots groups, government agencies and even donors, we notice that old cooperatives are being revived while new ones are being created at a rapid pace. But all parties involved are operating in an environment that is to a large extent culturally and institutionally influenced by past developments. The actors involved, as motivated as they might be to start anew or to avoid past mistakes, do not have unlimited room for manoeuvre since they are conditioned by past experiences, cultural habits and patterns, established relations as well as legal and institutional frameworks. So, history matters. While the objective of this book is to accurately describe the "state of the art" of cooperative action in Africa and to identify new and promising trajectories, we have to be conscious of the sensitive dependence of actors and policy-makers on initial, previous and prevalent conditions. It is for this reason that we have to delve into these historical conditions of the African cooperative sector using the background studies produced by Charles Kabuga (2005), Ada Souleymane Kibora (2005), Jan Theron (2005), Manuel Canaveira de Campos (2005) and Patrick Develtere (2005).

Why the cooperative traditions?

The reasons we attach such importance to the study of the traditions and past trajectories in cooperative development in Africa are twofold. First, the cooperative model in Africa is an inherited one; and second, the cooperative sector carries along a heavy legacy that conditions its path.

With regard to the first, the cooperative sector in Africa was introduced by external agencies, notably colonial authorities. Cooperatives were therefore often received as alien institutions. This was the case in all but a few territories. The British, French, Portuguese, Spanish, Germans and Belgians brought to their respective colonies their vision of cooperatives. Along with their view on the role of cooperatives in a colonial environment, they introduced mechanisms that would foster cooperative development, including legal frameworks, promotional schemes and funding systems. These colonial efforts set the tone for cooperative development in Africa. The cooperative sector thus did not emerge as a home-grown or spontaneous movement but rather as the result of colonial social and economic engineering. Hence, right from the beginning the cooperative sector in these territories had little or no links with existing pre-colonial, "traditional" or endogenous transaction systems in the realm of solidarity or economy. This was in spite of the fact that in all countries such systems did and do exist. An abundant literature shows that systems such as *idir* in Ethiopia, *tontines* in Cameroon and elsewhere in West Africa, *stokvels* in South Africa, work-sharing groups and burial societies in most countries have always involved large parts of the population. Unlike modern forms of cooperation and mutualism, these endogenous systems do not have built-in mechanisms for expansion or growth and are – in most cases – mobilized on an *ad hoc* or accidental basis. It is also remarkable that in countries that have not known extended periods of colonialism or any colonial rule at all, such as Ethiopia or Liberia, "modern co-operativism" has not evolved out of these home-rooted systems. In these countries, such co-operativism is the result of deliberate policy-making by state authorities that tapped into and borrowed from international experiences in cooperative development. We now know that "modern" cooperative ventures best thrive when the norms and values they rely on are congruent with those inherent in pre-existing or parallel systems (even if institutionally they are not congruent or linked). It is therefore of prime importance to understand how cooperatives were introduced, what cooperative philosophy was construed and how this related to cooperative behaviour, both social and economic, that existed in the region.

Secondly, cooperative development is much affected by what economists and other social scientists call "path dependency". Antecedent conditions and past choices or decisions determine the route that cooperative development takes. Institutions persist and are hard to get rid of even when they are recognized as being anachronistic or, worse, when they impede new choices or decisions. This is clear, for example, when we see how much cooperative development has been tied to the export crop strategy of authorities rather than to the marketing strategies of members. This, originally, was a deliberate choice by colonial agencies that saw cooperatives as mere instruments for their produce export strategy. Cooperatives had to help organize small and big farmers involved in the production of coffee, cocoa, bananas, cotton or other export crops and handled quality control, post-harvest treatment, transport and export in the name of colonial state authorities. Post-independence governments did not alter this, but rather generalized and reinforced this cooperative-export nexus by making agricultural cooperatives sub-contractors, executive agents or affiliates of the more powerful marketing boards. Another example of path-dependency is the specific government-cooperatives rapport that was established in most colonies. It made the government the prime patron of the cooperatives, contrary to the internationally accepted view that cooperatives are primarily membership, voluntary and autonomous organizations. Cooperative practitioners and policy-makers in Africa know very well how much government tutelage still stifles private cooperative initiative and innovation. The cooperative culture, with its own discourse, jargon and habits that characterize cooperative movements or sectors in a specific country, is also to a large extent tributary to a cooperative trajectory that started some decades ago. Studying these traditions helps us to understand why people in some countries sing a cooperative anthem at the end of each annual general meeting, while in other countries they will start with a prayer. Some countries will have a legalist cooperative culture, others will be more pragmatist. In some places cooperatives will be a masculine affair, while in others cooperatives will be one of those few places where feminine participation, but also feminine values, will be appreciated. In some regions cooperatives are seen and exhibit themselves as poor-men (or working-men) clubs with primarily social functions while in others cooperatives are presented as social and economic instruments of an entrepreneurial class. Thus, cooperative cultures are path-dependent.

Similarly, cooperative structures and networks are path-dependent. The cooperative sector consists of primary societies, secondary societies, federations, apex bodies, cooperative promotion agencies, cooperative training institutions *et cetera*. Cooperatives relate to government agencies, and are integrated or liaise with supranational or international bodies that may be cooperative or otherwise. This structural component of the cooperative sector is also to a great extent dependent on its historical trajectory and the many interactions with national and international agents that were involved in constructing the sector or movement.

While we admit that history matters a lot, we do not infer that cooperatives and cooperative sectors are fully and indefinitely locked into a certain stalemate tradition. If that had been the case, there would not be much variance and change. On the contrary, we see that the cooperative trajectories have changed over time and are indeed place-specific. They are neither linear nor irreversible, but amendable. People and their cooperatives are creative agents; they can see the parameters of the cooperative tradition they are part of, they can identify its traps and opt for piecemeal modifications or radical transformations.

Five cooperative traditions in Africa

It is tempting to trace the cooperative traditions to the colonial origins or experiences in Africa. In that manner we would simply have the British cooperative tradition, the French cooperative tradition, the Belgian cooperative tradition and the Portuguese cooperative tradition. This is particularly the case because these four colonial powers did, in different ways, introduce modern cooperation in their former colonies. As a matter of fact, it is not difficult to discover similarities in the cooperative systems in Kenya and Ghana, both former British colonies, much as it is relatively easy to compare Senegalese and Togolese cooperative experiences that originate from French colonialism.

Nevertheless, there are at least four good reasons why we should abandon this colonial traditions approach in the study of African cooperatives. For one, while it is true that colonial authorities directed the development of the cooperative sector in their territories, they did not do this in the same way in each of their colonies. Secondly, the reception of the cooperative model differed much from place to place. Thirdly, taking the colonial roots or sources of a model as the major references makes one believe that these are simply colonial prolongations of tested systems in the home country. But, as we will see, the colonial cooperative promoters did not believe that the cooperative experience from their own country could be easily repeated in the colonies. And, finally, the cooperative scenery has changed dramatically since the first cooperatives were introduced in Africa. Referring to the colonial traditions does not help us envision these changes.

We, therefore, suggest five traditions using a systemic characterization scheme to determine cooperative identity. The characteristics in this scheme can have colonial origins, but this is not necessarily true. If they originated in the colonial period, that does not mean they are "genetically" rooted or fixed patterns. These characteristics can be more or less evident and are not invariable.

Accordingly, we identify a unified model tradition, a social economy tradition, a social movement tradition, a producers' tradition and a sui generis tradition. We, however, hasten to point out that cooperative sectors in the African countries can tap from several of these traditions at the same time. As such, each cooperative sector is a unique configuration referring to one or more traditions and moulded by different players at different times.

The *unified model* tradition can indeed be traced back to the British attempt, both at home and abroad in the colonies, to develop a single cooperative movement. To that effect the protagonists of this kind of model suggest a multi-stage system with primary cooperatives at the bottom and a single apex body at the top. In between are secondary societies in the form of regional chapters, federations and unions that provide for the horizontal and vertical integration of the movement. The common denominator in this model is the legal form of cooperatives.

In the *social economy* tradition, which made strong inroads in many Francophone and Hispanic countries, a cooperative is just one of the many legal or institutional entities that bring together people sharing the same social and economic objectives. Mutual societies, associations, foundations and trusts are related forms and can perform the same functions. In this tradition, it is the social and economic objectives that are shared by the parties involved; not the virtues of a cooperative model.

The *social movement* tradition differs from both the unified model and the social economy tradition. In the social movement tradition, an interest group or established social organization such as a trade union, a women's association or a farmer's organization plays the pivotal role in bringing members together into a cooperative. The cooperative is an instrument, among many others, of collective action. The Belgian system of co-operation is very much embedded in this tradition and has influenced cooperative thinking and practice in Central Africa.

In the *producers' tradition*, cooperatives are seen as economic vehicles for agricultural producers. Thus, cooperatives are functional instruments of individual rural entrepreneurs or households helping them to procure quality consumables and to market their produce. The economic role of the cooperative, in this tradition, is seen as a stepping stone towards achieving the social objectives. This tradition is very well rooted in the Portuguese cooperative system and inspired the Portuguese colonial cooperative development strategy in Africa.

While all four traditions reviewed so far have been brought to the African continent by external – colonial – agencies, they have never fully covered the cooperative panorama in Africa. There remains room for the fifth cooperative tradition that we have labelled as *sui generis*, meaning self-generated or home-bred tradition. This is certainly the case in countries that were only to a limited extent exposed to colonialism such as Ethiopia, Sierra Leone, Liberia, or Egypt. In these countries modern cooperation was initiated by local agents who experimented with a blend of borrowed ideas and local adaptations to respond to socio-economic problems.

The kick-off

As may be clear from the foregoing, cooperatives came to the continent mainly through social and economic engineering by external agents. The question that arises is what conditions triggered the engineering of cooperatives by these agents? They seem to differ from one region to another and from one colonizer to another.

Towards a "one size fits all" cooperative in British colonies

For the Anglophone territories in Africa, Kabuga (2005) rightly asserts that cooperatives would neither have emerged at the time they did nor in the manner they did had it not been for the cash crops that were introduced by the British. The rapid development of these export crops came to be dominated by a few powerful and strongly established family firms of Asians and Europeans. Through middlemen, these firms bought, processed and then exported the crops. The role of the farmers was merely to produce the crops for which they were paid peanuts by these middlemen. In many ways, cooperatives started in Anglophone Africa as a protest against the disadvantageous terms of trade imposed on the peasants by the said middlemen. For example, in Uganda, as early as 1913, some farmers decided to market their crops cooperatively and were later followed by other associations of growers. In 1920, five groups of farmers formed the "Buganda Growers Association" that later became "The Uganda Growers

Cooperative Society". Its main aim was to market cotton and to present members' views to the government.

Similarly, the Kilimanjaro Native Farmers Association in Tanganyika (Tanzania) was formed in 1925 as the first ever indigenous association of African coffee farmers. They were struggling against the monopoly over the crop by European settlers.

In Ghana, cocoa was the crucial base for state revenue. By the 1920s, Ghanaians had discovered the advantages of pooling efforts to negotiate land rights and to share the burden of tending young cocoa trees. But European firms controlled the export trade. These firms, seeking to forcibly enlarge their share of the proceeds in cocoa exports, formed a secret buying combine whereby 14 of them dealing in cocoa would control prices paid to African brokers. This "price-rigging" scheme leaked out to cooperative groups, which played a leading role in the "cocoa hold-up" where farmers withheld their cocoa from the market to force a rise in prices. Organized groups like these were loathed by the British colonial administration because they presented a strong challenge to the political and economic status quo. This explains why the cooperative groups in Ghana and other Anglophone countries were initially denied legal backing.

Liberal colonial officers in Africa took inspiration from the British-Indian Pattern of Cooperation that had been developed in India and Ceylon (Sri Lanka) from 1904 onwards. The basic idea of the scheme was, as Münkner (1989: 103) observed, "to create autonomous, self-reliant cooperatives in the long run, but to generate the lacking initiative and technical know-how of the local population by the services of officials of a specialized government agency (Cooperative Department), headed by the Registrar". In the nineteen thirties and forties, Cooperative Societies Ordinances were enacted in much of colonial Anglophone Africa and Departments of Cooperative Development established. Thus, a cooperative tradition of constructive, non-antagonistic cooperation and "a one size fits all" was institutionalized. The Departments were to create, promote and advise cooperatives to run their affairs on internationally accepted cooperative principles. Registrars of Cooperatives were equipped with extended functions, discretionary powers and a sizeable staff of assistant registrars, auditors, accountants, and supervisors, which went well beyond those of the British Registrar of Friendly Societies at that time.

From semi-public cooperatives to mutual societies in the French colonies

Unlike Britain, France opted for direct intervention in the organization and administration of local structures in Africa. In Algeria, for example, the colonial authorities set up cereal banks among local communities to prevent food shortages and hunger as far back as 1875. A law of 1893 set the framework for the "Sociétés Indigènes de Prévoyance, de Secours et de Prêts Mutuels (SIP)". The experience with those "Native Provident Societies" in Algeria, Tunisia and Indochina inspired the imperial government to pass a decree in 1910 prescribing the establishment of provident societies in French West Africa. These native provident societies had a variety of tasks, notably to keep a stock of selected goods; to supply farm implements; to process agricultural produce; to serve as insurance against disaster and accidents; to grant loans; and to improve production methods. While the original idea was to encourage the traditional and spontaneous provident experiences through a modern cooperative and voluntary framework, the French authorities soon gave systematic and compulsory character to these initiatives. These semi-public institutions had a territorial base that went far beyond the village level. Their management was assured by colonial public servants.

After World War II, autonomous cooperative societies that ran parallel to these provident institutions were made possible by the extension of French cooperative legislation to the overseas territories. However, contrary to the British, the French did not intervene in the promotion and supervision of these cooperatives. Only when the emergent cooperative movement started to show political muscle did they shift gears by blocking the incipient integration of the movement and by getting involved in the daily operations of the cooperatives. Although many governmental and semi-governmental agencies got involved in cooperative development, this never resulted in a comprehensive cooperative strategy comparable to the British one. The French mainly relied on the methodology of "animation rurale" (rural animation) in the organization of cooperatives. It was a way of orchestrating the involvement of the peasantry in centrally designed agricultural plans. With the transformation of the provident societies into *Sociétés Mutuelles de Production Rurale* (Mutual Societies for Rural Production) and later into *Sociétés Mutuelles de Développement Rural* (Mutual Societies for Rural Development), the French made clear that their final objective was rural development and that cooperatives were not the only favoured legal institutional form.

The dual cooperative road in Belgian Central Africa

In the Belgian Congo as well as in the territory then known as Rwanda-Urundi, indigenous people were allowed to set up their own cooperatives from the 1920s onwards. The frame of reference was the very liberal Belgian metropolitan cooperative legislation that opened the door for semi-public enterprises called cooperatives in the colonies, which were to generate income for the established tribal administrative structures and produce additional benefits for the local population. This hybrid system resembled the (public) municipal cooperative companies that had been set up in Belgium (Lambert, 1963). In Central Africa, these cooperatives were involved in a wide variety of activities such as dairy, construction and the so-called tribal industries (pottery, oil pressing, and tanning). Because many of these public cooperative enterprises got caught in commercial battles with private European entrepreneurs, this system had to be reviewed in the 1940s. After World War II the Belgian colonial authorities started to promote indigenous cooperatives as vehicles for their social and educational policy as well as for their agricultural policy. Special cooperative departments were created within the national and the provincial authorities. The provincial governors were directly involved in the cooperative development strategy. They had to register new cooperatives and fix the prices that cooperatives were to pay their members for the produce. Characteristic of the paternalist approach of the Belgians, the governors also had to appoint the educational committees and the advisors to the cooperatives. Two participants of these four-member committees had to have Belgian nationality. The governor also appointed a "contrôleur" who was responsible for financial inspection and had the right of veto. Management was appointed by the district commissioner.

But the rather liberal legal framework and the original laissez-faire policy of the Belgian authorities at home also created scope for local actors in the colonies. Catholic missionaries, many of whom originated from families closely involved in the cooperatives of the catholic workers' and farmers' movements in Belgium, set up credit or savings cooperatives in the colonies. In other instances, indigenous cooperatives that got in trouble with colonial authorities because of their competition with Belgian businessmen received backing and support from the missionaries. When problems persisted and colonial authorities refused to recognize local cooperative societies or unions, missionaries and indigenous co-operators turned to pre-cooperatives, professional associations or unions to continue their endeavour.

Producer cooperatives in a corporative jacket in Lusophone Africa

The Portuguese-speaking countries in Africa – Angola, Cape Verde, Guinée-Bissau, Mozambique, Sao Tomé e Principe – only became independent in 1975. Until then, they were Portuguese colonies with separate administrative systems. Though the legal framework for cooperative development in Portugal and these colonies was created through the enabling legislation of 1888, the political regime in Portugal from 1928 to 1974 was not favourable for cooperative development as it negated the basic principles and values that underpin the latter namely, freedom of association; democracy; and autonomy. Portugal was a corporativist state with an economic and social structure that was appended to state-based corporations; thereby subordinating all civil society organizations, including cooperatives. Consequently, cooperative legislation was very restrictive and foresaw a heavy intervention of the state.

In Africa, particularly in Angola and Mozambique, agricultural cooperatives were merely functional appendages of rural extension work of semi-public agencies such as the Coffee Institute of Angola or the Cotton Institute of Mozambique. Because of state interventionism and quasi-monopoly, only big agricultural firms were able to set up viable cooperatives and associations. Such cooperatives were involved in export marketing of crops such as coffee, cotton and bananas or service delivery such as decortication of coffee, threshing of cotton or credit provision.

Home-grown cooperatives

It has already been pointed out that not all territories in Africa had colonial antecedents that sowed the seeds for a specific approach to cooperative development. Nevertheless, this does not mean that those places had to await the great independence movements that Africa has known to experiment with modern forms of cooperation.

In South Africa, for example, the cooperative tradition dates back to the 1920s when the first cooperative legislation was introduced. It distinguished between agricultural cooperatives and trading cooperatives, and this has remained a feature of the cooperative landscape since then. Jan Theron (2005) sees at least four separate sources of cooperative development in South Africa. Firstly, agricultural cooperatives benefited from a suite of measures aimed at promoting "white" farming. This included the establishment of agricultural marketing boards, on which white farmers were well represented, and which controlled the price at which a range of different agricultural products were marketed.

Secondly, the Afrikaner nationalist movement also promoted cooperatives as an appropriate mechanism for empowering poor Afrikaners, including small farmers displaced by the growth of commercial agriculture, particularly in the 1930s and 1940s.

By the 1980s two new cooperative traditions were emerging. One was agricultural cooperatives in the so-called homelands, often set up by officials of the homelands government. The other was cooperatives set up alongside trade unions and civil society organizations as part of a broader political struggle to end minority rule that was increasingly gaining momentum. This category included worker or producer cooperatives, consumer cooperatives and savings cooperatives. Cooperatives were thus seen as having a political as well as an economic objective, and also as a response to the lay-offs of workers and rising unemployment.

In Namibia, the development of cooperatives to a large extent mirrored developments in South Africa. A legislative framework was established through a 1946 Ordinance. Cooperatives registered in South Africa also operated in Namibia, and are still able to do so.

The colonial cooperative balance sheet

The colonial agencies in some parts of Africa occasionally invested a lot of human and financial resources in their ambition to create a viable cooperative sector. Subsequently, modern contractual cooperation became accepted as a separate business formula. However, in contradiction to the practice in their home countries, the cooperative sector in Africa was not seen as an independent socio-economic movement based on self-managed cooperative enterprises. Cooperatives and the cooperative sector as a whole were treated as instruments for propagating public economic and social policy. In the same vein, members joined cooperatives as matter of public policy rather than the result of voluntary individual motivation. Members belonged to a cooperative either to avoid problems with colonial authorities or to get access to certain services like marketing their produce through the only available channel. They did not regard themselves as the owners of the cooperatives. Consequently, the seeds for a system of cooperatives without co-operators were sown (Münkner, 1989).

However, this did not preclude the establishment of a widespread cooperative sector. Table 1.1 below gives an idea of the importance of the sector in the former British African colonies at the end of the nineteen fifties and, for most countries, on the eve of independence. Taking into account the demographic situation at that time, it is clear that in most British colonies the cooperative sector had a considerable penetration rate and touched upon many (rural) households. In Tanganyika, for example, 3.4% of the population was formally a member of a cooperative. The respective figures for Uganda and Kenya were 2.7% and 1.8%.

Table 1.1: Number of cooperatives and members in the British colonies (1959)

Country	Number of societies	Number of members
Nigeria	3 115	154 420
Sierra Leone	275	24 000
Gambia	55	4 389
Kenya	576	158 429
Uganda	1 598	187 860
Tanganyika	617	324 994
Zanzibar	67	5 161
N. Rhodesia	245	33 421
Nyasaland	87	7 763
Mauritius	343	32 420

Source: U.K. Information Service, 1961.

In all these countries, a unified cooperative model was tried out with primary societies, regional chapters and national secondary and apex bodies.

With regard to the French, they left a relatively less extended cooperative sector in their colonies by the time of independence. Using data for the period 1956-1963, Desroche (1964) came to the conclusion that less than 1% of the population of the former French colonies was involved in a cooperative. Only three former territories of French West Africa had higher, and impressive, rates. These were Mali (8%), Senegal (5%) and Guinea (2.4%). Desroche estimated that cooperative penetration in the former British part of Cameroon was two to three times higher than that of the former French part.

In general, the French left a tradition of strong and direct government involvement in mainly rural cooperative schemes. The colonial agencies supporting and supervising cooperatives had less staff at their disposal than their British counterparts and left a heterogeneous social economy sector with cooperatives, mutuals and other types of associations. The sector was also less integrated than that of the British colonies.

When they became independent, the Belgian territories in Africa had only a limited number of state-controlled cooperatives. In the case of the Congo, 83 cooperatives had been registered, of which 63 were agricultural cooperatives (Desroche, 1964). The latter were mainly linked to the so-called "paysannat organisé" (farmer collectives under the supervision of colonial administrators) and were involved in the marketing of new types of produce introduced by the Belgians, such as cotton, rubber, coffee or palm oil. The colonial state also established some ten to fifteen cooperatives in Ruanda-Urundi. Desroche estimated that the penetration ratio for the Belgian territories was a little above 1% of the then population. Alongside these cooperatives, many small scale cooperative-type undertakings existed as professional associations or unions and were patronized by missionaries.

The post-colonial cooperative experimentation

After independence cooperatives remained high or even got higher on the political agenda in most African countries, irrespective of their colonial tradition. The cooperative system and approach to cooperation were, however, not altered. As was the case in the colonial period, government-sponsored *casu quo* government-controlled cooperatives remained the norm. This era of experimentation, which simultaneously took place in Africa, Asia and Latin America, was characterized by five features which would become important imprints of the cooperative sector (Develtere, 1994).

First of all, there was an intensification and extension of government involvement in cooperative development. Cooperatives, because of their said potential to mobilize local human resources to the benefit of the entire nation and to transcend the existing class or ethnic divisions, were promoted by governments as part of their populist-nationalist strategy. Governments strengthened the administrative apparatus responsible for cooperative development and adjusted their cooperative legislation to fit the new strategy. While in most cases the role of promotion, control and guidance of the sector was vested in special cooperative departments or ministries, the planning process and the financial participation of the state became a matter of general government policy.

Second, under the wing of government, the power holders had full confidence in the cooperative sector and gave it a prominent place in their development rhetoric and strategies[1]. Cooperatives were hailed by a number of African leaders for their contribution to "village socialism" (Senghor of Senegal); "African socialism" (Nyerere of Tanzania); and higher productivity in agriculture (Houphouët-Boigny of Côte d'Ivoire). Because of this full confidence in the cooperative formula, they could be given special treatment and advantages – often monopoly or monopsony positions. This was the case, for example, in Uganda and Tanzania where cooperatives were granted a virtual monopoly in cotton ginning and coffee factories. But in reality the cooperatives were undermined by the governments. Governments set up state Marketing Boards to manage the export business, such that many rural cooperatives became mere agents of these statutory bodies. The Boards provided the necessary crop and marketing finance and merely arranged for the disposal of the crops domestically or in foreign markets. This happened in a context where the dominant development philosophy emphasized industrialization based on import substitution and relegated rural development to a distant second, if at all, in priority. At best, agriculture was seen as a means of providing low-cost food for the politically sensitive urban masses and to earn the much needed foreign exchange.

Third, in many countries governments shifted their initial policies of cooperative development from inducement to, more or less, coercion. In this sense, the cooperative sector lost its voluntary character completely and strictly became subject to political and ideological imperatives. Cooperative development was supposed to be both voluntary and rapid; but being voluntary, it was viewed to be slow and to be rapid, it was made compulsory. This antinomy was resolved in favour of the accelerated advancement of the sector. As early as 1961, for example, in Benin, Rural Renovation Cooperatives ("coopératives d'aménagement rural") were established by law for the cultivation of food crops and put under the tutelage of the state. In Haute Volta (now Burkina Faso), access to cultivable state land was reserved for those who accepted membership of a cooperative. In Tanzania after a special Presidential Commission of Inquiry (1966), sixteen cooperative unions and hundreds of societies were taken over by the State.

---

[1] There are a few notable exceptions though. Nkrumah, the first post-independence leader of Ghana was not enthusiastic about cocoa marketing cooperatives, which he considered to be socially and politically conservative.

Fourth, cooperatives were used as social control instruments. What happened in this regard is very much similar to what Korovkin (1990) called the political inclusion or the co-optive encapsulation of the popular segments into state-controlled functional organizations. In many countries a number of strategic political measures were used to discipline the cooperative movement: leaders were co-opted by the political system; the movement was used as a dispenser of patronage; competitive cooperative movements were not accepted; and cooperative apex bodies were not allowed or had to work in partnership with the authorities or the dominant party.

Finally, many governments of the young African nations attempted to diversify the cooperative sector. In quite a number of countries, governments experimented with different forms of pre-cooperatives. In some French-speaking African countries, these pre-cooperatives were registered under simplified cooperative legislation. In Senegal, for example, *Associations d'Intérêt Rural* (AIR) or producer groups were established for a period of two years. The management of these organizations was in the hands of public servants (Kibora, 2005). In Anglophone countries, probationary societies with provisional or deferred registration were stimulated (Münkner, 1989). In addition, many governments favoured multipurpose cooperatives and producer cooperatives with communal or cooperative ownership patterns. Along the lines of the social movement tradition, the Mobutu regime, for example, linked the cooperative and mutual movement to the single trade union, the *Union Nationale des Travailleurs du Zaïre* (UNTZa), which itself was a satellite of the single party, the *Mouvement Populaire de la Révolution* (Mahaniah, 1992).

Data from Desroches (1964) and Orizet (1969) show that the cooperative sector did expand considerably in the early nineteen sixties. It was estimated that by 1966 over 7,300 cooperatives were operational involving over 1.8 million people. The cooperative movements expanded enormously with lots of government resources flowing into them. In Uganda, for example, Young (1981) reports that the number of members doubled, the amount of cotton handled tripled and the total turnover in the cooperatives, by 1965, was 30% higher than the total revenue of all the local administrations in the country. This period has often been caricatured as a time of nationalization of the cooperative sector. However, as Gyllström (1988) described the Kenyan case, the governments never had sufficient resources to develop a completely government-controlled cooperative sector. He argues that "It was not simply a mode of organization imposed on a passive peasantry. Peasants did in many cases actively contribute to the establishment of societies. The mode of organization had, no doubt, been defined by government, but on the other hand this meant legal recognition and, hence, a possible means for improving income earning opportunities" (Ibid: 43). Hamer (1981) also gives evidence that in many cases in Africa, groups turned to the cooperative formula to oppose or countervail middlemen, while benefiting from some protection from the State in this struggle. In addition, local and international actors, like non-governmental organisations, the clergy or the traditional elite, did at times provide the necessary resources and political protection to shield the peoples' initiatives from too much state interference.

But with the amount of government support and backing it received, the drop height of the cooperative sector became particularly dramatic. The rapid expansion of the sector far outstripped the capacity of the cooperative officers to manage. The then practice of cooperatives being guided by illiterate committee members did not help either. Supervision of technical operations was beyond their capabilities. Loss of capable African cooperative leaders and managers to the political arena worsened the situation. As Kabuga (2005) notes, every Tom, Dick and Harry of questionable motives, integrity and competencies who vied for cooperative leadership could invade the sector. In that way, floodgates for nepotism, corruption, mismanagement and financial indiscipline were opened. In addition, farmers became increasingly sceptical when they realized that not they themselves, but state agencies and boards set priorities and targets; that extension work and *animation rurale* were meant to impose these conditions on them; and that – in the end – surpluses generated in the agricultural sector were ploughed into urban and industrial development projects. These factors were responsible for a rapid devaluation of cooperatives as a policy instrument for rural development. However, the essential development role assigned to the cooperatives rendered them too important to be allowed to die. Efforts to salvage them usually resulted in greater government control (Hussi et al., 1993).

In addition to government support, international organizations such as the International Labour Organisation and the International Cooperative Alliance also promoted cooperative development. In 1966, the ILO adopted "the Cooperatives (Developing Countries) Recommendation N° 127", which called for governments to develop a comprehensive and planned cooperative development strategy in which one central body would be the instrument for implementing a policy of aid and encouragement to cooperatives.

Government involvement and tutelage were seen as a temporary, but necessary, measure by these agencies.

Many other development organizations, bilateral agencies as well as multilateral, governmental and non-governmental, saw cooperatives as the preferred form of association and business to realize rapid social and economic growth. Of special importance were the programmes of the Nordic cooperative movements, the (cooperative) *Centrosoyus* of the USSR, the Israeli *kibbutz* cooperatives and the American and Canadian credit union movements. With the exception of the *Centrosoyus*, most of them accepted reluctantly that governments played a key role in cooperative development and sought ways for more cooperative autonomy.

Early critique and controversy

At the end of the nineteen sixties, the United Nations Research Institute for Social Development (UNRISD) carried out a research project on rural development and social change. Thirty-seven rural cooperatives in three Asian, three Latin American and six African countries were studied. The twelve African cooperatives evaluated were from Ghana, Kenya, Tanzania, Tunisia, Uganda and Zambia (Apthorpe, 1970; 1972). The researchers chose a scientific immanent approach to unveil the discrepancies between the myth and the reality of cooperation in the Third World (Fals-Borda, 1970b). This meant that the criteria used in assessing the performance of cooperatives were the economic and social goals which cooperatives, cooperative movements and cooperative policies set for themselves (Apthorpe and Gasper, 1982).

The results of this case study research were published by the institute in seven volumes (Apthorpe, 1970; 1972; Carroll et al. 1969; Fals-Borda 1970, 1971; Inayatullah 1970, 1972).

The researchers singled out two general problem areas concerning cooperative development in the developing world. The first problem was related to the diffusion, adoption and even imposition of certain alien models of rural cooperation. Secondly, the UNRISD team was disappointed with the performance and impact of cooperatives in the Third World.

With regard to the first, cooperatives were found to have been initiated and sponsored by external agencies. In the African countries studied, rural cooperatives were sponsored by numerous institutions including the World

Bank, the United States Agency for International Development, national governments, churches, political parties, and private individuals and organizations. The task of organizing cooperatives was, in most countries, taken on almost exclusively by the national governments. The capacity of governments to organize cooperatives seemed greater in those countries that had programmes of local development, such as community development and *animation rurale*. Political parties tended to interrelate with the cooperatives in order to extend their political influence and diffuse their ideology. Pressure was brought to bear on people to join the cooperatives, principally through three means: 1) direct compulsion and coercion; 2) the creation of a monopolistic situation in which the individual was deprived of certain economic benefits if he decided to stay out; and 3) the offering of inducements in the form of prospective benefits (Fals-Borda et al., 1976).

In terms of the performance and impact of cooperatives, the UNRISD team found that the activities of the cooperatives under review bore little relation to the dominant economic and social patterns. Their performance was found to be irrelevant in the wider context of social and economic change. Only a very small proportion of the total number of farmers was even touched by cooperatives, let alone effectively dependent on them. While the aims of the agricultural cooperative policies were commonly directed towards self-reliance; agricultural innovation and increased productivity; social and economic equalization; and structural change, the UNRISD study found that cooperatives did little to contribute to the achievement of these objectives. In many cases, cooperatives reinforced existing patterns of exploitation and social stratification or were carriers of new inequalities. The poor had seldom been reached by the cooperative programmes under review; the position of women was negatively affected under the cooperative development process; and the means of production did not really come into the hands of the collectivity. The general policies and the functioning of African cooperatives lay with government officials rather than with the formal leaders of the cooperatives. The "intercalary man" enjoyed considerable personal advantage. The researchers also concluded that in terms of agricultural innovation and increased productivity, no impressive achievements could be presented. Rural cooperatives had much difficulty in tackling the problems of productivity and equality simultaneously.

Despite many such setbacks, the researchers were of the opinion that the performance of African cooperatives in promoting local initiative and self-reliance had not been entirely negative. The cotton and coffee cooperatives, for instance, had at least brought in new forms of social organization at the local level. They also found significant local social participation, particularly when the cooperatives were small in scale, despite the high degree of identification they had with central governments.

The general policy conclusion of the UNRISD team was that one should question the wisdom of continuing along the dubious way so far taken, with its low probability of success and its waste of expectations, talents, resources and funds. The UNRISD study was subject to massive criticism and resulted in a sterile debate about the case-study methodology applied and about the definition of genuine cooperatives (Stettner, 1973).

New ways, old beliefs: further attempts at cooperative development

The UNRISD report, as well as the many hurdles encountered in the field, caused many to believe that the cooperative ideals could only be achieved using new approaches and methodologies. The ILO Recommendation 127 of 1966 had already set the tone in its observation that cooperatives were powerful instruments for social and economic development, but had to be seen as voluntary organizations. From that time on, the United Nations considered the cooperative sector as "1) an important element of the strategy for the Second United Nations Development Decade; 2) a means of broadening the basis for popular participation in the development effort; and 3) a means for the equitable sharing of the benefits of development" (Morsink, 1975).

This did not, however, result in a concerted or systematic approach to cooperative development. To the contrary, many different actors brought in their own approaches or experimented with new forms of cooperation. Government was less seen as the owner of the cooperative process than as the director.

In terms of objectives, cooperative development was no longer considered an instrument for realizing national economic and social objectives, but rather as an instrument for poverty alleviation and fulfilling the basic needs of the poor. Participation became a key ingredient of many cooperative projects and programmes. This participation had to be "spontaneous" and had to take place outside the confines of rigid bureaucratic structures. Insisting on the importance of grassroots participation, the new methodologies departed from the top-down approach applied during the colonial and immediate post-colonial period (Oakley & Marsden, 1984; Cernea, 1985). It was, however, generally accepted that external agencies, both governmental and non-governmental, had to give the impetus to grassroots participation and could trigger voluntary action. The basic difference from former efforts was that in the nineteen seventies and eighties "such interventions must aim at stimulating participatory development from below, even if the stimulus is from above" (Dadson, 1988).

So, donors and governments alike continued to prefer cooperatives as ideal instruments and institutional linkages through which participation could take place, but also through which funds could be channelled. In a 1986 review of World Bank-assisted projects, for example, it was shown that 50% of all agricultural projects in Africa involved cooperative organizations (Pohlmeier, 1990). Bilateral donors such as the Scandinavian countries devoted an even larger share of rural development expenditure to promotion of cooperatives. In this way, members of cooperatives became active partners of development projects, but they did not become the patrons and owners of their cooperatives. There is much evidence that donors were very weak in institution building because they were impatient or never really saw cooperatives as independent community organizations with their own agenda and rationale, but rather as implementing agencies for their projects (World Bank, 1986). The World Bank concluded from the review of over 100 projects that cooperatives were expected to perform additional functions, or to serve non-members, without sufficiently evaluating their institutional capacity to do so. Donors also treated cooperatives individually and did not see a need for strengthening the movement as a whole (Braverman, 1991; Develtere, 1994). Thus, cooperatives arguably remained "don-operatives".

But in many instances, cooperatives can also be said to have remained "gov-operatives". As Braverman et al. (1991) concluded, most cooperatives ended up as mere collecting agents of agricultural produce for public marketing boards; distribution channels for agricultural inputs; or as lending agencies for government- or donor-provided resources. They were hardly considered as private enterprises. Like quasi-non-governmental organizations, they were almost always subject to administratively imposed price controls and as such could not realize sufficient returns or profits. Their activities and organizational structures were heavily regulated by laws that were too detailed to be understood by the average member, especially when there was no serious effort at cooperative education.

Attracting so much attention from governments and donors, cooperatives became aid- or subsidy-lobbying organizations. Members and leadership developed a highly opportunistic, passive and instrumental attitude towards their cooperatives. Their financial contributions, in terms of share capital or membership fees, were minimal or completely absent. This led to undercapitalization of the cooperatives, with a bias towards external funding and the subsequent external accountability rather than internal accountability. Political patronage further eroded the autonomy and economic rationale of the cooperatives (Holmén, 1990). This, together with the profit constraints, led to widespread inefficiencies, mismanagement and irregularities in the sector.

At the same time, in the 1970s and 1980s, a number of developments took place that created space for a different approach to cooperatives. We can highlight at least four developments that – in our opinion – further marked the evolution of cooperative trajectories in Africa.

As was also the case in Latin America, Asia and the Caribbean the emerging trade union movement spurred a different type of savings and credit cooperatives. These credit unions had close institutional linkages with the trade union movement; attracted an urban, educated and salaried class; and were seen by their members as a vehicle for their upward social mobility. They did not consider themselves as conveyor belts for donor or government subsidies. Their operations were based on savings facilitated by the check-off system whereby savings were automatically deducted from the member's monthly salary. These experiences had a positive spill over effect on many rural credit and savings projects. The *Banques Populaires* in Rwanda are prime examples of this.

Secondly, a number of donors massively invested in cooperative education. These new efforts differed from previous ones in a number of ways. They were not solely investing in the training of governmental cooperative department staff and managers of federations and apex organizations. Training was also organized for cooperative managers, board members, supervisors and members. Examples of this kind of project were the ICA-directed Cooperative Education Material Advisory Services (CEMAS) and the ILO project on Material and Techniques for Cooperative Management Development (MATCOM). These and other training programmes combined theory with practice. The approach was job-oriented and adaptable to various circumstances (ILO, 1988).

Thirdly, in a number of countries a coalition of local cooperative leaders and donor agencies attempted to set in motion a process of deregulation of the cooperative sector. This led to some early attempts at legislative reform. But, in most cases, this was only debated and not realized. As long as governments continued to receive substantial international recognition and financial resources for their "pivotal role" in cooperative development, there was little or no incentive to reduce or dismantle the government institutions involved in control and supervision or to build institutions within the cooperative movement which could gradually take over these functions. For example, in Kenya the number of staff in the Ministry of Cooperative Development increased from 163 in 1963 to 1,868 in 1983 (Gyllstrom, 1988). Consequently, deregulation did not become a reality as a matter of explicit policy. It was realized gradually because some international (non-governmental) organizations started to work with alternative or parallel cooperative support institutions. The German Friedrich-Ebert-Foundation, for example, established independent support units as a "consulting office" run by FES itself or as a joint venture with a cooperative federation. Some European and North-American cooperative development agencies also started supporting cooperative movement organizations directly.

Finally, other non-cooperative or semi-cooperative organizations became increasingly popular with some governments, and more so with donors. This produced a shift in development discourse and practice. Village committees, community based organisations, peasant or farmers' associations, NGOs, non-profit associations, economic interest groups or women's groups were seen as alternative sectors for development. Some political parties, such as the Kenya African National Union in Kenya jumped on the bandwagon and promoted self-help groups (popularly known as harambee, a Kiswahili word that means "let us pull together" to accomplish the task). But in most cases, these government-sponsored or -initiated forms of participation treated people still as subjects, not as citizens (Bazaara, 2002). Some international agencies tried to transform development practice more radically. This was the case, for example, with the FAO-supported People's Participation Project that assisted NGOs in planning, implementing and evaluating pilot projects.

Structural adjustment and cooperative adjustments

The varying changes and adaptations in the history of the development of cooperatives in Africa saw the sector emerge in the early 1990s as an amalgamation of very different cooperative structures rather than a movement (Develtere, 1994). Having been created and shaped by external patrons, particularly governments and donors, it was acknowledged that the sector had both strong and weak points with regard to its viability in a liberalized economic environment. This prompted a set of important studies in the early 1990s – by the World Bank and the International Cooperative Alliance – on the feasibility of the African cooperative sector in the wake of market liberalization and political democratization.

In the period 1991-1992, the World Bank conducted a regional study on the development of cooperatives and other rural organizations in Africa. Six country studies provided the bulk of the material and arguments, namely Ghana, Kenya, Niger, Nigeria, Senegal and Uganda (Hussi et al., 1993; Porvali, 1993). The study concluded that in spite of the liberalization measures, the policy framework in many Sub-Saharan African countries continued to be characterized by interventionism, which gave government authorities a high degree of control over rural organizations; thereby compromising the self-reliant character of such organizations. In line with this policy framework, a complex legal framework inhibited the formation and operation of cooperatives. Regulation of markets and prices further restrained the commercial viability and business development potential of cooperatives as well as other farmer organizations.

The authors, however, insisted that genuine cooperatives still possessed a number of characteristics that made them significant contributors to rural development. It was argued that as member-owned and member-controlled business organizations, cooperatives provide their members with the advantages of economies of scale; link small-scale and medium-scale producers to the national economy; provide an element of competition that is often lacking in rural areas; contribute to rural stability; and form an effective means of channelling assistance to women. Based on an evaluation of past support policies and a number of successful cooperative projects, the World Bank research team subsequently advised that the Bank play a central role in assisting governments in the identification of legislative, policy and institutional reforms that would enable cooperatives and other rural organizations to evolve into efficient and sustainable organizations managed by their members and capable of providing competitive services. The study also emphasized that capacity-building measures should be included in all World Bank-supported projects involving cooperatives and other farmer groups. The World Bank study thus put the blame for a deficient cooperative sector in Africa on the inappropriate institutional environment and did not shy away from criticizing the role played by donors and lending institutions in perpetuating this scenario.

The ICA report, on the other hand, focused on the transformation of the African economies and societies and its impact on cooperative organizations (Birgegaard & Genberg, 1994). Faced with severe economic crises, most African countries had adopted the World Bank- and IMF-prescribed structural adjustment programmes in order to bring about stabilization and improve resource allocation. Alongside market liberalization and institutional reform measures that were embedded in structural adjustment programmes were monetary policy reforms that involved the imposition of credit ceilings and increased interest rates on loans. The latter policy particularly affected cooperatives because many of them had a high degree of indebtedness and low cost bearing capacity. Moreover, market liberalization struck cooperatives even harder, for it threatened their monopoly and monopsony position. The widening of trading margins when markets were liberalized attracted new actors, with the result that less competitive cooperatives lost market share and trading opportunities. However, some of these measures helped to strengthen the economic position of a few cooperatives. In Uganda, for instance, a major devaluation of the currency in 1992 gave coffee-exporting cooperatives a windfall profit that permitted bonus payments to the members.

In general, the ICA researchers concluded that all cooperatives – including the efficient ones – were going to lose market share. They argued that cooperatives were ill-prepared to face the challenges of structural adjustment programmes, particularly the liberalization of the economy. Among the many problems cooperatives had included the persistence of their low business efficiency; weak capital base; heavy indebtedness and limited credit-worthiness; the weak entrepreneurial capability of managers and board members; and the unbalanced organizational structures of the movement.

At the same time, the researchers observed that most African countries were in the midst of a process of political transformation characterized by increased pluralism and democratization. Combined with economic reforms, which reduced the role of the state, these changes opened the possibility for a disengagement of the cooperative movement from the state. This would possibly enable them to become truly popular organizations. They reasoned that the democratization of society at large could also facilitate successful democratization of the cooperative movement itself. In this, they joined a chorus of many co-operators, development practitioners and scholars who praised the opportunities offered by democratization for new civic engagement, collective action and civil society-State relations (Fuentes & Frank, 1989; Gentil & Mercoiret, 1991). Interestingly, many of these civil society and social movement advocates were passionate about the numerous new types of socio-economic ventures that were undertaken by popular groups and organized social movements (Defourny et al; 1999; Develtere, 1998). The donor community – including the cooperative development agencies – concluded that far more attention should be given to cooperative development outside existing and formal cooperative structures than had been the case before. It was clear again that the creeping wheel never gets the oil! The consequence was that not only did governments withdraw from the cooperative scene, but so did the donor community. The other chapters of this book will show the consequences of this deliberate policy decision.

Continuity and change in cooperative traditions

The discussion of cooperative development in Africa has so far traced the historical trajectories that have characterized the evolution of the sector in the past 100 years or so. The question that arises is what paths and traces have been left by these trajectories? How have they determined the nature of the cooperative sector that one finds in Africa today? How has the sector changed or departed from the historical paths?

The gradual erosion of the unified model

In terms of legal and administrative framework, it is clear that the unified cooperative model, which was introduced by the British in their colonies, still very much relies on a single cooperative law, a tiered structure and a specialized administrative unit (the Commissioner or Registrar of a Cooperative Department). Many of the cooperative laws were adapted in the course of the nineteen nineties referring explicitly to the Statement on Cooperative Identity of the International Cooperative Alliance. The cooperative structure that characterizes this model is a hierarchical one. Primary societies form secondary cooperative societies known as unions in some countries. The unions in turn form tertiary organizations known as national cooperatives. The tertiary organizations then form the apex organizations. In Tanzania, Ghana, and Zimbabwe, these apex organizations have formed federations. In most of Anglophone Africa, the administrative structure of the Departments of Cooperative Development was also hierarchical. Assistant cooperative officers were the ones who largely supervised the primary societies; the district cooperative officers handled the secondary cooperative organizations; while the headquarters handled all administrative duties but mainly took care of the national cooperatives, apex organizations and federations. With governments withdrawing from provision of cooperative support services since the mid 1990s to allow cooperative movements to become truly autonomous, this division of labour is changing. Flatter structures are being experimented with and many tasks are being handed over to the movement's organizations.

The setting up of Cooperative Colleges and Cooperative Development Centres in Anglophone Africa was another feature of the unified cooperative model. Tanzania has a college wholly dedicated to cooperatives. The Cooperative Colleges in Kenya and Uganda run cooperative and social enterprise programmes with a wider mandate.

Another feature of this model is that cooperative movements interface with their governments through their respective Ministries or Departments of Cooperative Development. The tradition has always been that the Commissioners or Registrars for Cooperative Development are ex-officio members on the boards of the apex organizations or federations.

In line with the unified model, cooperative movements in Anglophone Africa are subsequently affiliated to the International Cooperative Alliance through their apex organizations and federations. Agricultural cooperatives are often also members of the International Federation of Agricultural Producers (IFAP). Savings and Credit Cooperatives are affiliated to the World Council of Credit Unions (WOCCU) and its African member organization the African Confederation of Cooperative Savings and Credit Association (ACCOSCA). Through these international cooperative organizations, cooperative movements have developed partnerships with similar movements. Prominent are the collaborations with the Swedish Cooperative Centre (SCC), the Canadian Cooperative Association and the members of the American Overseas Cooperative Development Organization.

The social economy model expands

The social economy model took root in many Francophone countries. Parallel to the general promotion of agricultural cooperatives, sectoral measures were also taken to advance cooperation and mutualism in different fields.

Groupements collectifs, association *villageois, mutuelles*, producers groups and other pre- or semi-cooperative types of organizations were promoted. Contrary to the unified model, this tradition did not have a concerted or co-ordinated promotional strategy. Few countries had a comprehensive cooperative development plan. Cooperatives and other forms of organizations were subjected to numerous sectoral policies. They played a key role in cash crop marketing, hydro-agricultural projects or rural resettlements. *Animateurs* (extension officers) were responsible for the one-way communication from Government to the people. The many laws, regulations and model statutes pertaining to the social economy were all presented to the target groups in French, a language not mastered by the majority of the people concerned. Civil servants were seconded to the regional and national unions or even to the big agricultural cooperatives (Kibora, 2005).

A unique development in Francophone West Africa was the adoption of the so-called "PARMEC law" by the West African Monetary Union in 1993. The project to regulate all micro-finance institutions in the region was funded by Canada under the *Projet d'Appui à la Réglementation sur les Mutuelles d'Epargne et de Crédit* (PARMEC). All micro-finance organizations subsequently became subject to this law although only credit unions (*mutuelles de crédit*) and their network federations could be granted a full-fledged licence. This means that in fact the PARMEC law is a credit union (*coopec*) law. Other micro-finance institutions are subject to regulation through a special "convention cadre" agreement with the Ministry of Finance to which supervision of all credit union and non-credit union micro-finance is entrusted (Ouattara, 2004).

In the countries that follow the path of the social economy model, cooperatives are generally supervised in two different ways. First, general legal and administrative supervision is taken up by the Ministries of Agriculture or Social Affairs. Second, technical follow-up is the responsibility of the "technical" ministry. This is for example the case for housing cooperatives, health care cooperatives, handicraft cooperatives, fishermen cooperatives or sometimes even women's or youth cooperatives. In general fewer financial and human resources are attributed to these administrative bodies than is the case in the Anglophone African countries.

As we have seen, the French did not want a forceful cooperative movement to arise in their colonies and, therefore, hindered the development of federations in the sector. In most countries, a very complex and heterogeneous configuration of unions and federations emerged only in the post-colonial period. This was the result of disparate public sector or external NGO efforts to modulate the sector(s). The result has been the emergence of unions and federations mainly in the agricultural export sectors (fruits and vegetables, cotton, peanuts, coffee and cocoa). Also, the credit and savings cooperatives, health *mutuelles* and handicraft cooperatives in many countries have recently started a timid process of restructuring using different denominations such as confederation, council or national association. Very few linkages between these regroupings, however, exist.

In the social economy model, there are no national specialized cooperative colleges. The only specialized cooperative training institution is the *Institut Supérieur Panafricain d'Etude Coopérative* (ISPEC), based in Cotonou, Benin. It offers a broad training programme for a variety of target groups active in the social economy (cooperatives, trade unions, associations, *mutuelles* and other self-help groups). Cooperative training and promotion in these countries are also part and parcel of a much broader approach to the social economy in national and regional programmes set up by a variety of institutions such as the *Centre d'Etudes Economiques et Sociales de l'Afrique de l'Ouest* (CESAO), the *Institut Africain pour le Développement Economique et Sociale* (INADES) and the *Institut Panafricain pour le Développement* (IPD), which have bases in Burkina Faso, Côte d'Ivoire, Cameroon, Senegal and Togo.

This broader approach to cooperative and socio-economic development has also resulted in a variety of regional networks of social economy actors. Many of these networks rely heavily on a few very strong national movements or organizations and the support of committed development partners or regional authorities. They are relatively open and ever-changing. Mention can be made of the *Plate-forme Paysanne des Producteurs du Comité Inter-Etats de Lutte contre la Sécheresse au Sahel*; the *Association Africaine des Producteurs Cotonniers*; the *Réseau des Organisations Paysannes et de Producteurs de l'Afrique de l'Ouest* (ROPPA); the *Réseau Afrique Verte*; the *NGO 6S*; *Centre Africa Obota*; and *la Concertation*. Very few of the international partners of these social economy organizations do specifically insist on the cooperative identity of the national organizations. There is a strong presence of institutions and organizations of the Francophone and non-Anglophone world. The bilateral agencies of Switzerland, France, Belgium, Canada and Germany are prominently present. So are their national cooperative and mutual development agencies (DID and *Socodevi* of Québec; *Crédit Mutuel* and *Crédit Coopératif* of France, the Belgian health mutuals, and Agriterra of the Netherlands). In addition a wide variety of British, Italian, American and German organizations are very active on the scene.

The social movement model

The very liberal and dual cooperative system that the Belgians introduced in their African territories of Congo and Rwanda-Urundi also left deep traces. On the one hand, the promotion of cooperatives in independent Zaïre/Congo, Rwanda and Burundi was left in the hands of very marginal governmental agencies. On the other hand a large number of social movements and non-governmental organizations chose a cooperative formula to promote the interests of their members or target group. In Zaïre, the Mobutu regime put cooperative development under the national trade union federation (UNTZa). After the downfall of the single party and the single trade union system, the trade union movement continued to be one of the backbones of the cooperative sector in the country. It is no surprise that an atomized trade union movement also brings along a much atomized cooperative sector. Parallel to this, different churches and religious movements like the Catholic, Protestant, indigenous *Kibangist* church, the Baptist community and the evangelical movements stimulated cooperative development with the twin objectives of bringing material benefits to their adherents and forging loyalty towards their institutions. However, in the absence of a coherent cooperative legislative and policy framework, many of these cooperatives were not formally incorporated under the anachronistic cooperative law. They functioned, and continue to function, as *de facto* associations, NGOs or mutuals. This was also the case for the many cooperatives and mutuals that were established in the framework of regional development efforts, jointly undertaken by regional associations and international partners. A prime example is the *Centre de Développement Intégré* (CDI) in the Equator province that started as a local association in 1967 and has become one of the biggest development projects in the country. Hundreds of thousands of peasants are involved in one of the many structures of CDI and sell their soya beans, coffee and maize through them. Over 100,000 persons are due-paying members of Africa's biggest health insurance mutual set up by CDI (Develtere & Stessens, 2005).

A single cooperative movement did not emerge in Burundi. The Cooperative Department, set up with the commencement of the Second Republic in 1976, first supported the creation of consumer cooperatives and later of credit and savings societies. But the sector never really got roots. Only a couple of hundred cooperatives were created and very few were sustainable. The governmental *Centre de Formation Coopérative* was short-lived. Consequently, much room was left for private initiatives by religious organizations, social movements and non-governmental organizations. The *Fédération des Coopératives du Burundi*, for example, was an initiative of the Catholic Church.

In Rwanda the MRND Government tried to stimulate cooperative development, but this did not result in a coherent and assertive cooperative policy. Between 1960 and 1985, no fewer than eleven different ministries were responsible for cooperative development. Halfway through the nineteen eighties more than 1,300 primary societies were registered. Nevertheless, their vitality depended more on external assistance and the support of local non-governmental bodies than on genuine local participation. This was also the case for those cooperatives that were established under the umbrella of the single trade union federation (CESTRAR) and later by the competing trade union federations. Movements such as the Christian workers' movement, the young Christian workers and several farmers' organizations also set up their cooperative or socio-economic entities. The *Centre de Formation et de Recherche Coopérative* (IWACU) trained and coached volunteers and staff of cooperatives and other related types of organizations. The best developed cooperative structure was that of the *Union des Banques Populaires du Rwanda*, which exists to this day. As is clear from the chapter on Rwanda in this book, the level of integration of the sector is still minimal, but its strongest branches are the *banques populaires* and some cooperative trade federations.

While they have numerous contacts with the outside world through their respective social movement partners and through their working arrangements with numerous donors, the cooperatives in this social movement model have little or no contact with the international cooperative movement. In other words, this model relies on international ties with the workers' movements (e.g. the international trade union federations), the farmers' movements (e.g. International Federation of Agricultural Producers) or religious networks (e.g. World Council of Churches) rather than international cooperative organizations like ICA and WOCCU.

The producer model

As already pointed out, the producer cooperative model was introduced by the Portuguese in their African colonies. In all these countries, except in

Guinée-Bissau, the associational and cooperative sectors are linked to the Ministry of Agriculture. This is partly because for a long time, under the influence of state socialism, cooperatives were promoted as semi-public enterprises. In addition to this linkage, there is a national union of farmers or farmers' cooperatives in most of these countries to defend the interests of the rural population. This is the case, for example, with the Union of Peasant Associations (UNAC) in Mozambique and the Union of Angolese Peasant Associations (UNACA) in Angola. In Cape Verde, as will be seen in the chapter on this country, the national federation of cooperatives (Fenacoop) is in fact a federation of consumer cooperatives. In most countries these federations bring together cooperatives, pre-cooperatives and associations. In this way, the UNAC represents over 50,000 members who belong to more than 1,000 associations and cooperatives, 67 district unions and two central unions.

Support for the cooperative sector in the Lusophone countries comes primarily from a number of international non-governmental organizations. Very few local points of reference exist. A notable exception is the *Centro Moçambicano de Estudos Cooperativos* in Mozambique. Of particular importance for the producers' model is the work done by the *Instituto Antonio Sérgio do Sector Cooperativo* (INSCOOP), a public agency in Portugal. It is the principal promoter of the *Organizaçao Cooperativa dos Paises de Lingua Portuguesa* (OCPLP). The OCPLP organizes conferences and seminars on a regular basis. One of the promotional instruments of the INSCOOP and the OCPLP is the bulletin *Jornal Cooperativo de Lingua Portuguesa*.

Indigenous models

As for the remaining "indigenous models", it has been pointed out that each country has some home-bred systems of cooperation that evolved in interaction with the imported models. Only in the case of a few countries such as South Africa, Egypt and Ethiopia can one talk about modern cooperation in a local jacket. This of course does not exclude the import, copying or borrowing of foreign elements. In this way, for example, in both South Africa and Namibia, as in other countries influenced by British colonial practice, there is a Registrar of Cooperatives whose office is responsible for all matters pertaining to cooperatives (Theron, 2005). Whereas in South Africa the role of the Registrar has been considerably reduced in recent years, the Namibian legislation still envisages a more interventionist role of the Registrar. The Registrar in Namibia has considerable discretion on whether to register a cooperative and may even visit the premises of the proposed cooperative or meet with would-be co-operators before deciding on the registration. This difference in cooperative strategy is also exemplified by the fact that in South Africa cooperative development is ultimately seen as being the responsibility of the movement while in Namibia the Registrar's office and the Cooperatives Advisory Board appear to assume a more prominent role. In both countries an "established" cooperative sector, located primarily in agriculture or food manufacturing, was firmly allied to the old – white dominated – order. During the transition in South Africa and after independence in Namibia, many of the largest and best-known cooperatives converted to companies. Besides this, an emergent cooperative movement based on black economic empowerment has much difficulty in taking root. According to Theron, this can be explained by the fact that relatively few organizations in civil society facilitate the establishment of cooperatives. Notable exceptions in South Africa are the Dora Tamana Cooperative Centre and the Cooperative Policy and Alternatives Centre. Although both countries have taken separate and even opposite routes in terms of cooperative development strategy, their trajectories are still intertwined as is clear from the fact that cooperatives registered in South Africa are still able to operate in Namibia.

Conclusion

Modern cooperation has found many roots in African societies and economies. Alien models were introduced by colonial agencies as a mechanism for social and economic engineering. But, notwithstanding the fact that they were foreign models specifically designed for colonial purposes, cooperatives have become one of the main forms of popular economic and social organization. The positioning of the cooperatives in the economy and society at large as well as their organizational set-up depended on certain colonial traditions. As a result, we have witnessed the emergence of five different models: a unified cooperative model, a social economy model, a social movement model, a producers' model and an indigenous model. These models have been reinforced rather than transformed by the post-colonial governments. While in all colonial models co-operators were dependent agents, in post-colonial times they became clients of semi-public cooperatives up to the mid 1990s in many countries. The advent of a more competitive market environment in conjunction with a more democratic political opportunity structure made it possible to re-envisage cooperatives as private sector agents primarily driven by the (interests of the) members. In other words, co operators had the chance to become the real owners of their cooperative businesses and the real members of their cooperative associations. This new dynamism of the cooperative sector does not mean that there is a fresh start. The heritage of the models has not been cast out completely. On the contrary, the models survive in cooperative policy, cooperative organization, cooperative networking and cooperative culture. This provides us with a rich and diversified cooperative scenery. Interestingly, the models we have seen can not any more be traced back to colonial origins alone. In some countries, particularly in the Anglophone world, we still see the attempts to unite and streamline the cooperative sector as was envisaged by the unified cooperative model. In many others, new forms of cooperation are now accepted and even legally recognized. They get inspiration from the social economy model. The fact that many social movements, such as trade unions, farmers' organizations, regional movements and other interest groups have opted to provide services to their members through cooperatives and other related types of organizations allow room for the social movement model in many countries. Because of the prime role of agriculture in African economies, these cooperatives are often producers' organizations that rely heavily on a regulatory and governmental support framework. In this way, a producers' model brings inspiration. And, finally, in many countries cooperatives venture out to new areas and new challenges such as health care, social services, environmental protection or manufacturing. This gives scope for new and innovative home-grown models.

Bibliography

- Apthorpe R. (1970), *Rural Cooperatives and Planned Change in Africa: Case Material*, UNRISD, Geneva.

- Apthorpe R. (1972), *Rural Cooperatives and Planned Change in Africa: An Analytical Overview*, UNRISD, Geneva.

- Apthorpe R. and Gasper D. (1982), "Policy evaluation and meta-evaluation: The Case of Rural Cooperatives", *World Development*, Vol. 10, No. 8. pp. 651-668.

- Bazaara N. (2002), *Legal and Policy Framework for Citizen Participation in East Africa: A Comparative Analysis*, LogoLink Research, Sussex.

- Birgegaard L. & Genberg B. (1994), Summary of a report on Cooperative Adjustment in a Changing Environment in Africa, ICA, Geneva.

- Braverman A. et al (1991), *Promoting Rural Cooperatives in Developing Countries – The Case of Sub-Saharan Africa*, World Bank Discussion Papers 121, The World Bank, Washington.

- Canaveira de Campos M. (2005), *Coopérativisme dans les pays lusophones*, Essential Research for a Cooperative Facility, ILO, Geneva, Mimeo.

- Carroll T. et al (1969), *A Review of Rural Co-operation in Developing Areas*, UNRISD, Geneva.

- Cernea M. (1985), Putting People First: Sociological Variables in Rural Development, World Bank, Oxford University Press, New York.

- Dadson J. A. (1988),"Cooperative Reorganization: The Ghanaian Case", in H. Hedlund, *Cooperatives Revisited*, The Scandinavian Institute of African Studies, Uppsala.

- Defourny J., Develtere P. and Fonteneau B. (1999), *l'Economie sociale au Nord et au Sud*, De Boeck Université, Bruxelles/Paris

- Desroche H. (1964), 'Coopérativismes Africains: Jalons Inductifs d'une Recherche Comparée', *Archives Internationales de Sociologie de la Coopération*, 16, July-December, pp. 131-186.

- Develtere P. (1994), *Co-operation and Development*, Acco, Leuven.

- Develtere P. (1998), *Economie sociale et developpement – les cooperatives, mutuelles et associations dans les pays en developpement*, De Boeck Universitie, Bruxelles/Paris.

- Develtere P. (2005), *The Belgian Cooperative Tradition in the Congo, Rwanda and Burundi, Essential Research for a Cooperative Facility*, ILO, Geneva, Mimeo.

- Develtere P. and Stessens J. (2005), le Centre de Développement Intégral en République Démocratique du Congo, cheminement d'un projet vers l'économie sociale, HIVA, Leuven

- Fals-Borda O. (1970a), *Estudios de la Realidad Campesina: Cooperacio y Cambio*, UNRISD, Vol. 2, Geneva.

- Fals-Borda O. (1970b), "Formation and Deformation of Cooperatives Policy in Latin America", *Cooperative Information*, No. 4, pp. 7-29.

- Fals-Borda O. (1971), *Cooperatives and Rural Development in Latin America: An Analytical Report*, UNRISD, Vol. 3, Geneva.

- Fals-Borda O., Apthorpe R. & Inayatullah (1976), 'The Crisis of Rural Cooperatives: Problems in Africa, Asia and Latin America', J. Nash, J. Dandler. & N. S. Hopkins, *Popular Participation in Social Change*, Mouton Publishers, The Hague/Paris, pp. 439-456.

- Fuentes M. and Frank A. G. (1989), "Ten Theses on Social Movements", *World Development*, Vol. 17, No. 2. pp. 179-191.

- Gentil D. and Mercoiret M. R. (1991), "Ya-t-il un movement payson en Afrique noire? *Revue Tiers Monde*, XXXII, No. 128, pp. 867-886.

- Goussault Y. (1968), 'Rural 'Animation' and Popular Participation in French-Speaking Black Africa', *International Labour Review*, vol. 97, pp. 525-550.

- Gyllstrom B. (1988), "Government versus Agricultural Marketing Cooperatives in Kenya", in H. Hedlund (ed.), *Cooperatives Revisited*, The Scandinavian Institute of African Studies, Uppsala.

- Hamer J. H. (1981), "Preconditions and limits in the Formation of Associations: The Self-help and Cooperative Movements in sub-Saharan Africa", *African Studies Review*, Vol. 24, pp. 113-132.

- Haubert M. (1999), *L'avenir des paysans. Les mutations des agricultures familiales dans les pays du Sud*, Presses Universitaires de France, Paris.

- Holmen H. (1990), *State, Cooperatives and Development in Africa*, The Scandinavian Institute of African Studies, Uppsala.

- Hussi P. et al. (1993), *The Development of Cooperatives and Other Rural Organizations – The role of the World Bank*, The World Bank, Washington.

- ILO (1988), *Cooperative Management and Administration* (second, revised edition), ILO, Geneva.

- Inayatullah (ed.) (1970), *Cooperatives and Planned Change in Asian Rural Communities: Case Studies and Diaries*, UNRISD Vol. 6, Geneva.

- Inayatullah (1972), *Cooperatives and Development in Asia: A Study of Cooperatives in Four Rural Communities of Iran, Pakistan and Ceylon*, UNRISD Vol. 7, Geneva.

- Kabuga C. (2005), *Cooperative Tradition in Anglophone Countries, Essential Research for a Cooperative Facility*, ILO, Geneva, Mimeo.

- Kibora A. S. (2005), *Rapport de l'étude sur les traditions coopératives en Afrique – Le cas des anciennes colonies françaises, Essential Research for a Cooperative Facility*, ILO, Geneva, Mimeo.

- Korovkin T. (1990), *Politics of Agricultural Cooperatives: Peru, 1969-1983*, University of British Columbia Press, Vancouver.

- Lambert P. (1963), *Studies in the social philosophy of co-operation*, Cooperative Union, Manchester

- Mahaniah K. (1992), *Les coopératives au Zaïre, Ed. Centre de Vulgarisation Agricole*, Kinshasa.

- Morsink H. (1975), "Technical Assistance to Cooperatives: The Evolution in Priorities as seen by the United Nations", *Review of International cooperation*, Vol. 68, No. 6, pp. 190-199.

- Munkner H. H. (ed.) (1989), *Comparative Study of Cooperative Law in Africa*, Marburg Consult, Marburg.

- Oakley P. and Marsden D. (1984), *Approaches to Participation and Rural Development*, ILO, Geneva.

- Orizet J. (1969), "The cooperative movement since the First World War", *International Labour Review*, Vol. 100, pp. 23-50.

- Ouattara K. (2004), 'Implementation of the PARMEC Law for Regulation of Microfinance', *Finance*, July 2004.

- Pohlmeier L. (1990), *Recent Developments in the World Bank's Approach to Co-operative Support in Africa*, The World Bank, Washington D.C.

- Porvali H. (ed.) (1993), *The Development Of Cooperatives, Agriculture and Rural Development Series*, No. 8, The World Bank, Washington, D.C.

- Stettner L. (1973), "Coooperation and Egalitarianism in the Developing Countries", *ICA Review*, Vol. 66, pp. 203-218.

- Theron J. (2005), *The cooperative tradition in South Africa and Namibia, Essential Research for a Cooperative Facility*, ILO, Geneva, Mimeo.

- U.K. Information Service (1961), *Co-operation in the U.K. Dependencies*, Central Office of Information, London.

- World Bank (1986), *Rural Cooperatives in World Bank Assisted Projects and some Related Development Issues*, World Bank, Washington, D.C.

- Young C. et al. (1981), *Cooperatives and Development: Agricultural Politics in Ghana and Uganda*, University of Wisconsin Press, Madison.

Chapter Two – Renaissance of African Cooperatives in the 21st Century: Lessons from the Field

by Patrick Develtere & Ignace Pollet

As it has already been pointed out in chapter one, African politics from the 1960s through the 1990s onwards have not been particularly kind to cooperatives. Even if the failure of many rural cooperatives in Sub-Saharan Africa is often attributed to management problems and internal weaknesses, the major cause may be the non-viability of some of the activities imposed on them by governments (Hussi et al., 1993: 27). Many cooperatives in Africa had become fraudulent derivatives of the international cooperative tradition. They functioned as semi-public and bureaucratic enterprises rather than genuine, voluntary and private businesses. Nevertheless, the different studies that came to this conclusion in the early 1990s still underlined the theoretical and practical benefits that could be derived from modern cooperation in Africa. For instance, in their authoritative report, Hussi et al. (1993: 27) concluded that cooperatives remained "the preferred form of organization and perhaps the only organization with which rural people are familiar". Most studies not only blamed the governments for the abysmal condition of the cooperative sector, but also the donor community. The latter's preference for quick solutions and one-size-fits-all strategies had seen it excessively invest in non-viable and unadapted cooperative organizations.

In the 1990s political and investment preferences of governments and donors turned to more market- and private sector- oriented fields. A number of questions arose with regard to the development of cooperatives in this new era. Firstly, would this mark an end to the promotion of cooperatives as engines for development and see these organizations in Africa fall into oblivion? Secondly, would cooperatives benefit from some kind of benign neglect by governments and donors? Thirdly, would they survive their sudden contact with market realities and fierce competitors? Fourth, would this new situation help to unveil their real comparative advantages? And finally, would cooperatives benefit from the democratic wind of change that brought with it new civil society actors, many of whom also desired to change economic modes of production and exchange?

More than ten years since the World Bank study, there is sufficient evidence to conclude that the cooperative sector has not withered away. Signs unmistakably indicate that cooperatives are still playing a determining role in the structuring of African societies: they are important economic operators in many sectors; they mobilize significant capital and social commitment; and they continue to be recognized by governments and donors. Despite different recent and promising case studies (Myers 2004, Ofeil 2005, Duursma 2004; Adeyemo 2004, Birchall 2003, Evans 2002, Younoussi 2002, Kayenwee 2001), the extent and the significance of the African cooperative movement is very much unknown. Therefore, the basic ambition of this research is to take stock of the cooperative sector with a view to assessing its value, the obstacles it encounters as well as its potential.

Methodology

This study is informed by library and field research on the cooperative traditions in Africa. The library research took an overview of the recent literature on cooperatives in Africa. The results of this research can be found in chapter one of this book. Considerable effort was made to trace most of the relevant studies that were done on the African cooperative sector in the 1990s. It is apparent that research on this subject was not abundant in this period. When political and donor attention on cooperatives sneaked away, scholars also seem to have lost much of their interest in the topic.

The field research consisted of two consecutive projects. First a rapid appraisal by "cooperative insiders" was carried out. This took the form of a questionnaire filled out by either the apex body or the government department in charge of cooperatives in sixteen African countries. Thus, in addition to the eleven countries covered by the case studies in this book, we also collected information from Burkina Faso, Madagascar, Mozambique, Tanzania and Zimbabwe. This rapid appraisal served the double purpose of showing the state of African cooperatives "at a glance" and providing a starting point for the researchers of the in-depth country studies.

Second, in-depth field studies were carried out in eleven countries. These case study countries were chosen on the basis of four criteria. They had to allow for comparison with the World Bank study (Porvali, 1993) that was mainly based on Ghana, Kenya, Niger, Nigeria, Senegal and Uganda; hence the choice of these countries. We also looked for a set of countries that reflected African diversity in terms of regions and language groups (Anglophone, Francophone, Lusophone and others). This justified adding Rwanda, Cape Verde and South Africa to the list. We also chose to have Egypt and Ethiopia as two populous countries. And, finally, countries that are accessible in terms of data and information retrieval got preference over others. The combined population of the 11 case study countries represents 52% of the total population of the continent. Table 2.1 below shows the eleven case study countries as well as the sixteen rapid appraisal countries.

Table 2.1: Countries covered in the study

11 Case study countries	16 rapid appraisals
Ghana Kenya Niger Nigeria Senegal Uganda Rwanda Cape Verde South Africa Egypt Ethiopia	Same countries as for case studies *In addition:* Burkina Faso Madagascar Mozambique Tanzania Zimbabwe

The in-depth country studies were carried out by academically qualified local researchers who were briefed on the research issues and the methodology during a three-day workshop in Nairobi, Kenya. Their field research was executed from September to December 2005. The resultant individual country papers were subjected to an anonymous peer review process before the final results of the research were discussed during a second three-day workshop in Addis Ababa, Ethiopia.

The cooperative sector in Africa: extent, structure, vibrancy

The extent of the cooperative sector: figures and tendencies

The first questions that come to mind when we study the significance of cooperatives in Africa are certainly: how many cooperatives are operational in Africa? How many people do they represent?

To be able to answer these important questions, we need to clarify two methodological questions related to the validity and reliability of the available data.

First of all, whom do we take into consideration when we talk of a cooperative? For pragmatic reasons, it was decided that this study would rely on a rather broad definition of cooperatives. In accordance with *ILO Recommendation 193, cooperatives are defined as group-based, autonomous enterprises with open and voluntary membership and democratic governance*. To qualify to be a cooperative, the organization has to realize its objectives through economic transactions in a market environment.

The idea of this definition is to make a clear distinction between the profit sector at one end (traditional private companies) and non-economic associations at the other end (political and religious groups, trade unions, interest groups, etc.). Purists, however, will argue that many organizations which are covered by this definition cannot be identified as cooperatives, because they are not registered as such or because they would not even want to be considered as cooperatives. Still, the spirit of this book is that "being a cooperative in name" is less important than "being an open and democratically structured group of people who jointly carry out economic activities to the benefit of all members of the group and, by extension, the whole society". Economic activities or transactions may be in the productive sphere (e.g. joint purchasing of agricultural inputs or joint marketing of products) as well as in the redistributive sphere (e.g. saving and credit, mutual insurance). One good pragmatic reason to go beyond the *strict interpretation* of cooperatives as those legally incorporated lies in the fact that this would only work for the Anglophone countries. Indeed, the British left to their former colonies a unified model (one category, one legislation and one governmental department assuming the tutelage). In many French-speaking countries to the contrary, the distinction between cooperatives and other group-based organizations is hardly discernible. In their social economy tradition a wide variety of business models fit the ILO definition. Not only cooperatives, but also *groupements d'intérêt économique, associations villageoises, mutuelles* and even tontines are recognized as group-based economic actors. Table 2.2 below includes these groups in the number of cooperatives. Because these groups tend to affect or contaminate the actual number of cooperatives as conventionally defined, we present these figures in italics.

An equally important question concerns the reliability of the data. The assumption, fed by a blatant absence of statistics in the available literature on African cooperatives, is that figures may be often out of date, fragmentary and incomplete. They are based on estimations rather than the actual counting and they tend to represent different realities in different countries. Due to these difficulties, data on the number of cooperatives were scrutinized in two steps. First, during the rapid appraisal exercise that was executed by relevant government agencies or apex bodies, an inside evaluation of the extent of the sector was undertaken. Secondly, the eleven country researchers scrutinized these data and complemented them with alternative sources. In Table 2.2, we deliberately indicate the source(s) and give an assessment of their reliability. For two countries, Rwanda and Nigeria, it was not possible to find reliable national data. We, therefore, extrapolated the data we found for one single province (Ruhengeri in Rwanda) or state (Enugu in Nigeria). Because the said province and state are not representative of the two countries concerned, the figure we present is not more than a rough approximation.

Table 2.2 gives an idea of the presence and the relative importance of cooperatives in Africa by listing side by side the total population and the numbers of both cooperatives and cooperative membership. We learn from this table that there are some 150,000 collective socio-economic undertakings in the sampled countries that are considered to be cooperatives or cooperative types of business. This figure could be even higher if the semi-cooperatives in the Anglophone countries were also counted. For instance, the hundreds of burial societies and pre-cooperatives in South Africa are not included in this database. But, this figure could also be much less if we subtracted the dormant ones. Estimates from Kenya, for instance, indicate that as many as 35% of the registered cooperatives may be dormant. A recent count in Uganda revealed that only 47% of the registered societies could qualify as "active".

Table 2.2: Number of cooperatives and cooperative members in 11 African countries

Country	Pop. (million)	n of coops	n of members	Source & reliability
Cape Verde	0.47	300	6 000	Fenacoop (consumer coop federation – figures of 2002)
Egypt	73.4	13 100	10 150 000	General Cooperative Union (apex) 2005
Ethiopia	72.4	14 400	4 500 000	Federal Cooperative Commission (gov't), 2005
Ghana	21.4	2 850	2 400 000	all registered coops (GCC apex & Dep.of Coop, 2005) + 11 000 village assoc (1 300 are viable)
Kenya	32.4	10 640	3 370 000	Min. of Coop, 2004 (7 000 estimated active)
Niger	12.4	*11 300*	*332 000*	*incl. Pre-coops*; figures problematic (different departments, 2003)
Nigeria	127.1	*50 000*	*4 300 000*	Extrapolation of Enugu State figures, problematic (Dep. Of Coop, 2004)
RSA	45.2	5 000	75 000	Registrar's Office, 2005
Rwanda	8.5	*33 631*	*1 600 000*	Extrapolation of Ruhengeri province; *incl pre-coops and non-coops* (Care Internat, 2003)
Senegal	10.3	*6 000*	*3 000 000*	incl also GIE and pre- and non-coops (BS/OAP, Senegal Ministry of Agriculture, 2006)
Uganda	26.6	7 476	323 000	Uganda Coop. Alliance, 2004 Registrar (n of coops), 2005
Total	*429.8*		*30 136 000*	*(average penetration rate 7%)*

Source: UNFPA (figures 2003); this research (2005).

When we divide the number of members of cooperatives by the number of potential members (i.e. the total population), we get the penetration rate of the sector. This is also called the "cooperative density". In fact, to assess the penetration rate, figures about the active population would be more appropriate, but such figures would be even harder to come by and also less reliable[1]. In addition, we have to be conscious of the fact that in some countries non-active youngsters are involved in school cooperatives and non-active elderly people remain members of credit unions, burial societies or health care cooperatives.

Box 2.1: African cooperatives and co-operators in international networks

Statistics about African cooperatives are scarce. One of the main reasons for this is undoubtedly the low participation of African cooperatives in international apex organizations such as the International Cooperative Alliance (ICA), the World Council of Credit Unions (WOCCU) or the International Raiffeisen Union (IRU).

For instance, in the statistics from ICA (1996) dated from 1995, covering 26 associated cooperatives from 16 African countries, African countries made up 14 million members of a world total of 765,258,821. Thus, the African region made the smallest representation within the ICA. Only four countries, namely Egypt, Kenya, Senegal and Tanzania, had member organizations with membership of over one million.

On the other hand, only four countries, namely Kenya, Malawi, Rwanda and South Africa, are members of WOCCU (2005). In 2004, 3,027 credit unions representing over 2.5 million members were active in these 4 countries. Total WOCCU numbers for Africa are 7,856 credit unions with over 7 million members, comprising a small part of the world totals of over 43,000 credit unions with 136,000,000 members. Only two African countries, Egypt and Kenya, have members in the International Raiffeisen Union.

---

[1] E.g. the ECA, the United Nations' Economic Commission for Africa does not reveal any figures in that respect. Statistics derived from www.unhabitat.org indicate that about 55% of the African population is situated in the age category 15-64 years, a category which roughly corresponds with the "population at an active age". This category is still different from the "active population" which counts only the professionally active (excluding the unemployed, the sick and destitute and the non-active for other reasons, e.g. studying). As many Africans survive and work in a subsistence or informal economy the difference between "active" and "unemployed" is often academic. Activity indexes as known in many industrialized countries are impossible to produce in most of Africa.

Taking all our reservations into account, we come to an average penetration rate of 7%. This means that for every 100 Africans (including children and the elderly), seven people are likely to be members of a cooperative. Schwettmann (1997:5) arrived at a similar conclusion some ten years ago based on data collected by ILO missions in 30 African countries between 1989 and 1996.

Our figures thus show that the cooperative sector, despite a recent history that was not all that easy, still makes for a substantial presence in many African countries. There is evidence to infer that the cooperative density today is no lower than ten years ago. Taking into account the demographic evolutions on the continent, one would even be tempted to conclude that today more people are involved in African cooperatives or cooperative types of organizations than a decade ago. Reference to the World Bank studies of the early ninety nineties makes us also believe that the total number of active cooperatives as well as the number of people involved in Africa has increased. Data from four countries presented in Table 2.3 below illustrates this point.

Table 2.3: Evolution of number of cooperatives in selected countries

	Active coops		Members (millions)	
	1989-1992	2005	1989-1992	2005
Ghana	1 000	2 850	n.a.	2.4
Kenya	4 000	7 000	2.5	3.3
Nigeria	29 000	50 000	2.6	4.3
Senegal	2 000	6 000	n.a.	3.0

Source: Porvali (1993); this research (2005).

It appears that during the last century, at least in a number of countries, the cooperative sector was purified and revamped. Some old cooperatives were revitalized and survived the liberalization process. Insolvent and non-competitive cooperatives were closed down. There is a proliferation of new cooperatives that are less dependent on state support than was the case in the past. Membership is now free and keeps pace with demographic evolution and services rendered by the cooperatives. The latter can only be interpreted as an explicit support of large segments of the population for an approach which is in line with the international cooperative tradition.

On the other hand, the *differences between countries* are considerable. Some countries (Egypt, Senegal, Ghana, Kenya and Rwanda) have a cooperative membership penetration rate of over 10%, while others are struggling with around 1 or 2% (Niger, Uganda, Cape Verde).

Overall it would be fair to say that the cooperative sector is by far one of the most widespread popular sectors in Africa. In terms of membership, it outreaches or equals trade union or religious affiliation in many countries. But, as this study reveals again, cooperatives – in most cases – are part of a sector rather than a social movement and thus have much less cohesiveness, visibility and concomitant socio-political leverage.

It can also be observed that in some countries (Egypt, Senegal, Ghana) the *average size* of cooperatives tends to be large (about 800 to 1,000 members) while in others (Rwanda, Niger, Cape Verde and South Africa) a cooperative counts fewer than 50 members on average. The country studies reveal that large cooperatives can be found in "traditional" cooperative sectors such as agriculture and credit. The new generation of cooperatives involved in new crops, distribution, handicraft production, tourism or health and social services tends to be smaller in size. This would explain why cooperatives may be smaller on average in countries where they had to make a new start (e.g. Uganda, Cape Verde and partly South Africa) than in countries where cooperatives continued to operate in the traditional sectors (e.g. Egypt and Ghana).

Structure and integration of the cooperative sector

"Cooperation among cooperatives" is one of the key principles guiding cooperatives worldwide. By creating secondary structures, federations, unions, leagues, confederations and possibly a national apex body, a more integrated cooperative sector or network comes into being. The nomenclature for these structures differs from country to country and from one cooperative tradition to another. The way and degree of integration can also differ a lot. Horizontal integration takes place when "neighbouring" cooperatives involved in different activities work together. Agricultural cooperatives, for example, can make arrangements with rural financial cooperatives for pre-harvest credit provision within the same region. Vertical integration, on the other hand, happens when cooperatives in one and the same industry or trade seek mutual advantages through cooperation. Credit union leagues or federations, for example, can function as the financial centre; conduct operational audits; or re-insure the loan portfolio of the affiliated credit cooperatives. In many cases, federations of agricultural cooperatives are responsible for processing, packaging, marketing and exporting produce. Once these secondary or tertiary structures become operational and *speak out on behalf* of their affiliated cooperatives, the sector can take the shape of a popular movement. These structures bring social cohesion to the movement; streamline operations; and represent the movement.

At the next level downwards, secondary structures may claim their legitimacy by providing those services which single primary cooperatives cannot take up, such as training and technical assistance as well as representation and lobbying vis-à-vis government, donors and other social and political actors. On paper, secondary and tertiary cooperatives thus bring the benefits of economies of scale and leverage. The question is whether this has worked in Africa?

Previous research argued that it was inappropriate to talk about cooperative *movements* in most developing countries due to the absence of such integration (Develtere, 1993; 1994). The sector was far too fragmented and dependent on outside patrons (governments and donors) for the services that single cooperatives could not provide. If there were many federations or apex bodies, they were largely imposed on the sector by governments and other agencies that wanted to implement their blueprint for the cooperative sector (Hyden, 1988).

The question now remains what kind of cooperative system is in the making in Africa. Are the imposed federative and apex structures being replaced by self-organizing networks? Desrochers and Fischer (2005) provide a useful conceptual tool for understanding this. They suggest distinguishing between atomized systems, loosely structured consensual networks and highly integrated strategic networks. The key difference is that in a strategic network the traditional apex of cooperative federations becomes a "hub node" with the key function of strategic leadership. The hub is thus preoccupied with strategic planning and decision making for the entire network. For example, in strategic networks the primary societies are bound by network decisions. This might include mandatory pooling of resources and standardization of operations in areas chosen by the network. The central node can also be the prudential supervisor of the first-tier affiliates, be in charge of brand promotion or can introduce mechanisms of collective insurance designed to assist members in difficulties.

On the basis of our country studies, we conjecture that the previous model of imposed federative and apex structures (which we could call "dependent strategic networks") has been abandoned in most countries. Such structures have, however, not been replaced with voluntary and autonomous strategic networks as one would have expected, but mostly by voluntary and (relatively) autonomous consensual networks.

The different country studies make it clear that the archetypical movement model (apex – federations – unions – primary cooperatives) does not exist in practice. Egypt and Kenya come closest to this model but structures are often defunct or contested. In Egypt, the apex (General Cooperative Union) as well as the trade organized national unions (agriculture, consumers, fisheries, producers and housing) continue to be weakened by interference by the respective patronizing ministries. In Kenya, several secondary cooperatives suffer from severe mismanagement. This has resulted in, among other things, delays of payments to farmers for their produce. The market liberalization of the early 1990s has had a profound and often beneficial effect on the rapport between primary and secondary *casu quo* tertiary cooperatives and even on the performance of the former. Owango et al. (1998), for example, found that when the urban milk marketing monopoly of the Kenya Cooperative Creameries was lifted, the role of the unregulated raw milk market increased dramatically. But this also helped to increase real milk prices paid to producers by up to 50%. Large increases were observed in the provision of veterinary and artificial insemination services by the dairy farmers' cooperative societies. Their client-based production and credit facilities enabled them to compete effectively with the independent private sector. The apex body, having failed to represent secondary societies vis-à-vis government in demanding better services, seemed not to have added value. It fell subject to mismanagement and ethnic quarrels and became a largely redundant institution.

In Nigeria and Ghana, apex and secondary cooperatives (though economically viable) have been "hijacked" and staffed by the government. In Senegal as well as Niger, our round-up reveals an extended and rather inextricable pattern of unions representing cooperatives and other organizations ("groupements" and "associations"). Such unions are geographically and trade based, but are also sometimes based on both criteria. In Niger it is hard to assess the extent to which the existing federations of cooperatives are really representative, for the government holds on to a rather interventionist approach. Trade federations with both cooperatives and non-cooperatives as members are emerging in Rwanda (e.g. Ferwathé) and Uganda (e.g. Nucafe).

Both are countries where the old cooperative sector has, for different reasons, disintegrated. The newly launched Rice Cooperative Union (Ucorirwa) in Rwanda plays a major role in negotiating prices with the government. Ethiopia is yet to establish secondary structures, which means that cooperative societies there are still dependent on the government and donors for any attempt at representation and integration. In Cape Verde, the only integrative "structure" worth mentioning is Fenacoop, representing the various consumers' cooperatives. The South African cooperative sector has a rather fragmented image, with an apex body (NCASA) to which both secondary and primary societies can affiliate. Many cooperatives however – and this presumably applies to a good part of Sub-Sahara Africa – live and die without ever belonging to a secondary or tertiary structure.

Box 2.2: Cooperative networks in some African countries not covered in this study

Apart from the individual cooperatives, movements and networks that are present and active in the countries under review, Africa counts a number of very viable and vibrant cooperative initiatives.

The Cameroon Cooperative Credit Union League (CamCUL), for example, was established in 1968 as the umbrella organization of the credit cooperatives in the country. It presently (2005) represents some 168 credit unions with over 200,000 affiliates. The assets of the movement total over 37 billion FCFA; its savings portfolio amounts to 30 billion FCFA; and outstanding credit total over 20 billion FCFA. In 2000, the League established the Union Bank of Cameroon plc. Together with its affiliates, it holds 75% of the share capital of the UBC, the remainder being held by Rabobank of the Netherlands and the general public.

The CDI-Bwamanda in the Democratic Republic of Congo is another example of a highly integrated strategic network. The CDI (*Centre de Développement Intégral*) started in 1968 and remains one of the few surviving social economy organizations in the country. In addition, it is one of the few economic agents in a region of approximately 60,000 km2 in the northern province of Equateur. The organization employs over 550 people. A pivotal role is played by the commercialization of coffee, soya beans, corn and rice. Between 1975 and 2003 CDI-Bwananda bought over US$ 38 million worth of coffee and over US$ 17 million worth of other crops from over 100,000 farmer families. Coffee is largely sold through the Max Havelaar fair trade circuit. Benefits derived from these economic activities are re-invested in health care, social infrastructure and road maintenance. Some 115,000 persons are affiliated to the CDI Mutual Health Insurance Scheme (*mutuelle de santé*) (Develtere & Stessens, 2005).

Then there is the Groupements Naam, a farmers' movement that took root in the Yatenga Province of Burkina Faso. The movement, which is inspired by traditional and modern forms of cooperation, preaches development without destruction (*développer sans abîmer*). This fast-growing movement is now present in over 1,500 villages all over the country. It counts over 600,000 affiliates organized in 5,000 local groups. Its more than 85 unions are all represented by the *Fédération Nationale des Groupements Naam*. Each group is involved in a number of food production and marketing activities, self-help initiatives, adult education and the fight against drought. The groups create wells, dams, vegetable gardens, village woodlots and cereal banks. The Naam have also created the so-called Traditional Savings and Credit Banks. In 1976 the Groupements Naam were founding members of a regional movement of farmers, involving partner organizations in nine West African countries. The movement was called the Six-S, referring to their common goal to "savoir se servir de la saison sèche en Savanne et au Sahel" ("to know how to benefit from the dry season in the Savannah and the Sahel").

The *main tendencies* in this complex field seem to be three-fold. First, there is certainly a slow but irrevocable erosion of the unified cooperative model in those countries (mainly Anglophone) where they were introduced. In some countries, such as Tanzania or Egypt (Putterman, 1995; Aal, 1998), where the cooperatives were strongly linked with other government-controlled marketing boards, credit agencies and training institutions, it took years of tinkering with institutional details before the cooperatives were weaned from government. Gibbon (1992: 87) in his discussion of African agriculture under structural adjustment concluded that "Cooperatives ... in most parts of Africa are state-instituted and state-organized bodies, which have somehow escaped the agenda of reform". He concluded that "there has been unholy compromise to maintain a polite silence over cooperatives, between donors wanting to secure abandonment of single-channeled marketing organization and governments wishing to retain control of economically and politically important functions". But, more than ten years later, in every single country under review, this liberalization process has come with a loss of monopoly position for cooperative unions and boards.

Second, a viable alternative seems to be a progressive strengthening of trade- or industry-based structures. Bottom-up growth and consensual networking and integration is taking place between cooperatives involved in similar trades or industries. In the agricultural sector this has led to the creation of some very viable "movements" such as the previously mentioned Federation of Rice Producers in Rwanda, the Oromiya Coffee Producers Federation in Ethiopia or Nucafe in Uganda. The credit cooperative sector is also witnessing this tendency. Examples of these are the credit union federations in countries like Kenya and Senegal. Interestingly both the agricultural and the credit sector show that this emergence of voluntary and consensual networks also makes room for alternative movements competing amongst each other for member affiliation, market share and social influence. In Bénin, for example, no fewer than four different financial cooperative networks exist (Kaba, Gueyie & Sinzogan, 2005). In addition, each of them[2] has a rather low level of integration. Desrochers and Fischer (2005) use data for Benin, Senegal, Mali and Madagascar (and many other non-African countries) to conclude that for the financial cooperative sector, there is a strong interaction between efficiency and level of integration. Lower (higher) integration tends to improve the efficiency of financial cooperatives in markets with lower (higher) levels of maturity of the financial sector.

The third tendency we notice is the gradual blending of cooperatives and other economically active group-based organizations. In the 1990s, as we have seen, many donors shifted preferences from the formal cooperative structures to informal self-help organizations (Birgegaard & Genberg, 1994). But co-operators as well, in many countries, wanting to avoid association with a derelict cooperative system and the sullied image of the sector, invested in other types of organizations. This was certainly the case in those countries that already had experience with a more holistic social economy model. This was also very apparent in countries such as Ethiopia and Rwanda where the cooperative system was less strongly embedded in, or linked to, the state apparatus. Regime change in these countries wiped out most of the cooperative legacy. However, in other parts of Africa there were also experiments with self-help groups, community-based organizations or micro-finance institutions. Federations then did not insist anymore on the cooperative denomination per se, but welcomed and promoted other types of organizations.

---

[2] Fédération des caisses d'épargne et de crédit agricole mutuel (FECECAM), la Fédération nationale des Caisses rurales d'épargne et de prêts (FENACREP), les Caisses d'épargne et de crédit (CEC) and the Caisses villageoises d'épargne et de crédit autogérés (CAVECA).

The basic thrusts of the African cooperative sector

One of the objectives of this study was to become familiar with the inside of African cooperatives, particularly the kind of activities they are carrying out and the people belonging to them. To this end, each researcher interviewed key people of the cooperative sector, the government and the donor community. In addition, at least two more profound investigations took place in selected individual cooperatives. In selecting the two cooperatives for this purpose, the researchers looked for one cooperative renowned for its success and another one that faced structural weaknesses. In total some 27 case studies were generated in the eleven sampled countries.

Client-owned agricultural cooperatives dominate in numbers

Most cooperatives in Africa are *client-owned* rather than worker-owned and are related to *agricultural* activities. In the context of this study, we have defined worker-owned cooperatives as those in which the professional activities of the members coincide with the cooperative's activities. The existence of such cooperatives in Africa, as is the case elsewhere, is very much the exception rather than the rule. The South African case studies are some of the exceptional examples of worker-owned cooperatives. This is possibly the case because the political and ideological context in South Africa encourages the creation of such cooperatives just as the post-colonial political context in Benin, Tanzania, Niger or Guinea encouraged collectives[3].

The idea behind client-owned cooperatives is that the cooperative can support individual or household economic undertakings. Farmers, in other words, want to concentrate on their own farming business. They feel they are lacking the time, the knowledge and the social capital when buying seeds, fodder and fertilizers or selling their produce to the market. Handing over these activities to a jointly-owned cooperative protects them from losing income because of ignorance over prices or being cheated by untrustworthy traders. Most African cooperatives are unifunctional, though many call themselves "multipurpose cooperatives". The examples of Nguru Nsukka cooperative in Nigeria and Lume Adama Cooperative in Ethiopia show that providing farm inputs to members and marketing members' produce is often a difficult job for small and young cooperative entities, such that they get

---

[3] It would be plausible to assume that the South African cooperative movement is to some extent countercyclical. According to the typology of Melnyk (1985), most African cooperatives could be described as "coming from a socialist tradition and trying to find their rightful place in a liberal-democratic tradition". South Africa for obvious reasons totally missed out on the "socialist wave" during the 70s and 80s which explains the lesser degree of aversion to collective property in the new emergent cooperative movement.

overwhelmed to take on other functions. However, we still find in many cases that after a consolidation period – i.e. after the cooperative has managed to generate and set aside some of the surpluses – they tend to venture out into ancillary activities directly related to the core business of the cooperative. This was the case for the Rooibos tea cooperative in South Africa that started with storage, packaging and equipment. Others seek expansion in the field of credit, insurance, education or medical services. The examples of the El-Mehala Al-kubra Cooperative in Egypt as well as the Kuapa Kokoo Cooperative in Ghana indicate that these additional services of the cooperatives are developed at the explicit demand of the members. They bring benefits to the members as well as to the cooperative because they enhance social cohesion within the member constituency and guarantee greater loyalty of members to the cooperative business.

Savings and credit cooperatives dominate in financial strength

Over the last two decades, credit initiatives have been proliferating all over Africa and the world. They are very varied in operational terms. Lapenu and Zeller (2002) distinguish between cooperatives, solidarity groups, village banks and micro banks using individual contracts. But the sector is also very diverse in terms of integration. Many credit initiatives work in splendid isolation and only survive because of external assistance. Others belong to more integrated networks. In many countries (Kenya, Nigeria, Niger, Rwanda, Cape Verde) saving and credit cooperatives (SACCOs) are the second largest cooperative sector – and still expanding. Quite often a SACCO is grafted onto an existing organization (parish, trade union, company, etc.) or another cooperative (mainly agricultural cooperative). Very much like micro-finance institutes, SACCOs respond to the ever imminent need for access to capital by the poorer segments of society in Africa. Using a postal survey conducted by the International Food Policy Research Institute (IFPRI) in 1999, Lapenu and Zeller (2001) found that in Africa (contrary to other parts of the world) SACCOs were the predominant form of micro-finance institutions. Zeller (2003: 21) contends that the major comparative advantages of SACCOs or credit unions lie in their ability to service large numbers of depositors, and use these savings to provide a diversified range of loans to individual members. Another key strength is their ability to reach out to people who would otherwise remain excluded from the financial markets. He concludes that while most members of credit unions are non-poor, they also reach many poor people because of their breadth of outreach. Some of the credit unions reviewed in this study present impressive records in this regard. The Harambee

Savings and Credit Cooperative in Kenya has no fewer than 84,000 members, employs 235 staff and had a turnover of over 500,000,000 Kenya Shillings (equivalent to about US$. 7,100,000) in 2005. In the same country, Mwalimu SACCO presented even better figures in the year under review. With fewer members (44,400) it had a turnover of over 700,000,000 Kenya Shillings (about US$. 10,000,000). In Senegal over half a million people belong to one of the three largest credit and savings movements. In Rwanda, 398,799 persons or 12% of the adult population are affiliated to one of the savings and credit cooperative societies affiliated to the Union of People's Banks (*Union des Banques Populaires*). In 2004, their collective savings totaled some 44 million US dollars. In the same year, the 250 member societies of the Ghana Cooperative Credit Unions Association served over 156,000 cooperative shareholders, who had deposits of over 314 billion cedis and benefited from some 262 billion cedis in loans.

A myriad of other cooperatives

Apart from agriculture and credit, African cooperatives are involved in many more sectors. The Senegal chapter, for example, describes the strategic place of *housing cooperatives* for marginalized migrants in the suburban periphery of Dakar. In North and East Africa as well, housing cooperatives are of increasing importance in the context of the influx of rural masses into the big cities. In Ethiopia alone there are some 3,400 housing cooperatives. The Egyptian Housing Cooperative Federation has almost 2,000 member cooperatives that cater for 2 million members. In Kenya there are some 495 housing cooperatives. It is generally the case that the number of people housed by these cooperatives is relatively small in relation to the need for shelter. However, the number of informal self-help housing projects and NGOs that work along cooperative lines in urban as well as rural impoverished areas is certainly increasing.

In Cape Verde the *consumers' cooperatives* represent two thirds of the country's cooperative affiliates. The consumer cooperatives also have an important presence in Egypt where the relevant federation represents 4,320 consumer shops. Abdel Aal in his chapter on Egypt remarks that their business has been expanding quite a bit in the last couple of years. Consumer cooperatives are also well established in Uganda (with some 240 consumer cooperatives), Kenya (with some 180 societies) and Senegal (with over 120 consumer societies).

Transport cooperatives are also found in most of the countries under review.

There is a large number of them in Uganda (275). In several countries they are operating in the tourism and urban transport sectors. Of more recent vintage are a growing number of *handicraft, cottage industry and other small productive cooperatives*. As was mentioned earlier, only in a minority of cases are these cooperatives worker-owned cooperatives. This though is the case with the 400-plus and relatively successful Egyptian workers' cooperatives as well as with the new-wave black workers' cooperatives in South Africa. In many other countries the members have a more loose relationship with their "industrial" cooperative. This is the case for more than 1,500 handicraft cooperatives in Ethiopia, the craftsmen cooperatives and the Jua Kali ("Hot Sun") cooperatives of the informal sector workers in Kenya.

Further we see that cooperatives in most countries also penetrate new domains. In Ghana we note the special importance of *cooperative distilleries*. These societies benefited from a special piece of legislation, which enjoins all distillers and dealers in the local gin ("akpeteshi") to belong to a distillers' cooperative. This law permits the cooperative to collect taxes on behalf of the state. At the same time this tax collection exercise helps them to collect regular contributions from over 35,000 cooperative members. Through this research, we also discovered cooperatives in the mining sector, the recreational sector, engineering, basic infrastructure, educational services and health services. The social base, the employment effect and the economic performance of some of the cooperatives can be gauged in Table 2.4 below.

Table 2.4: The socio-economic base and performance of selected cooperatives

Country	Name and type	Members	Direct employees	Key figures	Main purpose	Other services
Cape Verde	UNICOOP de Fogo (consumers)	404	58	E2.8 million turnover	Consumer goods	Loans, house repair, funeral assistance
Egypt	Agricultural Production Coop Giza	145	145 (member-workers)	n.a.	Joint production	skills development, transport
Egypt	General Cooperative for Weaving and Spinning Workers	38 950	900	E.£69.2 million turnover	Consumer goods	
Ethiopia	Oromia Coffee Farmers' Union (sec.)	74 725	20	$ 8 million turnover 2 691 tons of coffee	Coffee marketing and exports	Coffee shops in Europe and US; founded a Coop Bank
Ghana	Kuapa Kokoo Ltd (cocoa marketing)	45 000	261	Sells 38 000 tons of cocoa per year	Cocoa marketing	savings and credit, community development, chocolate
Kenya	Githunguri Dairy Farmers Coop	6 000	300	80 000 litres of milk per day, Ksh 1 billion turnover	Milk marketing and processing	Animal feed; insemination; extension; credit
Madagascar[4]	Union FFTA Region Sofia (sec.)	2 351	n.a.	Capital in 2003: Fmg 659 mio	agriculture	joint purchasing of inputs & joint marketing
Madagascar	Union ROVA (sec.) Region Vakinankaratra	270	n.a.	Fmg 412 mio turnover in 2003	dairy collection & processing	
Mozambique	UGC (União Geral de Cooperativas Agro-Pecuárias de Maputo) (sec.)	6 600	1 250 (staff and workers)	n.a.	poultry production cooperative	Input; credit; health services; member education (95% women)
Niger	Groupements Mooriben (cereal banks) (tert.)	19 112	450	Covers 37% of food requirements	Grain storage	Input supply, credit, extension, radio

Nigeria	CICS Nigerian Police Cooperatives (sec.)	110 000	120		Credit & consumer items	
Nigeria	University Women's Coop Society	250	55	n.a.	Consumer goods	Nursery school
Rwanda	Union des Banques Populaires (sec.)	398 799	600	$ 44 million savings, $36 million loans, $1.5 million net profit	Savings and credit	Risk coverage
Rwanda	UCORIRWA National Union of Rice-growers (sec.)	40 148		Covers 35% of national rice consumption	Joint production & sale	Maintenance & infrastructure
Senegal	Housing Cooperative Mboro	400	30	CFA 800 million invested	Construction	Life insurance
Senegal	Fenajee Fédération Nationale des GIE de Pêcheurs (sec.)	45 000		Assets: 11 000 pirogues	Tools & credit for fishing & fish processing	Lobbying
South Africa	Rooibos Tea Cape Town	36	2	n.a.	Joint tea production	Member training, replication
Tanzania	Kasimana Agricultural Marketing Cooperative Society	160	6	T.Sh 176 million	Tobacco marketing	Distribution of inputs to members
Uganda	Jinja Teachers Savings and Credit Cooperative	600	2	$22,000 savings $19,600 loans	Savings and credit	Burial society, skills training
Uganda	Uganda Co-op Transport Union UCTU	44	95	$ 3.5 million	Joint transport	

Source: this research.

[4] Madagascar data: www.fert.fr holding FERT-Madagascar, *Rapport d'activités 2003 et Perspectives 2004. Un engagement professionnel et durable au coté des paysans malgaches*, Paris, 2004. Mozambique data: www.oxfam.ca/news/Mozambique/anniversary.htm (as retrieved on 11 Apr.)

Membership of African cooperatives: where are the poor and the women?

The available literature on African cooperatives is extremely scarce and mostly casuistic. But still when it comes to membership it generally advances two hypotheses. One is that the members' profile reflects the social stratification outside the cooperatives; inferring that cooperatives have limited potential for altering social relations in society. Poorer segments of the population would not find their way to the cooperatives. They might even be excluded from the. Secondly, and in line with the first, participation of women is said to be weak and mainly serves to legitimize and perpetuate existing inequalities.

Our findings bring some more perspective to this rough sketch. Most of the country studies indicate that cooperatives mainly operate in rural and urban areas where poverty prevails. For the whole of the sector it can be concluded that the rural poor smallholders constitute the bulk of the members. Many country studies also report the existence of poor-only cooperatives. They are created to enable members to do petty trading and support each other in periods of crisis or when in need of credit. Many of these cooperatives are not registered or recognized by the authorities in any other way. Many are also created for support-lobbying purposes by poor people who are aware of the donor or government preference for cooperative types of organizations. As suggested by social capital literature (Narayan & Pritchett, 1999; Maluccio, Haddad & May, 2000) it can be expected that the poor who participate in these cooperative groups gain important returns from their participation. These cooperatives can help to mitigate risks and vulnerability through (mostly informal and ad hoc) self-help practices or other mutually beneficial exchanges. But for several reasons most are not able to help members to break out of mere subsistence and the cooperatives themselves mostly remain stagnant. The homogeneous membership composition is in this regard a major structural hindrance, for capital formation is limited. The applied solidarity mechanisms are distributive rather than redistributive. The social relationships and, thus, social capital are restricted. Many have severe organizational and leadership capacity deficits. A few cases reported in our country studies contradict this pessimistic view. However we guess that the relative success of some Jua Kali ("hot sun") cooperatives in Kenya, the shoe shiners' cooperative in Uganda and the Young Christian Workers' cooperatives in Rwanda is related to the fact that some not-so-poor members adhere to and invest in these cooperatives. These can be better-off farmers or traders who join the cooperatives to acquire direct material and power benefits. But these can also be adherents or constituents who are not potential beneficiaries (donors, public servants, religious people). In other words, the social capital of these cooperatives extends beyond the group of the poor.

A large proportion of the cooperatives in Africa (and elsewhere) are constituted on a heterogeneous membership base, mixing poor and not-so-poor. The relevant question that arises in this regard is whether the poor also control their cooperatives. In one of the few detailed surveys done on this subject, Aal and Hassan (1998) found that among the membership of agricultural credit cooperatives in Egypt, 44.2% of the farmers were illiterate; but only 24.8% of the board members were illiterate. Also, board members tended to hold more land.

In many countries the mere fact that members have to pay up shares and sometimes need to pay yearly membership fees prevents the poorest from participating. Day labourers and vagabonds will find it hard to become members of a cooperative as they constitute an underclass, which is likely to be avoided even by poor farmers and cattle herders. The country case studies also indicate that many SACCOs attract the new lower-middle classes (public servants, nurses, teachers, small business people and professional groups). Even if they do reach rural and urban poor constituencies, as is the case in all countries under review, SACCOs tend to attract the somewhat better-off poor groups. A study by Petrie (2002) on Rwandan credit unions revealed that member households had higher monthly expenses (US$ 263[5]) than non-member households (US$ 162). But this study as well as our cases provides evidence that African credit unions do represent a considerable group of the poor. In this way they generate social relationships across social strata. They also generate social capital across other social divisions. Fredrick Wanyama, in the Kenyan country study in this book, for example, indicates that people from diverse ethnic backgrounds participate in the same financial cooperatives. This has positive effects in the sense explained by Narayan (1999) as both bonds and bridges (social capital among commons and others) are essential for social cohesion and poverty reduction.

As for *gender*, most cooperatives are initiated, composed and run by men. When there is a mixed composition, male members and directors tend to dominate the cooperative. For instance, 75% of the membership of Kenyan agricultural cooperatives is male. As Wanyama explains, this is directly related to the traditional male ownership of agricultural assets (land, livestock,

[5] Adjusted for business and farm expenditure

equipment ...). In other sectors such as SACCOs or consumers' cooperatives, women often have a more important position and role. This is reflected in both general memberships, positions on the board of directors, staff and management team. It is generally recognized that women are far more reliable when it comes to repayment of credit, which makes them more eligible to represent a household in a SACCO. In French-speaking West Africa, a fair share of the *Groupements d'Intérêt Economique* are women-only groups, for emancipation of women was one of the reasons to launch such groups. Donor preference for gender-based affirmative action is certainly not foreign to this, but some of these cooperatives play a considerable role in voicing the interests of the women. In Senegal, for example, 15,800 women are reportedly involved in ten women-only cooperatives that joined forces in the National Union of Cooperating Women of Senegal.

The only country where the gender composition is reversed is South Africa, where two thirds of the members in the registered "emerging" cooperatives (i.e. black-owned, as opposed to the established white-owned cooperatives) are women. This probably reflects the culture of militancy which many women acquired during and after the struggle against apartheid.

Maybe our *main conclusion* on membership characteristics is methodological rather than substantial: even at micro-level, there is an alarming *lack of data* on the constituency of cooperative initiatives. Without an elementary insight into the actual state of the membership, any policy directed towards cooperatives in Africa will be very speculative with regard to impact and strengthening of the movement.

The vibrancy of African cooperatives

Our rapid appraisal carried out in 16 countries indicated an upward tendency in terms of numbers of cooperatives. In some countries that do not have a strong tradition in cooperative development, such as Rwanda and Ethiopia, government and donor support is speeding up the organization of cooperatives. Nevertheless, our correspondents qualified the general economic significance of the cooperative sector as poor. Their main weaknesses were found in the domains of management, leadership, governance, access to capital and the ageing of key persons. The strengths reported were the members' commitment, the large social base of the cooperative sector and the willingness to revitalize old structures. Liberalization and deregulation still remained challenges to the cooperative sector, while donor fatigue with supporting the sector seemed to be a threat to cooperative development.

It is, however, intriguing to find out what makes some African cooperatives viable and vibrant while others are not. A comparative reading of the case studies led our researchers to the following ingredients for viable cooperatives.

Cooperatives are associations

Successful cooperatives are locally embedded voluntary associations. Members have a group identity and participate in the associative life of the cooperative. This they share with other types of organizations of the social economy (Defourny, Develtere and Fonteneau, 2001). It is generally accepted that the homogeneity of interests is a crucial factor for the social dynamics of the groups, but also for their business operations. People do speak out more easily when they have a common bond and share the same experiences. People also feel more comfortable to do business with the cooperative (and thus increase their business operations) when fellow cooperators do the same. To maintain a sufficient alignment of owner interests, cooperatives tend to constrain their activities to narrow lines of business (Skurnik, 2002). Frequent contacts and interactions among and between members, management and directors are essential for enhancing trust and loyalty. Some of the cooperatives in our sample invest a lot in member-relation management and give members that extra value that makes them loyal adherents. The Menshat Kasseb Cooperative situated in Giza (Egypt), for example, does not only process and market the members' farm produce. It also provides training courses, home economics lessons to female members, health care and special assistance to small and poor farmers (e.g. subsidized shipping to markets). Independent leaders or movement entrepreneurs, with a talent for professional organization, business economics and with a good rapport with members and external agents alike, are prerequisites to every successful cooperative. They have to articulate and defend the individual and collective interests of the community they represent.

Most of the vibrant cooperatives we reviewed also had an explicit mission statement and a clear vision as to the role of the organization, its challenges and its strategies. That this can even be realized in an environment that is not so hospitable for independent cooperative enterprises is exemplified by more than 400 Mooriben groups in Niger. Sanda Maman Sani reports that a determining factor of Mooriben's success is the sharing of a common vision and the sense of belonging to the same "extended family".

In addition, all successful cases studied show cooperatives that are very result-oriented and creative in finding solutions to the daily problems of the members. The majority engineered an organizational model that could guarantee member ownership and patronage, mobilize local resources and attract sufficient external support. Several combined different legal entities such as cooperatives, trusts, GIE or NGOs. Many explicitly go for an expansive strategy. They want to grow both as associations (in terms of reach) and as businesses (in terms of profitability, market share, etc.).

Cooperatives as businesses

As has been shown in previous tables, there are a number of very important cooperative enterprises on the African continent. The viable cooperatives we studied all produce significant financial and economic benefits for the members. Those dynamic cooperatives heavily rely and insist on local capital mobilization. Even if they started with an up-front capital injection by a development agency or government, they gradually derived more financial resources through their own business operations and through shares, loans and savings by the members. As was also concluded by a recent CGAP evaluation of World Bank and UNDP supported micro-finance projects (2006), groups that are working with their own money are much more careful investors and spenders. We conjecture that expense preference and other opportunistic behaviour by management and staff can only be offset if members have sufficient financial stakes in the business. Kaba et al. (2005), discussing the excessive liquidity situation of the credit unions in Benin, however, suggest that this might ultimately also make management rather conservative. They believe that managers of credit unions often prefer less profitable investments over more risky loans to certain categories of the cooperative constituency to avoid criticism from the majority of the members.

From our cases, we can also conclude that profitable cooperatives invariably function as demand-driven and market-oriented businesses. They seek market niches and marketable products; invest in quality management; and their pricing as well as interest rate policies are inspired by the prevailing market conditions (and not by some kind of altruistic rationale). Several, like NUCAFE reported by Mrema in his country study of Uganda, give business support to members and reward quality. In successful cooperative businesses, members receive significant and often predictable returns from their investment and transactions with the cooperative. Professional staff, if necessary coming from outside the members' constituency, is hired and personnel retention policies are applied. Finally, both management and members show preference for a growth oriented approach in terms of asset base, business turnover, market share and profitability. These findings of our profitable cases, again, are confirmed by other case studies (e.g. Yeboah, 2005; Tesfaye Assefa, 2005).

The governance nexus

The successful cooperatives under review also reveal that governance elements play a crucial role in harnessing the different associative and business forces at play in a cooperative. It is often inferred that agency problems are more prevalent, disturbing and acute in cooperatives than in other (non-investor owned) businesses. In other words, cooperatives would have inherent problems in defining who best takes the entrepreneurial lead in the organization: the members, the directors or management?

There is, however, no concluding theoretical basis or empirical evidence for this pessimistic view. In any case, the different patrons of a cooperative have to find interaction patterns that minimize decision-making costs. It is known that sufficient homogeneity of interests among any potential class of patrons (members, staff, financiers, etc.) is a major determinant of the costs of collective decision making. Transparency, democratic governance, internal accountability and control are necessary ingredients to build this homogeneity of interests and to limit free riding, sub-goal or opportunistic pursuit and other deviant behaviour. The case studies confirm that the institutional set-up of the cooperative model with its general assemblies, elected and co-opted boards of directors, management committees and different controlling agencies is well suited to make these interaction patterns conflict-low and to a certain extent predictable. As the example of the fast-growing Rooibos cooperative in South Africa, as described by Jan Theron in this book, shows this often implies a lot of member education, deliberations and internal debate in order to avoid the tendency of members to go for quick wins.

External patrons

Our case studies confirm that vibrancy comes from a suitable combination of genuine internal organizational and economic capabilities and adequate support. In Kenya, for example, the Githunguri Dairy Farmers Cooperative Society shows that an accommodative and cordial relationship with the local state bureaucracy can help prevent further government intrusion on the cooperative's business operations. International support in terms of a low-interest loan further helped the cooperative in expanding its operations considerably. The Kuapa Kokoo cooperative in Ghana and the Rooibos tea cooperative in South Africa show that fair trade arrangements can help cooperatives to penetrate the larger market. Collaboration between the fair trade agent Max Havelaar and the CDI network in northern Democratic Republic of Congo generated a surplus of almost 3 million US dollars between 1995 and 2003 for this war-torn region. Eshuis and Harmsen (2003) report that fair trade allowed the Kagera Cooperative Union in Tanzania to inject extra income into the region of approximately 5 million US dollars between 1991 and 2003. Without exception, our successful cooperative cases purposely increased collaboration with other cooperatives, but also with research centres, NGOs, support agencies and other external partners that could be helpful for the cooperative. Not one developed in isolation or limited its working relations to one particular partner. Each of them sought to empower the cooperative through a conscious search for opportunities, financial, human and social capital that could benefit the cooperative project.

The role of external patrons: governments and donors

The early 1990s witnessed the liberalization and deregulation of the economy in Africa, which was more or less imposed on the African countries through the structural adjustment programmes by the World Bank and the IMF. This new context was to fundamentally alter the relationship between governments as well as donors and cooperatives. Cooperatives were now to operate as independent business enterprises. In the 1993 World Bank study on cooperatives, the conclusion reflected this reality: "(...) the review showed that rural organizations can fully develop their potential as self-managed sustainable businesses only if the country's policy and legislative framework is favorable to private sector initiatives and group activities" (Hussi et al., 1993: 70). We have seen that donors were very instrumental in legitimizing and financing the patronizing of cooperatives by the State in the post-colonial era. They were equally instrumental in dismantling this system from the 1990s onwards. What then is the new role of the government and the donor community in cooperative development in Africa?

Legislation

Governments can take various attitudes towards cooperatives. They can provide a legislative and an institutional framework that could leave cooperatives on their own or interfere in the affairs of the cooperative sector. This interference can either be supportive or controlling. With regard to control, it can be "defensive" as a government attempts to keep all civil society-born initiatives in check, or it can be "instrumental" as a government tries to use cooperatives as a vehicle for its own economic policy. As it has been described in detail, most post-independence African regimes saw cooperatives primarily as instruments for government and state bureaucracy. Cooperatives in this sense were subjected to a political logic. After the authoritative 1993 report of the World Bank the cooperative sector was supposed to be exposed to the new private sector orthodoxy. The question therefore is whether governments have lost control of cooperatives and what effect this has had on the sector. It should be pointed out that the period during which the structural adjustment incentives came into effect coincided with the transition from authoritarian to relatively democratic regimes in a number of African countries. In Table 2.5 below, we provide a snapshot of governments' rapport with the cooperative sector in the countries under review. For each country we indicate the legal instruments pertaining to cooperatives; the main government agency responsible for cooperatives; the registration mechanism; and other support measures.

It is apparent in the table that in most African countries, the rapport between government and cooperatives was reconsidered during the 1980s and 1990s. It was generally felt that the then existing legislative framework was obsolete and in need of replacement. Different countries started a consultative process involving the cooperatives themselves in drafting a suitable legislation. Despite these attempts, the Progress Report of the sixth ICA Ministerial Cooperative Conference (1999) acknowledged the fact that this did not work out as planned. The main reasons for this were the lack of knowledge and capacity within the cooperative sector and the tendency of the government to arrogate the law-making process. Different international organizations such as the ILO, the ICA and some cooperative movements from the North stepped in and played a decisive role in creating a new generation of cooperative laws. The 1995 ICA Statement on the Cooperative Identity and the 2002 ILO Promotion of Cooperatives Recommendation (193) had a catalyzing effect on the efforts to change government-cooperative sector relations and the concomitant new legislative framework. The ILO's Cooperative Branch assisted a number of national governments in formulating modern, comprehensive cooperative development policies. Several African countries have explicitly adopted the new definition and

Table 2.5: Governmental involvement in the cooperative sector

Country	Legislation	Main actor	Registration	Support policy
Cape Verde	Constitution '75 Liberalization after 1990	Disappeared; Now: independent Forum Cooperativo	(disappeared, now by costly Notary Service)	No interference or support
Egypt	Constitution 1971 & sector-wise legislation 70s-80s	Different departments (sector-wise)	Meticulous but decentralized (various bodies)	Rather directive than supportive
Ethiopia	1978, 1995 and 1998 proclamations	Federal Cooperative Commission (FCA)	by FCA (required)	Training & technical support to unions / coops
Ghana	1968 restrictive (new law in the making)	Dept. of Cooperatives Registrar	Meticulous implementation	Promote SME to become coops; Accent on pre-coops
Kenya	1966, liberalized in 1997 (policy frame & act)	Dept. of Cooperatives (promotion) (sanctioning)	Commissioner for Cooperative Development	Controlling the "cooperative character"
Niger	Many laws and regulations; a.o. 2003 (rural assoc.); 2004 (credit assoc.)	Dispersed among various Ministries	costly and not encouraged	Decentralized tutorship (for categories of GIE and Coops)
Nigeria	1993 (federal) + state laws unrestrictive	Dep. of Coop (both federal & state level)	Department of Cooperatives	Interference (policy implementation)
RSA	1981 ("Old Act") 2005 ("New Act")	Registrar's Office	Attempts to map coops (finance, members)	Limited
Rwanda	1988 legislation defunct after 1994	Provisional ministerial Task Force	(not)	2005: Task Force legislation., training & promotion
Senegal	1983 (on coops) 1995 (mutuals & saving/credit associations.)	BSOAP "Bureau Suivi Org. Auto-promotion"	BSOAP	BSOAP may intervene on demand
Uganda	1991 (now obsolete)	Department of Cooperatives (defunct)	Loose implementation	No interference or support

Source: this research, country studies, 2005.

principles. A recent example of this is the 2005 South African Cooperatives Act. But as is clear from our overview, many African countries still rely on an outdated and often dysfunctional or obsolete legal framework.

Policy lines

Our country studies clearly illustrate that cooperative policy has been very erratic in most African countries. New policy lines are promulgated and programmes are developed in an inconsistent way. This was the case during the heyday of state bureaucratic control over the cooperative sector, but it doesn't seem to have changed much. This, in general, has created a climate of uncertainty for cooperatives and their promoters.

But what is certainly apparent is that most countries have moved from a situation where government and the state apparatus were heavily involved in cooperatives towards a situation where this is less so. The degree of distance the government and the administration now have from the cooperative sector differs from country to country. The progress and effects of this weaning process and the new state-cooperatives rapport has been the subject of a number of monographic studies (Owango & Lukuyu, 1998; Akwabi-Ameyaw, 1997; Putterman, 1995) and is well illustrated in our country studies.

In Cape Verde the cooperative sector has been radically abandoned by the government and left to its own regulation. This is in sharp contrast to the initial "Marxist" zeal when this republic was still young and the cooperative mode of production was solemnly proclaimed in the constitution. After 1990, liberalization was pushed through and the different state institutions promoting the cooperative sector soon disappeared from the scene. As Gomes Mendonça reports in his chapter, this left the sector in disarray. The number of cooperatives and their membership plummeted. The Foro Cooperativo, a non-governmental coalition of cooperatives, is having great difficulty in revamping the movement without proper cooperative legislation and state support.

In Uganda, the retreat of the government has led to a collapse of many cooperative societies as well as unions. At the same time, it has enabled a shift towards non-traditional cooperatives involved in new crops such as vanilla and oil-seed. In Ghana the story is complicated by the apparent fight for control between the Department of Cooperatives and the apex body

(GCC). Tsekpo in his chapter on Ghana observes that attempts have been made to re-orient cooperatives to work in a liberalized environment, but that these efforts are frustrated by the absence of a clear government policy; the lack of competent staff in government and cooperative movement institutions; and the preference of many donors and NGOs for other types of groups.

The Kenyan government also released its grip on the cooperative sector, only to see many of them falling into decay through mismanagement and outright corruption. Now the government involvement is facilitative rather than controlling. The supervision (by the commissioner) is separated from the support services (Department). As Wanyama shows in the Kenyan case study, some cooperatives managed to come out stronger and benefited a lot from their confrontation with a freer market and competitors.

Senegal presents yet another configuration. In his chapter, Fall argues that the economic crisis of the 1990s and the Structural Adjustment Programmes triggered a revival in the cooperative movements which were seen as a solution within the reach of those who were the victims of increasing vulnerability, including the urban middle class. Yet at the same time the legislative and regulatory framework, pertaining to cooperatives as well as to specific economic sectors, remains a serious obstacle for the cooperative movement. Fall calculated, for example, that housing cooperatives need five years to complete a housing construction project including 26 months of administrative formalities before the construction work can begin and 20 months after it has been completed.

Meanwhile, other governments have taken a *more pro-active attitude* towards the cooperative sector. Interestingly, this seems to be the case in countries such as South Africa, Rwanda and Ethiopia where during the 1990s, the political scene underwent severe changes. South Africa is still in the process of (literally) getting its act together when it comes to recognizing and monitoring its new and emergent cooperatives. A Cooperatives Development Unit was established and a Cooperative Development Policy adopted. This seems to be part of a government move to bridge the divide between the formal and the informal economy and to create employment for disadvantaged groups such as women and youth. Government preferences for cooperatives in South Africa might however differ from province to province. In Kwa-Zulu Natal a provincial policy foresees that ten per cent of procurement has to be allocated to cooperatives. The technical, financial and material support to the cooperative though, for the time being, is fairly limited.

Still in the phase of reconstruction after the civil war, the government in Rwanda has taken an interest in all forms of economic group initiatives, among them cooperatives. An interministerial task force is now operational in order to reorganize and strengthen cooperatives and "inter-groupements[6]" through adequate legislation, training programmes and support structures. Also, the privatization of tea-processing plants is presented as an opportunity for cooperatives as government agreed to award 10% of shares in these plants automatically to cooperatives.

In Ethiopia, the government has gone a step further. The governmental Federal Cooperative Agency seconds personnel to cooperative unions, while at local level, leaders of primary cooperatives often have key positions in the local authorities. The government also instituted cooperative studies in four universities. Lacking a proper movement leadership in the form of apex bodies or federations, cooperatives do not have much countervailing power against so much political interest.

Bureaucratic control seems to be one of the characteristics of government involvement in Egypt's extensive cooperative sectors. It has been pointed out that the cooperative sector in this country is built up alongside a number of economic activities, which all fall under different ministries. This prevents the cooperative movement from unifying, while the "suffocating" methods of the administration block the way to competitiveness. In addition, registration in Egypt is quite a rigorous process which may deter many from taking the initiative to form a cooperative.

Finally for Niger, Sanda Maman Sani speaks of an utterly confusing avalanche of laws and regulations affecting the cooperative scene over the years. They brought a mishmash of bureaucratic measures stifling much cooperative entrepreneurship. But the ill-equipped state bureaucracy has never been able to fully stop innovative social and economic engineering as has been shown by the over 400 dynamic Mooriben farmers' groups.

All in all, African governments' involvement from 1994 onwards has been showing the following trends:

- in quite a few countries, the liberalization policy has worked as a purification process, separating the viable cooperatives from the

---

[6] In Rwanda, "groupements" often correspond to village-based farmers groups. Through monitoring of collective use of tools and equipment and joint buying of seeds and fertilizers. Quite a few of these are NGOs, these groups are scaling up into inter-groupements which become the agents for credit, tending towards economic viability and qualify as candidates to become cooperatives.

mistreated and the weak;

- because of the proliferation of new types of social economy and pre-cooperative initiatives, the registered cooperatives have lost their privileged position;

- in many cases, government agencies meant to monitor or support cooperatives are too underfunded or too understaffed to play any significant role, other than registering; and

- in several countries, the government has re-discovered the potential of cooperatives as autonomous partners in fighting poverty and social exclusion.

Where do donors fit in?

The liberalization policy has been a case of too much too soon for many cooperatives, which either collapsed or have been struggling with a lack of financial and human resources ever since. The ones who managed to survive or to re-emerge often did so through support from donors. In our country studies, we see that African cooperatives are supported by four types of development partners:

- the large international or bilateral development agencies. The most prominent ones seem to be the World Bank, the ILO, the FAO and the German GTZ;

- cooperative movements from the North, such as CCA (Canada), SCC (Sweden), ACDI-VOCA (USA) and DGRV (Germany);

- the international cooperative structures such as the ICA and WOCCU; and

- northern development NGOs.

Comparing donor involvement in cooperative development on the African continent before and after the early 1990s, we observe a number of significant changes (see also Pollet & Develtere, 2004). First, support for the cooperative sector in Africa is still mostly channeled through government departments (e.g. in Nigeria, Kenya, Niger and Egypt); through apex bodies or secondary cooperatives (e.g. in Ghana, South Africa and Rwanda); or to support agencies such as cooperative colleges. But large cooperative development projects, such as the ones funded by the Nordic countries in East Africa and the ILO-ACOPAM projects in West-Africa in the 1980s and early

1990s have made room for more modest, national and local interventions.

Secondly, agencies have replaced a project approach with a more programmatic approach. For several agencies, programmes are open-ended and flexible toolkits that permit donors and their partners to achieve jointly-established objectives in a strategic manner. Many agencies have opted for long-term working relations with a selected number of cooperative partners in lieu of short-term commitments towards a broad range of cooperatives.

We also observe that a number of agencies (particularly agencies related to the northern cooperative movement) show preference for a network and systems approach in that they foster consensual networks among cooperatives and invest in adapting the policy, legal and fiscal environment in which their partner cooperatives have to operate. In addition, traditional methods of know-how transfer are increasingly being replaced by methods of knowledge acquisition. There are few that still rely on expatriate staff within cooperative structures. In this way, cooperative partners in Africa have increased ownership of the cooperative support programmes and determine their own knowledge needs.

In the past cooperatives were often reduced to being social and welfare institutions for certain disadvantaged groups. Nowadays most agencies stress the fact that cooperatives have to be considered as private economic actors that have to make a surplus or profit. Emphasis is now more laid on issues such as financial management, solvency, profitability, financial sustainability, market penetration or return on investment. This more business-oriented approach also goes hand in hand with new support tools such as revolving loans funds, bank guarantees, loans or equity capital. Commercial links are also promoted. An example is given by a Malian cooperative growing cotton in an eco-friendly way, sending it to an Indian cooperative that makes clothes from it, which are then sold in the outlets of the Swiss cooperative retail stores called Migros. While this is an example of south-south and south-north cooperative trade, most of the commercial activities in favour of cooperatives still take place within the fair trade sector which is mainly a corrective mechanism for south-north trade.

Cooperatives indeed have been identified by fair trade organizations as the preferred producers' form. Fair-traders and cooperatives are somehow akin in their pursuit of economic development in a spirit of justice and solidarity. In addition, cooperatives do provide basic institutional stability, an institutionalized sense of ownership and a potential for growth (Duursma,

2004; Develtere & Pollet, 2005). We also have to note the increasing awareness of the potential of fair trade within the northern cooperative movement. For UK consumer cooperatives, for example, fair trade is viewed as a key way of putting cooperative values into business practice. In the UK the cooperative sector now has over 150 own brand fair trade products (Shaw, 2006). Another remarkable venture is the Day Chocolate Company which was established in 1998 in the UK and in which the Ghana cooperative network Kuapa Kokoo has a 33% ownership.

Box 2.3: Comparative advantages of fair trade

Anna Milford (2004) compared two kinds of support to southern cooperatives: "traditional" subsidies and fair trade. She wanted to know whether the negative effects of traditional support (free-rider behaviour by members, lack of innovation, leaving the management burden to others ...) would also appear when the support came through fair trade. On the basis of case studies in Chiapas (Mexico) she came to the following tentative conclusions. (1.) The minimum price guaranteed by fair trade functions as a subsidy per unit sold. This makes the fair trade premium more market related and holds a self-correcting mechanism of some sort. Still, if management ignores the cooperatives' long term viability, risks of inefficiency, moral hazard and free riding remain immanent. (2.) The cases she studied did not show that cooperative members tend to lean back and rely on the fair trade premiums to guarantee them a decent income for years to come. This may have to do with the selection of the cooperatives (being 'fair-trade-able') or with the moral-boosting effect of non-economic activities (credit schemes and political activities) launched by the cooperative on the basis of the fair trade financing. (3.) Apart from these "efficiency" questions, another effect of fair trade was illustrated. The oligopsonic cartels seem to become destabilized because of the increased level of information among farmers. This means that small farmers who do not belong to the cooperative also benefit from the altered relations between producer and wholesale buyer. Cooperatives involved in fair trade in addition function as "barometers of exploitation", indicating to non-members the extent to which they are exploited by local purchasers.

Finally, cooperative development agencies belonging to the international cooperative movement are increasingly cooperating with each other and talking with UN agencies in the framework of the UN Committee for the Promotion and Advancement of Cooperatives (COPAC). But very few contacts exist between those agencies, the fair trade movement and important NGOs involved in cooperative development in Africa.

Significance of cooperatives for African societies

One of the motives for this study was to obtain some insights into the significance of the African cooperative sector in resolving some of the major challenges the continent is facing, namely employment creation, poverty reduction, the extension of social protection and the representation of the interests of the silent majority of poor people. This difficult task was tackled in a double manner. At the aggregate level indicators were sought from the existing literature that could function as proxies for the contribution of the cooperative sector to these challenges. The real potential for cooperatives was further investigated through the 27 case studies that were carried out.

Significance of cooperatives for employment

Three levels of employment effects can be distinguished: 1. *Direct effects or wage employment*: personnel and staff of primary and secondary cooperatives and of supportive institutions (*"induced employment"* through Government Cooperative Departments, Cooperative Colleges, etc.); 2. *Indirect effects or self-employment*: members of cooperatives whose membership has a substantial role in guaranteeing a decent income; and 3. *Multiplier or spillover effects*: non-members whose professional activities are only viable through the transactions they have with cooperatives (e.g. tradesmen or suppliers of agricultural inputs and fertilizers).

The 1997 ILO study (Schwettmann, 1997: 7) estimated that the cooperative sector in 15 African countries was responsible for 158,640 direct jobs, 5,937 indirect jobs and supported 467,735 self-employed people. As for the spillover effects, no figures were given. These are the only figures made available for over a decade, which again illustrates the difficulty in obtaining reliable data on employment in Africa. Some of our researchers were able to access government or movement reports that give some idea of the direct employment effect of the cooperative sector. Cooperatives are reported to employ a staggering 77,400 staff in Kenya, 28,000 in Ethiopia, 9,500 in Egypt, 3,130 in Ghana, 2,823 in Uganda and about 800 in Rwanda. On the basis of more detailed analysis, Wanyama and Lemma suggest for Kenya and Ethiopia, respectively, that employment in the sector might even be higher than the official figures provided and shows a slow growth. A number of researchers also refer to the fact that many cooperatives do create seasonal and casual work. On the basis of available data from grain marketing cooperatives and coffee farmers' cooperative unions, Lemma estimates that over 21,000 people are recruited for casual labour services every year by the Ethiopian cooperatives. Nyamwasa calculated that in Rwanda tea planters' cooperatives engage an impressive number of temporary workers (nearly the equivalent of 4,476 permanent employees on a yearly basis).

When it comes to figuring out the number of *self-employed* workers who rely for their employment or income on their cooperative membership, the numbers are higher, but also less conclusive. For each member the question can be raised: would he/she be able to carry out his/her job without belonging to the cooperative? Has membership of a savings and credit cooperative per se a substantial effect on the source of income of the member? It can be argued that in some cases it has. Take a member who gets a loan to set up or expand his/her small business. When it only helps a civil servant to beef up his or her consumptive capacities or other members to overcome seasonal fluxes in their income, it has little or no effect on their employment status. It is, however, more relevant in the case of farmers and their households who can access the market, thanks to their cooperative. Some country studies mention a figure for the number of people self-employed through cooperative membership: Ghana (209,145), Rwanda (150,000), and Uganda (between 6,000 and 15,000).

The spillover effect of the cooperative sector on the employment market is very diffused and difficult to estimate. Still, it is clear that several categories of people rely on the vibrancy of the cooperative sector for their income as they provide inputs (fertilizers, stationery, computers, etc.) to the sector or sell the products of the cooperatives in the marketplace.

In addition, a number of our researchers also point to the fact that cooperative members who rely on the cooperative for part of their income very often also employ other (seasonal and full-time) personnel in their farm or business. Tsekpo, for example, found that gin distillers affiliated to cooperative distilleries in Ghana have two assistants on average. This means that no fewer than 70,000 persons would gain their income in this way.

Compared to the traditional private sector and public sector, the contribution of cooperatives to employment and income support is not negligible in many countries. Several researchers found support for the idea that this contribution is on the increase (Ghana, Ethiopia, Rwanda, Egypt, Cape Verde, and Nigeria).

Significance of cooperatives for poverty reduction

We have already seen that the cooperative sector in Africa is very heterogeneous in terms of its class composition. Most draw their membership exclusively from the poor rural masses. The poorest, with few or no assets tend to exclude themselves or to be excluded. Many cooperatives also include not so poor people, such as micro-entrepreneurs or low-income wage earners. But even successful entrepreneurs or middle-income wage earners sometimes seek their benefits from a cooperative venture. The question that arises is whether cooperatives are poverty reducing and welfare enhancing instruments for all these categories. The question as to whether cooperatives also play a role in pushing for a comprehensive poverty reduction policy in their countries is also pertinent here.

So far, the impact of cooperatives on poverty reduction in Africa has not been studied in any systematic way. This stands in sharp contrast with the adjacent field of micro-finance that has been subject to numerous research initiatives and several overviews looking at the impact of different schemes and the effectiveness of aid to these (see e.g. Rosenberg, 2006; Goldberg, 2005; Develtere & Huybrechts, 2005). Nevertheless, practitioners, governments and development partners involved in cooperative development assume that cooperatives do have a significant potential to lift people out of poverty. Some, like Birchall (2003) even make the point that "cooperatives have the potential to reduce poverty and – provided their values and principles are respected – will do this more effectively than other forms of economic organization". The argument often goes that cooperatives change the institutional setting in which people work and live to the advantage of those who have fewer resources at their disposal. They pool the risks and enhance the risk-mitigating capacity of the members by bringing together their capital and capacities in a synergetic way. The beneficiaries are first and foremost the initiators (often those who have more social capital and business acumen) and the immediate followers who also join the cooperative. But it is argued that cooperatives have positive effects also on non-members and the broader environment. The group which is empowered by the cooperative and which is less poor or at least less vulnerable, thanks to the cooperative, shows the way ahead for people in similar circumstances. These non-members might also benefit from more affordable interest rates, higher wages, better infrastructure or even more equitable power relations that come as a consequence of the cooperative.

In addition, some authors insist on the cooperatives' potential to reduce transaction costs for the members who face incomplete markets, imperfect information and little government-provided institutional and physical infrastructure (e.g. Delgado et al 1997; Luttrell & Smith, 1994). Some cooperatives also help members confronted with the vagaries of world markets. On the basis of a case study of the Ethiopian coffee farmers' cooperatives, Myers (2004) concludes that they successfully position the small-holders in the unpredictable international coffee market.

Most of our country studies bring lively reports of the way cooperatives help to lift poor people out of poverty. The Jinja Teachers Savings and Credit Society in Uganda, for example, gave loans to its members for the payment of school fees. Thanks to this three children graduated in medicine, engineering and finance. They are now employed and provide financial assistance to their relatives and parents. The same kinds of stories about credit unions permitting members to pay school fees, to build houses, to invest in business and farming, and to meet family obligations resonate throughout the country papers. In addition to withdrawable savings deposit products and instant cash advances on salaries, many SACCOs facilitate cash flow in areas that commercial banks have shunned. Many papers also give illustrations of the impact of agricultural cooperatives. In Ethiopia, for example, the cereal banks provide farmers with better prices throughout the year. Since their introduction a few years ago they have stabilized the local grain markets in favour of the producers. In Nigeria, mention is made of "women only" cooperatives preventing social exclusion for this particularly vulnerable group.

But it is also clear from the case studies that cooperatives cannot do the poverty reduction job alone. The (extra) income they generate as well as the support and opportunities they provide are too little to lift their members out of poverty. Nyamwasa, for example, calculated that in three years the Rwandan rice growers' cooperatives were able to secure an almost tripling of the price for paddy rice. But still, on average each of the 40,000 cooperative members only gets US$ 0.60 per day out of his rice production, which is clearly insufficient to live on. Unfortunately, as Theron reports for the cooperatives in the poor South African provinces of Limpopo and Eastern Cape, they are often the sole source of income for an entire household. In KwaZulu-Natal 70% of the members of 32 cooperatives interviewed had never been employed at all prior to joining the cooperative.

We can thus conclude with Münkner (2001) that "cooperatives do not help the poor, but by working together, by pooling their resources, by submitting themselves to group discipline and by accepting to combine self-interest and group solidarity, the poor can solve some of their problems by way of organized self-help and mutual aid better than alone".

Cooperatives and the extension of social protection

We could describe *social protection* as all the safety mechanisms the social environment provides for an individual or communities in case of hazard or loss of income. It needs no argument that social protection in Africa is very low. Only a very small minority of wealthy people benefit from social protection systems such as health insurance. The small tax base, the prevalence of the informal economy and the institutional weaknesses of the African states hinder the establishment or extension of formal, centrally-organized and state-run social protection systems. The questions are, therefore, whether civil and private organizations such as cooperatives can provide alternative social protection mechanisms; the extent to which they already do so; and their performance in this regard.

It is very clear from the country studies that social protection is a new theme for the cooperative sector in Africa. Very few cooperatives and promoters of cooperatives have reflected upon it and research on the actual and potential contribution of cooperatives to social protection is non-existent.

Cooperatives, however, in different ways already touch upon this new area. First, cooperatives do provide a new framework or re-enforce traditional mutual support habits which are mostly event or hazard related. In numerous cooperatives members and personnel set up ad hoc solidarity mechanisms to cater for expenses related to wedding ceremonies, illness, death or funerals. These elementary solidarity mechanisms are similar to those that exist outside the cooperatives, which are common to most African social communities (village, neighbourhood, religious community, etc.). However, as Enete rightly remarks, cooperatives do re-enforce the prevalent informal social security systems because the extent of social protection is usually spelt out in the cooperative's constitution, whereas in typical African communities, the system is conventional. He also emphasizes that cooperatives are a much tighter community with stronger bonds. This enables the cooperatives to act faster and in a more coordinated manner.

At the same time, cooperatives as new and modern institutions of cooperation and solidarity do provide new mechanisms of social protection which complement these traditional institutions. Savings, of course, is one important strategy to mitigate risks. Contrary to other types of micro-finance institutions, SACCOs are savings-based groups. But also many other cooperatives, such as housing cooperatives and agricultural cooperatives, have a savings plan. Members can rely on their savings when they face temporary financial problems, for example in the case of illness. Or, they can ask for a loan. In many SACCOs these loans are insured (through an extra "micro-insurance" premium) so that the family does not have to cover the unpaid balance of the loan when the creditor – who is normally the main income earner – dies (Enarsson and Wiren, 2005). In addition, many cooperatives have established benevolent funds. Contrary to the traditional systems just mentioned, these funds benefit from regular member contributions. Members can only draw from them when they are in need.

Many SACCOs offer emergency loans to members. Wanyama says that these act as a fall-back for members to quickly respond to unanticipated socio-economic problems that may arise at any time. However, demand for such loans often exceeds the capacity of the available funds. Mrema describes how SACCOs in Uganda are trying to mitigate the effects of HIV/AIDS. Members of the cooperatives are seriously affected by this killer disease, but often do not benefit from the burial contribution schemes of the government. Therefore, they establish their own burial contribution funds to cover burial expenses for society members who die or who lose relatives. As is revealed in research by Evans (2002), SACCO members not only look to their cooperative for financial support but also for other services such as prevention information, testing services and legal advice.

In Ethiopia cooperatives are required to allocate 1 to 5% of their profit to a social fund. The funds are not necessarily earmarked for contingencies. Lemma gives the example of an Ethiopian coffee farmers' cooperative union that provides financial support to 21 students who are undergoing higher education in the country. In addition, the cooperative donates education materials and uniforms to 250 orphans every year. These support packages are part of the annual plan of the union. In the same country a number of cooperative unions have established HIV/AIDS clubs for raising awareness and enhancing the use of preventive and control measures.

Of more recent vintage are a number of micro-insurance initiatives set up by existing cooperatives. The *Forum Cooperativo* in Cape Verde, for example, has spearheaded the development of micro-insurance or mutual health organizations in the country. So far, 2,000 families have been brought into this system. This kind of new social economy initiative has been proliferating in West Africa. In a study of 11 Francophone African countries, 622 health micro-insurance schemes were identified. Some are independent mutual health organizations set up by individuals who want to get greater social protection through the pooling of risks and some kind of interest aggregation in the health system. Others are set up by health service providers themselves with the aim of recovering the costs of their services. Still other micro-insurance schemes are grafted onto existing organizations such as religious groups, trade unions, cooperatives and micro-finance institutions (see e.g. Fonteneau et al., 2006; Develtere et al., 2005).

Voice and representation

Is the cooperative movement capable of having a voice to defend the interests of its constituent members? And, does it play its legitimate role in representing the poor in the national political arena? These are the two remaining questions.

It is clear from our national reports that in almost all countries the cooperative sector has not as yet found an alternative for the imposed and government-patronized federations and apex bodies that represented the sector in the post-colonial period. In any case, most federations and apex bodies are dormant and have folded up in most of the countries. In a few countries, like Egypt, Kenya and Ghana, they still exist but don't have much clout and have trouble in getting rid of their old image of government-run apexes or even agents of government. Except for a few countries, the apexes have not been replaced by consensual "bottom-up built" structures. The movement is as a consequence much fragmented and cannot speak with one voice. Only in Cape Verde, South Africa and Senegal have we seen the emergence of real movement-based platforms. However, both *Foro Cooperativo* in Cape Verde and the National Cooperative Alliance of South Africa remain very loose and ill-funded structures only representing a fraction of the movement.

A promising phenomenon though is the rapid development of federative structures bringing together cooperatives involved in one trade or industry. Most countries have a league or federation representing the savings and credit cooperatives. But in countries such as Rwanda, Senegal and Kenya there are very dynamic federations covering a great majority of the national cooperatives involved in specific agricultural crops, housing or fishery. Our empirical evidence shows that these federations do function well to the extent that they have a significant economic plus-value for the affiliated cooperatives. Also, they seem to be able to aggregate the interests of their members and at times to lobby the government successfully as the Rwandan Union of Rice Growers showed when it was able to secure significant increases in the price for paddy rice.

Notwithstanding this promising perspective we have to conclude that the cooperative movement remains much atomized, lacking vertical and horizontal structures. As a consequence, interest aggregation remains very weak and the voice of the cooperative constituency is very timid and hardly ever heard. Thousands and thousands of primary cooperatives remain under-represented.

This observation helps us to answer our last question. Authors like Birchall (2004) claim there is a role for the cooperative movement in representing the poor. In this book as well we find a host of arguments for having cooperatives represented at the negotiating table when governments work out plans to reduce poverty. We have seen that cooperatives do represent a significant group of poor and vulnerable people; mainly operate in poverty-stricken areas; and are important protective mechanisms for the not so poor. It is no exaggeration to say that hundreds of thousands of poor Africans only have their cooperative to represent their interests. However, it appears that cooperatives have not been and are still not recognized partners in the Poverty Reduction Strategy programmes. Yet these programmes are designed for and insist on the participation of all relevant national stakeholders, particularly civil society. Very few cooperatives have participated in the design of the national Poverty Reduction Strategy Papers (PRSPs) or are involved in the implementation of them. Evaluations of these programmes hardly ever mention the role played by or even the potential role of cooperatives (e.g. Booth, 2003).

Increasing the participation of cooperatives in designing and implementing PRSPs in African countries was the subject of a workshop organized by the ILO and the ICA in Tanzania in 2003. In line with our previous observations, the workshop concluded that participation of cooperatives in the PRSP process was seriously hampered by the absence of cooperative apex bodies representing the movement. This is certainly part of the answer. However, other segments of civil society, such as women's organizations, community based organizations and NGOs, also often lack national and representative bodies that can function as the mouthpiece for the entire group. We believe that there are three additional reasons for this lack of voice on behalf of the cooperative sector in the poverty reduction processes.

First, cooperative members tend to focus on local matters. They do not see why and how their cooperative should participate in public policy making at the national level. Several surveys amongst members, professional staff and leaders of cooperatives clearly show that cooperative members regard their cooperative as the source of a decent income, not as a bargaining instrument. (FAO, 1996; Bingen 2003). In contrast, professional staff and leaders of the cooperatives usually cited benefits such as contacts with NGOs, access to formal credit institutions, training and participating in policy debate. Civic participation, democratization and decentralization mean little or nothing in the everyday lives of the vast majority of poor cooperative members.

Secondly, the international partners of the African cooperatives have not paid much attention to the subject. Most vocal civil society organizations that are involved in PRSP processes are seriously backed in this by their partners. Advocacy and lobbying have become key components of most programmes that support civil society organizations. Cooperatives and their international partners focus on the economic and social dimensions of development, which is their comparative strength. They have been negligent as to the political component. Or maybe, they have become afraid of it because of past experience?

And, finally, governments have forgotten about cooperatives as representative groups of the poor. They equate civil society with the new social and political forces and elites that show concern for the new issues such as poverty, gender, democratization and sustainable development. Contrary to the cooperatives, these are often vocal groups with high visibility who do not shun political debate and conflicts. They are able to play the short-term political game because of their high (international) credibility and the significant resources at their disposal. But, governments and others should realize that cooperatives play the long-term game because they rely on local credibility and the pooled resources of the poor.

Conclusion

The cooperative movement is again gaining momentum in Africa. Despite the legacy of state dominance and suffocation of the sector; the recent deregulation and liberalization; and the new donor fashions, we see a sector that is still quite extensive. Notwithstanding the scarcity and dubious nature of data on the subject, we were able to make a fair guess that there are some 150,000 collective socio-economic undertakings in the 11 countries in our sample. Most of them are registered cooperatives, but increasingly new types of social economy organizations (community based organizations, mutual help organizations, trusts, member-owned micro-finance and micro-insurance institutions) perform similar functions and operate in the same way. In many countries – and not only the Francophone countries that have a long social economy tradition – these new organizations are integrated in the larger cooperative movement. Out of every 100 Africans, seven belong to a cooperative type of organization. For many it is the only group they belong to and that helps them to make a better living. In most countries we observe a net increase in both the number of cooperatives and membership compared to a decade ago.

But the cooperative panorama is not the same as it was ten years ago. Much has changed since. In most countries governments have departed from the scene leaving the cooperatives to the forces of the market. Government agencies following up on cooperative matters have been downsized. Their competencies have been reduced considerably in many countries. The revision and adjustment of the cooperative laws and regulation to the new realities have been completed in a few countries, are under way in several, but are, strangely enough, not an issue in quite a few places. The previous government-run apex bodies have been dismantled or play no significant role any more. The same goes for the many unions and federations that linked up cooperatives with state marketing agencies and governmental economic policies. They have been replaced in some countries with federations and unions that have grown in a bottom-up way. These create real plus-value for the affiliated cooperatives and their members as they perform necessary economic and financial functions and lobby in the interests of their constituency.

The main cooperative sub-sector is still composed of client-owned agricultural cooperatives. Most of them are unifunctional and concentrate their operation on the handling of one crop, but many venture out into ancillary activities such as credit or insurance. Over the last decade we have seen a spectacular growth of the savings and credit cooperative sector in almost all African countries. These SACCOs are often integrated in secondary structures. Interestingly in many countries we see different savings and credit union movements side by side and sometimes involved in a healthy competitive struggle with each other. Besides these two main thrusts of the African cooperative sector, there are hundreds of other cooperatives involved in housing, consumer goods, health care, transport or tourism. In every single country under review there were many small cooperatives, but always also some very big and fast growing cooperative groups or networks. Vibrant cooperatives invariably have a vivid associative life, a strong understanding of business and growth as well as the ability to mobilize internal and external patrons (members and outsiders) in their planned activities.

Cooperatives do make a significant contribution to employment creation and income support. They have a considerable number of people on their pay roll. But they also support many self-employed members who in addition very often also employ other full-time and temporary workers. Cooperatives also work quite exclusively in poverty-ridden areas and count a majority of poor people amongst their members. They have the advantage though of not excluding the not so poor and capitalize on the expertise, the social capital and the financial contribution of this group. This helps poor people to cooperate out of poverty. Although it is a completely new concept for the cooperative sector, many cooperatives seem to be venturing out into new areas such as social protection. Thus, they build on the existing traditional principles of self-help and mutual help, but also develop new systems of risk pooling and social security such as social benefit funds, micro-insurance and mutual health organizations.

This renaissance of the cooperative movement in Africa has not as yet been noticed by many, not even by many cooperators in the field. It, therefore, seems that giving voice to this silent group of cooperative entrepreneurs might be the key challenge for the immediate future.

Bibliography

- Aal A. M. H. (1998), 'Farmers and Cooperatives in the Era of Structural Adjustment', in: N. S. Hopkins & K. Westergaard (Eds.), *Direction of change in Rural Egypt*, The American University in Cairo Press.

- Adeyemo R. (2004), *Self-help Farmer Cooperatives' Management of Natural Cooperation*, 32(1), pp. 3-18.

- Akwabi-Ameyaw K. (1997), "Producer cooperative resettlement projects in Zimbabwe: Lessons from a failed agricultural development strategy", *World Development*, 25, 3, pp. 437-456.

- Attwood D. & Baviskar B. (1988), Who shares? Cooperatives and rural development, Oxford University Press.

- Bingen J. (2003), *Community-based producer organizations: a contribution to the West Africa regional program action plan for the initiative to end hunger in Africa*. Bethesda: Abt Associates Inc.

- Birchall J. (2003), *Rediscovering the cooperative advantage*, Geneva, ILO.

- Birchall J. (2004), *Cooperatives and the Millennium Development Goals*, ILO Cooperative Branch, Geneva.

- Birgegaard L. & Genberg B. (1994), *Cooperative Adjustment in a Changing Environment in Africa*, ICA, Geneva.

- Booth D. (ed.) (2003), *Fighting Poverty in Africa: Are PRSPs Making a Difference?* Overseas Development Institute, London.

- Charmes J. (1998). *Informal sector, proverty and gender, a review of empirical evidence*, Washington D.C., The World Bank.

- Cracogna D. (15-17 May 2002), *Legal, judicial and administrative provisions for successful cooperative development*. Paper for the expert group meeting on supportive environment for cooperatives, Ulaanbaatar, United Nations and Government of Mongolia.

- Defourny J., Develtere P. and Fonteneau B. (2001), *The Social Economy: North and South*, HIVA/CES, Leuven/Liège.

- Delgado Ch., Nicholson Ch. & Staal S. (1997), 'Smallholder dairying under transaction costs in East Africa' in *World Development*, 25, 5, pp. 779-794.

- Desrochers M. & Fisher K. (2005), 'The power of networks: integration and financial cooperative performance', *Annals of Public and Cooperative Economics* 76, 3, pp. 307-354.

- Develtere P. (1993), "Cooperative Movements in Developing Countries: Old and New Orientations", *Annals of Public and Cooperative Economics*, Vol. 64, No. 2, pp. 179-207.

- Develtere P. (1994), *Cooperation and Development*, ACCO, Leuven.

- Develtere P. & Huybrechts A. (2005), 'The impact of microcredit on the poor in Bangladesh', *Alternatives*, 30, pp. 165-189.

- Develtere P. & Pollet I. (2005), *Cooperatives and Fair-trade*, COPAC Open Forum paper, Berlin.

- Develtere P. and Stessens J. (2005), le Centre de Développement Intégral en République Démocratique du Congo, cheminement d'un projet vers l'économie sociale, HIVA, Leuven

- Develtere P., Doyen G. & Fonteneau B. (2005), *Micro-insurance and health care in developing countries*, Cera, Leuven.

- Duursma M. (2004), *Community-Based Microfinance Models in East-Africa*, SNV-Tanzania, Dar es Salaam.

- Eisenhauer J-M. (1995), Malawi union of savings and credit cooperatives member service survey, Madison, WOCCU.

- Enarsson S. & Wiren K. (2005), *Malawi Union of Savings and Credit Cooperatives*. CGAP Working Group on Microinsurance: Good and Bad Practices, Case Study n°8.

- Eshuis F. & Harmsen J. (2003), *Making Trade Work for the Producers: 15 years of Fairtrade Labelled Coffeee in the Netherlands*, The Max Havelaar Foundation, Utrecht.

- Evans A-C. (2002), *The unpaved road ahead: HIV/AIDS & microfinance, an exploration of Kenyan credit unions*. Madison, WOCCU.

- FAO (1996), *People's participation in Ghana: a post-project study of sustainability.*, Rome, FAO [FAO: http://www.fao.org/waicent/faoinfo/sustdev/PP¬direct/PPre0007.htm].

- Fonteneau B., Galland B. & Schmitt-Diabaté V. (2006, forthcoming), 'The community-based model: mutual health organizations in Africa', in: Churchill C. (ed.), *Microinsurance and Poverty*, Munich Re/ILO/CGAP, Munich/Geneva/Washington.

- Galor Z. (2005), *Failures of Cooperatives*, published at www.coopgalor.com and at www.developmentgateway.com.

- Gibbon P. (1992), 'A Failed Agenda? African Agriculture under Structural Adjustment with Special Reference to Kenya and Ghana', *The Journal of Peasant Studies*, 20 (1), pp. 50-96.

- Goldberg N. (2005), *Measuring the impact of microfinance: taking stock of what we know*, Grameen Foundation USA, Washington.

- Hussi P., Murphy J., Lindberg O. & Brenneman L. (1993), *The Development of Cooperatives and Other Rural Organizations. The Role of the World Bank*, The World Bank, Washington D.C.

- Hyden G. (1988), 'Approaches to cooperative development: Blueprint versus Greenhouse', in D. W. Attwood & B. S. Baciskar, *Who Shares? Cooperatives and Rural Development*, Oxford University Press, Delhi, pp. 149-171.

- ICA (1996). *ICA's membership by region*, Geneva, ICA. [University of Wisconsin-Madison: http://www.wisc.edu/uwcc/icic/orgs/ica/what-is/ICA-1995-Statistics--1996-1.html].

- ICA (4-6 August 1999), *Progress Report*. Paper for the Sixth ICA African Ministerial Cooperative Conference, Swaziland, ICA.

- ICA/ILO (2003), *The role of cooperatives in designing and implementing poverty reduction strategies*, Geneva, ICA/ILO.

- ILO/ICA (2005), *The Global Cooperative Campaign against Poverty*, Draft version, Geneva.

- Jutting J. (2003), 'Do community-based health insurance schemes improve poor people's access to health care? Evidence from rural Senegal', *World Development*, 32, 2, pp. 273-288.

- Kaba L., Gueyie J. & Sinzogan C. (2005), *Les institutions de microfinance au Bénin: contexte organisationel et efficience*, Montréal.

- Kayenwee C. (2001), 'Ghana: Ghana Cooperative Pharmaceuticals Ltd', in M.F. Countre, D. Feber, M. Levin & A.B. Nippied (eds.), *Transition to cooperative entrepreneurship: case studies from Armenia, China, Ethiopia, Ghana, Poland, Russia, Uganda and Vietnam*, ILO & ICA, Geneva.

- Lapenu C. & Zeller M. (2002), *Distribution, growth and performance of the micro-finance institutions in Africa, Asia and Latin-America: a recent inventory*, International Food Policy Research Institute, Discussion Paper n° 114, Washington.

- Luttrell M. & Smith H. (1994), 'Cartels in an 'Nth-Best' world: the wholesale foodstuff trade in Ibadan, Nigeria', *World Development*, 22, 3, pp. 323-335.

- Maluccio J., Haddad L. and May J. (2000), "Social Capital and Income Generation in South Africa, 1993-98", *Journal of Development Studies*, Vol. 36, No. 6, pp. 54-81

- Mauge K. (1997), *Etat des lieux des lois sur les coopératives et sur les autres organisations d'auto-assistance à caractère économique dans dix pays d'Afrique francophone*, Geneva, ILO.

- Melnyk G. (1985), *The Search for Community : From Utopia to a Cooperative Society*, Black Rose Books, Montréal.

- Mercer C. (2002), 'The discourse of Maendeleo and the politics of women's participation on Mount Kilimanjaro', *Development and Change*, 33, 1, pp. 101-125.

- Milford A. (2004), *Coffee, Cooperatives and Competition: The Impact of Fair Trade*, Chr. Michelsen Institute, Bergen.

- Mugisha J. & Kwasa S. (2005), *Status of Rural Producer Organizations in Uganda*. Report prepared for ICRAF/RELMA, Nairobi.

- Münkner H. & Shah A. (1994), *Creating a Favorable Climate and Conditions for Cooperative Development in Africa*, International Labour Office, Geneva.

- Münkner H. (ed.) (2001), *Best Practice: Innovative Approaches to Cooperative Solutions of Housing Problems of the Poor*, Marburg Consult, Marburg.

- Myers A. (2004), *Old Concepts Revisited: Are Cooperatives the Way Forward for Smallholder Farmers to Engage in International Trade?* London School of Economics & Political Science, London.

- Narayan D. (1999), *Bonds and Bridges: Social Capital and Poverty*, World Bank Poverty Group Working Paper, July 1999.

- Narayan D. and Priychett L. (1999), *Cents and Sociability: Household Income and Social Capital in Rural Tanzania*, World Bank, Washington DC.

- Ofeil K. (2005), 'Participative Schemes and Management Structures of Ghanaian Cooperatives', in *Journal of Cooperative Studies*, 38.3, December 2005, pp. 14-26.

- Ouattara K. (2003), *Microfinance Regulation in Benin*, Washington, World Bank.

- Owango M. & Lukuyu B. (1998), 'Dairy cooperatives and policy reform in Kenya: effects on livestock service and milk market liberalization', *Food Policy*, 23, 2, pp. 173-185.

- Pollet I. & Develtere P. (2004), *Development Co-operation: How Cooperatives Cope*, Cera-Foundation, Brussels.

- Porvali H. et al. (1993), *The Development of Cooperatives and Other Rural Organizations*, World Bank, Washington.

- Petrie R. (2002), *Rwanda Credit Unions Member and Non-member Survey 2002*, WOCCU, Madison, Wisconsin.

- Putterman L. (1995), 'Economic reform and smallholder agriculture in Kenya', *World Development*, 23, 2, pp. 311-326.

- Resources for Sustainable Development in Southwest Nigeria, *Journal of Rural*.

- Rosenberg R. (2006), 'Aid effectiveness in microfinance: evaluating microcredit projects of the World Bank and the United Nations Development Programme', *CGAP Focus Note*, 25, April.

- Schwettmann J. (1997), *Cooperatives and Employment in Africa*, Discussion paper, International Labour Office, Geneva.

- Shaw L. (ed.) (2006), *Co-operation, social responsibility and fair trade in Europe*, The Co-operative College, Manchester.

- Skurnik S. (2002), 'The role of cooperative entrepreneurship and firms in organizing economic activities – past, present and future', *The Finnish Journal of Business Economics*, 1/2002, pp. 103-124.

- Stessens J., Gouët C. & Eeckloo P. (2004), *Efficient contract farming through strong Farmers' Organisations in a partnership with Agri-business*, HIVA, Leuven.

- Tchouassi G. & Tekam Oumbe H. (2003), 'Microfinance et réduction de la pauvreté, le cas du crédit du Sahel au Cameroun', *Revue internationale de l'économie sociale*, 288, pp. 80-88.

- Tesfaye A. (2005), *Revitalizing Market-Oriented Agricultural Cooperatives in Ethiopia*, ACDI-VOCA, Addis Abeba.

- Weihe T. (2004), *Cooperatives in Conflict and Failed States*, U.S. Overseas Cooperative Development Council.

- WOCCU (2005), 2004 Statistical Report, Madison, WOCCU.

- X. (2004), 'Le rôle de la sociéte civile Rwandaise dans le DSRP', *Dialogue: revue d'information et de réflexion*, 234, pp. 45-55.

- Yeboah G. (2005), 'The Farmapine Model: A Cooperative Marketing Strategy and a Market-Based Development Approach in Sub-Saharan Africa', *Magazine of Food, Farm and Resource Issues*, 1st Quarter 2005 – Choices 81, American Agricultural Economics Association (www.choicesmagazine.org).

- Younoussi B. (2002), *Les organisations paysannes nigériennes en mouvement; Diagnostic participatif rapide de 20 organisations paysannes*, CASPANI, Coopération française, Niamey.

- Zeller M. (2003), *Models of Rural Financial Institutions*, Institute of Rural Development, Georg-August University, Göttingen.

Annexes

Annexe 1 – Figures on number of cooperatives and members based on the Rapid Appraisal

Please note that these figures are presumably less accurate than the figures listed in Table 2.2 (based upon the Country Studies). They are shown for reasons of comparison only.

Country	Pop. in mio. (CIA)	no of coops registered	no of members	source & estimated reliability
Ghana	21.4	2 200	2 300 000	Ghana Cooperative Council (apex), 2005
Nigeria	127.1	50 000	5 000 000	Federal Cooperative College, 2005
Kenya	32.4	10 800	5 700 000	(active coops: 7000) Coop. College Kenya, 2005
Uganda	26.6	7 377	400 000	(active coops: 1500) UCA, 2005
Ethiopia	72.4	9 790	5 200 000	Registrar's Office, 2005
RSA	45.2	700	500 000	NCASA (apex, 2005) – "members" is estimate; 3600 unregistered coops (estimate)
Egypt	73.4	13 162	11 000 000	General Coop Union, 2005
Rwanda	8.5	33 631	1 600 000	extrapolation of Ruhengeri province; inc. pre-coops and non-coops (Care Internat, 2003)
Niger	12.4	13 000	500 000	Different federations, 2005 (very rough estimate – breakdown: 150 000 members of coops and 350 000 members of non-coop associations)
Cape Verde	0.5	300	6 000	Fenacoop (consumer coop federation – figures of 2002)
Senegal	10.3	1 350	1 500 000	Incl. also pre- and non-coops; UNCAS (Coop College, 2005)
Burkina F.	13.4	30 000	955 000	Min. of Agr., coop section – only agric.coops (2002)
Madagascar	17.9	620	6 800	Min. of Commerce, estimates (2005)
Mozambique	19.2	n.a.	n.a.	(UNCA, National Union of Peasants)
Tanzania	37.7	5 730	600 000	4 trade apex; n of members is a rough estimation
Zimbabwe	12.9	3 960	175 000	Registrar's Office

Source: UNFPA (2003 figures); this research programme

Chapter Three – The Qualitative and Quantitative Growth of the Cooperative Movement in Kenya

by Fredrick O. Wanyama

Introduction

The ever growing consensus that the crisis in African development is partly a function of the centralized "top-down" approaches that characterized development efforts up to the 1980s has given credence to the acclaimed suitability of people's organizations in the fight against poverty. The various types of people's organizations that are expected to spearhead the development process and defeat poverty include cooperatives (Uphoff, 1993; Holmen and Jirstrom, 1994). The latter organizations, by virtue of their nature, are increasingly being presented as a pre-condition for successful anti-poverty work (Birchall, 2003; 2004). Nevertheless, there seems to be a dearth of updated empirical literature on the actual activities of cooperatives in the development process, more so in Africa, since the early 1990s.

In Kenya, current literature on cooperatives is rare despite the fact that the government recognizes the sector as a major contributor to national development (Republic of Kenya, 1997a). Most of the literature dates back to the early 1990s (e.g. Hedlund, 1992; Hussi et al, 1993; Lindberg, 1993), with only a handful of works being written since the mid 1990s. Among the few recent studies, none takes a broad comprehensive perspective of the cooperative movement in the country to give one an insight into what its status is in the overall development process. What exist are isolated small studies focusing on specific sectors of the movement like dairy cooperatives (Staal et al, 1997; Owango et al, 1998); savings and credit cooperatives (Evans, 2002); and agricultural marketing cooperatives (ICA, 2002). In the circumstances, the current overall state of the cooperative movement in Kenya is not well known to development scholars, commentators and practitioners.

The purpose of this study is to obtain qualitative insights into the strengths and weaknesses of the cooperative movement in the country with a view to assessing the real and potential impact of cooperatives on reduction of poverty through creation of employment; generation of economic activities; enhancement of social protection; and improvement of the voice and representation of vulnerable groups in society. It is envisaged that the performance of cooperatives in these respects would significantly depend on their scope, vibrancy, support and sustainability.

Being a qualitative rapid assessment study, data were collected using semi-structured interviews with key informants in the cooperative sector, first, at the national level. These included respondents from the office of the Commissioner of Cooperative Development in the Ministry of Cooperative Development and Marketing; the Kenya National Federation of Cooperatives (KNFC); the Cooperative College of Kenya; the Cooperative Bank of Kenya; the Cooperative Insurance Company of Kenya (CIC); the Kenya Union of Savings and Credit Cooperatives (KUSCCO); and the Kenya Planters Cooperative Union (KPCU). Interviews were also held at the International Cooperative Alliance (ICA) Regional Office for Africa in Nairobi.

At the society level, two cooperative societies were visited for in-depth interviews with leaders and members. These were Githunguri Dairy Farmers Cooperative Society in Kiambu district and Kamukunji Jua Kali Savings and Credit Cooperative Society in Nairobi. In addition, informal discussion was held with a professor at the Institute for Development Studies, University of Nairobi, who is a leading commentator on cooperatives in Kenya. These primary data were supplemented with secondary data from official records and reports of cooperative organizations and published books and articles.

A four-tier cooperative sector

The fact that agriculture is the main economic activity in Kenya has led to the classification of cooperatives into two broad economic sectors, namely agricultural and non-agricultural. Agricultural cooperatives are mainly involved in the marketing of produce, an activity that has seen some of them get into the manufacturing sector through primary processing of produce before it is marketed. These cooperatives are organized according to the crop or produce that they handle, the key ones being coffee, cotton, pyrethrum, sugarcane and dairy. In addition to these, there are also fishery, farm purchase and multi-produce cooperatives in the agricultural sector. Whereas fishery cooperatives play the role of marketing members' fish, farm purchase cooperatives mobilize resources to purchase land for the members.

In the non-agricultural domain, cooperative activities are found in the financial, housing, insurance, consumer, crafts and transport sectors. In the financial sector, savings and credit are the predominant activities of cooperatives while cooperatives in the housing sector have the provision of affordable shelter as their key activity. Consumer and craft cooperatives market respective commodities for a profit while cooperatives in the transport sector engage in savings and credit activities. It is important to note here that cooperatives have also spread to the informal sector. There already exist some Jua Kali (Kiswahili for "hot sun", in reference to the open air environment of informal enterprises) cooperative societies that are confined to savings and credit activities. It is, therefore, apparent that cooperatives are found in the leading socio-economic sectors of the country.

The cooperative movement in Kenya is organized into a four-tier structure that links up cooperative societies at the local level to the national level. The structure consists of primary societies, secondary cooperatives or cooperative unions, national cooperative organizations and one apex cooperative organization. Currently, the apex organization is the Kenya National Federation of Cooperatives, whose membership includes national cooperative organizations as well as some cooperative unions. It is through KNFC that the Kenyan cooperative movement is expected to be linked to the world cooperative movement.

It has already been mentioned that Kenya has an activity-based cooperative system. This manifests itself in the organization of national cooperative organizations (NACOs) that are based on specific types of activities such as banking, insurance, dairy, savings and credit, housing, coffee, among others. Currently, NACOs include KUSCCO, CIC, KPCU, the Cooperative Bank of Kenya, Kenya Cooperative Creameries (KCC), National Cooperative Housing Union (NACHU), and Kenya Rural Savings and Credit Societies Union (KERUSSU). Members of these organizations are mainly cooperative unions, but not to the exclusion of cooperative societies. It should be pointed out here that the Cooperative College of Kenya is also one of the NACOs, but it is essentially a government institution, having been started in 1969 as a department of the Ministry of Cooperative Development before its transformation into a semi-autonomous government parastatal through an Act of Parliament in 1995.

Cooperative societies are affiliated to cooperative unions, once again according to the activities or agricultural produce marketed. Consequently, in the agricultural sector, there are produce-oriented cooperative unions that collect produce from societies for primary processing and marketing. These unions also provide the societies with other centralized services like farm input supply, administration of production credit, accounting, staff training and member education. In addition to these activity-based unions, there are also District Cooperative Unions. These are area-based cooperative unions that bring together societies dealing with different types of activities within their geographical area of operation (Republic of Kenya, 1997a: 13). Most of these unions are agriculturally based and their role is to provide a range of support services to their members that would have otherwise been provided by activity-based unions.

This structural organization has seen a proliferation of cooperatives in the country. The total number of cooperatives in Kenya in 2004 stood at 10,642. Whereas agricultural cooperatives were the predominant type up to the early 1990s, non-agricultural cooperatives have since surpassed the number of agricultural cooperatives. Savings and credit cooperatives (SACCOs) constitute over 70% of the non-agricultural cooperatives and they have totalled more than all the agricultural cooperatives since 2003. Table 3.1 below summarizes the number of cooperatives in Kenya by type between 1997 and 2004.

The table shows a general growth in the number of cooperatives over the years, but the main area of significant growth has been the non-agricultural sector, especially SACCOs. It should, however, be noted that these are cumulative figures that exist in the register, with some of the cooperatives being dormant. For example, all cotton cooperatives have remained dormant since the virtual collapse of cotton production in the early 1990s, partly due to the low producer prices and the poor marketing chain that left farmers not paid for their produce over long periods of time (Wanyama, 1993). Active cooperatives were estimated at about 7,000. It was not possible to establish the exact number of active and dormant cooperatives because the registers in the Ministry are not maintained in that form. Nevertheless, some crude indicators could serve to illustrate the level of dormancy. For instance, among agricultural cooperatives, the ICA study of marketing societies in 2001 indicates that 31% were dormant (ICA, 2002: 7); while the government's annual returns for the same year indicate that 3,173 agricultural cooperatives were active and 1,075 (representing 25%) were dormant (Republic of Kenya, 2002: 147). With regard to SACCOs, KUSCCO records indicate that 2,600 out

Table 3.1: Number of cooperative societies and unions in Kenya by type, 1997-2004

Type of Society	1997	1998	1999	2000	2001	2002	2003	2004
Agricultural								
Coffee	279	308	335	366	462	474	487	498
Cotton	78	78	86	86	71	71	59	59
Pyrethrum	65	66	71	73	152	152	140	142
Sugarcane	98	99	108	112	112	112	149	149
Dairy	313	323	331	337	332	332	239	241
Multi-produce	1 342	1 446	1 504	1 560	1 593	1608	1794	1 798
Farm purchase	677	698	717	731	624	624	109	109
Fisheries	72	74	79	82	82	84	64	65
Other agricultural	860	915	968	1 002	944	956	1 125	1 154
Total Agricultural	**3 784**	**4 007**	**4 199**	**4 349**	**4 372**	**4 414**	**4 166**	**4 215**
Non-Agricultural								
SACCOs	3 169	3 305	3 538	3 627	3 925	4 020	4 200	4 474
Consumer	-	189	194	197	206	208	180	180
Housing	-	424	440	468	442	440	229	495
Craftsmen	-	73	91	104	102	102	85	86
Transport	-	35	36	36	32	32	28	28
Other non-agric.	1 276	551	564	572	600	712	1316	1068
Total Non-agric.	**4 445**	**4 577**	**4 863**	**5 004**	**5 307**	**5 514**	**6 038**	**6 331**
Unions	83	85	89	89	89	89	93	96
Grand Total	**8 312**	**8 669**	**9 151**	**9 442**	**9 768**	**10 017**	**10 297**	**10 642**

Source: Ministry of Cooperative Development and Marketing, Statistics Unit.

of the total number of 4,474 were active as at 31st December, 2004. If these figures are correct, then about 42% of the SACCOs were dormant at the end of 2004.

With regard to membership, some of our respondents estimated it at about 5 million. However, statistics at the Ministry of Cooperative Development and Marketing indicate that cooperatives in Kenya had a total membership of 3,377,000 at the end of 2004. About 72% of the membership belonged to non-agricultural cooperatives. Once again, SACCOs had the largest membership among the non-agricultural cooperatives. Out of 2,453,000 members of these cooperatives, about 2 million were SACCO members. These figures include dormant members, whose exact number we could not establish. The magnitude can, however, be illustrated by Githunguri Dairy Farmers Cooperative Society. Out of the cumulative figure of about 12,000 members that are in the register, 6,000 are active. The implication is that about 50% of the members of agricultural cooperatives could be dormant.

The data nevertheless show a general decline in the growth of cooperative membership, particularly in the agricultural sector. For instance, whereas the membership of agricultural cooperatives was 1,554,000 in 2000, it had fallen to 924,000 in 2004. SACCOs also suffered a similar fate. Their membership of 2,670,000 in 2000 had fallen to 1,575,000 in 2004. Whereas the decline in membership in agricultural cooperatives could be attributed to the general poor performance of the agricultural sector, public and private sector reforms after the liberalization of the economy that led to the retrenchment of employees saw SACCOs lose their members.

Members of cooperative societies cut across ethnic backgrounds, the rural-urban divide and professional categories. Whereas members of agricultural cooperatives are largely rural dwellers and they include both large- and small-scale farmers, the majority of the members of non-agricultural cooperatives live in the urban areas. In these settings, there are people from diverse ethnic backgrounds participating in the same cooperatives. The proliferation of SACCOs, particularly in the urban areas, has significantly integrated people from different professional and income categories in cooperative activities. High-ranking professionals employed in organizations, around which SACCOs are formed, find themselves in the same cooperative with their juniors. Thus, it is the services rendered by cooperatives that form the basis for people joining cooperatives in Kenya rather than ethnic and professional bases. Indeed, SACCOs are even being formed among the self-employed people in the informal (Jua Kali) and agricultural sectors, which is a complete departure from the past where these cooperatives were only formed among the employed in the urban areas who could make their share contributions through a payroll check-off system.

Despite the fact that membership in cooperatives is voluntary and open without any discrimination by gender, membership in Kenyan cooperatives is generally skewed in favour of males. Though the exact figures of female cooperative members are not available, some studies in certain types of cooperatives provide some indicator of their participation. For example, a study of agricultural marketing societies in 1995 showed that only 22% of the total members were active female members (Karlen, 1995). This percentage increased to 26 in 2001 (ICA, 2002: 11), but it still falls far below that of males. Possible explanations for this are cultural factors that tend to exclude women from ownership of property, particularly in the agricultural sector where farmers (and, therefore, recognized members of societies) are the owners of land. Although women are the dominant producers in this sector, men are the majority shareholders of the agricultural societies because they are the legal owners of the family land on which women work. In other economic sectors where such forms of discrimination do not exist, like in wage and salaried employment, female membership in cooperatives, especially SACCOs, is higher (Republic of Kenya, 1997a: 5). But still the proportion of females falls below that of males because the number of women in employment is lower.

There are variations with regard to the performance of cooperatives in the country. Whereas the performance of agricultural cooperatives has generally been on the decline since 2000, that of non-agricultural cooperatives, especially SACCOs, has been on the rise. Using turnover (income) as an indicator of cooperative performance, Table 3.2 below illustrates this point.

Table 3.2 indicates minimal turnover for cotton cooperatives despite the fact that cotton production in Kenya ceased in the early 1990s, leaving cooperatives in this sector dormant. In the absence of an explanation from our source of the data, we doubt the accuracy and reliability of the figures for cotton cooperatives in the table. Nevertheless, the table shows that the performance of agricultural cooperatives, with the exception of dairy cooperatives, has generally shrunk to the extent that the turnover of SACCOs almost doubles the combined income of all agricultural cooperatives. That SACCOs are the prime movers of the cooperative sector is illustrated by the fact that their turnover in 2004 constituted 62% of the total turnover of all cooperatives in the country. The financial strength of SACCOs has seen them

Table 3.2: Total turnover of cooperative societies and unions in Kenya, 1998-2004

(Kenya Shillings, Millions)

Cooperative Type	1998	1999	2000	2001	2002	2003	2004
Coffee	7 188	7 661	7 741	6 928	2 976	2 538	2 492
Cotton	5	5	5	3.8	3.2	1.0	1.0
Pyrethrum	128	129	129	122	122	114	102
Sugarcane	332	340	345	344	341	218	209
Dairy	1 501	1 530	1 529	1 268	1 325	1 290	1 400
Multi-produce	126	128	129	225	226	83	84
Farm purchase	58	59	60	60	60	0.5	5
Fisheries	5	6	7	7	6	522	339
Other Agricultural	288	288	292	296	296	239	256
Total Agricultural	9 631	10 146	10 237	9 254	5 355	5 005	4 888
SACCOs	3 381	3 386	3 389	4 882	4 886	8 261	8 359
Consumer	8	9	9	8	8	2	4
Housing	7	8	8	8	10	54	47
Craftsmen	40	42	43	42	43	158	144
Transport	25	26	26	25	24	2	3
Other Non-agric.	52	54	56	56	57	27	32
Total Non-agric.	3 515	3 527	3 533	5 023	5 030	8 504	8 589
Unions	197	198	269	389	389	963	983
Grand Total	13 343	13 871	14 039	14 666	10 774	13 509	13 477

Source: Ministry of Cooperative Development and Marketing, Statistics Unit.

become the majority shareholders in the Cooperative Bank of Kenya, thereby occupying the position that was previously held by agricultural marketing societies. The relatively poor performance of the latter has been attributed to the general recession in the agricultural sector since the early 1990s, but part of the problem could be the liberalization of the cooperative sector without adequately preparing the cooperatives. We return to this point later.

Government and the development of cooperatives

A fundamental characteristic of the Kenyan cooperative movement is its close association with the state to the point of developing a dependent relationship. It will be recalled that the first cooperatives in the country founded in the colonial era were moulded by the colonial government to suit the interests of the white settlers through strict legislation that restricted the participation of Africans in these enterprises (Cooperative Bank of Kenya, 1993: 3). At independence, the government sought to use cooperatives as instruments for promoting economic development especially in the rural areas. It had, therefore, to ensure the emergence of strong, viable and efficient cooperatives by directing the formation and management of these institutions from above. This state-controlled promotion of cooperative development was formalized by the introduction of a single legal framework for all types of cooperatives in 1966 via The Cooperative Societies Act, Cap. 490.

As per the intentions of the government, the main content of this legal framework was strict supervision of cooperatives by the state. With the formulation of the Cooperative Societies Rules in 1969 that stipulated the operational procedures for all cooperatives, the law gave the Commissioner for Cooperative Development unrivalled powers in the registration and management of cooperatives. Besides giving the Commissioner power to register, amalgamate and deregister cooperatives, he/she had to approve annual budgets of cooperatives; authorize borrowing and expenditure; audit their accounts; monitor financial performance; and could even replace elected cooperative societies' officials by management commissions at his/her pleasure (Manyara, 2003: 17). All employment issues in cooperatives fell within the mandate of the Commissioner as he/she had to approve remuneration, salary or other payments to staff or members as well as approve the hiring and dismissal of graded staff. Even labour matters in cooperatives were subject to the discretion of the Commissioner as the Trade Union Act was expressly excluded from applying to cooperatives.

A significant consequence of such overwhelming government control was the disappearance of a member-based, member-controlled and self-reliant cooperative movement guided by internationally acclaimed principles and ideals. Members' participation and control declined (Republic of Kenya, 1997a: 10). Administrative regulations imposed by the Cooperative Societies Rules impaired the flexibility required for running cooperatives as business enterprises (Hussi et al, 1993: 35).

Economic liberalization that followed the implementation of Structural Adjustment Programmes (SAPs) from the mid 1980s, however, rendered this legal framework irrelevant in the development of the cooperative movement. The new economic environment required government withdrawal from the cooperative sector in order to facilitate the growth of commercially autonomous and member-based cooperative organizations. To this end, the government had to adopt a policy of liberalizing the cooperative sector. Subsequently, the government published Sessional Paper No. 6 of 1997 on "Cooperatives in a Liberalized Economic Environment" to provide the new policy framework for the necessary reforms. The role of the government was redefined from controlling to regulatory and facilitative in nature. The main duties of the Ministry of Cooperative Development were confined to (a) registration and liquidation of cooperative societies; (b) enforcement of the Cooperative Societies Act; (c) formulation of cooperative policy; (d) advisory and creation of a conducive environment for cooperative growth and development; (e) registration of cooperative audits; and (f) carrying out of inquiries, investigations and inspections (Republic of Kenya, 1997a: 11). The aim of this new policy was to make cooperatives autonomous, self-reliant, self-controlled and commercially viable institutions. The monopoly of cooperatives in the agricultural sector was removed, with the result that cooperatives were now to compete with other private enterprises on the private market. The ICA cooperative principles of voluntary and open membership; democratic member control; member economic participation; autonomy and independence; education, training and information; cooperation among cooperatives; and concern for community were formally incorporated in the policy.

This new policy obviously required significant changes in the legal framework of cooperatives. Consequently, the 1966 Cooperative Societies Act was repealed and replaced by the Cooperative Societies Act, No. 12 of 1997. Like Sessional Paper No. 6 of 1997, the new Cooperative Societies Act served to reduce the involvement of the government in the day-to-day management of cooperatives. A very liberal law, it granted cooperatives "internal self-rule" from the previous state controls by transferring the management duties in cooperatives from the Commissioner for Cooperative Development to the members through their duly elected management committees (Manyara, 2004: 37).

For instance, cooperatives were no longer required to seek the permission of the Commissioner to invest, spend or borrow. They were now free to borrow against the whole or part of their properties if their bye-laws allowed them to do so, provided the annual general meeting approved. The Act empowered the members to be responsible for the running of their own cooperatives, through elected management committees. Like other business entities, cooperatives were mandated to hire and fire graded staff without the Commissioner's consent (Republic of Kenya, 1997b).

As much as this liberalization was a welcome move in the development of an autonomous, self-managed and sustainable cooperative movement, cooperatives were not prepared for the new era. The sector was left without a regulatory mechanism to play the role that the government had previously played. Consequently, the immediate impact on cooperatives was mainly negative. The newly acquired freedom was dangerously abused by elected leaders to the detriment of many cooperative societies. Cases of corruption; gross mismanagement by officials; theft of cooperative resources; split of viable cooperatives into small uneconomic units; failure to surrender members' deposits to cooperatives (particularly SACCOs) by employers; failure to hold elections in cooperatives; favouritism in hiring and dismissal of staff; refusal to vacate office after being duly voted out by cooperative officials; conflict of interest among cooperative officials; endless litigations; unauthorized cooperative investments; and illegal payments to the management committees were increasingly reported in many cooperatives (Manyara, 2004: 42-43).

However, there were some exceptions to this trend. Some of the cooperatives made commendable gains from the liberalization. For instance, Githunguri Dairy Farmers Cooperative Society benefited from a focused and well-intentioned management committee that took office in 1999 to use the new freedom to turn around the performance of the Society. With the power to hire and fire staff, the committee hired professional staff to steer the day-to-day management of the cooperative. It also used the power not only to borrow, but also to borrow against the society's property to get a loan of about 70 million Kenya shillings from OIKO Credit of the Netherlands to put up a dairy processing plant, which has seen a tremendous turnaround in the fortunes of the cooperative. This could not have been easily done under the previous state control. A similar pattern was also reported in Limuru Dairy Farmers Cooperative Society in Kiambu district.

Nevertheless, the general negative impact of liberalization on the majority of the cooperatives compelled the government to intervene with a new legal framework. The Cooperative Societies Act of 1997 was amended through the

Cooperative Societies (Amendment) Act of 2004. The main content of the amended Act was to enforce state regulation of the cooperative movement through the Commissioner for Cooperative Development. Though the independence of the Commissioner from politics was improved by making him an appointee of the Public Service Commission of Kenya rather than the Minister for Cooperative Development, his/her power over cooperatives was increased.

For instance, the Commissioner has to approve a list of auditors from which cooperatives can appoint their auditors at the annual general meeting; he/she may convene a special general meeting of a cooperative which he may chair, directing the matters to be discussed; the Commissioner may suspend from duty any management committee member charged in a court of law with an offence involving fraud or dishonesty pending the determination of the matter; he/she can dissolve the management committee of a cooperative that, in his/her opinion, is not performing its duties properly and appoint an interim committee for a period not exceeding ninety days; the Commissioner can call for elections in any cooperative society; he/she can attend meetings of cooperatives and require every cooperative to send to him/her at a proper time, the notice and agenda for every meeting and all minutes and communications of the meeting; and the Commissioner may also require that cooperatives update their bye-laws (Republic of Kenya, 2004a).

Most of these provisions should, however, be understood in the context of the mismanagement of cooperatives that followed the liberalization of the movement. The intention of the Act is to promote the development of cooperatives in tandem with ILO Recommendation 193 of 2002. It restricts the role of the government to creating policy and a legal framework for the development of cooperatives; improving the growth and development of cooperatives by providing the requisite services for their organization, registration, operation, advancement and dissolution; and developing partnerships in the cooperative sector through consultation with cooperators on policies, legislation and regulation.

Registration of cooperatives continues to be the main role of the Commissioner for Cooperative Development. The requirements and procedure for registering cooperatives have been spelt out in the revised Cooperative Societies Rules of 2004, which also outline the operational procedures of all cooperative societies in Kenya. Application for registration of a cooperative is made on a prescribed form that is obtained from the Commissioner's office in Nairobi. The application fee is five hundred Kenya shillings while the registration fee is three thousand Kenya shillings (Republic of Kenya, 2004b). These fees are generally affordable for cooperatives and the registration process is fair given that applicants have the right to appeal against a refusal to register. The significance of registration for pre-cooperatives is that the cooperative movement in Kenya was founded on the basis of legislation that provides for the legal existence of cooperatives. Consequently, all cooperatives are required to conform to the existing cooperative law in the country.

Some cooperatives ailing, others very vibrant and sustainable

The point has already been made that most of the cooperative societies in Kenya have their origin in state-controlled promotion of cooperative development. In order to transform the rural economy by integrating the smallholder farmers into the national cash economy, the government took the initiative to direct the formation and management of these institutions from above. In the circumstances, people joined cooperatives not on the basis of their common bonds and mutual trust, but due to the directive from above that those engaged in similar economic activities join cooperatives. For instance, in the agricultural sector, it became mandatory for cash crop farmers to join these institutions if they were to market their produce. Even the SACCO movement has its origin in government advice and encouragement (Republic of Kenya, 2002: 147). This government practice served to undermine the bottom-up character of cooperatives, with adverse implications for the growth and sustainability of some of the institutions.

The case of Kamukunji Jua Kali Savings and Credit Cooperative Society in Nairobi's informal sector clearly illustrates the adverse impact of government promotion of cooperatives. The SACCO was formed in 2001 as a result of government advice that Jua Kali associations form cooperatives to provide credit services to the artisans. The SACCO is thus an offshoot of the Kamukunji Jua Kali Association that was registered under the Societies Act in 1994 to protect the artisans from City Council harassment. The SACCO, however, seems to have been formed in anticipation of government assistance rather than members' common bonds, mutual trust and self-interest. Out of about 2,000 members of the Association, only 50 are members of the SACCO; 20 of whom are dormant. The reason for this small active membership is the lack of trust, for there is fear among most of the artisans that the officials of the SACCO might embezzle their funds. Consequently, it has a share capital of only 52,000 Kenya shillings that is too little to advance reasonable credit to the members. It continues to operate without staff given the low level of activity.

This should not be interpreted to mean that all cooperatives formed as a result of government initiatives are not vibrant. The case of Githunguri Dairy Farmers Cooperative Society, formed in 1961 through state initiatives illustrates a contrasting success story. Its membership now stands at 12,000 from the initial 31. Its initial activity of collecting milk from members to sell to Kenya Cooperative Creameries (KCC) has blossomed since the completion of its own modern milk processing plant in 2004. It collects and processes about 80,000 litres of milk daily, up from 25,000 litres in 1999. It has eighteen vehicles for transporting milk from 41 collection centres in Githunguri Division of Kiambu District to its plant in Githunguri town. The plant produces four main branded products that are sold in Nairobi: packed fresh milk, yoghurt, ghee and butter.

Besides this activity, the cooperative also provides productive services to its members. These include artificial insemination, extension services and animal feeds in its 31 stores that straddle its area of operation. These services are made available to members on credit that is recovered from the sale of their milk. These activities have seen tremendous improvement in milk production by members, to which the cooperative has responded by offering competitive prices and paying promptly for members' produce to further motivate them while at the same time buying all the milk. It sells some of the milk to other processors in Nairobi. The turnover of the cooperative in 2005 was over one billion Kenya shillings, with a share capital of over 100 million Kenya shillings.

The expansive activities of the cooperative are taken care of by a staff of about 300 employees who are recruited on the basis of an employment policy. Whereas the lower level staff is recruited from within the division, management staff is sought nationally and appointed on the basis of professional qualifications. It is significant that unionsable employees have formed a trade union, which has entered a collective bargaining agreement (CBA) with the cooperative. This is increasingly enabling the cooperative to attract and retain staff compared with the era of state control when there was no employment policy but the discretion of the Commissioner of Cooperative Development. As already alluded to, the success of this cooperative was attributed to the proper management system put in place by a management committee that took office only in 1999.

Similar vibrancy is to be found in cooperative societies that have largely been formed as a result of the demonstrative effect of good examples. A case in point is the mushrooming of SACCOs in the formal wage employment sector. These employer-based cooperatives now stand out as the most vibrant in the country rather than the agricultural marketing cooperatives that were dominant up to the end of the 1980s. Statistics in Table 3.3 of the ten leading SACCOs (in terms of annual turnover) in 2005 serve to demonstrate their vibrancy.

Table 3.3: Top ten SACCOS in annual turnover, 2005

Name of SACCO	Membership	Number of Staff	Annual Turnover (in Kshs.)
Mwalimu SACCO Ltd.	44 400	219	711 562 812
Harambee SACCO Ltd.	84 920	235	514 276 669
Afya SACCO Ltd.	44 879	283	483 599 495
Ukulima SACCO Ltd.	35 048	138	284 707 899
Kenya Bankers SACCO Ltd.	14 800	54	246 000 000
Stima SACCO Ltd.	14 789	38	235 500 000
Gusii Mwalimu SACCO Ltd.	13 042	48	219 506 484
Kenya Police SACCO Ltd.	6 575	74	156 790 546
UNEP SACCO Ltd.	2 501	7	148 790 782
Teleposta SACCO Ltd.	16 319	58	146 638 556

Source: Annual Reports of the SACCOs.

The vibrancy of SACCOs is further illustrated by the fact that they have replaced agricultural marketing cooperatives as the leading shareholders, due to their financial strength, in the Cooperative Bank of Kenya – the fourth largest bank in Kenya. With proper management and leadership integrity, SACCOs stand a higher chance of sustainability than agricultural cooperatives for two reasons. First, they largely rely on their own financial resources to transact their activities, thereby avoiding the pitfall of dependency. Secondly, being in the financial sector, their services will always remain in demand unlike agricultural cooperatives that are dependent on the performance of the agricultural sector. Indeed, the increasing decline of agricultural cooperatives has to do with the recession in the sector, which has seen a sharp drop in the production of certain crops like cotton, pyrethrum and to some extent coffee.

But the main challenge to the sustainability of SACCOs remains management. Many of these cooperatives have not injected professionalism into the recruitment of staff, resulting in poor retention of qualified staff. For instance, this is the main problem facing the Harambee SACCO, which is arguably the largest savings and credit cooperative society in Africa. The figures in Table 3.3 show that it has the largest membership and staff, but its turnover is lower than that of Mwalimu SACCO. Whereas Mwalimu recorded an average monthly check-off (in lieu of share contributions and loan repayments) of 440 million Kenya shillings in 2005, Harambee SACCO had 320 million Kenya shillings. The relatively lower performance of Harambee was attributed to management problems.

Whereas cooperative societies can be said to be vibrant in the economic sphere, they have little to offer in the organization of non-economic activities. They organize one members' education day annually to enlighten members on their activities and the virtues of cooperation, but the single day has proved inadequate to serve the purpose of education and training. With the exception of some SACCOs that have benevolent schemes to assist their bereaved members, cooperatives have little regard for the social welfare of their members. Though some of the financial services that they offer eventually translate into the provision of such services – such as when school fees loans help members to put their children into school – cooperative societies do not directly address members' social welfare issues like leisure, gender equality and workers' rights.

Departing from the unified cooperative tradition

As may be apparent, vertical integration has been a feature of the cooperative movement since its inception. Cooperative societies have always been affiliated to activity-based and district cooperative unions. The latter are then affiliated to national cooperative organizations, which are members of the apex cooperative organization. This vertical structure has seen the evolution of a vibrant cooperative movement over the years, but not without some problems in the recent past.

Agricultural cooperatives in particular have had the most problems in their vertical integration. The point has already been made that the decline in the production of cotton and pyrethrum in the late 1980s has seen most of the cooperative societies in these sectors remain dormant. The unions have been severely affected in this regard. For instance, Luanda Cotton Farmers Cooperative Union in Busia District had to close down its ginnery that had just been rehabilitated in 1992 following the collapse of cotton production.

In the dairy sector, cooperative societies were affiliated to Kenya Cooperative Creameries (KCC) that monopolized the processing and marketing of milk up to the early 1990s. However, KCC's poor financial performance in the late 1980s and early 1990s forced it to pay cooperatives, and subsequently the producers, milk prices that did not keep pace with the cost of production. This was due to inefficiency in KCC's collection and processing operations as well as the political directives regarding prices of milk to consumers. The problem of low prices to producers was compounded by delayed payments by KCC to cooperatives for milk supplied, sometimes taking several months. This forced producers to shift more sales to the informal raw milk market, thereby drastically reducing supplies to KCC (Staal et al, 1997: 785; Owango et al, 1998:174). The persistent poor performance of KCC saw it sold to politically connected private investors in 2000 after it failed to pay Kshs. 220 million owed to its employees and a bank loan of Kshs. 400 million. Since the mid 1990s, dairy cooperative societies have been functioning independently without a union. It is in these circumstances that some of them like Githunguri and Limuru dairy cooperative societies have put up their own milk processing plants. It is significant, however, that the government repossessed KCC from the private investors in 2003 and it is being rehabilitated as a state corporation before being handed back to the cooperative movement.

The coffee sector is also sliding into a similar fate given the poor performance of the Kenya Planters Cooperative Union (KPCU). Part of the problem in KPCU can be attributed to the liberalization of the coffee sector in the early 1990s that introduced new coffee millers and marketing agents to compete with the union as well as the central coffee auction system that is long and characterized by delayed payments, poor management seems to be the key problem. For instance, KPCU is owed Kshs. 2 billion by politicians, businessmen and large plantation owners - some of whom are the main competitors to the union. This debt has seen KPCU unable to pay farmers promptly for their produce. It is this delayed payment that is triggering some cooperatives affiliated to the union to market their coffee through private agents, thereby denying the union income and vibrancy. The situation for

KPCU is likely to worsen when the proposed direct marketing system is introduced, for more players will enter the market to pay farmers cash on delivery of their produce. Cooperative societies are likely to start operating outside KPCU, as some of them are already doing, thereby destabilizing the vertical integration of the movement.

Nevertheless, non-agricultural cooperative unions have remained vibrant, particularly those in the financial sector. For instance, KUSCCO brings together 2,600 active SACCO societies with a membership of two million while KERUSSU has 45 active rural SACCO societies with a membership of 1,430,390. These unions serve as the mouthpieces of the respective SACCOs in the country; a role that continues to see them attract rather than lose membership. KUSCCO also provides common shared services like education and training; business development, consultancy and research; risk management; and the inter-lending programme for SACCOs called Central Finance Programme, which have enhanced the vertical integration of the sector. It is in this regard that the sector has been said to be the largest SACCO movement in Sub-Saharan Africa (Evans, 2002: 13).

Horizontal integration of the cooperative movement has, however, not been as pronounced as vertical integration. Nevertheless, it is noticeable that companies wholly owned by cooperatives have been formed to carry out specialized and investment functions for the entire cooperative movement. One example is the Cooperative Insurance Company. Initially started as an insurance agency to secure insurance cover for cooperatives in 1972, it was formally licensed as a composite company in 1980 to provide risk protection to cooperative property like vehicles, factories and buildings as well as SACCO savings in the event of the death of borrowers. It is owned by 1,495 cooperative organizations that have put in more than Kshs. 200 million as share capital. Many cooperative societies have found it easy to invest in the company because they need a minimum of 1,000 shares, each share valued at only Kshs. 20. Besides providing risk insurance, the company also provides awareness in risk protection and management to cooperatives.

The other example of horizontal integration is the Cooperative Bank of Kenya. Started in 1968 for the purpose of mobilizing savings to offer banking services and affordable credit to the cooperative movement, the bank has restricted shareholding to the cooperatives and (since 1996) individual members of cooperative societies duly recommended by their societies. To retain its association with the cooperative movement, 70% of the shares are held by cooperatives while individual members of societies hold only 30% of the shares and are not entitled to attend the annual general meeting of the bank. The bank's prosperity was attributed not only to prudent management, but also to the willingness by cooperatives to increase their share capital to meet the Banking Act's legal requirement on the capital to deposit ratio that has variously been adjusted upwards over the years. This has helped to keep out private shareholders who might have bought out the bank as has been the case in other African countries. Since the liberalization of the cooperative movement, the bank has modernized its services to effectively compete with other banks and financial institutions, resulting in increased profitability. For instance, in 2004 the bank made a pre-tax profit of Kshs. 365 million, up from Kshs. 183.4 million in 2003. By September 2005, the bank had recorded a commendable pre-tax profit of Kshs. 608 million – the highest profit since its establishment. The bulk of the bank's credit facilities are offered to cooperatives, particularly SACCOs. For instance, it lends about Kshs. 3.5 billion annually to SACCOs for lending on to their members in school fees loans.

In addition to horizontal integration through these national cooperative investments (NCIs), it is significant that rural SACCOs are steadily being formed by various agricultural cooperative societies and unions to provide financial services to their members. This diversification of activities by agricultural cooperatives could help to resuscitate a sector that is fading away due to the recession in agriculture.

At the apex level, KNFC has not been as vibrant. The organization was formed in 1964 to promote cooperative development, unite the cooperative movement and represent cooperative interests on all matters of policy and legislation. Its principal role was to be the spokesman of the cooperative movement in Kenya. However, poor management over the years saw it deviate from its core business into other activities like education and training as well as research and consultancy that were already being performed by some of its members. The liberalization of the cooperative sector worsened matters for the falling giant as corruption and ethnicity became the main driving forces in the election of the board of directors. Such a board would then appoint incompetent chief executives with the intention of looting the organization.

This turn of events led the Minister for Cooperative Development and Marketing to dissolve KNFC's board of directors and replace it with an interim one in May 2005 following an inquiry report that implicated the executive director in corruption and gross mismanagement. By that time, its membership had shrunk from over 8,000 to just over 600. The institution was bankrupt and could not pay its workers. Property and printing equipment worth millions of shillings had been vandalized or stolen. The organization had even failed to pay its membership fees to the ICA. The interim board of directors is currently putting in place measures to revive the organization and restore members' control.

Great potential for cooperative growth

Kenya has thousands of member-based self-help groups straddling the rural and urban sectors. These groups exist to satisfy the social and economic interests of their members. They are found in several sectors of the economy, including poultry, livestock, crop farming, savings and credit, small-scale business, pottery and handicraft, knitting and tailoring, among others (Wanyama, 2003: 110). However, there is no vertical or horizontal organization that integrates the activities of these groups. In the circumstances, these groups do not have a mechanism for pooling their resources to provide services that are beyond the capacity and capability of a single group. The demand for such services by their members has occasionally provided the opportunity for the formation of cooperatives.

For instance, in western Kenya, a number of self-help groups have been formed to enable members to acquire exotic cows for increased milk production at the household level. In the long term, such members have been able to produce more milk, but have not been able to find a suitable market for it. In order to effectively market members' milk, some of these groups have transformed themselves into multi-produce marketing cooperatives. A case in point is Emarenyo Zero-grazing Self-help group that was formed in 1994 in Butere Division of Butere-Mumias District.

The organization was initially a self-help group to facilitate exchange of experiences, information and resources in the management of their "zero-grazing" dairy cattle and poultry farms. With increased production of milk and eggs among the members, the immediate problem became how to market the produce. In 1998, it transformed itself into Emarenyo Multi-purpose Cooperative Society in order to focus on marketing dairy produce. It subsequently opened its membership to any interested person in Butere Division, subject to paying membership fees and a minimum share contribution of Kshs. 10,000 within two years. By 2002, the cooperative had 82 members, 42 of whom were women. It had set up a store in Butere town where it collected members' produce for marketing. It sold milk to dairy processors in Kakamega town as well as to local consumers. Eggs were sold on wholesale terms to local traders. In the same premises, it stocked animal feeds and veterinary medicine for sale to the members and the general public. Members could purchase these on credit terms, with their share contributions and proceeds from the sale of their produce serving as collateral for the credit. Thus, what was essentially a self-help group is now a multi-produce marketing cooperative society due to the lack of a proper marketing infrastructure for members' produce (Wanyama, 2003: 138-9).

This case shows the enormous potential that exists for the transformation of the numerous self-help groups into cooperatives for the purpose of providing specialized services to their members. This can effectively be done through awareness creation as to the possible investments and benefits that members stand to gain by pooling their resources into activity- and regional-based cooperative ventures. But this would have to be complemented with training in entrepreneurship and cooperative management skills.

Besides the formation of new cooperatives on the basis of the existing self-help groups, the potential for growth in the cooperative sector can also be enhanced by strengthening the existing cooperatives. In the agricultural sector, a major impediment to the growth of these institutions is the low production of various products due to a host of factors like lack of credit, lack of farm inputs and extension services, poor quality produce, low producer prices and delayed payment to farmers (ICA, 2002: 23-24). This has served to demoralize farmers from producing more, with some abandoning the production of some crops (like cotton) altogether. A resuscitation of agricultural productivity by addressing these problems would increase demand for markets and hence cooperative services.

There are also problems that are specific to cooperatives. Key among these are managerial issues like poor record keeping because of inadequate training of society staff; delayed production of management reports and audits; lack of qualified staff; and poor decision-making on the part of the management committee. These are issues that can be addressed through training. The Cooperative College of Kenya, which was established by the government to train leaders and members of the cooperative movement, has over the years played this role. Unfortunately, the number of trainees from cooperatives at the College has been declining since the liberalization of the movement mainly because most cooperatives, especially in the agricultural sector, have been unable to pay fees for their staff just as government sponsorship to cooperatives and the College for training has been declining. On the other hand, most cooperatives have been poor at retaining trained staff partly due to the poor remuneration that used to be determined by the Commissioner for Cooperative Development. Furthermore, the training programmes at the College have always targeted staff rather than members of the cooperatives, who would be elected to management committees to make managerial decisions. To overcome these difficulties, there is a need for balanced training of staff, management committee leaders and members to make all aware of their respective responsibilities in the management of autonomous, independent and self-reliant cooperatives.

Whereas these management problems affect both agricultural and non-agricultural cooperatives, SACCOs have additional problems that are specific to their nature. The core business of these cooperatives is to mobilize saving for the purpose of advancing credit to the members. Given that their vibrancy depends on how much money they are able to loan out to members, they need to build larger loan portfolios that may be beyond members' savings and share contributions. Assistance in funding the building of such a loan portfolio would make more loan packages available to the members at lower interest rates, thereby enhancing the growth of the cooperative sector. Some of our respondents argued that SACCOs can be more vibrant if they can get a stabilization fund to cushion the high interest rates that they are forced to charge their members to meet operational costs while at the same time generating a profit. The fund, given to a SACCO as a working capital support grant, would thus enhance the liquidity of SACCOs, which could result in increased availability of funds to loan to members or even a reduction in interest rates on loans.

It is nevertheless significant that despite the problems that bedevil cooperatives, there are a number of good practices that are triggering the formation of other cooperatives. The point has been made, for example, that the vibrancy of the SACCO movement has seen agricultural cooperatives start rural savings and credit activities to replace their dormant marketing activities.

From assistance through government to direct support to the movement

Donors to the cooperative movement in Kenya are mainly cooperative agencies from developed countries and international organizations. Their support to cooperatives includes capital provision, institutional capacity building, education and training, and supporting the development of an enabling environment for the effective operation of cooperatives.

There are two significant cooperative agencies from the developed countries. First is the Swedish Cooperative Centre (SCC). It funds programmes for capacity building and institutional development of cooperatives. Such funds are directly channeled to the cooperative movement rather than through the government as was the case under the Kenya Nordic Cooperative Development Programme (KNCDP) that has been phased out. SCC has supported capacity building and curriculum development at the Cooperative College of Kenya; it has funded KNFC to host cooperative consultations on the implications of the Cooperative Societies (Amendment) Act of 2004; it is supporting initiatives to revive the institutional capacity of KNFC; and it is also funding, to the tune of about Kshs. 30 million annually, the Intensive Cooperative Management Improvement Scheme (ICMIS) whose objective is to improve the management of selected cooperative societies through training of their staff and management committees. In addition, SCC funds cooperative member education through specialized programmes. For example, it has funded Community Empowerment and Economic Development through Cooperatives (CEEDCO), a local NGO operating in Kiambu District, to educate members of Githunguri Dairy Farmers Cooperative Society on the value of cooperatives in development and their role as members of these enterprises.

The second agency is the Canadian Cooperative Association (CCA). Like SCC, it focuses on capacity building and organizational development. Besides its support to KNFC to host cooperative consultations on the implications of the Cooperative Societies (Amendment) Act of 2004, it is funding the ICA Regional Office for Africa's Policy and Research Programme to translate the policy and legal framework in Kenya into a language understandable to all co-operators. The ICA Programme is in the process of simplifying the Cooperative Societies (Amendment) Act, 2004 and the Cooperative Societies Rules, 2004 before translating the simplified English versions into Kiswahili. It also intends to set up a cooperative web site from which the cooperative movement could access all cooperative information in the country; all these courtesy of CCA funding.

A number of international institutions also support cooperatives. First is the European Investment Bank. It recently donated two million Euros to the Cooperative Bank of Kenya for lending on to rural SACCOs. The second institution is the World Bank. It funds cooperative activities through government ministries responsible for agricultural development. For instance, it has funded the Smallholder Coffee Improvement Project (SCIP) through the Ministry of Agriculture. The funds were channeled to coffee cooperatives through the Cooperative Bank of Kenya under an agreement with the said Ministry and the Treasury. Third, there is the International Fund for Agricultural Development (IFAD). It supports rural SACCOs in information technology training through the Cooperative Bank of Kenya. Fourth, the United States Agency for International Development (USAID) has funded WOCCU to provide management technical assistance to credit unions in Kenya (Evans, 2002). USAID is also indirectly supporting cooperatives through its funding of capacity building initiatives in the Strategy for Revitalizing Agriculture (SRA).

These few examples of the donors in the cooperative movement in Kenya clearly show that most donors now prefer to fund capacity building initiatives rather than the capitalization of cooperatives. Much as this could strengthen self-reliance in cooperatives, the question of a poor capital base for cooperative enterprises will remain a challenge. It is also significant to note that most donors are now channeling resources directly to the cooperative movement rather than to the government.

The impact of donor support is, however, yet to yield the desired results. Decades of training in the cooperative movement through KNCDP significantly improved management skills among staff in cooperatives, but, as already pointed out, all trained staff have not been retained in the movement; thereby leaving the capacity of the affected cooperatives unchanged. Above all, the training has always targeted staff rather than management committees and members who become the key decision-makers. With regard to capital support, cooperatives have abused credit schemes funded by donors through defaulting on repayment. For instance, most of the cooperatives defaulted on their loans under SCIP I and II. Perhaps it is this experience that has seen many donors reduce their capitation support to cooperatives and also change their focus from capital provision to institutional capacity building.

Cooperative valuation of institutional linkages

Cooperatives in Kenya are linked to a multiplicity of institutions at the governmental and movement levels. With regard to the government, the point has been made that the Ministry of Cooperative Development and

Marketing has over the years been very close to the cooperative movement. This relationship has been evaluated by cooperatives differently at varying periods. Before the liberalization of the sector in 1997, the role of the ministry, particularly the Commissioner for Cooperative Development, was generally perceived by cooperatives to be a burden due to the strict controlling influence. This perception now varies among cooperatives. The point has been made that liberalization opened some cooperatives to massive corruption and mismanagement while others found space to rejuvenate themselves. Whereas the former category of cooperatives, in which leaders are misappropriating resources, continue to find the role of the government (as provided for in the 2004 Cooperative legislations) a burden, those cooperatives that are performing fairly well find the role of government to be supportive and collaborative. Perhaps the latter perception should be understood in the light of the changed role of the government, which is now regulatory rather than controlling.

Within the cooperative movement, the point has been made that the apex organization has fared poorly. This has seen many cooperatives disengage from KNFC, leaving it with a paltry membership relative to the past. Consequently, the status of this organization has seen many cooperatives regard it as a liability and, therefore, a burden to the cooperative movement since it has failed to play the role for which it was set up.

As already mentioned, the Cooperative College of Kenya has played a key role in training the staff of the cooperative movement. The College has also occasionally designed members' education programmes as well as courses for management committees of cooperatives at the request of specific cooperative societies. Indeed, most if not all trained staff in cooperatives went through the College. Due to this close association with the movement, the College tends to be identified more with the movement than the government that funds most of its activities. Cooperatives, therefore, appreciate the supportive and collaborative role of the College.

Cooperatives in Kenya are also linked to international cooperative promotion organizations. Top among these is the ICA, whose role is to represent, unite and support the development of autonomous and viable cooperative organizations globally. Through its three members in Kenya, namely the Cooperative College of Kenya, the Cooperative Insurance Company and the Cooperative Bank of Kenya, the ICA is appreciated by cooperatives as a partner in advocating the appropriate policy and legal environment. The presence of the ICA in Kenya would have been better felt through KNFC, the apex organization for all cooperatives but it is, unfortunately, not a member due to its failure to pay its membership fees.

Besides being a member of the ICA, the Cooperative Insurance Company is also a member of the International Cooperative and Mutual Insurance Federation (ICMIF). CIC has found this organization important for solidarity and, most importantly, a provider of mutual support in reinsurance services.

In the savings and credit sector, KUSCCO is affiliated to the African Confederation of Savings and Credit Cooperatives (ACCOSCA), the African Rural and Agricultural Credit Associations (AFRACA), the World Council of Credit Unions (WOCCU) and the International Raiffeisen Union (IRU). In addition, KUSCCO is also a member of the East African Regional Association of SACCOs comprising Uganda, Rwanda, Burundi, Kenya, Tanzania, Eritrea, Ethiopia, Seychelles and Democratic Republic of Congo. KUSCCO has joined all these international and regional organizations to forge solidarity and mutual support.

Estimating the employment effect of the cooperative movement

Cooperatives are generally regarded to be key generators of employment in Kenya, but such claims are rarely supported with statistical figures. The available data, however, show a relatively slow growth in wage employment in cooperatives. Whereas the number of wage employees in cooperatives in 1999 was 72,100, it stood at 77,400 in 2003 (Republic of Kenya, 2004c: 261), thus creating slightly over 5,000 jobs in five years. If these figures are anything to go by, then cooperatives are not the significant wage employment creators.

However, these figures could as well be an underestimation of wage employment in cooperatives. For instance, in the agricultural sector, total wage employment figures are difficult to come by, but a study in 2001 showed that there were only 11,311 permanent employees in the sector (ICA, 2002: 14); yet Githunguri Dairy Farmers Cooperative Society alone had 250 employees. Githunguri's wage employment increased to 300 in 2005. Whereas the Cooperative College has 104 permanent employees, the Ministry of Cooperative Development and Marketing has slightly over 1,300 staff. In the financial sector, the Cooperative Bank alone employs over 1,200 while CIC has over 600 employees. Just ten top SACCOs (in terms of annual turnover) that have been highlighted in Table 3.3 above bring together a total workforce of 1,154 yet there are over 2,600 active SACCOs spread across the country. These estimates imply that the total number of employees in cooperatives could be more than the above stated estimates.

Employment estimates in the cooperative sector cannot be based on wage employment alone, but also on the income that the sector generates for people. In 2004, SACCOs had a total membership of about 2 million, 1,575,000 of whom were considered active. The other non-agricultural cooperatives had a total membership of 878,000, about 50% of whom were estimated to be active. Cooperatives in the agricultural sector had a total membership of 924,000, about 50% of whom were estimated to be active. The implication is that about 2.5 million people directly derive at least an income from their membership of cooperatives.

In addition to these, there are people who get part of their income from manufacturing and marketing goods that are purchased by cooperatives, for instance, office stationery used in cooperatives, particularly SACCOs; packaging paper used by dairy cooperatives to pack products; machinery for primary processing of agricultural produce like coffee and milk; and farm inputs stocked in cooperative stores. Then there are people who earn some income by marketing products from cooperatives. For instance, dairy cooperatives produce various products like fresh milk, ghee, butter and yoghurt while other agricultural cooperatives market coffee, fish, pyrethrum, eggs, etc. Consequently, it can be safely estimated that over three million people derive a significant part of their income from the activities and services of cooperatives in Kenya. This represents over ten per cent of the current estimates of the country's total population.

Employment opportunities in cooperatives

Before the liberalization of the sector, employment terms in cooperatives were not competitive enough to attract and retain qualified staff basically because these were at the discretion of the Commissioner. This, however, changed when liberalization required cooperatives to compete with private firms in the production and marketing of goods and services. As the case of Githunguri Dairy Farmers Cooperative Society shows, cooperatives are now putting in place employment policies that emphasize competitive sourcing and remuneration of staff to enhance their competitive edge in the market. This has the potential of creating more attractive working conditions in the cooperative sector than in the past.

In addition to such policies, more employment opportunities could be generated by revitalizing the agricultural sector. For instance, the cotton sector is currently dormant yet some of the cooperative unions have ginneries and plants for manufacturing soap, animal feeds and oil from cotton seeds. A case in point is Malaba-Malakisi Cotton Farmers Cooperative Union in Teso district that is virtually closed because cotton is no longer grown by farmers for reasons that have already been given above. Luanda Farmers Cooperative Union in Busia District has a modern and efficient ginnery in East Africa, but it is also closed for the same reason. The pyrethrum sector is also performing below expectation. The processing activities of agricultural cooperatives in Kenya were estimated to employ just 6,854 people in 2003 (Republic of Kenya, 2004c: 262), yet their potential far exceeds this. In short, increased agricultural productivity has the potential of generating more employment opportunities in the cooperative sector.

In the financial sector, there are also some opportunities and challenges in cooperatives with implications for employment creation. For instance, SACCOs could diversify their traditional products of savings and credit by introducing new products like Front Office Service Activity (FOSA), education accounts, holiday and Christmas accounts and children's accounts. They also need to improve their performance by increasing their capitalization to meet the growing demand for loans; introducing information technology in the management of their activities; developing a competitive business model by reducing transaction costs and improving the quality of services; and improving leadership integrity by electing the right calibre of leaders – which can be done through member education. Furthermore, KUSCCO estimates that the SACCO movement has a potential of 10 million members, but only 2 million have been recruited. There is a need to expand the outreach to members. All these would enhance the vibrancy of SACCOs and hence generate additional employment opportunities.

The other factors that generally affect the performance and vibrancy of cooperatives have already been highlighted. Solutions to such leadership, management and capital problems stand a chance of unlocking the enormous employment potential in cooperatives.

A significant contribution to poverty reduction

Though state-directed formation of cooperatives initially targeted (but without an outright policy) the so-called agriculturally high potential areas, these institutions are now found in both the low and high potential areas. The SACCO movement is quickly spreading from its traditional urban and wage employment sectors into the rural and informal sectors. Some of the urban- and employer-based SACCOs like Mwalimu (for teachers) and Harambee (for employees in the Office of the President) have opened branches outside Nairobi, with Front Office Services (including withdrawable savings deposit products and instant cash advances on salaries) that facilitate cash flow in areas that commercial banks have shunned. The income that is associated with the activities of these cooperatives has benefited not just the members, but also local businesses and people. The contribution of cooperatives to poverty reduction should be appreciated in this light.

It is also significant that the income generated from cooperative members is mainly used to address long-term poverty reduction measures. For instance, the main type of back office loan offered by most SACCOs (at interest rates of 1 to 1.5% on reducing balances for a 12-month period) is for paying school fees (Evans, 2002: 22-23). This has afforded many members of these cooperatives an opportunity to educate their children, with a view to reducing poverty in their families following the children's employment in the future. At Maseno University SACCO, members have obtained development loans to build houses, invest in businesses and farming and meet other family obligations, besides paying school fees. All these are efforts towards poverty reduction.

Even more revealing about the contribution of cooperatives to poverty reduction are the lamentations of cotton farmers of western Kenya. They narrate how much easier it was to educate their children and meet household obligations like clothing before the collapse of cotton farming in the late 1980s than it is now. It is the cotton cooperatives that made this possible, yet they remain dormant today. Members of Guthunguri Dairy Cooperative Society expressed similar sentiments. They were happy with their cooperative for facilitating the marketing of their milk and paying them competitive prices promptly. This had enabled them to pay school fees, buy clothes, buy household furniture, buy food, improve their farms and build better houses. They could not afford to do these easily before the late 1990s when the cooperative witnessed a turnaround in its performance that improved the marketing of members' milk and supply of animal feeds and medicine to members on credit.

Rudiments of social protection

As business enterprises, particularly in the liberalized competitive market, cooperatives in Kenya have little concern for the social protection of people in society. This is in spite of the fact that social protection is expressly included in the ICA cooperative principle of concern for the community. Neither do the state and non-governmental actors use cooperatives as a basis to initiate systems of mutual social protection in society. Nevertheless, rudiments of social protection are found in the activities of some cooperatives.

One of these is found in both the back office and front office activities of SACCOs. With regard to back office activities, SACCOs offer emergency loans to their members for a term of twelve months. This acts as a fall-back for members to quickly respond to unanticipated socio-economic problems that may arise at any time. However, most cooperatives usually have limited funds for such loans, resulting in the inability of SACCOs to effectively respond to increasing demands for emergency loans as is the case at Maseno University SACCO. In the front office service activities, SACCOs have introduced cash salary advances that are popularly referred to as "instant loans". Under varying conditions, SACCOs approve and pay these advances in less than one day, and often within five minutes (Evans, 2002: 18). It is in this regard that instant loans are increasingly becoming more popular than emergency loans though their repayment terms are shorter and interest rates higher. The popularity of these loans has, however, outstripped the available funds in most SACCOs.

Secondly, some SACCOs have introduced benevolent funds to which members contribute regularly and only draw from when they are bereaved. The schemes define the relatives at whose death the member would get assistance to meet the burial expenses as well as the respective amount of money he/she would be entitled to. In the event of a member's death, his/her immediate family gets assistance from the fund to meet burial expenses.

Thirdly, the core business of CIC is to give protection against risks in the cooperative sector as well as for individuals. It is significant that CIC has also developed a micro-finance insurance scheme specifically for covering savings of micro-finance institutions (MFIs) in case a loan recipient dies before completing repayment. The importance of the scheme is that it is protecting the funds of the "poor segments of society". Nevertheless, the insurance protection is a business and is only available to those who are able and willing to pay the requisite premiums. The only exception to this is CIC's corporate social responsibility programme that allocates limited funds annually to provide social services to the community. This is done by donating such funds to institutions to be used for a specific service. For instance, CIC donates money to hospitals to bail out patients who are genuinely unable to pay their medical bills. But such funds are limited and discretionary.

Many voices, but not heard

The point has been made that KNFC is the spokesperson of the cooperative movement in Kenya as well as its representative in national and international circles through appropriate networking and linkages. Its key mandate is to lobby and advocate for favourable policy and legal changes in the cooperative sector. However, the leadership and management problems that have bedeviled the organization, forcing the Minister to intervene and dissolve its board of directors in May 2005, have seen KNFC ineffective in improving the voice and representation of the cooperative movement in the country.

To the extent that the organization had been brought to its knees, it failed, for example, to effectively participate and influence changes to the 1997 Cooperative Societies Act that produced the Cooperative Societies (Amendment) Act, 2004. It was after the amended Act had been enacted that it started mobilizing donor support to hold consultations on the implications of the Act – too late in the day. Perhaps this also explains the absence of cooperatives in national development debates like the preparation of the country's Poverty Reduction Strategy Paper (PRSP) (Hanmer et al, 2003). We did not come across any significant participation or recognition of cooperatives in our 2003 survey of non-state actors that took part in the PRSP and negotiations for the Cotonou Agreement that established trade and development partnerships between African, Caribbean and Pacific (ACP) countries and the European Union (Develtere, Hertogen and Wanyama, 2005). Moreover, KNFC ceased to be a representative of the cooperative movement in international circles when it failed to renew its membership with the ICA, thereby losing a key network and linkage at the international level.

In the circumstances, NCOs and Cooperative Unions could become more effective speakers and representatives of the cooperative sector than KNFC.

For instance, KUSCCO now stands out as the mouth-piece of SACCOs in Kenya and the advocate of the sector in all matters that affect the development and growth of SACCOs. In the recent past, it was vocal in opposing the retrenchment of employees as that would affect the membership of SACCOs. It has also demanded to be involved in poverty reduction and HIV/AIDS awareness programmes. Even more significantly, KUSCCO was recently involved in the formulation of the yet to be debated and enacted SACCO Act that sets out to make special provisions for the registration and licensing of SACCOs; prudential requirements; standard forms of accounts; corporate governance; amalgamations, divisions and liquidations; establishment of a SACCO Regulatory Authority; savings protection insurance; and setting up a Central Liquidity Fund, among others. We have already indicated the various regional and international organizations in which KUSCCO represents the SACCO movement.

However, the cooperative unions in the agricultural sector are not as active as KUSCCO; nor do they have the same capacity and competencies to persuade, lobby and advocate for their respective sectors as KUSCCO does. Perhaps this is due to the fact that cooperatives in this sector do not consider giving priority to the voice and representation of their members in their activities.

Conclusion

The purpose of this discussion has been to highlight the status of the cooperative movement in Kenya with a view to assessing the real and potential impact of cooperatives on reduction of poverty through creation of employment, generation of economic activities, enhancement of social protection and improvement of cooperative voice and representation.

The discussion shows that the foundation and growth of cooperatives in the country have been guided by a deliberate government policy and legal framework. The content of this framework has, however, been changing over the years from strict state direction and control to the current liberal posture of minimal state regulation and supervision. It is this legal and policy environment that has seen a phenomenal growth in the number and membership of cooperatives, particularly up to the early 1990s. Thereafter, the growth trend has witnessed a reduction in the number and membership of agricultural cooperatives that were initially predominant and a significant increase in the number and membership of non-agricultural cooperatives, particularly SACCOs. Thus, whereas the vibrancy of SACCOs is on the rise, that of agricultural cooperatives, perhaps with the exception of dairy cooperatives that have responded to the void created by the fall of KCC, is declining. Whereas this turn of events could be attributed to the liberalization measures of the mid 1990s that culminated in the poor performance of cooperatives, part of the problem has to do with the recession in the agricultural sector that triggered the search for alternative income in the financial sector.

This pattern of growth is also reflected in the contribution of cooperatives to employment creation and income generation. Though the movement as a whole has been characterized by a slow growth in wage employment creation, agricultural cooperatives seem to be more affected than SACCOs. Nevertheless, the income that members derive from these institutions is significant in the livelihoods of a large proportion of the Kenyan population. The income has been particularly valued by cooperators for its contribution to items including paying school fees, meeting domestic expenses, building improved shelter, investing in small-scale enterprises and farming, meeting medical expenses, and buying household furniture. In addition, the spillover effect of cooperative ventures has afforded many local people who are not members of cooperatives income opportunities. All these have seen cooperatives regarded as significant contributors to poverty reduction, though there remains enormous potential that can be explored.

Cooperatives have, however, not fared as well with regard to social protection. They mainly operate as business entities with little concern for communal social welfare. Thus with the exception of some SACCO activities like emergency and instant loans that cushion members from unexpected problems as well as benevolent funds that take care of burial expenses for bereaved members, cooperatives have not lived up to the ICA principle of concern for the community. With regard to voice and representation, cooperatives have not featured in national debates on development and poverty reduction. KNFC has generally failed the cooperative movement as its mouthpiece and representative, but the consolation is that unions and national organizations like KUSCCO are increasingly taking up the challenge of representing the interests of their respective cooperatives in policy-making circles.

It is, therefore, fair to conclude that the performance of the cooperative movement remains below expectation, but that there is potential for improving its status in order to enhance its capacity to contribute to poverty reduction. We finish this article by putting forward some of the key suggestions for rejuvenating the movement.

- Agricultural productivity is the main factor affecting the vibrancy of cooperatives in the sector. Consequently, the revival of the production of some crops as well as improvements in the level of production will also resuscitate cooperatives in the sector.

- All cooperatives face management problems despite many years of staff training by the Cooperative College of Kenya with donor support. There is need for balanced training that focuses on all actors in a cooperative, namely staff, management committee and ordinary members in order to make all aware of their rights and responsibilities in cooperatives.

- There are also leadership problems in all cooperatives. To enhance leadership integrity, member education needs to be intensified to sensitize them about the need to elect leaders of sound calibre.

- Although cooperatives need to be self-reliant, the reality is that most of them do not have the requisite capital to enable them to compete in a liberalized market with private firms. In agricultural marketing, this may see private firms take over the marketing of produce to the disadvantage of cooperatives as the fears of KPCU over the introduction of the direct marketing system for coffee confirm. There is, therefore, a need for donors to balance the current preoccupation with institutional capacity building with capital support, which should be channeled directly to the cooperative movement rather than the government. This should also apply to SACCOs that face high demand for loans from their members but whose capitalization is low.

- SACCOs need to diversify their activities from the traditional savings and credit to new products like front office service activities, education accounts, Christmas accounts and children's accounts.

- SACCOs also need to modernize their management systems by adopting information technology in their management to reduce transaction costs and improve the quality of services to their members.

Sources

This article is based on a series of documents and interviews carried out during the autumn of 2005. The author wishes to thank the following persons: Mr. S. O. Bango, Cooperative Bank of Kenya; Mr. Ada Kibora and Mrs. Ann Njoki Mutisya, ICA Regional Office for Africa; Mr. James Bango, Kenya National Federation of Cooperatives; Mr. Francis Munyao, Cooperative Insurance Company; Mrs. Esther Gicheru and Mrs. Cecilia Kiongo, Cooperative College of Kenya; Mr. J. K. Njage and Mr. Kyangu, Ministry of Cooperative Development and Marketing; Mr. John Kilonzo and Ms. Gladys Wambiri, Githunguri Dairy Farmers Cooperative Society; Mr. Gilbert Ndere and Mr. Fredrick Otieno, Kamukunji Jua Kali Savings and Credit Cooperative Society; Mr. Eric Kathanga, Kenya Planters Cooperative Union; and Prof. Patrick O. Alila, Institute for Development Studies, University of Nairobi.

Bibliography

- Birchall J. (2003), *Rediscovering the Cooperative Advantage: Poverty Reduction through Self-help*, ILO, Geneva.

- Birchall J. (2004), *Cooperatives and the Millennium Development Goals*, ILO, Geneva.

- Cooperative Bank of Kenya (1993), *Cooperative Banking in Kenya*, The Cooperative Bank of Kenya, Nairobi.

- Develtere P., Hertogen E. & Wanyama F. (2005), 'The Emergence of Multilevel Governance in Kenya', *LIRGIAD Project Working Paper No.7*, Catholic University of Leuven. (Available at www.hiva.be/docs/nl/).

- Evans A. C. (2002), 'The Unpaved Road Ahead: HIV/AIDS & Microfinance: An Exploration of Kenya Credit Unions (SACCOs)', *Research Monograph Series n°21*, World Council of Credit Unions, Madison, Wisconsin.

- Hanmer L., Ikiara G., Eberlei W. & Abong'o C. (2003), 'Kenya', in D. Booth (ed.), *Fighting Poverty in Africa: Are PRSPs Making a Difference?*, Overseas Development Institute, London.

- Hedlund H. (1992), *Coffee, Cooperatives and Agriculture: An Anthropological, Study of a Coffee Cooperative in Kenya*, Oxford University Press, Nairobi.

- Holmen H. & Jirstrom M. (1994), 'Old Wine in New Bottles? Local Organization as Panacea for Sustainable Development,' in H. Holmen & M. Jirstrom (eds.), *Ground Level Development: NGOs, Cooperatives and Local Organizations in the Third World*, Lund University Press, Lund.

- Hussi P., Murphy J., Lindberg O. & Brenneman L. (1993), *The Development of Cooperatives and Other Rural Organizations: The Role of the World Bank*, The World Bank, Washington, D.C.

- International Cooperative Alliance (ICA) (2002), *Status of Agricultural Marketing, Cooperatives in Kenya*, ICA-ROECSA, Nairobi.

- International Labour Organization (2002), *Recommendation 193 of the ILO on Promotion of Cooperatives*, ILO, Geneva.

- Karlen L. (1995), *Active Marketing Societies in Kenya, Unpublished Consultancy Report*, Ministry of Cooperative Development and Marketing, Nairobi.

- Lindberg O. (1993), 'Kenya: Review of the Cooperative Sector with Special Emphasis on Coffee Cooperatives', in H. Porvali (ed.), *The Development Of Cooperatives, Agriculture and Rural Development*

Series, No. 8, The World Bank, Washington, D.C.

- Manyara M. K. (2003), *The Development of Cooperative Law and Policy in Kenya*, Nairobi.

- Manyara M. K. (2004), *Cooperative Law in Kenya*, Nairobi.

- Mudibo E.K. (2005), 'Highlights of the SACCO movement and current trends in the Kenya Union of Savings and Credit Cooperatives (KUSCCO)', KUSCCO, Nairobi.

- Owango M., Lukuyu B., Staal S. J., Kenyanjui M., Njubi D. & Thorpe W. (1998), 'Dairy Cooperatives and Policy Reform in Kenya: Effects of Livestock Service and Milk Market Liberalization', *Food Policy*, vol. 23, n°2, pp. 173-185.

- Republic of Kenya (1997a), Sessional Paper n°6 of 1997, *Cooperatives in a Liberalized Economic Environment*, Government Printer, Nairobi.

- Republic of Kenya (1997b), *Cooperative Societies Act*, Government Printer, Nairobi.

- Republic of Kenya (2002), *Economic Survey 2002*, Central Bureau of Statistics, Ministry of Finance and Planning, Nairobi.

- Republic of Kenya (2004a), *The Cooperative Societies (Amendment) Act*, Government Printer, Nairobi.

- Republic of Kenya (2004b), *The Cooperative Societies Rules*, Government Printer, Nairobi.

- Republic of Kenya (2004c), *Statistical Abstract 2004*, Central Bureau of Statistics, Ministry of Planning and National Development, Nairobi.

- Republic of Kenya (2004d), *Economic Survey 2004*, Central Bureau of Statistics, Ministry of Planning and National Development, Nairobi.

- Staal S., Delgado C. & Nicholson C. (1997), 'Smallholder Dairying Under Transactions Cost in East Africa', *World Development*, vol. 25, n°5, pp. 779-794.

- Uphoff N. (1993), 'Grassroots Organizations and NGOs in Rural Development: Opportunities with Diminishing States and Expanding Markets', *World Development*, vol. 21, n°4, pp. 607-622.

- Wanyama F. O. (1993), *Politics of Rural Development: The Performance of Cotton Cooperatives in Busia District, Kenya*, Unpublished M.A. Thesis, University of Nairobi, Kenya.

- Wanyama F. O. (2003), *Local Organizations for sustainable Development: The Political Environment of Community-Based Organizations in Western Kenya*, Unpublished PhD Thesis, Maseno University, Kenya.

Chapter Four – Growth Without Structures: the Cooperative Movement in Ethiopia

by Teigist Lemma[1]

Introduction

Cooperation among people and communities is an inherent element of many cultures and has existed for many decades in various urban and rural economies of Africa. The gradual transformation of such cooperation enabled the formation of cooperatives as institutions that allow people to systematically pool resources in order to achieve a defined set of goals. The growth and development of cooperatives, however, has been constrained and challenged by various policies and procedures adopted by different governments. Currently, cooperatives have gained due attention particularly in the development discourse as well as programmes designed to reduce poverty. These programmes consider cooperatives as viable institutions for employment generation, increasing the income of the poor and thereby reducing the levels of poverty in Africa.

This study sets out to assess the real and potential impact of the Ethiopian cooperative sector in creating employment, reducing poverty, enhancing social protection and improving the voice and representation of vulnerable groups. A serious limitation to the study is the shortage of literature and reliable data on cooperatives in Ethiopia. At first sight this is surprising since powerful institutions have overseen the performance of the sector during the last three regimes. Nevertheless, the restructuring of government institutions in the different regimes resulted in the misplacement of documents on cooperatives. The decentralization reform implemented by the present regime

---

[1] *Teigist Lemma is a graduate of Addis Ababa University and holds a B.A. in Economics and an M.Sc. in Human Resources Economics. She has worked in government and various non-governmental institutions in the areas of early warning, food security, project and programme planning and evaluation, gender, HIV/AIDS, community based organizations and health micro-insurance systems. She is currently working as an independent consultant.*

has also affected the smooth flow of information from lower to higher levels. The study, therefore, makes use of the very disparate information available at the Federal Cooperative Commission (FCA) and some cooperative unions as well as a wide variety of published and unpublished documents.

In addition to this, we also conducted qualitative field research on one primary cooperative and two cooperative unions, one of which is the pioneer union. The information gathered and the analysis made of these cooperatives were checked and complemented with interviews with officials of the FCA, staff of the ILO and two NGOs that are very active in this field (Volunteers in Oversees Cooperative Assistance – VOCA – and Self Help Development International – SHDI). Also, discussions were held with staff and leaders of the Oromiya Cooperative Bank, the Oromiya Coffee Farmers' Union and the Sidama Coffee Farmers' Cooperative Union.

The history of Ethiopian cooperatives in a nutshell

The history of cooperatives in Ethiopia goes back to the imperial regime. The first proclamation on cooperatives was issued in 1961 (FCA, 2005). From the limited documents available, it is apparent that few cooperatives were functional in the 1960s and 1970s. These were mainly established by coffee and sesame producers. Also, savings and credit cooperatives (SACCOs) were organized by employees of Ethiopian Airlines, the Light and Electric Power Authority, the Commercial Bank, the Highway Authority and Telecommunications. One study indicates that there were about 149 cooperatives in 1974. They consisted of 94 multipurpose cooperatives, 19 SACCOs, 19 consumers' cooperatives and 17 handicrafts cooperatives (Lelisa, 2000).

The emergence of a large number of cooperatives was observed during the centrally controlled economy which lasted from 1974 to 1991. The new cooperatives largely focused on savings and credit as well as the supply of government-subsidized consumer supplies and agricultural inputs. According to information from the Ministry of Agriculture (MoA), at the height of the regime there were about 10,524 primary cooperatives with membership of 4,529,259. The formation of cooperatives during this regime was conducted without respecting the principle of voluntary membership. All were organized on the socialist principle of collective farming and all members were required to contribute an equal amount and have an equal share. Moreover, all households under the designated Kebele[2] were required to be members of cooperatives without which certain basic supplies would not have been accessed at affordable prices. The large majority of the cooperatives during this period were providing services to their members only.

After reform and liberalization in 1989, the agricultural and consumer cooperatives could not maintain their objectives of supplying subsidized tradable items. Many were not able to withstand market competition and as a result they either collapsed, became non-functional or continued to operate in a very inefficient way. This led to a serious misconception as to their potential for employment and poverty reduction. Cooperatives were not accepted as suitable instruments by those concerned with poverty reduction among the poor masses. The offices that were established in various ministries to support the cooperative sector, such as in the Ministry of Agriculture and Relief and Rehabilitation Commission, were ill-equipped to perform a good job. In this way, the cooperative sector was left by and large unattended until 1994. In that year the Agricultural Cooperative Society Proclamation was enacted. The Proclamation was further amended in 1998. This, according to the ILO, created a fertile ground for reorienting and strengthening all types of previously established cooperatives as well as for the formation of new cooperatives (ILO, s.d.).

The said Proclamations provide for primary cooperatives/societies to be organized by a minimum of ten people engaged in agriculture. Due to the decentralization policy, they are largely organized within the geographic boundaries of their respective regions although not limited by them. All cooperatives are currently owned by members and provide services mainly to their members with a gradual extension of their services to non-members.

According to the legislation, the next highest level of integration of cooperatives is the cooperative union that is formed by primary cooperatives engaged in similar produce/activity, but without geographic limitations. Cooperative unions in turn can form their federations in line with their product specializations or engagements. At present, the highest level in the country is formed by the cooperative unions. No national leagues or federations have been established so far.

At primary level, the management boards of cooperatives are elected by the general assembly for a two- or three-year term. The elected board member(s) can serve for a maximum of two terms. At union level, the general assembly

---

[2] The administrative structure in Ethiopia is classified as regional, zonal, Wereda (equivalent to district) and Kebele administrations. Kebele is, therefore, the lowest administrative structure and was formerly known as Peasant Association.

is constituted by representatives of primary cooperatives. These can either represent individual members or the member cooperative itself. The former is the practice in Oromiya Region where the representatives speak and vote on behalf of 100 to 200 individual members of primary cooperatives while the latter is the case in Amahra Region.

A rapidly expanding cooperative movement

Based on the documentation of the Federal Cooperative Agency (FCA), we estimate that there were over 7,366 cooperatives in 1991 out of which 3,771 were farmers' cooperatives, 684 saving and credit cooperatives, 2776 housing cooperatives and 119 handicrafts cooperatives. By 2005 about 14,423 cooperatives were known to exist in the country.

Cooperatives exist in various sectors in the economy and have a larger presence in the service, agriculture and industry sectors. About 80% of the primary cooperatives operate in the service sector located in both rural and urban areas. The service sector is dominated by housing (35%), multipurpose (32%) and saving and credit cooperatives (31%). The high number of housing cooperatives can be explained by the fact that government requires that in urban areas plots for housing construction can only be accessed through housing cooperatives. Most of these cooperatives facilitate the acquisition of the plots and mortgages from public banks. Some of these cooperatives extend their objectives and provide community services such as waste collection, employing security guards, recreational services, road construction, setting up burial societies and other activities with a focus on close neighbourhood.

The multipurpose cooperatives are involved in agricultural production and marketing as well as the supply of consumer goods. The available data indicate that there are about 24 primary multipurpose cooperatives operating in urban areas. Although development agencies would like to see these cooperatives become unifunctional and specialized cooperative enterprises, the leadership of these cooperatives wants to maintain the ongoing engagements in different areas.

Saving and credit cooperatives are widespread due to the demand for credit and financial services. The main objective of these cooperatives is to provide financial services to their members who are generally organized in self-help groups for income generation or small businesses. In the agriculture sector,

SACCOs are linked with the agricultural extension activities of the government and NGOs. The SACCOs working with Self Help Development International (SHDI), for instance, are involved in an extension programme promoting vegetable production and poultry. In addition, the agriculture bureaus as well as other input supplying agencies have been using cooperatives as the most relevant avenues for reaching the farmers, to disseminate information and facilitate the supply of agricultural inputs through credit. Previously the agricultural bureaus themselves used to supply inputs in the absence of cooperatives.

Out of the total of 14,423 cooperatives about 6% of the primary cooperatives are in agricultural production namely in grain, coffee, vegetable, dairy, fish, irrigation and honey production.

In the industry sector, cooperatives are involved in handicrafts and salt production and marketing. The majority of the cooperatives in handicrafts are organized by NGOs working with group based schemes.

In addition, a good proportion of the cooperatives in handicrafts (1,584 cooperatives), housing (3,427 cooperatives), construction (182 cooperatives) and recreational services (two cooperatives) are believed to operate in urban areas. Cooperatives are highly promoted in the Addis Ababa, Amhara, Oromiya, Southern Nation and Nationalities Peoples (SNNP), Harari and Dire Dawa regions that are mainly agricultural and industrial. Regions whose main engagements are livestock, herding and hoe culture such as Afar, Somalie, Gambela and Benshangul Gumuz regional states have a smaller number of cooperatives as shown in Figure 4.1 below.

Figure 4.1: The spatial distribution of cooperatives in Ethiopia

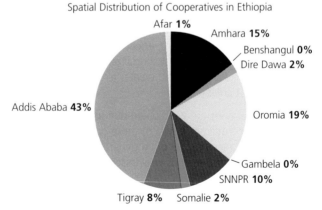

Spatial Distribution of Cooperatives in Ethiopia

Afar **1%**
Amhara **15%**
Benshangul **0%**
Dire Dawa **2%**
Addis Ababa **43%**
Oromia **19%**
Gambela **0%**
SNNPR **10%**
Tigray **8%**   Somalie **2%**

The number of cooperatives, as well as the size of membership, indicates that the large majority of the population and areas have not yet been able to explore and utilize the potential services of cooperatives. The agricultural sector, for instance, is a source of livelihood for about 85% of the total population in the country. The available data show that only about 8% of the rural population belongs to a cooperative. In absolute terms, the present number of members is close to what was achieved during the socialist regime in the 1980s, namely over 4.5 million. However, there is marked progress in reviving the sector with restructured as well as newly created cooperatives now being more oriented towards genuine cooperative principles. Due to the reorientation and success of some cooperatives, there is a growing interest among the population in cooperative undertakings. An indicator for this is the fact that the technical support provided to applicants and functioning cooperative projects falls short of fulfilling the demand for it.

Regarding gender, specific attempts have not been made to either increase the participation or empowerment of women as most cooperatives target households. The available data show that female members of cooperatives account for just about 14%. Nearly all are female heads of households. Otherwise, married women are members of cooperatives through their spouses. In many cooperatives the female group is represented by two to three members who serve on the boards due to policy prerequisites.

Although figures are not available, it is believed that there is a good number of cooperatives organized by women. Handicraft cooperatives and SACCOs seem to be the preferred form of women's cooperatives. It is generally accepted that these cooperatives benefit from better and more effective management as well as accountability and responsibility than male-dominated cooperatives. Most cooperatives, however, do not incorporate activities that can economically and socially engage and empower women. In addition, cooperatives effect payments to the male heads of households who have the upper hand at home in financial and other family decisions. This is very likely to maintain and even reinforce the customary social division of labour which in turn may contribute to an inefficient and lopsided wealth creation impulse in society. Table 4.1 below serves to illustrate the dismal participation of women in the cooperatives of various regions of the country.

Table 4.1: Cooperative members by region and gender

Regions	Male	Female	Total
Addis Ababa	185 713	122 163	307 876
Afar	768	154	922
Amhara	1 290 476	154 656	1 445 132
Benshangul	6 215	589	6 804
Dire Dawa	6 900	2 748	9 648
Harari	1 601	779	2 380
Gambela	195	2 067	2 262
Oromiya	1 307 716	145 302	1 453 018
SNNPR	827 387	108 332	935 719
Somalie	6 528	2 267	8 795
Tigray	255 534	85 633	341 167
Total	**3 889 033**	**624 690**	**4 513 723**

Source: Proceedings of the national consultation meeting on the Annual Report on Cooperatives for the year 2004/05, July 2005.

The formation of cooperative unions is a new phenomenon in Ethiopia with the first agricultural union, Adama Lume Farmers Cooperative Union, established as recently as 1997. Currently there are 104 unions that bring together about 13% of the primary cooperatives in the country. The existing data show that about 91% of the cooperative unions are in agriculture. The year 2005 recorded about a 100% increase in the number of unions in one year. This was due to the promotional efforts of the government to increase the number of unions. This trend is expected to continue in the coming few years as the government is committed to promoting the sector by establishing 600 cooperative unions and 24,000 primary cooperatives.

The catalyst role of the Federal Cooperative Agency

The government of Ethiopia has recognized the economic and social importance of cooperatives for increasing employment as well as reducing poverty. Although the repercussions and approaches of the policies on cooperatives vary, the governments of the previous and current regimes have attempted to encourage and improve the sector's performance as well as the coverage of cooperatives in the country.

The latest Proclamation on cooperative societies (1998) defines a cooperative as "a society established by individuals on a voluntary basis to collectively solve their economic and social problems and to democratically manage [the] same". The Proclamation provides cooperatives with the right to engage in productive or service provision activities that can be determined by the bye-laws of the cooperative. This Proclamation is issued in compliance with ILO Recommendation 193 and the ICA minutes of 1995.

The Federal Cooperative Agency (FCA) was initially set up as a temporary office under the Prime Minister's Office (PMO). The government established FCA with a mandate of overseeing the appropriate implementation of the legislation on cooperatives, designing policies and legal procedures consistent with the international conventions on cooperatives and ensuring the coherence of the cooperative policy with other policies relevant to the sector. The policies and laws that directly affect the functions of cooperatives are those on land, investment, labour and employment, customs and taxation, financial regulations and directives. Recognizing the need for tailoring the provisions on relevant laws and policies, the FCA had produced specific procedures on labour and employment, credit management, store and warehouse management, auditing and accountancy, marketing and on the structure of cooperatives.

Ethiopia being a federal state, the structure of FCA reflects the different administrative levels in the country (federal, regional, zonal and wereda). The cooperative promotion offices within regions (i.e. regional, zonal and wereda levels) provide training of trainers (TOT), training to leaders of cooperatives, technical support (facilitation and seconding managers of cooperatives and cooperative unions until they are able to cover costs) and auditing services. At the federal level, the FCA is providing technical advice to the regional offices and unions. Although it has not materialized, it is also responsible for registering and providing technical support for unions that have member cooperatives from two or more regional states.

FCA is also mandated to register cooperatives with a view to providing them with legal personality to act and/or enact as per the legal provisions stipulated in the Proclamation and legal codes. Cooperatives acquire their legal certificate from the regional offices and the process takes about 15 days. They are required to pay Br. 60 for registration and Br. 30 if they lose their certificate of registration. Cooperatives are required to submit the minutes of the founding meeting, the bye-laws of the society, names, addresses and signatures of the members, the members of the management committee and members of the societies for registration and acquisition of the legal certificate. In addition, they are expected to file a description of whether the registered members of the cooperative have met the requirements of membership in accordance with the Proclamation and their respective bye-laws, business plans and financial statements that indicate the amount of capital owned.

The enforcement of the Proclamation that details the specifics of the bye-laws seems to be very strictly applied in some regions. According to the information of local NGOs working with cooperatives, the bye-law as allowed by the proclamation is not flexible enough to accommodate the interests of cooperatives. For instance, changing the number of terms for serving on the board from two to three and engaging in activities other than their specialization unless undertaken in a minor way are not allowed. If a cooperative plans to include another major component, it needs to re-register. According to the NGO experts, some cereal and seed banking cooperatives feel their activities are limited by the procedures.

FCA is expected to have institutional links with various government institutions. The three-year strategic plan of FCA, for instance, indicates that the Council of People's Representatives, the Ministry of Agriculture, the Ministry of Capacity Building and the Ministry of Economic Development and Finance are the most important institutions that can have direct and indirect influence on cooperatives at all levels. In addition, regional offices are expected to work with other line offices. In Oromiya Region, for instance, the Women Affairs Office, as well as the Youth, Sports and Culture Bureau, the Disaster Prevention and Preparedness Commission and the Enterprise Development Agency are expected to provide normative support to cooperatives and unions. At Wereda levels, there are more government agencies such as the Agriculture Desk and the Ethiopian Agricultural Research Organization that have direct links with the cooperative sector. At lower levels, the development agents are also playing key roles in disseminating information, providing technical support and mobilizing the community.

Ethiopia has not yet adopted a policy on cooperative development and the final draft (that is expected to be ratified soon) is being used as a de facto policy. This policy provides suitable conditions for strengthening the cooperative sector by detailing the policy objectives related to poverty reduction, the promotion of cooperatives in local and international markets, cooperation with government, non-government and international institutions and the promotion of the participation of women and disadvantaged groups. It also outlines the strategies for promotion, structures and financial regulations of cooperatives; curriculum development, training and research, audit and inspection and participation of cooperatives in the social and economic sectors. In addition, it provides a framework for the role of the government, international institutions and NGOs. The government formulated a five-year cooperative development programme in 2000.

On the road to viability and sustainability

As indicated earlier, most of the cooperatives initiated during the 1970s and 1980s were established through government directives that violated the core principles of cooperatives. Cooperatives as well as members were required to operate respecting the principle of socialist collectivization where both production and sales of produce were conducted collectively. Moreover, membership of a cooperative was compulsory. Although the leadership was supposed to be established through elections, nearly all leaders were political activists. Moreover, cooperatives were nearly the only suppliers of basic consumer supplies and inputs. Some cooperatives had reached an advanced stage of rural modernization in terms of service provision to members during this regime.

The Yetnora grain producers' cooperative in Amhara Region can be cited as one example of the cooperatives that were outstanding in this regard. According to the former chairperson[3], the cooperative had a total capital of Br. 17.4 million with a total annual turnover of Br. 1.6 million before its liquidation in 1991. It possessed a dump truck and a small truck, three tractors, two pickups and one land cruiser. In addition, it was able to construct two schools (elementary and high school), a clinic and hotel with 42 bedrooms. It was also generating income from a slaughter house with 50 employees as well as from an oil processing plant. In an effort to provide enhanced services to its members, it set up a woodwork atelier, a dairy farm, a bee-keeping farm, a kindergarten, a bakery, a telephone centre, a post office, a petrol/gas station and four flour mills. In the sphere of social protection, it established a home for the elderly. As a model cooperative, it had received support from the government, donors and other institutions. The cooperative started facing problems of competitiveness after the reform

---

[3] Interview held by Ato Worku G/Silassie upon the request of the author.

towards a mixed economy in 1989 and totally disintegrated after the fall of the Marxist Dergue regime in 1991. The infrastructure of the cooperative was abandoned and taken over by the government. The high political influence, absence of voluntary membership, participation, common bond and trust made the cooperative vulnerable to the negative effects of the change in the political and economic system.

Some cooperatives established during this regime, however, were able to continue to operate sub-optimally in the 1990s while they underwent restructuring. The Dibandiba primary cooperative society is an example. The cooperative was established in 1969 with the objective of supplying consumer items and fertilizer under the auspices of the Ministry of Agriculture of the time. It covered 12 peasant associations and all their members; 1,568 farmers were automatically affiliated to the cooperative. After its restructuring, this cooperative extended its operations to grain marketing, grain flour mill service and the supply of agricultural inputs. It eventually became one of the four founding members of the Adama Lume Farmers' Cooperative Union.

Since 2000, Dibandiba has been struggling to maintain its activities. Its active members in grain marketing decreased to about 22% of the initial membership mainly due to the competitive prices farmers are offered by private traders. The capacity of the cooperative to withstand the challenges of private traders is limited. The cooperative collects grain only from farmers who can bring it to its office. But farmers find lower transaction costs by selling grain to private businessmen who collect at farm gates. As a result, the turnover from grain marketing declined from Br. 400,000 in 2000 to Br. 303,970 in 2005. On the other hand, this primary cooperative is doing well in the supply of agricultural inputs as it is the sole supplier in the locality. Its supply of fertilizer and seed, for instance, increased from 4,439 and 109 quintals in 2000 to 5,087 and 153 quintals in 2005 respectively. The cooperative owns a store for grain and agricultural inputs and a grain mill.

The Dibandiba primary cooperative has six staff employed on short-term renewable contract terms. The manager of the cooperative is seconded by government and works closely with the leadership of the cooperative. All leaders of the cooperative serve the Kebele Administration (local political administrative structure). Although the reform brought relatively more democratic leadership in cooperatives, its neutrality from politics has not reached the desired level. It is obvious that in the case of this cooperative the leadership has symmetrical access to decision making in both the Kebele and the cooperative, so ensuring the neutrality of the cooperative from political influences turns out to be complex.

As indicated earlier, those cooperatives which survived the transition period were able to reorient their approach and form unions. The Adam Lume Grain Farmers' Cooperative Union was established in 1997 by four primary cooperatives. This cooperative union covers three weredas in Oromiya Region and currently has 21 members out of the 30 primary cooperatives in the area. Primary cooperatives are required to pay Br. 5,000 for registration for membership. The union is administered by a management board composed of 164 representatives from member cooperatives.

The union's services include the supply of agricultural inputs, marketing of produce, the rental of tractors, transport of produce, a flour mill and storage and credit services. In addition, it acquired three stores (with a capacity of 20,000 quintals) and an office with basic facilities. Its total turnover substantially increased from Br. 5,799,173 in 2000 to Br. 32,557,212 in 2005. Its 17 full-time, 21 temporary staff and 150 casual labourers serve about 16,955 farmers.

A recent development in the cooperative sector in Ethiopia is the involvement of the cooperative unions in international trade. In 2005, three grain farmers' cooperative unions in Amhara and Oromiya Regions imported 100,000 metric tons of fertilizer at Br. 406 million, thanks to a loan guarantee from their respective regional governments. The cooperatives successfully supplied the input and completed the repayment of their loans. This exercise demonstrates the vitality and competence of cooperatives in the open market particularly in importing fertilizer.

Similar vitality is found in the coffee producing farmers' cooperative unions that are established as a result of the fall in world coffee prices and its adverse effects on the livelihood of the coffee farmers. There are five coffee cooperative unions established in the major coffee producing regions – Oromiya and SNNP Regions. One of these, the Oromiya Coffee Cooperative Union, was established in 1999 with a membership of 34 primary cooperatives (with 11,334 farmer members). It started operating with a share capital of Br. 825,000. Currently, it has 101 primary cooperative members and its share capital has substantially increased to Br. 11,812,582. Similarly, its total turnover increased from Br. 2,271,157 in 2001 to Br. 67,207,846 in 2005. This union is rigorously monitoring the quality and origin of the coffee to sustain its competitive position in the market. The cooperative unions in coffee marketing get support from the government and NGOs to increase their export capacity. In 2004, for example, they received loans amounting to Br. 17 million through a loan guarantee provided by the American NGO, VOCA.

Unlike the experiences during the former regime, cooperatives are now in an open and competitive market environment. Although the communities that experienced failure during the previous regime still doubt the viability of cooperatives, the successes of the existing cooperative societies and unions are triggering the interest of many groups in various parts of the country. The continuation of the existing democratic practice is believed to contribute substantially to the confidence of the general population as well as to the growth of the sector. All stakeholders in the cooperative sector recognize well enough that cooperatives have to be initiated and owned by their members. Since the sector was not given adequate emphasis in previous decades, it requires strong support in terms of human and financial resources until such time as federations and unions have a strong institutional basis to take over some of these responsibilities.

First moves towards the integration of the cooperative movement

Vertical and horizontal integration are important tools that enable cooperatives to realize their potential by pooling resources as well as working collectively to attain their common vision and goals. Although cooperative unions have only been set up in Ethiopia for a decade or so, their effort to create a network was successfully realized through the establishment of the first cooperative bank a few years ago.

The formation of Oromiya Cooperative Bank started in 2002 as a project and was later registered as commercial bank. The bank is authorized to have capital of Br. 300 million out of which 40% is paid up capital. It started operation in 2005 and has since opened seven branches in different parts of Oromiya Region. With its 140 full-time employees, the bank provides deposits, medium and short term loans, money transfers and foreign banking services. From 1 July to 31 December 2005, the bank was able to extend loans amounting Br. 152 million to cooperative societies and unions. Its current loan portfolio indicates that 96.6% of loans are extended to cooperatives. The emergence of this cooperative bank has given hope for the other regions such as Amhara, SNNP and Tigray to set up their own banks.

Cooperatives in coffee production have informal networks for their promotional activities. The Oromiya and Sidama Coffee Farmers Cooperative Unions work closely together to promote their products and mutual values in the European and US markets. In addition, the grain farmers' unions, such as Adama Lume and Merekeb in Oromiya and Amhara Region respectively, exchange supplies with the objective of promoting their mutual business objectives.

Although there is a consensus on their relevance, cooperative federations have not yet materialized. The process of setting up a Federation of Grain Farmers Cooperatives started in the last two years and its realization is expected to be finalized in 2006. The Coffee Farmers Unions seem ready to set up their federation in the near future. The government, in this connection, has a long-term plan of establishing 17 federations in line with production specializations; ten in agriculture (federations of coffee, grain, livestock and other producers' cooperatives), four in the urban sector (federations of housing, industrial, tourism and other service cooperatives) and three in finance (federations of insurance, SACCO and banking services cooperatives).

Limited donor involvement

The dynamic of the cooperative movement in Ethiopia is very much a self-propelled process. Unlike many other sectors in Ethiopia, the cooperative sector benefits little from international aid. Among the international and multilateral donors, the International Labour Organization (ILO), the International Fund for Agricultural Development (IFAD) and the United Nations Development Programme (UNDP) have been supporting the sector for a long time. The ILO has been supporting the cooperative sector through capacity building and technical support since 1994. It was actively involved in designing the Proclamation on cooperatives. Its resources were also used for experience-sharing tours organized for officials and experts as well as cooperative leaders. ILO has also been implementing HIV/AIDS projects in three coffee-growing zones of Oromiya Region where there is high labour mobility. Considering cooperatives as work places, the ILO has provided training and technical support for leaders of cooperative unions to address HIV/AIDS issues in collaboration with the member primary cooperatives. This project has been able to reach about 189 primary cooperatives with over 140,000 members.

IFAD has been supporting cooperatives mainly engaged in irrigation farming and saving and credit activities. It channels the resources through the government and the Rural Financial Intermediation Programme-RUFIP that is implementing a seven-year programme in favour of rural institutions including cooperatives. This programme mainly focuses on capacity building and training of promoters.

The UNDP has also been helping the cooperative sector through the Ministry of Agriculture and the Regional Cooperative Bureaus. The UNDP resources are mainly used to enhance the capacity of the cooperatives for agricultural output marketing. It also financed training of promoters and leaders of cooperatives.

The United States Agency for International Development (USAID) and the support of the Irish Government are channeled through VOCA-Ethiopia and SHDI, respectively that exclusively work with cooperatives. Action Aid, SNV-Netherlands, Farm Africa, World Vision, Concern Ethiopia, Plan Ethiopia and SOS Sahel work with cooperatives in conjunction with their other development programmes.

VOCA has been working with cooperatives since 1997 through the government structures and was actively involved in the restructuring of cooperatives to become member-owned and -controlled, democratic and transparent. It provides technical support to improve the economic capacity of cooperatives and provides ten days' to six months' training to cooperative leaders and promoters. In Ethiopia, VOCA is the first and only NGO that works exclusively with cooperatives.

SHDI started working with group loans in 1999 and shifted to promotion of savings and credit cooperatives in 2000. It has been supporting seven unions and over 140 primary cooperatives in the Oromiya and SNNP Regions.

There are also a number of local NGOs working with cooperatives, like HUNDEE and Facilitators for Change. Many local NGOs have a special focus such as seed and grain banks, SACCOs or handicrafts. Most NGOs work directly with communities and continue to provide technical support until cooperatives start operating effectively and autonomously.

Multiple institutional links give strength to the cooperative sector

At national level, cooperatives have links with various government institutions such as the Ministry of Agriculture, the Ministry of Industry, the Women Affairs Office and the Labour and Social Affairs Office. These working relations exist at lower levels as well. It is evident that the policies and developmental work of some Ministries have a profound effect on the cooperatives concerned. The Ministry of Agriculture, for example, implements the Agricultural Marketing Improvement Programme (AMIP) including components that specifically target cooperatives such as infrastructure development, store/warehouse construction, capacity building and finance for credit.

The government has instituted cooperative studies in four universities namely in Alemaya, Awassa, Jimma and Tigray Universities that have opened cooperative departments since 2002. These universities have plans to graduate about 800 students with first degrees and diplomas in 2006. In addition, they registered students for post-graduate education in 2005. These efforts are expected to substantially improve the qualified human resources available for the cooperative sector. The curriculum of these higher learning institutions was designed in close collaboration with FCA, VOCA and SHDI. The departments for cooperative studies are with the Faculties of Agriculture in Tigray, Ambo and Awassa and the Faculty of Business and Economics in Alemaya. As there has not been a uniform approach to define the scope of the discipline, there is a concern that association of cooperative studies with either of the disciplines may unintentionally affect or misdirect the focus necessary for promoting the profession.

Cooperatives were able to participate in the exhibition organized by the Chamber of Commerce in Addis Ababa in 2005. Some cooperatives are indeed taking initiatives to establish contact with the various economic and commercial operators. Some grain farmers' cooperative unions in Amhara and Oromiya Region, for instance, have contacts with industries that can and do purchase their products.

Some micro-finance institutions enter into agreements with cooperatives to provide financial services. The Dedebit, Amahara and OMO micro-finance institutions, for instance, are providing financial services in places where access to credit is not available. Cooperatives consider the service as essential as most farmers do not have alternative sources of finance. They believe this arrangement is temporary. The future plan is that all cooperatives need to set up their own SACCOs in order to provide better financial services to their members.

The cooperative sector as a major employer

The cooperative sector is believed to be effective in generating employment and it is currently one of the major employers in the country. According to FCA figures, cooperatives employed 28,000 people all over the country in 2005. It was also indicated that the annual wage expenditure incurred by the cooperatives in the same period was Br. 26 million excluding the employees of the Oromiya Cooperative Bank. There seems to be underreporting of employment as each primary cooperative is required to employ a minimum of three staff namely an accountant, a store keeper and a guard at the very initial stage of establishment. By this calculation, the employment figure could easily reach 43,270 people. In addition, the cooperative unions are expected to employ about 1,870 staff based on an average of 18 staff[4] per cooperative union. If these estimates are considered, the cooperative sector in 2005 employed about 47,576 people including the 2,295 and 139 employees of FCA and Regional Bureaus, and the Cooperative Bank respectively.

Apart from wage employment, cooperatives are also major supporters of self-employment in the urban as well as rural areas. The SACCOs, which often extend small loans to micro-entrepreneurs and cooperatives in handicrafts and the service sector, are expected to generate self-employment for about 400,000 people all over the country. In addition, the members of cooperatives in the agriculture sector are expected to fully or partially generate their income through cooperative activities. Based on the experience of the Dibandiba primary cooperative where about 22% of the members actively participate in cooperative activity and generate income, about 900,000 people in the agriculture sector are estimated to generate part of their income through their cooperatives.

Another group that benefits from the employment opportunities of the cooperative sector is the people providing casual labour. Each grain marketing cooperative union is estimated to employ an average of 80 casual labourers every year while the coffee farmers' cooperative union employs an average of 3,000 casual labourers per year (for loading and unloading). Based on this estimate, over 21,000 people are recruited for casual labour service every year by the cooperatives. This estimate does not include those who are involved in labour intensive agricultural activities such as picking coffee. Traditionally people living in chronically food insecure or deprived areas use temporary migration as their coping mechanism and are engaged in this kind of temporary labour.

---

[4] Calculation based on the employment data acquired from three cooperative unions (Adama Lume Grain Farmers', Oromiya Coffee Farmers' and Sidama Coffee Farmers' Cooperative Unions).

Based on the above and with the omission of migratory casual labour employment, it can be safely estimated that about 1.4 million people are fully or partially generating their income through cooperatives in Ethiopia. In addition to this, the formation of new cooperatives will create extra avenues for generating employment. According to the plan of the FCA, the number of cooperative unions and primary cooperatives is to increase to 600 and 24,000 respectively in the coming five years. Considering the existence of 300 cooperative unions, 24,000 primary cooperatives in the coming few years and 30% active members per cooperative, the cooperative sector has the potential to fully or partially engage about 2.4 million people excluding the migratory labour employment opportunity.

Cooperatives are currently offering competitive salaries to their staff. Managers and accountants contacted indicate that the salary they receive from cooperatives is competitive enough to keep them satisfied. The cooperatives and cooperative unions contacted, for instance, employ their staff on a renewable annual contract basis and offer employment privileges as per the labour law of the country. The Adama Lume Farmers' Cooperative, for instance, is reviewing its employment benefit package in order to provide its staff with better benefits. The review according to the leaders will focus on annual leave, compensation and the establishment of a provident fund. This indicates that cooperatives and cooperative unions have started to look into their employment policies. Such efforts are expected to attract job seekers as well as retain the staff employed in the cooperatives.

Working with the poor and the poorest

Cooperatives in rural and urban Ethiopia are largely organized to assist poor and disadvantaged groups. Most cooperatives initially start with the objective of providing a service to a group of people who have problems of access to economic resources. The multipurpose cooperatives, for instance, supply consumer items at prices lower than the market and have the objective of protecting members from paying high prices. This undoubtedly has the positive effect of lowering household consumption expenditure.

Agricultural cooperatives are also organized to protect members from being vulnerable to unfavourable price changes. With the fall in coffee prices in the late 1990s for example coffee farmers were selling their assets to fulfill their basic needs. The coffee farmers' cooperatives try to cushion the effects of price volatility and continuously try to penetrate alternative and better markets. The same holds for the grain producers' cooperatives that play an important role in providing farmers with better prices throughout the year. This effort reduces the seasonal price fluctuation and stabilizes the local grain markets in favour of the producers. Grain farmers have witnessed that grain prices have not fluctuated much in recent years and even if they did, they have the option to sell to cooperatives at better prices.

Cooperatives, therefore, help their members to acquire better prices for their products and assist them to at least maintain their income and economic status. As per their objective, they also work towards increasing the income of their members through providing services for improved production, technology, human resource capacity and marketing that would directly help members to acquire more return for their products. They increase the incomes of members by distributing 70% of the profits (as dividend payment) generated from the business or marketing activities. In the case of Dibandiba Primary Cooperative, for example, an average of Br. 60 was distributed to 345 members in 2005 in the form of dividends. It can thus be safely said that the contribution of cooperatives in reducing poverty levels is tremendous.

SACCOs, handicraft cooperatives and other organizations, including self-help groups, also enable their members to generate income from productive employment. Moreover, SACCOs require members to build on their savings. In this way they can acquire more loans for running their small businesses and have sufficient savings for future consumption.

Cooperatives generally do not explicitly target the poorest. However, they mix the poorest with the less-poor members. They care about the wellbeing and economic problems of all their members. Due to their cohesive nature, they address the issues of poverty at an individual level through various means such as providing opportunities for casual labour, waiving contributions and mobilizing resources from members to support the very poor.

Social protection: complementary to the traditional institutions

Experience of cooperation among people residing in close neighbourhoods has been a tradition of many cultures in Ethiopia. Various communities organize traditional institutions that commonly have the objective of pooling risks. They mobilize financial, material and labour resources and the most widespread forms of such institution are Equb, Idir, Debo and Jige. Equb is a traditional rotating saving scheme while Idir is a social insurance system (burial society). Debo and Jige mobilize labour for peak farming seasons and labour intensive activities. All of these have maintained their services for many decades and, unlike cooperatives, they have not been able to adopt certain business principles to promote their role in other gainful economic activities.

A few development institutions have been attempting to work with Idir and some have been successful in refurbishing them into cooperatives. Bringing such institutions into the domain of cooperatives, in Ethiopia, has not gained adequate attention. It is very obvious that the transformation of the existing traditional institutions into viable cooperatives has not been explored.

At the same time, cooperatives as new and modern institutions of cooperation and solidarity do increasingly develop social protection mechanisms not so much as alternatives, but as complements to these traditional institutions. For instance, all cooperatives are required to allocate 1-5% of their profit to a social fund. Though most cooperatives emphasize objectives other than social protection, encouraging efforts of promoting social protection are observed in some cooperative unions. The Yirga Chefe Coffee Farmers Cooperative Union can be cited as an example. This cooperative union provides financial support to 21 students who are undergoing higher education in the country. In addition, 250 orphans are provided with education materials and uniforms every year. These support packages are already part of the annual plan of the union. In addition, in 2005 it extended financial support amounting to Br. 15,000 for the development association of the locality.

Some cooperatives spend their social fund to promote access and availability of basic social services and infrastructures. The fund is then used to construct community infrastructure such as roads, schools, health clinics or watering points. The Dibandiba Primary Cooperative made a contribution of Br. 7,500 for the construction of a watering point and the purchase of chairs for a school. It has also a plan to contribute to the construction of a bridge at a location where its members have a problem during the rainy season.

Via the HIV/AIDS project implemented by the ILO, five cooperative unions in Oromyia Region have established HIV/AIDS clubs for raising awareness and enhancing the use of the HIV/AIDS prevention and control measures among members. This effort has specifically helped cooperatives to distribute condoms. It also created a forum for exchanging experiences with PLHAs and disseminating information on the disease (though the distribution of translated manuals on HIV/AIDS prevention and control). This is an area that could enhance the role of cooperatives in social protection in the future.

Here again we see that cooperatives complement the concern for the welfare of the community already exhibited through traditional insurance institutions. A survey of idirs in Addis Ababa (Pankhurst and Tesfaye, 2006) suggests that 244 idirs were involved in some form of HIV/AIDS related work in 2002. This is about six per cent of the total number of idirs in the region but represents about a quarter of those idirs that are involved in "new" development activities.

Voice in the air

At national level, the cooperative sector is represented by FCA as no other independent federation or apex body exists in the country. The recently drafted poverty reduction paper (PRSP) indicates that cooperatives play a significant role not only in creating an improved marketing system and providing market information, but also in other agricultural development works. However, cooperatives and unions only participated in the discussions on the PRSP or on the food security programmes on an ad hoc basis. Although FCA has been facilitating their participation in the various forums, the voice and representation of cooperatives at the national level have not been sufficient. The cooperatives do not (as yet) have a proactive strategy when it comes to lobbying at the national level and their lobbyists are ill prepared.

At regional level, however, the participation of cooperatives and their unions is better but still very irregular. Cooperative unions have been attempting to use the available opportunities to lobby and advocate for the sector through their experienced and persuasive leaders.

In the last few years, development partners and FCA have used the print and electronic media to educate the public on the importance of the cooperative sector. The FCA also uses print media (Addis Zemen, Fortune and Reporter newsletters) to inform on cooperative success stories. With the support of SHDI, Ethiopian Radio last year launched a weekly programme on cooperatives in Amharic. In this programme, interviews, human interest stories and other relevant information about cooperatives are disseminated.

One of the relevant opportunities for voice and representation of cooperatives is organized civil society. The cooperatives in Ethiopia have weak links with this dynamic and expanding community. According to our respondents so far there has not been much effort made to establish relationships with the civil society actors such as the employers' federation, the trade unions and the NGO networks. Still, these organized social movements have the potential to promote the issues of voice and representation, social protection, gender etc. that have great relevance for cooperatives.

The fact that cooperatives are very much left out of public policy making has much to do with the general political and social atmosphere. A recent study on the Ethiopian economy indicates that the participation of the rural population in the planning and implementation of agricultural policies, and the monitoring and evaluation of government policies and development programmes has been insignificant (EEA, 2005). The recent planning process of the Plan for Accelerated and Sustained Development to End Poverty (PASDEP) had missed the participation of cooperative unions. The tendency towards a top-down approach to development was due to the inherent characteristics of the previous regimes, particularly concerning rural policies and programmes. Although the absence of an apex body could be a reason, the participation of selected cooperative unions would have an impact on their voice and representation. But also a genuine commitment to valuing the contribution of farmers in development discourse and process needs to prevail among the government institutions and development agencies before the demand for more participation can become effective.

Conclusions

The Ethiopian government was able to provide an ample platform for cooperatives and the cooperative sector to engage in various sectors of the economy as well as to establish structures at different levels. According to the current policy environment and Proclamation, cooperatives can be formed at primary, union, federation and league levels. In the interests of promoting the sector, the government has established FCA to oversee its performance.

Since the last reform, the government has been providing benevolent support for the sector and cooperatives have been able to use the support effectively in renewing their structures and reorienting their activities consistent to the cooperative principles adopted by the ICA. FCA has also worked within the framework of Proclamation 147/98 and prepared procedural manuals to assist the promotion of cooperatives at lower levels and made tremendous efforts to promote cooperatives in all the regions.

Although the availability of data limited exhaustive analysis about cooperatives and the sector, it is apparent that the cooperative sector in Ethiopia reaches millions of people. The sector is expanding very rapidly in terms of new cooperatives, share of the market and membership. Its contribution to employment creating, income support and enhancement of welfare is significant.

The development of second and third tier structures (unions, federations, and apex) as well as collaborative arrangements between cooperatives is now needed to realize and promote the visibility of the sector, to strengthen its advocacy and lobbying capacity and to realize economies of scale.

Finally, the links between cooperatives and the cooperative movement and the networks of NGOs and civil societies that promote specific development issues such as gender, street children, urban development, human rights, etc, are minimal. Establishing a network at national and regional levels for such issues will enhance the voice and representation of the cooperatives and their contribution to promoting development concerns.

Sources

The author wishes to thank the following people for their valuable information during the interviews: Mr. Haile Gebre, Mr. Abraham Ijeta, Ms. Yisgedulish Bezabih, Mr. Getachew Alemu, Mr. Abey Meherka, Mr. Fisha Dibissa, Mr. Shewaminale Minase, Mr. Wesen Mulu and Ato Zebenay (all at FCA); Mr. Lelisa Chelchisa (ILO); Mr. Liko Tolessa (Oromiya Cooperative Bank); Mr. Hune (VOCA); Mr. Belew Demene and Ms. Fetia Mohamed (SHDI); Ato Zegeye Asfaw (UNDE); Ato Bekle Mossisa (consultant); Mr. Teferi Abera, Mr. Dellu Ayisanew and Mr. Dereje Ketema (Dibandiba Primary Cooperative); Mr. Assefa Lemma, Mr. Demere Demissie and Mr. Fekadu Alemu (Lume Adama Farmers' Union); and Mr. Dessalegn Jena (Oromiya Coffee Farmers' Cooperative Union).

Acronyms

AMIP	Agricultural Marketing Improvement Programme
DPPC	Disaster Preparedness and Prevention Commission
EARO	Ethiopian Agricultural Research Organization
EC	Ethiopian Calendar
FCA	Federal Cooperative Commission
NGO	Non-Governmental Organization
PMO	Prime Minister's Office
SHDI	Self Help Development International
SNNP	Southern Nation Nationalities Peoples

Bibliography

- Birchall J. (2003), *Rediscovering the cooperative advantage: Poverty reduction through self-help*, ILO, Geneva.

- Birchall J. (2004), *Cooperatives and the Millennium Development Goals*, ILO, Geneva.

- EEA (2005), *Report on the Ethiopian Economy*, vol. 4, 2004/05, Addis Ababa.

- FCA (2000), *Cooperative Development Program*, Unpublished document (Amharic), Addis Ababa.

- FCA (2003a), *Strategic Planning of the Cooperative Sector* (2004-2006), Unpublished document (Amharic), Ministry of Rural Development, Addis Ababa.

- FCA (2003b), *Three Years Strategic Plan* (2004-2006), Unpublished document (Amharic), Ministry of Rural Development, Addis Ababa.

- FCA (2004), *Draft Policy on Cooperatives*, (Amharic), Addis Ababa.

- FCA (2005), 'Cooperative' in *Annual Magazine*, vol. 2, n°1, (Amharic), published by Public Relations Section, Ministry of Rural Development, Addis Ababa.

- FDRE (2004), *Rural Development Sector Millennium Development Goals Needs Assessment*, Addis Ababa.

- ILO (s.d), *Transition to Cooperative Entrepreneurship: Case studies from Armenia*, Geneva.

- LAFCU (2004), Lume-Adama Farmers' Cooperative Union leaflet, Modjo, Ethiopia.

- Lelisa (2000), 'Cooperative Entrepreneurship in Transition Economies: the case of Amecha Multi purpose agricultural cooperative', unpublished, submitted to ILO, Addis Ababa.

- Pankhurst A. & Tesfaye T. (ed.) (2006), *Social Responses to HIV/AIDS in Addis Ababa, Ethiopia with reference to Commercial Sex Workers, People Living With HIV-AIDS and Community-Based Funeral Associations in Addis Ababa*, Department of Sociology and Anthropology, Addis Ababa University, Addis Ababa.

Chapter Five – Uganda: Starting All Over Again

by Herment A. Mrema[1]

Introduction and approach

In Uganda 38% of the population lives below the poverty line, and the average income per capita is now approaching the level achieved in 1970. Poverty remains a predominantly rural phenomenon. Between 80 and 85% of the Ugandan population live in rural areas and largely depend on the agriculture sector for their livelihood. Agriculture is the most important sector of Uganda's economy, employing about 80% of the workforce and it is estimated that land holding per household is less than one hectare. Coffee is one of the major export crops, accounting for over half of the export revenues. Over the last decade, the structure of the economy has been changing. The share of agriculture fell from 51% of GDP in 1992 to 33% in 2003, as a result of drought and declining prices. The service sector grew from 35% of GDP in 1993 to 45% in 2003. The industrial sector expanded rapidly from 13% in 1993 to 22% of GDP in 2003.

In Uganda, cooperatives were set up as early as 1913 (Shafiq Arain et al., 1967). These were mainly agricultural cooperatives marketing coffee and cotton. Prior to liberalization policies the Government of Uganda played a significant role in the regulation and control, but also in the management, of the cooperative movement to the extent that cooperatives perceived themselves to be part of government rather than the private sector. Liberalization policies introduced in the early 1990s allowed for fierce competition, particularly in crop marketing. Most of the cooperatives could not withstand this new turn of events. As a result the majority of the crop marketing cooperatives collapsed and the remaining few are struggling.

This study aims to obtain qualitative information on the strengths and weaknesses of the cooperative movement in the country with a view to assessing the real and potential impact of cooperatives on employment

---

[1] Herment A. Mrema combines his professional habitat in the National Union of Coffee Agribusinesses and Farm Enterprises (NUCAFE) with consulting work in farmer empowerment programmes in Uganda and Tanzania.

generation and their contribution to the reduction of poverty as well as to social protection in Uganda.

For this research, which is largely qualitative, data were collected by way of semi-structured interviews with key informants in the cooperative sector. Respondents were selected based on their perceived roles and responsibilities in the cooperative sector. Respondents included the Commissioner of Cooperatives who is also the Registrar in the Ministry of Trade, Industry and Tourism; the Uganda Cooperative Alliance; the Uganda Coffee Development Authority; the Uganda Savings and Credit Union; the Cooperative College; and the Uganda Transporters Cooperative Union.

In addition, at society level two cooperative societies were visited for in-depth interviews with their leaders and members. These were Uganda Shoe Shine Repair Savings and Credit Cooperative and Jinja Teachers Cooperative Savings and Credit Society Limited. There were also discussions with the Busia Savings and Credit Society and the Kibinge Coffee Farmers Association in Masaka District. Additional data were obtained through key informant interviews and relevant publications.

From governmental involvement to liberalization: a brief history

Cooperatives in Uganda have had a long history, marked by a gradual expanding of activities (from sheer agricultural marketing to savings and credit, livestock, fishing, handicraft industries etc.) as well as a persistent avoiding of registration out of fear for government control (Kabuga and Kitandwe, 1995; Mugisha et al, 2005). The post independence era saw the departure of cooperative leaders for politics creating a leadership vacuum. By employing people who had ulterior motives other than commitment to serving cooperatives, floodgates for mismanagement, nepotism and corruption in cooperatives were opened. This led to discontent over operations of cooperatives in a number of areas and a successive series of laws which paradoxically brought the control of societies to the Registrar and in a later phase exclusively to the Minister. As a result, members lost their last bit of control over their cooperatives to managers, politicians and government officers. When the Uganda National Liberation Army (UNLA) took over power in 1979, donors wanted to assist in rebuilding the country. The Swedish Cooperative Centre (SCC) assisted the Uganda Cooperative Alliance (UCA) and just as the situation began looking rosy, political turmoil in the early

1980s affected many institutions, cooperatives being no exception (Kabuga and Kitandwe, 1995; Mugisha et al, 2005). In 1986, when the present National Resistance Movement (NRM) government took over administration of this country, there was hope of restoring cooperatives. By 1987 competent staff were hired, more donors notably USAID and SIDA took an interest in cooperatives and provided more funding. In 1988, a Cooperative Agriculture and Agribusiness Support (CAAS) project was launched. A provision was made to recognize UCA as the apex body for all registered cooperatives in the country. This, however, has not been possible due to the formation of yet another politically motivated body to take over the role of the apex body, the Agricultural Council of Uganda.

The liberalization of the economy in the early nineties made the previous legal framework irrelevant for the development of the cooperative movement. The liberalization policies required government to withdraw its active intervention in the regulation of the economy including the cooperative movement. It implied that cooperative members were given autonomy to commercially operate their cooperatives with minimal intervention from the government (enacted in the Cooperative Societies Statute, 1991, and the Cooperative Societies Regulations, 1992). At the same time, the monopoly of cooperatives in the agricultural sector was removed. Cooperatives were now expected to compete with other private enterprises on the private market.

The new law effectively transferred the management duties in cooperatives from the Commissioner for Cooperatives to the members through their duly elected committees. The committees were now empowered to assume most of the functions earlier performed by the Commissioner of Cooperatives such as making decisions to borrow funds and invest in a formally agreed venture, without consulting the Commissioner of Cooperatives. They were free to borrow against the whole or part of their properties if their bye-laws allowed them to do so, provided the annual general meeting approved.

Even though liberalization was a welcome move in the development of an autonomous, self-managed and sustainable cooperative movement, cooperatives were not prepared for the new era. The changes did not take into account how the vacuum left by the departure of the Commissioner would be filled. Members were not educated to appreciate the impact of the departure of the Commissioner as far as regulatory and management aspects were concerned, what would be the new roles and obligations of the committees, and how the members could effectively own their cooperatives without losing ownership to a few individuals on the management committee. As a result, the management seriously abused their powers resulting in massive corruption, mismanagement, theft, failure to hold elections, failure to surrender members' deposits, failure to hold elections on time, favouritism and dismissal of staff, refusal of cooperative officials to vacate office after being duly voted out and all sorts of conflicts. This resulted in the collapse of a large number of cooperatives and unions (Kayongo, 2005).

The cooperatives visited for this study were obviously among those which survived the turmoil, but their relation with the government remains tense. The Registrar of Cooperatives normally provides a guarantee for loans given to savings and credit societies for onward lending to the societies' members and many societies have been beneficiaries of this arrangement. The cooperative societies acknowledged that the loan guarantee service is the major service that societies enjoy from the Department of Cooperatives. But they felt that they were not getting other necessary services from the Department of Cooperatives such as membership development, training, regular inspections and management advisory services.

In response to this, the Registrar of Cooperatives underlined that the Government's attitude towards cooperatives is positive but the Government has been constrained with funds and competing priorities. The adoption of the farmer group-association/cooperative model by the Minister of Finance, Planning and Economic Development as a preferred vehicle for wealth creation to eradicate poverty as mentioned in the Rural Development Strategy is put forward as a clear indication of Government support for the cooperative movement. However, the capacity of the Department of Cooperative Development to take up this task is limited. Numbering 13 staff in 1998, today it consists of only the Commissioner, the Assistant Commissioner and a senior officer.

The cooperative sector today: facts and figures

In terms of activities, the cooperative movement could be classified in two broad categories: agricultural and non-agricultural. An agricultural cooperative is mainly involved in marketing of produce and to some extent in value addition which entails processing of produce before it is marketed. These cooperatives are organized according to the specific crops that they handle, the key traditional ones being coffee, cotton, dairy, tea, tobacco, and sugar cane. Others are multipurpose such as Area Market Cooperatives which are involved in more than one crop and provision of services such as input supply, technical advice, processing and marketing of more than one product.

The non-agricultural cooperatives are varied. In the financial sector, savings and credit are predominant activities of cooperatives, while housing cooperatives provide members with affordable shelter, transport cooperatives provide transportation as a service to the public including cooperative members, and in the hospitality sector some cooperatives operate hotels and lodges. Although savings and credit are provided as a separate product or service by credit unions, other cooperatives also such as shoe shine and repair cooperatives, transport and housing cooperatives often provide them.

The structure of the cooperative sector in Uganda is comparatively flat. Neither the Uganda Cooperative Alliance nor secondary and tertiary cooperative organizations are superior or above their owners. Primary societies can directly affiliate to the Uganda Cooperative Alliance. They can also re-create other structures that serve their needs and interests effectively and efficiently. The cooperative sector is divided into six categories which are:

1) Umbrella Organizations which are responsible for education, training, publicity, information, coordination, representation, advocacy and resource-mobilization for cooperatives;

2) Cooperative Finance Services, which are basically SACCOs offering rural finance services and potential progenitors of future regional and national cooperative banks;

3) Cooperative Marketing Services, which like other private sector players have to be competitive in the domestic and external markets;

4) Area Cooperative Enterprises, which are associations of primary cooperative societies of all types in an area which can be a sub-county;

5) Cooperative Service Centres; these are District Unions which are best suited to providing such services as inputs, implements, processing, consultancy, marketing and extension services;

6) Cooperative Carriage and Distribution Services which provide the cooperative movement with competitive transport services.

The most recent statistics on the sector are those for the year 2000.

Table 5.1: Number of registered societies 1998–2000

YEAR	1998	1999	2000
Primary Societies	6 244	6 299	6 353
Unions	37	37	37
Total	6 281	6 336	6 390

Source: Department of Cooperative Development – Annual Report (2000).

As shown in Table 5.1, the number of unions has remained constant from 1998 to 2000 while the number of primary societies increased by 109 in the same period. According to the Registrar of Cooperatives by 2005 there were a total of three active National Unions and five active Regional/District Unions compared to 37 existing in the year 2000. The total number of registered societies is 7,476 out of which 1,600 are SACCOS. The total number of active or "non-dormant" societies is however estimated not to be higher than 3,500.

In the annexe, we include two tables listing the number of cooperatives and members for some sub-sectors. Both tables indicate a growth pattern which seems to be more pronounced in terms of members than in terms of societies. This might be an indication that existing cooperatives are attracting new members. This is mostly the case in the non-agriculture sectors, which itself coincides with the growth of the non-agricultural sectors in the economy.

The total number of cooperative members is about 7.7 million, 1.8 million of whom are from the savings and credit sector[2]. Contribution to GDP has been reported to be about 60% (MFPED, 2004).

Table 5.2 below indicates a 14% (6.1 billion Uganda shillings) increase in the total assets of the cooperative movement for the period 1998 to 2000.

---

[2] figures for the year 2000, including the "dormant" societies.

Table 5.2: Financial position of the cooperative movement in Uganda, 1998-2000 (in Uganda Shillings)

	1998	1999	2000
Number of Societies	6 281	6 336	6 390
Number of Members	6 998 795	7 171 488	7 705 968
Share Capital	2 897 501 500	2 966 049 770	3 073 388 630
Reserves	16 534 920 600	16 489 119 712	16 366 213 463
Deposits	1 200 453 617	1 361 640 743	1 561 640 743
Other Liabilities	10 891 009 872	25 236 226 375	24 034 501 308
Total Liabilities	42 368 793 672	46 053 036 600	48 476 880 625
Fixed Assets	32 794 236 200	39 936 201 300	27 857 900 729
Loan to Members	8 231 286 300	11 837 419 800	14 465 495 600
Total Assets	**42 368 753 672**	**46 053 036 600**	**48 476 850 625**

Source: Department of Cooperative Development – Annual Report (2000).
Exchange rate: Ug Shs 1800: US $ 1.00 (Feb 2006)

Vibrancy of cooperatives in the different trades

In most cases, people joined cooperatives because they were advised by government, were provided with certain incentives or they did not have the choice since it was a mandatory requirement by government (Kabuga, 1994) and not on the basis of their common bonds and mutual trust. This practice serves to compromise the bottom-up character of cooperatives, with adverse implications for the growth and sustainability of some of the cooperative institutions. As explained above, lack of ownership by members and value addition contributed to slow growth of cooperatives. Furthermore the liberalization, particularly in crop marketing, adversely affected the growth and strength of the cooperative movement. However despite the weakness of the marketing cooperatives according to available data, overall the cooperative unions recorded turnover (income) growth from 5.0 billion in 1998 to 6 billion in 2000 (Dep. of Coop. Development, Annual Report 2000). Between 1998 and 2000, agricultural marketing cooperatives expanded their scope by incorporating other non-traditional crops such as sim sim and sunflower seeds as well as financial services. There was still a presence of cooperative unions in coffee, cotton, tobacco, non-traditional cash crops, micro-finance and savings and credit, and service cooperatives. We take a brief look at these different sectors.

Coffee:

From the year 2000 only Bugisu Cooperative Union was engaged in coffee export. The Union was financed by HSBC Equator Bank of USA at competitive rates which made it feasible to participate in export trade. In 1996 Bugisu finally closed business by renting out its coffee mills, stores, hotels and sold/leased out some of its strategic buildings in Mbale to a debtor who pre-financed BCU in 2000-2005 but the cooperative made huge losses and could not pay the debt.

Other cooperative unions such as Kigezi Coffee in Rukungiri, Banyankole Kweterana Cooperative Union in the West, East Mengo in Mukono, Busoga Growers in Jinja/Iganda/Kamuli, Bunyoro Growers in Masindi, West Mengo Growers in Mpigi and Wamala Growers in Mubende District handled some coffee which they sold locally to exporters located in Uganda. Other cooperatives have ceased to operate since they could not be competitive and reliable suppliers and farmers opted to sell to private buyers who were paying prompt cash and sometimes a higher price than offered by cooperatives. Table 5.3 below shows the number of unions and primary societies which sold coffee as well as their turnover from 1998 to 2000. The turnover shows a significant increase. Due to lack of data, it is not clear whether the increase is due to volume or price increase from 1998 to 2000. The number of unions remains the same but primary societies increased by 53 during this period. But by the end of 2005 all the above cooperatives had closed business, leased their operations or reduced their operations to one single crop.

Box 5.1: Farmer group – association model

The farmer group – association model is an emerging and promising model that has been experimented with in the Ugandan coffee sector for some years now. Farmers' groups are organized into production units that adopt uniform practices so that they can bulk their produce for processing and marketing through their marketing associations with the assistance of their union. The associations coordinate group access to appropriate technology, credit and inputs. The associations are organized into an umbrella union whose main functions are lobbying, advocacy, access to marketing agencies, appropriate technologies, credit, and links to certification and verification programmes. The main difference between this association model and the cooperatives is that farmers retain ownership of their produce. The associations and the union are paid on performance for services provided in the process of value addition and marketing. The sales proceeds are paid directly to the group accounts. The group members are few with an average of 30 members per group. So, they know each other very well and it is to their mutual benefit to protect each other. The groups of farmers in Bushenyi, Masaka and Mpigi organized under NUCAFE sold 125 tons of green coffees in 2005 and earned a net profit of over UG Shs 650 per kg.

Table 5.3: Coffee unions, membership and turnover 1998–2000 (Ug Shs)

	1998	1999	2000
Number of Unions	6	6	6
Membership (Primary Societies)	459	487	512
Turnover	5 200 000 000	6 000 000 000	7 000 000 000

Source: Department of Cooperative Development – Annual Report (2000).

Tobacco:

In the year 2000 there were three registered cooperative unions in Uganda dealing in tobacco – namely West Nile Tobacco, Middle North Tobacco in Gulu and North Kigezi Tobacco in Rukungiri. Of these only West Nile Tobacco Cooperative Union in West Nile was in operation. But it faced fierce competition from British American Tobacco and Mastermind Cigarette Company. The two companies opted to deal with farmers directly instead of working with cooperative unions. All three tobacco cooperative unions wound up business three years ago. Table 5.4 gives an idea of the number of primary societies affected by this.

Table 5.4: Tobacco union membership and turnover 1998–2000 (Ug Shs)

	1998	1999	2000
Number of Unions	3	3	3
Membership (Primary Societies)	91	93	95
Turnover Shs	100 000 000	130 000 000	150 000 000

Source: Department of Cooperative Development – Annual Report (2000).

Non-traditional cash crops:

The cooperative unions ventured into non-traditional crops as a diversification strategy to survive the competition. Lango Cooperative Union ventured into the sim sim export business in the year 2000. The venture was quite profitable for the union but it did not last long before the traders got interested and out-competed the union. Now, with the exception of Lango, East Acholi and West Acholi Cooperative Unions all the others have closed. Sebei Elgon Cooperative Union handled wheat which they grew at their farm at Kabyoyo and from other farmers in Kapchorwa and sold locally to Uganda Grain Millers in Jinja. Societies in northern, eastern and mid western Uganda marketed maize, sunflower, millet, cassava and beans which they sold to schools and other buyers.

Table 5.5 shows that the number of primary societies involved in non-traditional crops increased slightly but sales turnover increased substantially.

Table 5.5: Cooperatives in non traditional crops 1998–2000 (Ug Shs)

	1998	1999	2000
Number of Unions	1	1	1
Membership (Primary Societies)	650	660	690
Turnover Shs	100 239 320	114 655 210	135 918 354

Source: Department of Cooperative Development – Annual Report (2000).

SACCOs and service cooperatives:

According to available data turnover in the service cooperatives recorded an increase of 600 million from 1998 to 2000. The major growth was recorded in the savings and credit societies. But other segments of the sector also showed substantial operations. The Uganda Cooperative Transport Union, for example, had about 105 trucks of which 60 are hired by the World Food Programme on a long-term contract.

Table 5.6: Turnover in the service cooperative 1998–2000 (Ug Shs)

	1998	1999	2000
Number of Unions	2	2	2
Membership (Primary Societies)	83	97	105
Turnover Shs	4 600 000 000	4 800 000 000	5 200 000 000

Source: Department of Cooperative Development – Annual Report (2000).

At the primary level as well, we see that many cooperatives are facing an uphill struggle. The Uganda Shoe Shiner and Repair Savings and Credit Cooperative Society which was established in 1975 still exists despite the fact that it is not as vibrant as it was before liberalization of the cooperatives in the 1990s. Total membership has decreased from 370 in 1993 to 120 in 2005. Full-time membership has dropped drastically from 124 in 1993 to 70 in 2005. Part-time members dropped from 246 in 1993 to 50 in 2005. The society used to make brushes, buy raw materials in bulk and provide them to members on credit. This business has stopped due to low recovery rates. The main services now being provided to members are savings and credit.

The Jinja Teachers SACCO, a young society registered in 2002, is showing positive growth. Membership has increased from 41 (nine female and 32 males) in 2002 to 600 by 2005 (308 females and 292 males). All are primary school teachers in Jinja District. The society has managed to maintain an interest rate of 1.5% (18% per annum) compared with the prevailing lowest commercial rate of 36% per annum. The loans repayment rate is 98%. The society's assets increased by 33 million (471%) from 7.9 million to 40.4 million in 4 years. Loans outstanding increased by 27 billion (675%) from 4.0 million to 31.5 million Ugandan shillings.

Box 5.2: The Jinja Teachers Savings and Credit Cooperative Society Ltd

The Jinja Teachers' Savings and Credit Cooperative Society Ltd was established in 2002. Its main objective is to enhance social, economical and professional advancement of all teachers working in the Jinja District in Uganda. Both primary and secondary school teachers are allowed to become members of this savings and credit society but for the time being only primary school teachers are active members. The current membership of the Society stands at 600 (308 female, and 292 males) compared to 41 (nine females and 32 males) when it was established.

When the Society was established the requirements to become a member consisted of the payment of an application fee of Ug Shs 2,000, a membership subscription fee of Shs 3,000 and the buying of ten shares with a value of Ug Shs 5,000 per share. Currently the membership application fee has increased to Ug Shs 5,000, the membership annual subscription has increased to Ug Shs 10,000 and the cost of a share has increased to Ug Shs 20,000. The interest rate charged on loans to members was 1.5% per month when the society started. The cooperative relies on a check-off system. A member is required to sign an agreement with his employer and the society which commits the employer to deducting a certain sum of money as a monthly contribution. The society started its operations in a temporary classroom but now they have a modern office in the middle of Jinja town. The number of staff has increased from one to two, and the savings and credit society has continued to maintain an interest rate of 1.5% (18% per annum). The interest rate charged by the society is very low compared to interest charged by other financial institutions.

The society's assets increased by Ug Shs 33 million (471%) from 7.9 million to 40.4 million in 4 years. Loans outstanding increased by Ug Shs 27 million (675%) from 4.0 million to Ug Shs 31.5 million. (Annual Report 2002 and 2005). Approximately 80% of the loans extended to members are to meet consumption needs such as school fees; medical expenses or to buy consumable items. A few members are borrowing to finance business or enterprises for income generation activities.

Members of cooperatives: who and why?

The membership of cooperative societies is comprised of people of various backgrounds, wealth, social status and education levels. Members of agricultural cooperatives are largely rural dwellers and they include both smallholders and medium size land-holding farmers. The majority of non-agricultural cooperative members live in the urban areas. High-ranking professionals employed in organizations around which SACCOS are formed find themselves within the same cooperative as their junior staff.

On average women make up only about 24% of the total number of members (UCA, 2005). This trend is linked to several cultural and socio-economic factors. First, membership in agricultural cooperatives is in most cases reserved for the heads of households or the owners of land. Men thus have an edge over women. Secondly, even in employee-based cooperative societies females are fewer because traditionally women are underrepresented in the formal sector labour market (UCA 2005).

Why do people belong to a cooperative or why don't they? There is only scant information that can help us to answer this question. Based on a recent survey, Mugisha *et al.* (2005) list the five major benefits that were echoed by the cooperative members: (i) skills and knowledge acquired through training were cited by 43.8% of the members. 94% of the respondents attended training workshops on crops, livestock and environmental conservation issues; 40% of these workshops were organized by Rural Producer Organizations (RPOs); (ii) easier access to credit through revolving fund schemes and other sources was mentioned by 10.5% of the respondents. Credit was expected to boost members' spirits as well as their capital base invariably improving their productivity; (iii) planting materials received through their RPOs were mentioned by 6.5% of the respondents. These were mainly coffee plantlets and maize seeds; and (iv) social interaction and networking that have greatly improved their social wellbeing and, like skills and knowledge, also boost their confidence.

Mugisha *et all*. (2005) also report that farmers involved in groups received higher prices for their commodities than those who were not. Still 74% of the co-operators claimed to sell their coffee without the assistance of the RPOs. The results of this research are summarized in Table 5.7 below.

Table 5.7: Direct benefits obtained by farmers from RPOs (perception)

Benefits	Percentage (n = 116)
Credit from SACCOs	53.9
Savings	32.9
Better farming techniques	11.8
Price information	2.4

Source: Mugisha *et al.*, 2005.

Table 5.8: Second-order benefits obtained through RPOs by women and men (perception)

Benefits	Female (%) N = 65	Male (%) N = 88
No benefit	3.1	1.1
Seed given by RPO	7.7	5.7
Skills through training	49.2	39.8
Social interaction	6.2	3.4
Income improved	4.6	4.5
Improved food security	1.5	2.3
Sale of our crops	1.5	10.2
Credit access	10.8	10.2
Saving with the RPO	1.5	3.4
Group work	1.5	3.4
Improved welfare	1.5	1.1
Others	10.9	14.9

Source: Mugisha *et al.*, 2005.

Cross-gender analysis of the data in Table 5.8 shows that women have the impression of having benefited slightly more than men in terms of skills learned and social interaction. The sale of crops through the farmers' organization seemed to be more important for the male group than for the women.

Support from home and abroad

The most important international partners of the cooperative movement in Uganda are the Swedish Cooperative Centre (SCC), the Canadian Cooperative Association (CCA) and the Norwegian Society for Development (Norges Vel). These donors who have been around for the last ten years have been highly appreciated in particular in the area of capacity building, training and savings mobilization. These donors are part of the movement to movement support which had a positive impact when compared with support from other donors. The donors relate well with the Uganda cooperative movement and they provide a holistic technical support which builds to sustainability.

The Netherlands and the Common Funds for Commodities (CFC) have been providing support to the Warehouse Receipt systems being implemented by the Registrar of Cooperatives in close cooperation with the Uganda Coffee Development Authority and Cotton Development Organization. The European Union has been providing funds for the Commodity Exchange project being implemented by the Uganda Cooperative Alliance. Recently, the European Union provided the Uganda Cooperative Alliance with funds to build its capital base for lending on to its members. The donor communities' main interest has been towards provision of support towards capacity building, technical assistance, training, and member education but with little provision of capital.

Still, sustainability of donor funded projects has been questioned as most of the donor funded projects are said to lack reference to demands and needs. Even if they are demand-driven, the timing of funding is sometimes delayed. Ownership by the beneficiaries may be nominal, as they are not fully involved in the design and development of the project proposals.

Exporters are being funded under the USAID programme and European Union to organize producers as out-growers who are linked to selected exporters. This practice which is only for selective exporters is resented by many other exporters as it creates unfair competition, with the negative effect of distorting the real market prices.

Apart from the government involvement (which has been pointed out in preceding paragraphs), typical "home" institutions to provide assistance to cooperatives would be the Uganda Cooperative Alliance and the Cooperative College.

The Uganda Cooperative Alliance depends on its own source of income to fund its recurrent expenditure. The Alliance managed to transform itself by diversifying its concentration from traditional agricultural cooperatives into non-traditional agricultural cooperatives such as vanilla, bee keeping, small scale processing, financial services, food processing and area market enterprises. Cooperatives in these sectors were encouraged to become members of the apex body without necessarily passing through unions (UCA 2005 annual report). UCA also represents the Ugandan Cooperative Movement in the International Cooperative Alliance.

The Cooperative College previously came under the Ministry of Tourism, Trade and Industries but was transferred to the Ministry of Education and Sports in 1999. Since then it has maintained positive collaborative links with the cooperative movement. The Cooperative College has played a key role in training the staff of the cooperative movement. Occasionally and on demand the college designs member education programmes as well as courses for management committees of cooperatives. According to the college statistics 300 students graduate from the school each year.

The savings and credit associations in Uganda are affiliated to the African Confederation of Savings and Credit Cooperatives (ACCOSCA) and the World Council of Credit Unions (WOCCU) and benefit from many capacity building initiatives of these networks.

Employment in the cooperative sector

Table 5.9 below provides information on the number of people directly employed by the cooperative sector. The level of employment in the cooperative sector is estimated to be a total of 2,823 (UCA, 2004) which is small compared to the potential of the sector. Out of the total of 2,823 estimated employees 2,089 are males and only 734 are females (26% of the total).

Table 5.9: Number of employees by each cooperative level and category

	Males		Females		Total
	No.	%	No	%	
Primary Society	1 652	71.5	659	28.5	2 311
Area Coop Societies	38	73.1	14	26.9	52
District Union	397	86.7	61	13.3	458
National Union	2	100.0	0	0	2
Total	2 089	74.0	734	26.0	2 823

Source: UCA census, 2004.

In addition the cooperative sector does have a significant supportive effect on employment. An estimated 7,500 families are dependent on their agricultural cooperative for their income. Over 11,000 people (UCA, 2005) in the non-agricultural sector get income support due to the fact that they are cooperative members.

There are of course many more members who indirectly derive their income from activities related to the cooperative movement such as processing, packaging, insurance, banking, production of machinery, stationery, office equipment and other supplies used by the cooperative movement. There are people who are involved in marketing and distributing cooperative products such as milk, honey, sugar, foods and eggs. Cooperatives are also users of inputs such as fertilizers, seeds, drying materials, heavy and light equipment which require labour to produce them.

Although prior to liberalization the cooperative movement was more active with people working for the movement, it was inefficient, expensive and the farmers were paying for these inefficiencies. Some time back coffee farmers were paid as low as 20% of the free on board (fob) price of their coffee (UCDA Annual report, 1991/92). This means 80% of farmers' earnings were spent within the cooperative movement and the state apparatus. After liberalization farmers are now being paid 60–70% of the free on board price of their coffee (UCDA Annual Report, 2004/05). At its peak, the cooperative movement was employing over 35,000 people. Cooperative members and not cooperative staff seem to have benefited from the new wind. This can also be observed at the primary cooperative level. The Jinja Savings and Credit Society, for example, which started with one employee now has two. But the indirect effect of its growth is more impressive. Members who borrowed and paid for their professional advancement training have increased their salaries from an average of 150,000 to 200,000 Ugandan shillings per month. In addition, with the loans provided by the society some have started poultry, dairy and grocery businesses which are currently employing 50 full- time employees.

Cooperatives: contributing to the poverty reduction and social protection challenge

Cooperatives are perceived by many as vehicles in the fight against poverty. Typically for African organizations, social protection mechanisms are built in by the members. This is also the case with cooperatives. Members put aside funds to assist each other in case of death, fire where property is lost, sickness, and even where labour is required for harvesting or planting on the farm of a member who is sick, too old or has been overwhelmed by an unexpected bumper harvest. Therefore, the cooperative principle of concern for the community is part of the society values, is accorded its due importance and is provided for.

But cooperatives, more than any other type of economic or social institution, are oriented towards wealth creation and social protection of members of the community at large. This is practised in different ways.

Loans provided by SACCOs, but also by many other cooperative societies, directly and indirectly contribute to social protection and to the quality of life of the members concerned. Many types of loans have a significant risk and vulnerability mitigation impact. This is the case, for example, with the credits provided in times of need, sickness or disaster. The Jinja Teachers Savings and Credit Society whose members are seriously affected by the killer HIV/AIDS disease does not benefit from the burial contribution scheme within the District Council. Therefore the society has established its own burial contribution fund to cover burial expenses for any society member who dies or who loses family members.

The cooperative can also help members and their families to be lifted out of poverty. The same Jinja Teachers Savings and Credit Society reported that three of the members who borrowed and paid their children's school fees have seen their three children graduate in medicine, engineering and finance. These children are now employed and provide financial assistance to their relatives and parents. Another example is found in the Kibinge Masaka District where some farmers are certified under the Utz Kapeh programme.

They are employing labour and paying the wages recommended by the Utz Kapeh code which has resulted in employees earning higher wages than they used to earn. The higher wages have in some way contributed to poverty reduction. Due to backward and forward linked benefits in coffee production, processing and marketing Kibinge farmers will earn at least 30–40% more than the FOB prices previously received for their coffee. The additional income from the sale of value added coffee at a negotiated price will bring more money into the community which means that their purchasing power will increase.

Member ownership of the cooperative group, but also member education, which are key in every cooperative, enhance the capacity for members to understand their rights and obligations in the cooperative and society at large. The fact that a member feels empowered to own and to have a say in his/her assets gives him/her the opportunity to add value to his/her assets and in the end to command a better price for his/her products or services.

Indirectly, the services provided by cooperative unions also have the potential to contribute to wealth creation and social protection. For example, bulking and marketing services provided to members allow the member to earn higher income from increased bargaining power due to collective action and economies of scale. Also, active cooperatives and cooperative unions, which exhibit social and economic dynamism, can function as magnets that attract other investors to the region or the sector.

Concluding remarks

In Uganda, at certain moments in its history, the cooperative movement has proven to be a viable tool to harness the resources of individuals into a bigger pool. Cooperatives can be used to raise the financial resources required to capitalize a business which has been identified provided the core values of the cooperative movement are applied. Like elsewhere in Africa, the Ugandan Government is now interested in putting in place a regulatory framework which will make cooperatives more independent from government interventions. The present liberalization process, in particular in the areas of crop marketing, comes as an opportunity for the cooperative movement. Provided the members are empowered to add value up the chain while maintaining ownership, and provided the cooperatives have better access to information technology (improving market information and quick decision making), members will come out stronger in terms of personal income, and cooperatives will gain in terms of cohesiveness.

Still it is true to say that, in the past, lack of ownership has been the most important reason for the failure of cooperatives. Formation of cooperatives did not involve the members from the beginning, members were not adequately educated on why they should have a cooperative and they did not take an active role in the decisions that affect their cooperatives. Furthermore, governments had enacted Cooperatives Acts to serve the interests of the government instead of the co-operators. The office of the Registrar of Cooperatives had powers to appoint the senior staff of cooperatives which in effect rendered members powerless to make decisions affecting their cooperatives. The challenge of the cooperative movement in particular in the agriculture sector is therefore to deal with the issues of ownership. But this also requires all actors within the cooperative movement to think as "we" instead of "me" to keep the spirit of cooperation alive and effective. This would seem quite a challenge.

Sources

This article is based on a series of documents and interviews, carried out during the autumn of 2005. The author wishes to thank the following people: Rwasa Stephen and Dr. B. Kiiza, Makerere University; Mayanja Kizito, Uganda Coffee Development Authority; Mr. Frederick Mwesige, Commissioner of Cooperatives/Registrar of Cooperatives; Serwaji Kassim, Uganda Shoe Shine and Repair Savings and Credit Cooperative; Charles Kabuga, Consultant; Leonard Msemakweli, Uganda Cooperative Alliance; David Kalenderi, Jinja Teachers SACCO; Patrick Kayongo, Deputy Registrar; Fred Msaja, Busia Savings and Credit Society; Merv Exner, Canadian Cooperative Association.

Acronyms

ACCOSCA	African Confederation of Savings and Credit Cooperatives
CFC	Common Funds for Commodities
NAADS	National Agricultural Advisory Services
NUCAFE	National Union of Coffee Agribusinesses and Farm Enterprises
RPOs	Rural Producer Organizations
UCA	Uganda Cooperative Alliance
UCUSCO	Uganda Cooperative Savings and Credit Union Ltd.

Bibliography

- Bitanuzire S. (2004), *Farmers Organizations in Rwanda – Building Of A New Structure*, Kigali, unpublished paper.
- Department of Cooperative Development (2004), *Annual Report 2004*, Kampala.
- Department of Cooperative Development (2000), *Annual Report 2000*, Kampala.
- Jinja Teachers Savings and Credit Society (2002), *Annual Report 2002*, Jinja.
- Jinja Teachers Savings and Credit Society (2005), *Annual Report 2005*, Jinja.
- Kabuga C. (1994), "New Legislation Driven by Cooperatives in Uganda, in : Farmer Empowerment through Farmer Organizations: Best Practices", The World Bank, AFTES Working Paper, N° 14, Washington.
- Kabuga C. & Kitandwe J.W. (eds.) (1995), *Cooperatives: Past, Present and Future*, Uganda Cooperative Alliance Ltd, Kampala.
- Kabuga Ch. (2005), *Cooperative Tradition – Uganda*, unpublished paper.
- Lwasa S., Kiiza B. & Semana A., (2001), *Plan for Modernization of Coffee Farm-to-Market Chains: Farm Level Organisations' Demonstration Project*, a Report prepared for the Private Sector Foundation /World Bank, Kampala.
- Ministry of Finance, Planning and Economic Development (2004), *Background to the Budget 2004/05*, Kampala.
- Mugisha J. & Lwasa S. (2005), *Status of Rural Producer Organisations in Uganda*, Report prepared for ICRAF/RELMA, Nairobi.
- Mugisha J., Kiiza B.A., Lwasa S. & Katongole C. (2005), *Governance and Business Performance of Rural Producer Organization in Uganda*, Report prepared for NOARD.
- Pekka Hussi H. et al. (1993), *The Development of Cooperative and Other Rural Organization*, World Bank, Washington.
- Shafiq A. et al. (1967), *Commission of Inquiry into Cooperative Unions 1966*, Government of Uganda, Kampala.
- Stessens J. & Gouet C. (2004), *Efficient Contract Farming through Strong Organisations in Partnership with Agribusiness*, HIVA, Leuven.
- Uganda Cooperative Alliance (2005), *Annual Report 2005*, UCA, Kampala.
- Uganda Cooperative Alliance (2004), *Cooperatives Census 2004*, UCA, Kampala.

Appendices

Appendix 1. Classification of the types of societies per sub sector 1999–2000

S/N	Type of Society	Number of Societies	
	Non Agriculture	**1999**	**2000**
1	Micro-Finance	20	20
2	Savings and Credit	660	690
3	Multipurpose	435	436
4	Consumer	240	240
5	Transport	274	275
6	Hides and Skins	65	65
7	Millers	17	17
8	Carpentry	16	16
9	Housing	10	17
10	Engineering	9	10
11	Brick Making	3	3
12	"Enguli" (local brew)	21	21
13	Mining	13	14
14	Cottage Industry	43	43
16	Hand Craft	13	13
17	Processing	21	21
18	Bee Keeping	3	3
	TOTAL	**1 863**	**1 904**
	Agricultural		
1	District Union	32	32
2	National Union	5	5
3	Agricultural Marketing	3 953	3 960
4	Ranching	218	221
5	Dairy	54	57
6	Fishing	68	68
7	Poultry	10	10
8	Mixed Farming	123	123
9	Horticulture	10	10
	Sub Total	**4 473**	**4 486**
	Grand Total	**6 336**	**6 390**

Source: Department of Cooperative Development (2000).

Appendix 2: Classification of Memberships per sub sector

S/N	Type of Society	Number of Societies		% change
	Non Agriculture	**1999**	**2000**	**% change**
1	Micro-Finance	1 250	2 830	126%
2	Savings and Credit	775 450	1 857 050	139%
3	Multipurpose	75 740	107 610	42%
4	Consumer	10 690	12 960	21%
5	Transport	315 200	326 300	3%
6	Hides and Skins	270	230	(14%)
7	Millers	470	320	(31%)
8	Carpentry	450	300	(33%)
9	Housing	690 000	920 000	33%
10	Engineering	257	260	1%
11	Brick Making	120	135	12%
12	"Enguli"(Local brew)	100	70	(30%)
13	Mining	200	150	(25%)
14	Cottage Industry	77 500	37 000	(52%)
16	Hand Craft	156 000	110 000	(29%)
17	Processing	189	165	(12%)
18	Bee Keeping	30	60	100%
	TOTAL	**2103 916**	**3 375 440**	**60%**
	Agricultural			
1	District Union	4 232	4 243	2%
2	National Union	3 955	3 855	(2%)
3	Agricultural Marketing	3 046 535	3 864 355	26%
4	Ranching	158 750	183 950	15%
5	Dairy	1 950	2 200	12%
6	Fishing	500	470	(6%)
7	Poultry	400	450	12%
8	Mixed Farming	1 250	1 005	(19%)
9	Horticulture	350 000	270 000	(22%)
	SUB TOTAL	**3 567 572**	**4 330 528**	**21%**
	GRAND TOTAL	**5 671 488**	**7 705 968**	**35%**

Source: Department of Cooperative Development (2000).

Chapter Six – The Cooperative Sector in Ghana: Small and Big Business

by Anthony K. Tsekpo

Introduction

This study is a brief survey of the cooperative sector in Ghana. It is essentially to provide a snapshot of what has happened to cooperatives in the last decade or so. The methodological approach is essentially qualitative. The main inputs were responses to a short questionnaire submitted to the Department of Cooperatives by the Cooperative Branch of the ILO, extensive review of administrative documents and other secondary sources and interviews with stakeholders across the cooperative sector in Ghana.

Specifically, key officers in the three establishments that form the lead agencies in the cooperative movement in Ghana, namely the Department of Cooperatives, the Ghana Cooperatives Council and the Cooperative College were interviewed. In addition secondary data gathered from these agencies form the basic raw materials for the narratives in this report. Although there is little consistent data from the three establishments, it is apparent that important policy initiatives are in progress towards the reform of the cooperative sector. Perhaps the most important of these policy initiatives is the new Cooperative Bill. The lead agencies undertook joint action to get the Bill to its current stage. In anticipation of a new operating environment when the bill is passed into law, the Ghana Cooperative Council with the help of the World Bank-sponsored Agricultural Sector Investment Programme (AgSSIP) has drawn up a strategic plan to reposition itself to be of service to the associations, district and regional unions and primary societies.

To complement data gathered from the lead agencies and obtain a clearer understanding of the links between the apex body, the Department of Cooperatives and the primary societies, in-depth field studies were undertaken in a primary society, a regional association, and a federation. The potential of pre-cooperatives was also examined as the Department of Cooperatives is involved in formation of such groups in conjunction with the Ministry of Food and Agriculture. These field studies covered Kuapa Kokoo as a model cooperative, located in Kumasi, to learn useful lessons to guide primary societies that were described very often as moribund. Furthermore, the Zagyuri Community Women's Group, a pre-cooperative which operates along cooperative principles was also studied to draw attention to the potential of the several groups operating in the informal economy as a possible launching pad for the cooperative movement in Ghana. Interviews were also conducted with the two executives of the Ashanti Regional Union of the Cooperative Distillers Association to obtain an assessment from the middle tier of the movement. Finally, since credit unions are the most vibrant cooperatives in the country, it was considered appropriate to hear from the credit union association (federation) and the University of Ghana Cooperative Credit Union about the magic formula for success.

Cooperatives in Ghana: a heterogeneous sector

The formal cooperative tradition in Ghana dates back to the 1920s when the British colonial government introduced the concept to the cocoa sector. However, the basic concept of cooperatives already existed in the country in various forms and was known as "Nwoboa" among farmers in the Akan speaking communities (Kayenwee 2001; Department of Cooperatives, 1990). Today cooperatives are found in almost every sector of the economy and embrace people from all strata of society. Some of the leading sectors where cooperatives had significant presence include distilleries, poultry, crop production and marketing, pharmaceutical production and marketing, fisheries, marketing and distribution of household consumer durables, transport, savings and credit mobilization, textiles and dress making, printing etc. The various types of cooperatives have been classified into four broad categories by the Department of Cooperatives (DOC) and the Ghana Cooperative Council (GCC), namely agricultural cooperatives, industrial cooperatives, financial cooperatives and service cooperatives.

The cooperative movement in Ghana is very heterogeneous given the diversity of sectors in which members operate. It is often described as a pyramid. Technically it is a three-tier structure within federations or national associations and a four-tier structure at the overall movement level comprising:

i)   Several primary societies spread all over the country in different sectors of the economy at the base;

ii) District and/or regional (secondary) cooperatives also known as unions;

iii) National associations of cooperatives in the same narrow sector or trade also known as federations; and

iv) Ghana Cooperative Council at the apex (see Figure 6.1).

Figure 6.1: Structure of the cooperative movement in Ghana

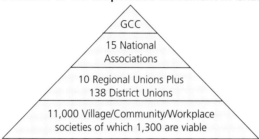

The national associations, currently about 15 in number are brought together to form the apex of the movement under the auspices of the Ghana Cooperatives Council. The current broad classification of the registered cooperatives is as in Table 6.1 below.

Table 6.1: Distribution of registered cooperatives

Cooperative	As at December 1988	As at June 2005
Agricultural Cooperatives	4 998	1 463
Industrial Cooperatives	1 733	815
Financial Cooperatives	40 440	277
Service Cooperatives	3 075	297
Total	10 246	2 852

Source: GCC (sd) Secretary General's Report to the Fourth Congress (1987-1989) and DOC (2005)

It is evident from the figures in Table 6.1 that the number of primary societies has decreased significantly. The rapid decline in registered cooperatives may be the result of the fact that as at 1989 the registered cooperatives may have been bloated with a large number of inactive societies. Indeed a World Bank Technical Department (Africa Region) Report observed that out of a total number of 10,585 cooperatives, only 1,000 were in operation at the end of

1989 (see Porvali, 1993). The account rendered in the World Bank report will suggest that the observed decline in reported cooperatives between 1988 and 2004 in Table 1 might signal a growth in active cooperatives from 1,000 in 1989 to 2,852 in 2004. This trend is consistent with the report presented by Oppong-Manu (2004) which put the number of registered cooperatives in Ghana at 2,200 (1,080 agricultural cooperatives, 740 industrial cooperatives, 241 financial cooperatives and 139 service cooperatives).

The current classification of cooperatives as agricultural, industrial, financial and service as depicted above hides a large amount of information with respect to the scope of activities, membership and ownership. Overall, as in many jurisdictions, cooperatives in Ghana are member-owned organizations, which are democratically controlled. Other cooperative principles that feature very well in the cooperative movement in Ghana are freedom of participation by members, delivery of service to the community and surplus sharing. However, one of the most important elements of cooperatives that is missing from the vocabulary of most primary societies in Ghana is the joint ownership of means of production. As we shall see later in this paper absence of common property among members of primary societies is a hindrance to the progressive development of cooperatives in Ghana.

In the absence of any central databases on the sociological profile of members of cooperatives in Ghana, it is fair to assume that the spatial distribution of cooperatives makes it possible for members to come from all social strata of the Ghanaian population. The agricultural cooperatives most of the time comprise simple rural farmers, the majority of whom are in the food crop sector.

The cooperatives in the industrial sector are often classified into small-scale manufacturing and food processing but the dominant group is the distillers. Until 2002 this group included all distributors and retailers of locally distilled gin, "akpeteshi". The scale of operation among the group varies from a few litres of the product to people who handle large quantities of the drink. The socio-economic, including demographic, characteristics of the members of the distillers' and retailers' cooperatives is very diverse. Similarly handicraft and certain groups which are workers' cooperatives have variable profile membership.

The financial cooperatives are made up of credit unions and "susu" collectors cooperatives, which are small, geographically-based savings cooperatives. The credit unions are categorised into workplace unions, parish or church unions and community credit unions and these are the links that bind the members of a specific group together. These groups could be people living in the same community, or people within some establishment, or people within the same profession, etc. Credit unions, which numbered approximately 260 at the end of December 2004, are distributed throughout all the ten regions of Ghana. It is fair to assume that the membership of unions is representative of the population of the communities/districts/establishments in which they are located. These groups are always made up of people of different socio-economic profiles from those found in the country.

The service cooperatives form another diverse group, comprising transport cooperatives, pharmaceutical cooperatives and different consumer cooperatives. The membership of these cooperatives is as diverse as witnessed in the other segments of the cooperative movement.

The fact that the cooperative concept has had its most widespread application in agriculture is reflected in agricultural cooperatives forming approximately 46.2% of registered cooperatives as at December 2004. Agricultural cooperatives are engaged in food production, storage, marketing and processing. A core function for cooperatives in food production is the purchasing/supply of input services to members of primary societies. On average, agricultural cooperatives perform no fewer than two of the three functions. Some of the service activities they undertake include land preparation; seed procurement and distribution; harvesting of crops; processing and marketing of produce; sourcing of funds and agricultural machinery; and training of farmers.

In addition to production related services and activities undertaken by agricultural cooperatives, the cooperatives discharge their social responsibility by assisting members in times of need. In instances such as funerals, weddings, naming ceremonies, sickness and hospitalization, members pool resources together to support the individual in need.

Despite the widespread use of the cooperative concept, there is very little information on the economic significance of the cooperative sector to the economy. The GCC and the Department of Cooperatives estimate that there are approximately 2,400,000 members in the cooperative sector. This approximates to 25% of the economically active population. However, the weak linkages between the primary societies, the district/regional unions and the federations make it difficult to verify the veracity of this figure.

Information on the assets and finances of these cooperatives is difficult to come by except for the Ghana Cooperative Credit Unions Association (CUA). At the end of December 2004 assets of the credit unions totalled ¢348 billion (CUA, 2005).

Managers of the cooperative movement, officers of the DOC and other independent observers of the state of cooperatives in Ghana often suggest that the poor performance of cooperatives and also the current structure of the cooperatives may be attributed to the involvement of government in cooperative activities including the introduction of cooperatives. Patronage often disorients cooperatives, making them consider themselves as subvented organizations rather than member-owned and democratically controlled enterprises with a mission to produce and share surplus among members.

The role of the government: many experiences and questions

It is often argued that the bane of cooperatives in Ghana dates back to the attempts in the First Republic to hoodwink cooperatives to toe the line of government. This attempt culminated in the takeover of the assets of the cooperative movement. Since then governments have considered cooperatives as a tool for mobilizing the population into groups that could form the channel for government support for improving resource pooling and output maximization (DOC, 1990).

Getting rid of old legislation?

The domineering attitude of the state towards cooperatives is evident in the Cooperative Societies Decree 1968, National Liberation Council Decree (NLCD) 252. The first paragraph of the Decree alludes to the appointment of a Registrar. Indeed the extensive powers given to the Registrar under the law include registration, the power to issue directions of a general or specific nature with respect to accounts and type of books to be kept and returns to be submitted to the Registrar, settlement of disputes, audit inspection and enquiries and dissolution of registered societies.

Even though the Cooperative Societies Decree, NLCD 252 is 37 years old, it remains the only legislation regulating the conduct of cooperatives. It is therefore relatively easy to make reference to a single source legislative framework with respect to cooperatives in Ghana. The legislation defines cooperatives as any "society which has as its object the promotion of the economic interest of its members in accordance with cooperative principles" and permits the registration of such societies as limited liability companies.

Under NLCD 252, application for registration shall be made to the Registrar of Cooperatives. It is required that, for a primary society, the application be signed by at least ten persons qualified for membership. District or regional unions and associations may be formed by at least two societies and must have their application to the Registrar signed by persons duly authorized by each society according to the member society's bye-laws. The law confers on members of societies the power to make bye-laws to regulate the conduct of the societies, but more significantly, the law recognizes registered cooperatives to be bodies corporate with perpetual succession and may sue and be sued in the corporate name under which it is registered.

In the area of financial management and transactions, which is critical to the success of cooperatives in a market economy, the law appears restrictive. The Registrar is expected to control the granting of loans by for instance prescribing a maximum loan which may be made by a society to any member without prior consent. The Registrar is also empowered, by means of a general or specific order, to prohibit or restrict the lending of money on the security of immovable property by any registered society. The law also forbids the attachment of shares or interest of a member in the capital of a registered cooperative. Investment of funds may be in Government of Ghana securities, shares of other registered cooperatives and securities of other banks registered under the Laws of Ghana. In exceptional cases the Registrar may sanction investment or deposit of funds in any other manner approved by the Registrar. NLCD 252 allows also for government assistance to cooperatives. Subject to regulations that the government may formulate, the government may grant loans to, take shares in or give financial assistance in any other form to any registered cooperative.

The attitude of government towards cooperatives

Members of the cooperative movement often suggest that the difficulties of cooperatives stem from government domination and the issue of wrong signals with respect to government assistance. Government support for the cooperative movement is through the provision of subventions to DOC, the Cooperative College and the GCC to undertake education and promotion of cooperatives in the country. However, the one thing that is common to all these three institutions is massive under-funding. Thus, all three institutions do not have the full complement of staff to execute their mandate effectively. Perhaps more difficult is the fact that the staff in these establishments do not have the resources to make them functional. Located in the Ministry of Manpower,

Youth and Employment, which is one of the under-funded sectors in Ghana, the institutions suffer from poor budgetary allocations to the sector Ministry and this is reflected in their output and performance.

The under-funding of the governmental cooperative institutions is made more problematic by the bitter history of government involvement in cooperatives. In 1960, government took over assets of the Cooperative Bank and handed them over to the Ghana Commercial Bank. Similarly, government took over the resources of the Ghana Cooperative Marketing Association in 1961 and handed them to the United Ghana Farmers Council (DOC, 1990: 85; Taylor, 2003). These takeovers were accompanied by the dissolution of the Department of Cooperatives for championing the cause of the dissolved cooperatives particularly the Ghana Cooperative Marketing Association (DOC, 1990: 86). The suit against the Bank of Ghana by the GCC following the liquidation of the second Cooperative Bank is another reference point when it comes to the bad memories of government interference with cooperatives. Council members and staff of the apex body also believe that the powers of the DOC are excessive and are inimical to the independence of cooperatives. However, DOC staff counter the argument by pointing to the weak management and deficiencies of the movement. For example it was pointed out that most staff of the movement completed the basic cooperative course in the 1960s and have not since undergone any refresher courses or upgraded their skills. In recent times courses being mounted by the Cooperative College are patronized rather by people outside the cooperative movement. On average, close to 75% of trainees at the college were private individuals (see Table 6.2).

Table 6.2: Patronage of courses mounted by Cooperative College

Target group	1999	2000	2001	2002
Coop societies staff	12	15	33	8
DOC staff	60	0	0	0
Private individuals	48	40	72	22
Total	120	155	105	30
Percentage from Movement	10	27.3	31.4	26.7

Source: DOC Annual Report, various issues.

DOC is perhaps the most effective of the three apex institutions responsible for the promotion and development of cooperatives. It has district officers in most of 138 local government administration areas in Ghana. However, staff of the department complains that their work is frustrated when government officials advise groups to form cooperatives to qualify for such facilities as may be available under the poverty reduction lending. The main effect of the way cooperative formation is engineered by public officers is that communities and individuals equate cooperatives with the formation of groups to secure funding from government, NGOs and other donors. Therefore many cooperatives stop holding together and may break up when they cease to receive funding or when they fail to attract any funding. The situation is made more precarious with the liberalization of the agricultural inputs market. Since the liberalization of the agricultural inputs market, cooperatives can only anticipate financial help from the state and other agencies through micro-finance schemes. Many NGOs which are filling in the gap of delivering agricultural inputs since liberalization have no preference for cooperatives, as they often prefer to experience the dynamics of group formation as part of their activities.

The DOC also contends that it receives little cooperation from other Ministries, Departments and Agencies (MDAs) that have resources to promote small and medium enterprises. Often, some of these MDAs invite the DOC to mobilize individuals into pre-cooperatives but their effort is frustrated when these same agencies bypass the DOC, which is tasked with mobilizing citizens into viable cooperatives, to do their own disbursement. Hopefully, the situation will improve as the DOC proves its worth with the decentralized local government framework.

A new policy on cooperative development

A new outlook on cooperative development is widespread among all the stakeholders in the sector. Under the poverty reduction strategy government has indicated the importance of cooperatives as a strategy for poverty reduction. The government policy is to promote cooperatives as a way of encouraging individual small and micro-enterprises to pool resources to expand their output (Republic of Ghana, 2000). This is part of the effort to create employment, improve incomes and reduce poverty especially among vulnerable groups. Further to this, the policy aims to re-orient the general perception of cooperatives towards business/market skills as a way of increasing incomes and attracting more people to join cooperatives. The broadening of decentralization is likely to promote cooperatives, as the new Local Government Law includes the Department of Cooperatives among the decentralized agencies.

In practice, the emphasis has been on pre-cooperatives, namely farmer-based organizations. Through the Department of Cooperatives and Ministry of Food and Agriculture, a long-term strategy has been outlined to ensure that all cooperatives and farmer-based organisations operate as going concerns that can compete effectively with other forms of businesses (DOC, s.d.). It is the expectation of the DOC that in the long run, cooperatives will take full responsibility for the management of the enterprises they set up, and operate as business enterprises applying best business practice in their operations.

In this regard, a new cooperative bill, which has gone through various phases of development and will soon be passed into law, is very detailed on management including financial management of cooperatives as well as cooperative principles. A significant inclusion under financial management is the proposal for the establishment of a Cooperative Development Fund towards education and training in cooperatives, including funds for the Cooperative College, the promotion of cooperative activities, the fulfilment of the international obligations of cooperatives and any other matters that may be determined by the Cooperatives Council.

As a boost to the cooperative development policy, it is important to observe that the cooperative registration policy has been kept very simple. Although the registration systems under the current law and the current bill remain very low cost and timely, there is no incentive for pre-cooperatives to register to become cooperatives because of the wrong message about cooperatives. As indicated above, communication about cooperatives puts them in a position to seek to take advantage of resources from government, donors and NGOs alike. Pre-cooperatives are positioned to do exactly the same. Once the needs of pre-cooperatives are satisfied, there is no incentive for them to take the next step of becoming cooperatives.

Many small, some big; many dormant, some very vibrant

The cooperative movement in Ghana cannot be said to be vibrant. However, efforts are underway to improve the situation and make cooperatives sustainable (see the proposal for strengthening the GCC dated September, 2000). The difference between registered cooperatives and active cooperatives as depicted in the decline in the number of cooperatives from 10,246 in December 1988 to 2,852 in 2004 (see Table 6.1) is a pointer to the poor performance of cooperatives in Ghana. Only a few of the active cooperatives can be considered as successful and for that matter sustainable in outlook. Credit unions are among the most successful cooperatives – thanks to the World Council of Credit Unions (WOCCU) revitalization programme to help credit unions become competitive, secure in capitalization and economically viable (Ofei, 2001). Until recently, the distillers' cooperatives were also counted among the successful cooperatives, but with a split in the association and primary societies forming splinter unions, the current performance of the distillers' cooperatives is far from successful. High input cost is another major factor affecting the vibrancy of the cooperatives. A recent survey of the pharmaceutical cooperatives shows that they also achieved great success through resilience (Kayenwee, 2001), having survived for 30 years of transition from the state controlled economic regime to the liberalized market regime.

Links with the four-tier structure

One way of assessing the vibrancy of the cooperative movement is to assess the links between the various tiers of the cooperative movement. In Ghana the link is rather weak, primary societies have little interaction with the district/regional unions. On the other hand the district/regional unions are loosely linked to the association, which does not have any strong bonding to the apex body, the GCC, either. This situation is often blamed on poor member participation. As a result of the high illiteracy rate among members, a few members control the activities/operations of the societies to the neglect of the majority. This explains the state of despair and lack of commitment from the general membership. In addition many of the members are poor and the cooperatives operate as micro-enterprises. Their contribution towards the running of higher levels of the cooperative movement takes away the little surplus they are able to generate. As a result, the general feeling among societies is that higher levels of the cooperative movement are irrelevant. At the apex level, the dependence on government subvention obscures the need to cultivate the societies to the point where they can sustain the cooperative movement. However, the recent policy of government to wean the movement off subvention has galvanized the GCC into planning for the provision of services to the societies and the affiliated associations (see GCC, 2000).

Scope and scale of economies among cooperatives

The evidence is that most cooperatives in Ghana remain very small and for that matter are not able to take advantage of scope and scale economies. The assets base of these cooperatives is such that they are not able to hire managerial staff. Thus, the administrative function was taken up by volunteers who must often train themselves with their own resources. Cooperative officers interviewed in the northern part of the country observe that the level of poverty in the communities is reflected in the scope of operation of the societies. Cooperative members are so poor they are not able to contribute towards the training of cooperative officers. However, unlike southern parts of the country individual elected officers are not able to sponsor their own training at the Cooperative College. Thus, most cooperative officers in the northern part of the country are not trained even in the basic cooperative principles. Furthermore, district officers do not even have the means necessary to go round the societies to give sufficient in-service training to the elected officers, making the management of cooperatives very weak. The outcome is that cooperatives in the northern parts of the country in particular are vulnerable to manipulation by ill-informed officers.

Market orientation

Apart from the credit unions which have adjusted to the liberalized environment and are doing brisk financial intermediation, production and service cooperatives appear to suffer from the old orientation that positions cooperatives to take advantage of government and donor resources. The FAO observed that the decline in government assistance to the agricultural sector, coupled with governmental decentralization and liberalization of market conditions have led to a dramatic fall in public services to rural areas, to a weakening of farmer organization, business competitiveness, increased rural poverty and restricted national economic growth (FAO, 2003). In the situation where production cooperatives do not perform joint marketing, the absence of subsidized inputs has limited their role to the search for credit.

The distillers' cooperatives benefited from Act 239 which enjoins all distillers and dealers in alcohol to belong to a distillers' cooperative. This law which permitted the association to collect taxes on behalf of the state also made it possible for the distillers' cooperatives to collect regular contributions from the membership. In the process the distillers' association acquired property mainly in the form of office buildings across the country. However, since the court challenge which led to the disintegration of the association, the income base of the association has dwindled.

The story is not all bleak; the experiences of Kuapa Kokoo, the pharmaceutical cooperatives and credit unions show that cooperatives can be viable and perform in a market-oriented economy (see Kayenwee, 2001, Ofei, 2001). The successful cooperatives point to the fact that effective management is an important element in sustainability of cooperatives in a market-orientated economy. Cooperatives that have a management with clear vision are able to identify opportunities for generating surplus and investing the surplus to take care of the community and also distribute surplus to members.

Non-economic activities

It is not an exaggeration to argue that most producer/service cooperatives remain functional as a result of their engagement in non-economic activities. They make regular contributions to raising funds to enable them participate in the social engagement of their members. They sympathize with members who are grieving and rejoice with those who are rejoicing. Thus, they join in and make contributions to members during sickness, funerals, weddings, naming ceremonies, etc. In the absence of any social insurance schemes covering the majority of these cooperative members who operate largely in the informal economy, members treasure these non-economic activities as a social support system.

A gender-friendly movement

There are barely any statistics in the cooperative sector that indicate the gender composition of membership of societies. But what is evident is that most of the producer cooperatives and farmer-based organizations include women. The trend is that most groups which were formed to take advantage of credit schemes have a high number of women. Micro-credit operators have intimated that women are better at repayment of credit facilities granted them. Indications of female participation in the cooperative movement can be seen in the conversion of Manya Krobo Fish Dealers Association, an all women group which was registered as a company limited by guarantee, to a cooperative in December 1999. The story of Zagyuri Community Women's Group, a pre-cooperative with 60 members shows how active women are and the potential of females in the cooperative movement.

The credit unions have a strong gender representation, as seen in the CUA Gender and Development (GAD) programme which is a research resource that advocates for gender sensitization within the credit union system. GAD operates a revolving micro-credit to women (¢90 million credit to women in

2002). GAD also operates youth savings clubs in senior secondary schools and teacher training colleges (¢5.5 million savings mobilized by these youth clubs in 2002).

Perhaps the strongest signal yet of the active involvement of women in the coop movement is that a female co-operator occupies the chair of the Ghana Cooperative Council. Aba Smith was a member of the board of the Cooperative Credit Unions Association (CUA) Ltd. in the past. She is currently an ex-officio member of the CUA board and on the board of the International Cooperative Alliance as one of Africa's two representatives on that board.

How vibrant is the cooperative sector and movement?

As indicated earlier in this paper the movement is divided into four sectors, namely:

- Financial service sector, made up of credit unions and "susu" collector cooperatives
- Agriculture sector cooperatives made up of food farming and marketing cooperatives, poultry and livestock cooperatives, fishing and fish marketing cooperatives, food processing and marketing cooperatives and cash crop marketing cooperatives
- Service sector cooperatives, made up of transport cooperatives, pharmaceutical cooperatives and consumer cooperatives
- Industrial sector cooperatives, made up principally of local gin (akpeteshie) distilling and retailing cooperatives

Each type of cooperative is organized at primary, district/regional and national levels. At the primary society level, the main strategy is about how to obtain quality inputs at minimum cost. Agriculture cooperatives, for example, organize tractor services to prepare the land for planting; where feasible they use the group to obtain credit and inputs at lower per unit costs. The same trend runs through the activities of other cooperative sectors.

While local gin distillers and retailers have a vertically integrated activity, the same cannot be said about agricultural cooperatives where different societies are engaged in production of different crops whilst others are engaged in marketing. The absence of integration or any other form of coordination among the cooperatives may be attributed to a common weakness – lack of the requisite skills by most managers.

Limited horizontal integration of cooperatives

Horizontal integration gives expression to the sixth principle guiding cooperatives, namely cooperation among cooperatives. At the level of values, this principle expresses solidarity. At the level of business practice, the principle emphasizes the point that cooperatives will serve their members most effectively when they work together (Birchall, 2004:18). While the scope and scale economies in the principle of integration among cooperatives at the secondary level do not take much to explain, such cooperation is yet to take place among cooperatives in Ghana.

Although these cooperatives come together in district/regional unions, at national associations, cooperation to boost the output of members is not emphasized. Primary societies and district/regional unions often see the national association or federation as quasi government agencies that provide useful services but do not belong to them (Birchall, 2004:15). Unfortunately this type of feeling is reinforced by the provision of subvention by the state to support these associations. In addition to the state support, the undemocratic practices which are rife in these associations make members of cooperatives and the primary societies distance themselves from the association. There are examples of DOC using its authority to compel some associations to call meetings, a directive some recalcitrant associations decide to contest in court. While one such association decided to take the Registrar of Cooperatives to court, 23 primary societies from the association decided to disassociate itself from the court case, a clear sign of disagreement between the association and member cooperatives on the principle of democratic control.

The poor integration and/or cooperation among the 15 central unions (federations) make them have very little shared activity. This situation is often blamed on the lack of resources (see Porvali, 1993). However it is important to observe that the Ministry of Manpower Youth and Employment, DOC, GCC and other stakeholders did collaborate on the cooperative development policy, revision of the cooperative law and the drafting of a new credit union bill, all of which promise to rejuvenate the cooperatives.

Weak district and regional unions

The district and regional unions are weak and internal democracy is not one of their strong values. The Ashanti Regional Manager of the Ghana Cooperative Distillers Association intimated that the unions do not generate their own income and rely on the societies. As a result, the activities of breakaway unions that do not excessively rely on members' contribution tend to make members of the traditional union believe that their welfare is not maximized. The regional office exemplified a very weak management which only bemoans the lack of resources to undertake any activity including cooperative education for officers.

Ghana Cooperatives Council (GCC)

The GCC is the apex body of the cooperative movement at the national level. It is headed by the secretary general who reports to the national executive committee. Membership of the GCC is made up of national associations. However not all the national associations are active. In recent times it has been difficult to count more than ten active affiliated national associations on the GCC. Staffing is one of the major problems of the apex body. Currently the total staffing position is 25 of which 15 are located in the head office in Accra and one located in each of the ten administrative regions of Ghana. The staffing situation is blamed on funding. Affiliated members are not able to fulfil their financial obligations to the apex body and the subvention is not adequate to finance the GCC to perform as expected. The current level of activity at the GCC is as a result of government determination to take the GCC off subvention. Thus, under the Agricultural Services Sub-sector Investment Programme (AgSSIP) resources have been made available through the Ministry of Food and Agriculture (MOFA) to the GCC to help organize farmer-based organizations into viable member-owned organizations and also to equip the GCC to render meaningful service to cooperatives for a fee. Also the GCC is pursuing active collaboration with other stakeholders to promote the new legal framework for cooperatives.

Alliances for action

The cooperative movement has not been active in building alliances. Very little exists beyond cooperation with MOFA under the aegis of the AgSSIP to promote farmer-based organizations. Perhaps the little that exists in the form of alliances beyond the MOFA arrangement includes collaboration between the financial sector cooperatives and the Ghana Micro Finance Action Research Network (GHAMFIN) and EMPRETEC Business Forum (Ghana). However, it is important to observe that the GCC's affiliation to the ICA has been very strong, despite the difficulty with the payment of its subscription.

An expanding cooperative sector

The current outlook of cooperatives may suggest that the sector has a significant potential for growth (see Figure 6.1). If the cumulative record of registered cooperatives is taken by sector, it shows that the agriculture sector is the most intensive sector for cooperative development (see Figure 6.3). The potential shown by the agriculture cooperatives is the outcome of a number of initiatives in the agriculture sector that identify the cooperative mode of organization as the route to poverty reduction and improved production. These activities include the AgSSIP mentioned above and Village Infrastructure Programme (VIP), also located in MOFA in which the DOC is involved in group formation and management. The groups formed have access to financial assistance from the VIP to enable them to undertake projects.

Figure 6.2: Registered cooperatives: 1998-2002

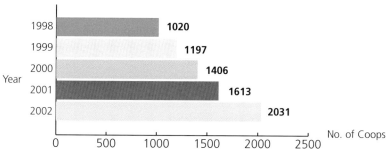

Figure 6.3: Distribution of cooperatives by sector: 2002

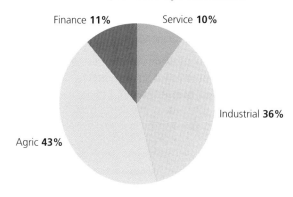

Source: Republic of Ghana, Annual Report 2001-2002, Department of Cooperatives, May 2003.

The association of group dynamics with DOC often has a snowball effect leading to some groups eventually registering as cooperatives. Another project involving the DOC and MOFA is the small-scale irrigation scheme. The small-scale Irrigation Development Project is aimed at facilitating the process whereby six thousand smallholder farmers would increase crop production by cultivating 2,590 hectares under irrigation and improve water management. As at the end of 2002, seventeen out of thirty-one irrigation farmers' groups in selected beneficiary communities were registered as cooperatives (DOC, 2003). In recent times the DOC also collaborated with MOFA to implement an Adventist Development and Relief Agency (ADRA) funded an agro-forestry project and an integrated development of an artisanal fisheries project.

Credit unions have also witnessed considerable growth in savings mobilization, loan advances to members, membership and number of credit unions. Data from CUA Ltd indicate that the number of credit unions moved from the 220 recorded in 2002 to 250 in 2004. A snapshot of recent growth indicators in the credit union movement is presented in Table 6.3 below.

Table 6.3: Growth indicators CUA Ltd

Year	No. of CU	Membership	Deposits ¢ billion	Loans ¢ billion	Assets ¢ billion
2000	200	76 356	55.0	38.0	68.4
2001	220	96 052	84.6	59.4	98.6
2002	220	125 000	150.2	88.3	200.0
2003	240	132 000	206.0	142.0	250.0
2004	250	156 000	314.0	262.0	348.0

Source: CUA (2005): 50 Years of Credit Unionism.

The growth of agriculture cooperatives and the role of DOC in organizing groups have the potential to cause an explosion in cooperatives. As it is, the groups which currently operate using cooperative principles may be convinced at a future date about the benefit of formal registration. The outcome of such a decision will be a rapid growth in cooperatives. The potential will be greatly enhanced by a large number of NGOs which are also actively promoting member-based organizations as evidenced in the case of the Zagyuri Community Women's Group.

Growth of cooperatives, fair trade and micro-finance

One of the areas where cooperatives and pre-cooperatives in Ghana are fairly weak is in the generation of surplus for members and community. However, the activities of Ghana Cooperative Pharmaceuticals Limited and also Kuapa Kokoo and its link with fair trade have demonstrated that growth of the cooperative sector can be enhanced greatly if the sector embraces fair trade (see Kayenwee, 2001).

Box 6.1: Kuapa Kokoo Limited: a symbol of success and hope in the Ghanaian cooperative sector

The rational for selecting the story of Kuapa Kokoo is in keeping with the understanding that the cooperative model is valid for all times. Kuapa Kokoo was initiated at the time the cooperative sector in Ghana can be said to have been on the decline. But more importantly, the cooperative came on the scene during the era of liberalization. The pioneers identified opportunities associated with the process leading to the liberalization of internal marketing of cocoa and positioned the cooperative to undertake a really profitable venture. Thus the misconception that cooperatives are organs for socialist mobilization subject to manipulation by government gave way to a market-oriented organization poised to take maximum advantage of economic opportunities. One of the pillars in the Kuapa success story is therefore the identification of the potential in the fair trade model. Indeed in order to take maximum advantage of the economic environment, Kuapa Kokoo which started as a limited liability company using a cooperative model was transformed into an organization best characterized as a mix of a cooperative, a limited liability company and a trust.

Kuapa Kokoo started operation in 1993 and is partly registered as a cooperative with approximately 45,000 members in 1,650 village societies. It currently employs 261 workers. The cooperative is multipurpose in character, comprising

- Farmers Union – a production cooperative.

- Kuapa Kokoo Ltd – farmer owned private licensed cocoa buying company i.e. the commercial and trading wing of the farmers' union.

- Kuapa Kokoo Farmers Trust – a trust company for managing premiums from sales to fair trade companies abroad.

- Kuapa Kokoo Credit Union – promoting savings and making credit easily accessible to members.

- Day Chocolate Company – manufacturing wing.

Governance of Kuapa Kokoo can be described as democratic in the true sense of the cooperative tradition. It is made up of a 3-tier structure with elected officers at all levels, namely village society, area council and national executive council. Seven members of the cooperative are elected as officers at village society level and they in turn elect three (3) of their number to the area council. Currently, the area councils number about 28. Each area council elects one member to the national executive council. The national executive council elects four (4) of its members to the board of Kuapa Kokoo Limited and another four (4) to Kuapa Kokoo Farmers Trust. Apart from elected officers the company employs professional management staff to carry out the day-to-day administration of the company and to produce value for money.

The success of Kuapa Kokoo can also be traced to useful exploitation of good external relations including cooperation with donors, links with NGOs, the Cooperative College of the UK and other external partners such as fair trade agencies. Furthermore, continuous education by the Research and Development Department of Kuapa Kokoo has aided primary societies to consistently improve the living conditions of farmers. In addition to engendering high bonding and solidarity among union members the village societies also provide community service in the form of potable water and school blocks.

The existence of a real organic link between the different tiers of the organisation gives Kuapa Kokoo a distinct strength that is missing from the wider cooperative movement. Kuapa Kokoo provides a useful model for production and marketing/service cooperatives. The credit unions attached to the cooperatives gave the financial power to members to secure inputs and also take care of their social needs when they need extra finances to do so without relying on other financial intermediaries. The other part of the success story is the quality management services provided by skilled managers to Kuapa Kokoo.

If the fair trade concept can be integrated with micro-finance activities, the growth of the cooperative sector could be enhanced tremendously. Already the impact of micro-finance activities can be felt on the growth of cooperatives and this explains their desire to benefit from one micro finance activity or the other. It may be argued that the desire to take advantage of micro-finance schemes gave birth to a significant number of cooperatives and almost all pre-cooperatives which happen to be operating along democratic principles and therefore form the potential for swelling the growth of the cooperative sector.

It is important to observe that whilst successful groups can metamorphose into cooperatives the greatest problem facing cooperative development and growth in Ghana is the impression created by politicians that for individuals to access credit they must form cooperatives. The outcome of this view is that most cooperatives seek resource inputs particularly credit believing that it is the only legitimate activity of the group. Once the credit or resource is secured or it is clear that such resources cannot be obtained, the groups cease to exist. This may account for the large number of cooperatives registered and the few that are active. For example only 609 out of 2,031 registered cooperatives prepared their accounts for audit in 2002. It is, however, important also to indicate that the use of audited accounts as performance indicators among cooperatives may be affected by inadequate resources available to the DOC to perform the audit. It is known that, in some instances, regional cooperative officers also fail to forward the accounts submitted to them to Accra for audit. However, failure to prepare and submit accounts for audit is a clear indication that societies are not very vibrant.

Support for cooperatives?

Government to government cooperation

As in all sectors of the economy donor activities proliferate in the cooperative sector but they are not crystallized into very conspicuous activities. They range from advocacy to technical assistance to farmer-based organizations. At the GCC, organizations like USAID, CLUSA and BUSAC supported advocacy workshops on the new cooperative bill and policy development and workshops on market access and development of cross-border trade in the sub-region. Also, the World Bank, the International Fund for Agricultural Development (IFAD) and the African Redevelopment Fund (ADF) of the African Development Bank are supporting the GCC through the AgSSIP to start a business development unit that will enable the council to render such services as audit and training to affiliated associations, cooperative societies and beyond. Such a development is meant to generate resources for the council and promote its bid to become independent of government whilst strengthening primary societies and district unions. The support programme included the supply of vehicles, computers, photocopiers and other resources as well as staff training to enable the GCC to operate a sustainable apex institution.

The rural financial services project at the Ministry of Finance has also provided resources to the GCC to educate cooperatives to embrace micro-finance and inculcate a savings culture among co-operators. The facility, which operates through rural banks, has seen a total of 104,438 members of agricultural, industrial and service cooperatives benefiting from the micro-finance scheme operated by the GCC at the end of 2002.

The credit union movement in Ghana has also benefited from technical and financial support from the Canadian Cooperative Association (CAA), Canadian International Development Agency (CIDA), World Council of Credit Unions, Ministry of Finance-supported Rural Financial Services Project, the German Technical Cooperation (GTZ), Bank of Ghana, International Finance Cooperation (IFC) and the United Nations Development Project (UNDP). The USAID also funded Ghana Susu Collectors Cooperative Association to the tune of ¢6,772 million for capacity building and institutional strengthening.

It is apparent from the nature of donor support that apart from the exchange between the CCA and the CUA Ltd, donor support did not take the form of movement-to-movement support. The greater proportion of donor support was technical support to production through government departments that are not directly responsible for the development of cooperatives, namely Ministry of Finance, Bank of Ghana and Ministry of Food and Agriculture. For example the Cooperative Programme of USDA Rural Development has been working in Ghana since 2000 to help extend western cooperative models to Ghana with the ultimate objective of helping farmers make the transition to commercial food production. The project offers technical assistance and training some of which is extended to the Cooperative College but it is a formal government-to-government relationship between USDA and MOFA (Dunn, 2004). However, it is important to acknowledge that the government's desire to revamp the cooperative sector is captured in the AgSSIP which made provision to pass on significant resources to the GCC (Republic of Ghana, 1999:9). Similarly resources were made available to the DOC and the Cooperative College to support their statutory functions. However because of the depth of resource constraint in the GCC, DOC and the Cooperative

College the level of resources transferred into the donor supported schemes is unable to make a significant impact on the performance of the institutions concerned.

Finally, donor support for the development of the new cooperative policy, cooperative bill and the credit union bill must be commended as they help to tackle the root cause of the non-performing cooperatives. The new policy and the draft laws aim to make cooperatives market friendly whilst promoting the independence of the cooperative movement from government control.

Governance and institutional support for primary societies

In Ghana the basic unit of the cooperative movement is the primary society, the supreme decision making body of the primary society being the assembly of members at a general meeting. At the district/regional level, the primary societies in specific and/or allied economic activities operating in a particular administrative zone of the country form a district/regional Union. Next in order is the association of regional unions in specific and/or allied economic activities coming together to form a national association. At the apex of the movement is the Ghana Cooperative Council (GCC), which is the melting point of primary societies, district/regional unions, and national associations. The GCC is responsible for implementing decisions of the quadrennial congress.

In this structure members of primary societies expect that the unions, associations and the council will provide voice and representation around the policy table as they interact with government departments. Ultimately, members of cooperatives expect significant improvements in efficiency, output, and standard of living when institutions higher up the movement's structure perform their functions effectively. However, the stakeholders suggest that institutions higher up the structure have failed to deliver on their mandate. The district/regional unions in particular are not visible and sometimes appear to overlap or to be in competition with the national associations. This explains why the financial cooperatives adopted a two-tier system whereby primary societies were given direct affiliation to CUA by paying affiliation fees and subscription to CUA shares. The primary societies in the cooperative credit union are therefore directly represented at the biennial conferences, CUA's Board of Directors and committees by delegates, removing the non-performing regional chapter as the unions are called among the financial cooperatives.

Stakeholders have suggested that the unions and associations have relied on government subvention to function more as a secretariat than as developmental or promotional institutions. For instance in the budget year 2000, the GCC had a total of ₵107,215,500.00 of which ₵97,537,500.00 constituted personnel emoluments. Indeed all operational funds of the GCC in that year came from government (GCC, 2000:3). The perception that middle and upper tiers of the cooperative movement are subvented make primary societies reluctant to pay their subscriptions to institutions higher up the movement hierarchy.

The GCC admits its weaknesses and attributes the situation to the decline of the cooperative movement as a whole and over-dependency on government support. Weak management, lack of coordination and undue interference by authorities is the way the GCC characterized the state of the movement in its proposal for strengthening the body dated September 2000. The foregoing characterization by the Ghana Cooperative Council confirms the views expressed by staff of the Department of Cooperatives.

Perhaps the greatest challenge for creating a supportive cooperative structure that will be appreciated by members is the tendency for the GCC, the national associations and governmental departments to rely on multilateral and bilateral donors and non-governmental organisations to provide resources to strengthen and reform their structures to respond to the liberalized environment. Hopefully, the outcome of these restructuring activities will improve the services rendered to the primary societies by institutions higher up the movement hierarchy. However, a critique of the strategies adopted so far will suggest a conflict of interest when the DOC is involved in the implementation of activities within cooperatives such as mobilization while at the same time being the regulator, supervisor, and auditor. In addition, whilst the reform effort is targeted at making the cooperative sector independent from government intervention, the greater challenge is to make the cooperative movement a successful market-oriented institution that does not neglect the social needs of the poor.

Does the cooperative sector in Ghana make an impact?

Cooperatives: supporting self-employment

Employment generation (through the diversification of activities and choosing products with higher economic returns to the producers e.g., value-addition through agro- processing, etc.) is one of the cornerstones of cooperative development in poor countries with a high agriculture content in their economies. Where a large number of people, including youth and women, are involved in agriculture-related activities cooperatives could become the focal points for the dissemination of information to the community. By networking with parallel institutions, centralized institutions and members and providing better access to market information, cooperatives can provide greater business opportunities to their members and thereby increase output and employment (Cracknell, 1996).

In Ghana it is practically impossible to have a direct estimate of employment generated in the cooperative sector as a result of an acute deficiency in employment information in Ghana (see Tsekpo, 2005). The situation is made more difficult by the weak management capabilities of the cooperative movement. The absence of analytical skills in the movement has also manifested itself in the weak presentation of data and inconsistent issue of annual reports. Table 6.4 gives a rough estimate of employment in the cooperative sector in addition to self-employed membership of the cooperatives. The estimates are based on annual reports of the DOC.

It is important to observe that membership of some cooperatives may be crudely equated to self-employment in which case the lower portion of the table can be taken as an indicator of the employment and/or socio-economic potential of the cooperative sector.

The major obstacle to estimating employment in the cooperative sector is that the majority of cooperative societies in the agricultural and industrial sector remain in the informal economy. The cooperatives have not succeeded in transforming the informal operations as yet and hence the difficulty of isolating the employment effects of the activities in the cooperative sector. Capturing informal employment has always presented a major measurement problem; however, one certainty about informal employment in Ghana is that it correlates highly with poverty (Tsekpo, 2004).

Table 6.4: Estimated in employment/self-employed cooperative members

Sector	2000*	2002**
Ghana Coop Distillers/Retailer Assoc.(staff)	1 987	1 933
Ghana Cooperative Pharmaceutical Ltd. (Staff)	17	14
CUA Ltd. (staff)	328#	488#
Kuapa Kokoo Ltd. (staff)	200	261
Ghana Coop Poultry Farms Assoc. (staff)	15	15
Pioneer Coop Cold store Complex (staff)	21	21
Ghana Coop College	12	12
Department of Cooperatives	387	364
Ghana Cooperative Council	19	25
	2 986	**3 133**
Ghana Coop Distillers/Retailer Assoc. (membership)	35 670	35 392
Ghana Coop Distillers/Retailer Assoc. (Assistants 2 per member)	72 000	72 000
Ghana Cooperative Pharmaceutical Ltd. (membership)	184	176
Kuapa Kokoo Ltd (farmers)	35 000	35 000
Ghana Coop Transport Societies (membership)	0	28 800
Pioneer Coop Coldstore Complex (membership) Agricultural Cooperatives (432 soc*20; 878*20)	17	17
(Estimated at 20 members per society)	8 640	17 560
Ghana Cooperative Fisheries Association Ltd. (membership)	_	15 000
Ghana Cooperative Marketing Association Ltd. (membership)	_	5 200
	151 511	**209 145**

Source: Based on Estimates in DOC annual Reports * Annual Report: 1999-2000 published May 2001; ** Annual Report: 2001-2002 published May 2003. # CUA Ltd, Computer Services Department.

Employment generation potential of cooperatives

The greatest potential for employment generation is in the area of agricultural service cooperatives. Developing the potential of agricultural service cooperatives is consistent with Ghana's vision of improving methods of production and processing of agricultural produce in Ghana's Growth and

Poverty Reduction Strategy (GPRS II). This realization explains the attention given to the sector in terms of promotional programmes by donors and government alike. However, the experience from the case studies presented in the appendix and elsewhere (see Hussi, Murphy, Lindberg and Brenneman, 1993) would suggest that to maximize the potential of agricultural services cooperatives for employment then critical consideration must be given to sound management. A management capable of servicing cooperatives particularly to move pre-cooperatives to become fully fledged cooperatives where they are schooled in cooperative principles and the dynamics of market organizations is a pre-requisite for success.

To illustrate the point above, the Zagyuri Community Women's Group was initially formed by 30 women with assistance from the Opportunities Industrialization Centres Ghana. The progress made by the group attracted other women in the community. However, for effective group dynamics it was undesirable to increase the number significantly. Consequently, a second group of 30 was formed to make the current total of sixty. The women in this group and officers at Opportunities Industrialization Centres Ghana indicate that if management capacity improves, the group could take on additional women in the community who desire to be part of the progress being made by the group. The management of Kuapa Kokoo also observed that the success story of the farmers' cooperative was infectious as membership grew from 2,000 in 22 villages to about 45,000 in 1,200 villages in the five major cocoa growing regions in a little over a decade.

Cooperatives and poverty reduction

Poverty reduction is the main objective of Ghana's economic and social development programme. Indeed the medium-term development framework as captured in the Growth and Poverty Reduction Strategy indicates that the agro-industrial link is expected to be the main lever for Ghana's poverty reduction strategy. This is the result of the fact that most of the rural population earn their incomes from farming. Thus, the AgSSIP programme is expected to contribute to widespread poverty reduction through supporting technological change, innovation in crop, livestock and fish farming, forestry production and in agro-processing, thereby improving returns to all production factors, including land and labour. The programme envisages strengthening producer organizations such as cooperatives and farmers' groups to provide better services to members to facilitate technology adoption by improving access to input and facilitating marketing.

Assess to micro-finance is considered a vital element in poverty reduction as it improves the ability of small-scale farmers and micro-enterprises to secure inputs and thereby maximize their output. The credit unions are in pole position to provide micro-finance and this recognition led to their active participation in the Ghana Micro Finance Network (GHAMFIN). Table 6.5 below shows the regional distribution of the value of resources mobilized by credit unions and the magnitude of loans outstanding in the books of the credit union at the end of 2004. Indeed this represents a great potential for financial resource mobilization.

Table 6.5: Portfolio of cooperative credit unions association, December 2004

Region	Shares	Savings	Loans Outstanding	Total Assets
Great Accra	2 939 122 096	62 886 244 989	38 207 187 930	76 965 406 756
Ashanti	5 099 096 017	72 620 136 703	60 680 982 712	90 586 351 397
Brong Ahafo	1 844 851 024	26 531 136 487	19 307 254 056	33 613 451 376
Central	2 266 498 706	44 532 740 832	33 003 476 527	65 191 944 524
Eastern	1 491 849 960	26 977 159 838	20 824 181 111	33 175 195 655
Tema	8 179 719 598	36 727 835 694	31 079 375 794	50 975 262 914
Northern	522 220 170	6 495 281 302	5 090 677 005	7 958 392 251
Upper East	156 986 161	4 096 155 569	3 475 636 331	5 145 484 819
Upper West	411 918 692	6 143 820 880	4 492 821 859	7 594 944 658
Volta	1 297 290 350	18 233 486 889	14 638 910 156	23 816 041 172
Western	1 581 315 029	25 908 774 600	19 301 699 335	29 977 844 129
Total	25 790 867 803	331 152 773 783	250 102 202 816	425 000 319 651

Source: CUA Ltd, Computer Services Department.

At the primary society level, the management of the University of Ghana Cooperative Credit Union also indicated that members of the credit union frequently accessed loans to support informal businesses. These informal businesses are known to offer part-time employment to housewives and domestic assistants in the University Staff Village whilst providing supplementary income to workers of the university community. Indeed the University of Ghana Cooperative Credit Union after a study of the uses to which loans and withdrawals by members are applied listed business as one of the nine substantive uses to which members direct their funds. Other categories to which members apply funds taken from the credit union include household goods, housing/rent/building, school fees, funerals, medical bills, transport, emergencies and personal. It is apparent that regardless of the amount, resources devoted to the areas listed will have a significant effect on poverty reduction.

The resolve of the primary societies to work towards poverty reduction is also demonstrated by the mission statement of the University of Ghana Cooperative Credit Union as follows: "University of Ghana Credit Union is a financial cooperative. Its purpose is to provide competitive and quality financial services to its members at reasonable costs; and to build a sustainable financial institution based on sound business principles and also to raise the standard of living of its members, their dependants and the community at large". Indeed the commitment of the cooperatives and pre-cooperatives studied towards poverty reduction can also be seen in their contribution to the development of community infrastructure such as a budgetary allocation to the university hospital by the University of Ghana Credit Union, a financial contribution to school building, safe water systems and so on by Kuapa Kokoo and the Zagyuri Community Women's Group.

Cooperatives and the social protection challenge

Social protection among cooperatives is largely an informal activity; movement staff is in the formal sector and by law are protected under the Social Security and National Insurance Scheme because they are in an employer-employee relationship. But members of primary societies who operate mainly in the informal sector often constitute themselves into mutual help groups with their own rules that are guided by regulations that are often not legally constituted. These groups make donations to members during illness, death, naming and wedding ceremonies. Some have argued that the solidarity enjoyed by members of these groups is one of the motivating factors prompting individuals to join cooperatives. The Zagyuri Community Women's Group and Kuapa Kokoo confirm the existence of the mutual help packages for members. Although work place cooperatives like the University of Ghana Cooperative Credit Union do not have formal packages for mutual assistance, the provision of parting gifts to members who exit the "Common Bond" as a result of retirement or separation from the university constitute an ample demonstration of solidarity. Credit unions are generally predisposed to social protection by providing resources for social obligations such as to bury the dead, educate the children, to receive good medication, to improve housing and to fulfil some other social obligations (CUA, 2005:31).

Cooperatives and voice

Currently GCC is supposed to give a voice to co-operators. However, its capacity to do as expected is limited. For instance whilst cooperatives were identified in the Ghana Poverty Reduction Strategy I as a conduit for improving agriculture and employment (see ICA and ILO, 2005), the GCC as the voice of the movement was at no time involved in the consultative process leading to the formulation of the strategy. Consequently, the AgSSIP investment in the GCC is to improve the capacity of the GCC to promote popular participation of primary societies in the governance of the GCC and district associations. Improving the productivity of cooperative members and the profitability of their activities will make their organizations viable and interest them in the activities of the movement. The challenge is how to overcome the funding difficulties currently experienced by the GCC. The poor finances adversely affect both the human resource base as well as the resources for effective administrative work.

Conclusion

Despite the realization that cooperatives hold promise for improving agricultural output and employment the sector is currently less vibrant than expected. This state of affairs may be attributed to weak government policy on cooperative development. In recent times, attempts have been made to re-orient cooperatives to work in a liberalized environment but there is no clear statement on their role in the national economy. The provision of adequate resources to the DOC and the GCC to carry out their mandate and interface with other government departments for promoting small and medium-scale enterprises will be necessary to make the institutions effective in the discharge of their functions.

It is also important to observe that the weak movement portrayed in this paper is due to the absence of a real organic link between the different tiers of the cooperative movement. The apex bodies are on subvention and lack the full complement of staff and resources to be efficient and to render useful service to the primary societies. On the other hand the primary societies position themselves to take advantage of programmes and projects brokered by the lead agencies particularly in the area of finance. Once the lead agencies cease to supply any inputs the primary societies stop reporting to them on their performance.

The absence of social protection schemes in the informal sector make people look to cooperatives as a source of solidarity in times of need. Thus, many societies keep together because of social action more than economic factors. This is indeed evident in the weak primary societies remaining as informal sector operators, which are not able to generate any surplus as a cooperative. Most of the time these societies tax their members to provide community service.

To end on a bright note, the experiences of Ghana Cooperative Pharmaceuticals Ltd and Kuapa Kokoo provide a useful model for production and marketing/service cooperatives. The credit unions attached to these cooperatives give the financial muscle to members to take advantage of their activities. The other part of the success story is the quality management provided by skilled managers to the two cooperative societies. The latter observation is also true of the credit unions. There is also potential for growth in the cooperative sector given the large number of member-controlled groups that use cooperative principles even though they do so currently to attract micro-finance.

Sources

This article is based on a series of documents and interviews, carried out during the autumn of 2005. The author wishes to thank: Mrs. Aba Smith and Mr. Newton Addo (Ghana Cooperative Council); Mr. Kweku Mensah Arthur and Mr. Isaac Oppong Manu (Ghana Cooperative College); Mr. J. Acheampong Arthur (Credit Union Association Ltd.); Mr. K. Ohemeng-Tinyase (Kuapa Kokoo); Ms. Awah Mahama (OICT Zagyuri Community Women's Group); Mrs. Philomena Dadzie (University of Ghana Cooperative Credit Union); Mr. J.B. Donkor and Mr. Francis Gyamfi (Ghana Cooperative Distillers Association, Ashanti Region); Ms. Edith Dzidzonu and Mr. George Somuah (DOC); Mr. John K. Nyako (DOC, Accra Metropolitan Assembly); Mr. K. Adjei, Mr. Andrew Alegewe and Mr. Isaac Bondzie (DOC, different district offices).

Bibliography

- Birchall J. (2003), *Rediscovering the Cooperative Advantage: Poverty Reduction through Self-help*, ILO, Geneva.
- Birchall J. (2004), *Cooperatives and Millennium Development Goals*, ILO, Geneva.
- Cracknell M. (1996), *Cooperatives in the Context of Globalization and Liberalization* on http://www.fao.org/sd/rodirect/roan0001.htm, posted March 1996.
- CUA Ltd. (2005), *Ghana Cooperative Credit Union: 50 Years of Credit Unionism*, Jirapa.
- Department of Cooperatives (1990), *History of Ghana Cooperatives: 1928-1985*, Nsamankow Press, Accra.
- DOC (s.d.) *The Cooperative as a Business*, Educational material prepared by the DOC.
- Dunn J. R. (2004), *USDA co-op development efforts support commercial farming in Ghana*, http://www.findarticles.com/p/articles/mi_moKFU/is_3_71/¬ai_6276239/print.
- FAO (2003), *The changing context: 'Cooperatives make development happen!'*, http://www.copacgva.org/idc/fao-idc2003.htm, posted: 4 July 2003.
- GCC (2000), *Proposal for Strengthening the Ghana Cooperative Council.* (Business Plan of Action), revised September, 2000, unpublished document.
- GCC (2000), *Secretary General's Report to the Seventh Congress of the Council – 29th August 2000*, GCC, Accra.
- GCC (sd), *Secretary General's Report to the Fourth Congress (1987-1989)*, GCC, Accra.
- Hussi P., Murphy J., Lindberg O. & Brenneman L. (1993), *The Development of Cooperation and other Rural Organization. The Role of the World Bank*, The World Bank, Washington D.C.
- ICA & ILO (2005), *Cooperating out of Poverty: The Global Cooperative Campaign Against Poverty*, Geneva.
- Kayenwee C. (2001), 'Ghana: Ghana Cooperative Pharmaceuticals Limited', in Ed. M-F. Countre, D. Feber, M. Levin, & A-B Nippied, *Transition to Cooperative Entrepreneurship: Case studies from Armenia,*

China, Ethiopia, Ghana, Poland, Russia, Uganda and Vietnam, ICA and ILO, Geneva.

- NDPC (2005), *Growth and Poverty Reduction Strategy: The Coordinated Programme for the Economic and Social Development of Ghana (2006-2009)* Draft 1.2.

- Ofei K. A. (2001), 'Retooling Credit Unions: the Case of Credit Union Association of Ghana', *IFLIP Research Paper 01-3*, ILO, Geneva.

- Oppong-Manu I. (2004), *Cooperatives and Cooperative Education in Ghana: Perspective from a Cooperative Educator*, A Paper Presented at the Centre for Cooperatives, University of Wisconsin, 16 September 2004.

- Porvali H. (1993), *Ghana: Review of Cooperatives and other Rural Organisations*, Report n° 12027, Africa Region, World Bank, Washington DC.

- Republic of Ghana (1999), *Roles and Impact of AgSSIP on Poverty Reduction*, prepared by GCC for the Tenth Correlative Group meeting on Ghana, Accra, November 1999.

- Republic of Ghana (2000), *National Cooperative Development Policy Framework*, Ministry of Employment and Social Welfare, April 2000.

- Republic of Ghana (2003), Annual Reports (1999-2000), Department of Cooperatives, GFC Assembly Press, Accra.

- Republic of Ghana (2003), Annual Reports (2001-2002), Department of Cooperatives, Klymacs Ventures, Accra.

- Taylor M.P. (2003), 'Ghana: Building Better Co-op Law', in *Cooperative Business Journal*, June 2003.

- Tsekpo Anthony (2004), *Wages, Incomes and Employment for Poverty Alleviation in Ghana*, A Report prepared for TUC (Ghana) & ILO.

- Tsekpo A. (2005), 'Employment: The Missing Link in Ghana's Macroeconomic Framework', *Ghana Trades Union Congress Policy Bulletin*, vol. 1, n° 1, July 2005.

Chapter Seven – Political and Genuine Cooperatives in Enugu State, Nigeria

by Anselm Enete[1]

Introduction

A cooperative society, according to Okonkwo (1989) is an association of individuals who voluntarily come together to solve their common economic needs through self-help. In other words, people join cooperative societies to become prosperous. Even a rich country, with the most benevolent and paternal government cannot do for its citizens a fraction of what they can achieve for themselves by organization on a cooperative basis (Puri 1979). For instance, farmers' cooperative societies are formed to bring in more agricultural inputs and produce marketing services to members, increase competition in the agricultural service sector and provide savings and credit services to members, among many other functions (Porvali 1993).

The history of cooperative societies in Nigeria dates back to the early 1930s when Mr. C.F. Strickland was appointed by government to study the possibility of introducing cooperatives in Nigeria. His report, which was accepted by government, was followed by the Nigerian cooperative society ordinance in 1935 and the regulations for the running of cooperative societies in 1936. Pioneer cooperative societies, particularly cocoa and palm produce farmers' organizations then started. By the end of 1944, there were up to 181 cooperative societies in Nigeria, thus showing encouraging progress. The Cooperative Federation of Nigeria (CFN) was also formed the same year (Okonkwo 1989).

Today, estimates put the number of cooperatives in Nigeria at about 50,000 with no reliable information on individual membership and further structure.

---

[1] Anselm Enete is currently a Lecturer at the Department of Agricultural Economics, University of Nigeria, Nsukka. From 1994-1998, he was a Research Fellow with the Collaborative Study of Cassava in Africa (COSCA), which was based at the International Institute of Tropical Agriculture (IITA), Ibadan, Nigeria. From 1999–2004, he was at the Catholic University of Leuven (Belgium) where he completed a PhD programme in Agricultural Economics.

This may be attributable to the fact that Nigeria has a federal structure with each federating unit independent in matters of cooperatives. Ten years ago, Porvali (1993) also noted that there are hardly any systematically compiled data at the Nigerian national level on cooperatives.

The purpose of this study is to give a qualitative overview of the cooperative sector in Enugu State of southeast Nigeria. The study will highlight the strengths and weaknesses of the cooperative sector in the state by assessing the role of government, the vibrancy of the cooperative movement, the potential of the cooperative sector to generate employment, reduce poverty and enhance social protection.

The information for this write-up was collected through a structured questionnaire and some unstructured interviews with key informants in the cooperative sector in Enugu State. First at the Department of Cooperatives, the officer responsible for the registration of cooperatives was interviewed. Secondly, based on choice, a structured questionnaire was given to the executive secretary of the cooperative federation of Enugu State, which he filled in and returned. Thirdly, the principal of Enugu State Cooperative College and the divisional cooperative officer in charge of Nsukka Division were interviewed.

At the primary society level, the secretary of the Amagu Omo Umulokpe Farmers Multipurpose Cooperative Society, a leading member of Uzondu Cooperative Society, three leading members of three cooperative societies[2] and the secretary of the Lions Micro-credit Society, University of Nigeria, Nsukka, were interviewed.

Cooperatives in Enugu State: a fact file

In Enugu State, there are 6,985 registered cooperatives with about 70,000 members, as at October 2005. Just as agriculture is the dominant economic activity in Nigeria (CBN, 2003), agricultural cooperatives dominate non-agricultural cooperatives in Enugu State (Table 7.1). The number of registered cooperatives increased at a phenomenal speed especially between 2003 and 2005. This could be because there is now a relatively better environment for the cooperative movement than during the military regime.

The major activities of the agricultural cooperatives include procurement of

---

[2] The three societies of which he is a member are: Nguru Nsukka Farmers Multipurpose Cooperative Society, Modern Farmers Multipurpose Cooperative Society, Nsukka and Pigree Farmers Cooperative Society, Nsukka.

fertilizer, securing of loans from government and exchange of labour. Except for the Amagu Omo Umulokpe Farmers Multipurpose Cooperative Society that helps members in the marketing of their farm produce, the other agricultural primary societies studied do not engage in agricultural marketing on behalf of members. While all the agricultural cooperative societies are located in villages or semi-urban areas, all the non-agricultural cooperative societies are found in urban areas.

Table 7.1: Number of cooperative societies by type: 2000–2005

Year Type	2000	2001	2002	2003	2004	2005
Agriculture	793	871	1 025	1 842	3 615	6 115
Non-agriculture	235	238	250	258	821	870

Source: Department of Cooperatives, Enugu State.

The state operates a three-tier system in which primary societies are affiliated with secondary societies at the local government level, which in turn are affiliated with the cooperative federation, the apex body of Enugu state. With 17 local governments in the state, there are therefore 17 secondary societies. With the number of local governments fixed at 17 (at least for now), the number of secondary societies has remained static over the years while the number of primary societies has shown remarkable progress since 2000, probably because government grants to poor people are most often routed through cooperatives.

About 90% of the registered cooperatives in Enugu State are agricultural. The remaining 10% is shared equally between credit cooperatives and produce marketing cooperatives. The profile of the membership of cooperatives in Enugu State is predominantly rural smallholder farmers. They are also among the poorest segments of society (World Bank 2000).

The changing role of government

In general, the current legislation guiding the registration and operations of cooperative societies in Nigeria consists primarily of the Federal Government's "Nigerian Cooperative Societies Decree 90 of 1993". However, each state government has the power to legislate on matters of cooperatives. The 1993 legislation established the director of cooperatives both at the federal and state levels and the Department of Cooperatives, whose parent ministry varies from one state to the other. In Enugu State, it is under the Ministry of Human Development and Poverty Reduction. The law basically does not restrict cooperatives to any particular activity, as long as the overall objective of the association is the promotion of the socio-economic interests of its members. However, the state, through the director of cooperatives, still influences greatly the management of cooperatives. The director can decide on matters like the number of shares a member can hold or the tenure of office of management committee members. In Enugu State for instance, cooperative department personnel are seconded to manage all the secondary cooperative societies in the state and the state apex body. The state cooperative college is just an integral part of the Department of Cooperatives.

As a result of this, the cooperative development policy has been moulded by the inclination of the federal and state governments to use cooperatives as a tool for implementing their policies. Many cooperative societies have been formed through government directives to certain categories of government officials to form a given number of cooperatives in their villages of origin. In some other cases, cooperatives spring up in response to government promises of providing subsidized services to members. These two categories could be referred to as "political cooperatives" which usually do not stand the test of time.

However, since the advent of civilian administration (1999) in the country, the overall government policy has shifted towards privatization and liberalization. In Enugu State for instance, government employees no longer run the affairs of primary societies (at least not directly), although they are still directly involved in the management of secondary societies and the apex body as noted above. And in line with the recognition of the potential of cooperatives in the fight against poverty, the state government created in 2004 a separate ministry whose major responsibility is cooperative development. In addition, government supports cooperatives through tax exemptions, promotion and technical assistance in management and controls cooperatives through registration, monitoring and supervision. All the people interviewed (from the Department of Cooperatives down to the primary societies) during this research describe the registration requirements of cooperatives in Enugu State as all right. This suggests that the direct involvement of government in cooperative business is with the best of intentions, although in this case, government best intentions do not always translate into the best conditions for cooperative development. Recommendation 193 of the ILO seems strange to most people involved in cooperative business in the state under review.

Cooperatives: not many private initiatives as yet

The memberships of political cooperatives are usually hurriedly put together with no special bond or mutual trust. Hence, they most often die prematurely. For instance, Chisom Edem-ani Women Farmers Multipurpose Cooperative Society and Nru Nsukka Women Farmers Multipurpose Cooperative Society, both with a membership of ten women were formed in 2001 but by 2004, they had already ceased to exist.

However, there is a fairly good bond, based on mutual trust and common objective among the membership of primary societies whose formation was engineered from among the members and not from the government. This is because they tend to withstand the test of time better. For instance, the Uzondu Cooperative Society in Nsukka with a membership of 100 has lasted for over thirty years. Similarly, the University Women Cooperative Society (University of Nigeria, Nsukka) has lasted for over twenty-five years. Adeyemo (2004) noted that cooperatives have proved the most effective and superior organization on account of their honest service and loyal patronage of their members.

The vibrancy and sustainability of cooperatives in Enugu State can best be gauged by the increase in the number of cooperatives registered annually rather than by the growth in membership, the latter most of the time remaining static. For instance, the three cooperative societies remained virtually the same in terms of membership except for losses through death and they have each existed for more than five years. In addition, the scale of operation of most societies is very low. Although there is no reliable figure available indicating their rate of turnover, respondents indicated it to be rather low. Most of the societies do not employ any permanent staff either.

The above underscores the point being made by one of interviewees that most people form cooperatives only because of the financial and technical assistance expected from government or its agencies. The society as a body therefore becomes poorly developed, since it is just looked upon as a conduit for credit. Puri (1979) observed that wherever cooperatives rely too heavily on finances from outside, their autonomy becomes vulnerable, so that financial self-reliance is a necessary condition for self- regulation within the movement.

Box 7.1: Two genuine cooperatives

(a) **The Lions Micro Credit Society, University of Nigeria, Nsukka.**
This society started in 2001 with the aim of mobilizing credit for poor
members of the society and also engaging in foodstuff storage and
distribution. Five members founded the society with an initial share
capital of about $19. Today, the society has grown to 122 members
with a share capital of about $11,450. At the moment, they advance
credit to about 20 persons per year at an average of $6 per credit
recipient and charge a 5% interest rate.

(b) **The University of Nigeria, Nsukka (UNN) Women Cooperative
Society.** This society started in 1980 as an offshoot of the National
Association of University Women with the aim of protecting,
projecting and serving the interest of women in the society. Today, the
society has grown from about ten members to over 200 members. It
has established a supermarket that employs about two people, a
nursery school that employs about 15 people and a children's library,
all of which serve the university community in particular and the wider
society in general.

These two societies have one thing in common; they were all established on
the basis of genuine problem solving cooperation and not on the priming
of any external force like the government. And this is the essential
ingredient for successful and vibrant cooperative development.

As a result of the above, the affairs of most societies (management,
accounting, public relations, marketing, etc.) are entirely handled by officers
elected from the membership, despite their limited skills in these areas. These
elected officers can sometimes hijack the affairs of the organization for their
selfish ends. A case in point is the Uzondu Cooperative Society in Nsukka that
has split into two factions with both factions in a legal tussle over the control
of the society.

However, the affairs of the secondary societies and the state apex body are
managed by government employees seconded to them by the government.
This may also not be conducive for cooperative development. Hussi et al.
(1993) noted that in order to make cooperatives effective private sector
enterprises, their freedom to operate without undue interference with their
management and business activities must be ensured. The greater the degree

of government interference in cooperative enterprise, the greater the degree of incompetence and failure.

Regarding input marketing, the government has retained a central role in the distribution of fertilizer – the major input commonly sourced by most farmers. The cooperatives have had little or no impact in this respect. This may not only be because of the generally small size of farmers' cooperatives, but also because the members of these societies are smallholder farmers, thus putting the farmers' cooperatives in the position of helpless buyers like any other individual. Further, integration among cooperatives is not yet a common feature, perhaps also because government employees manage the affairs of cooperatives at the secondary and the apex levels. The result of this is perhaps poor business acumen and managerial deficiencies, also reflected in the negligible impact of cooperatives on agricultural produce marketing which is controlled almost entirely by private traders.

However, most societies practice democratic equality because every member has just one vote/voice in the body irrespective of the number of shares held in the society. The cooperative manual for field staff in Enugu State puts it thus – irrespective of variations in the amount of shares held in a cooperative society, every member has an equal voice in the affairs of the society. Every member of the society is encouraged to buy as many shares as possible but not more than one fifth of the total number of shares.

Because of their size, many societies also do not have any permanent property (i.e. landed property) of their own. Such societies use one of their members' houses for their general meetings.

With regard to membership training, there are frequent government sponsored seminars and workshops at the secondary and the apex level. In addition, the Department of Cooperatives sends out field staff to every community, their duties including the organization of periodic education and training for the members of primary societies.

Limited level of integration

The primary cooperatives studied very much live in perfect isolation. Still a number of joint activities are developed by the cooperatives in Enugu State. Some form of vertical integration is taking place with regard to fertilizer procurement, other farm inputs and farm produce marketing. The activities across sectors include loan procurement and educational activities organized by the federations, both at the secondary and apex levels.

At the secondary level, the cooperatives are staffed with employees of government. Their activities include providing technical assistance to, monitoring and supervision of, primary societies, guiding pre-coops into becoming full coops, organizing seminars and workshops for the membership of primary societies, promotion of the activities of cooperatives in local government. None of the secondary societies studied directly engaged in any economic activity either for itself or on behalf of primary societies.

Similarly, the state apex body is staffed with government employees on secondment from the Department of Cooperatives. The executive secretary of the body, who was interviewed during the course of this research listed the activities of the federation as: (a) lobbying the government on behalf of cooperatives, (b) promotion of the activities of cooperatives, (c) providing technical assistance and training to cooperatives, and (d) linking cooperatives to donors. The effectiveness of the first function here is open to question because it may be difficult for government to lobby itself. The state apex body is also reportedly not politicized because it is not controlled by the political party in power.

Some of the institutional changes that have affected the cooperative sector in Enugu State for instance include the abolition of regional cooperative laws in favour of the National Cooperative Act of 1993; the phasing out in 1998 (at the national level) of the certificate in cooperatives being awarded by cooperative colleges in favour of the National Diploma (ND) in Cooperatives; the revitalization of the state-owned Cooperative College; and the creation of the Ministry of Human Development and Poverty Reduction in 2004, in which the Cooperative Department holds sway. There was also at national level the merging (in 1998) of the two previous Departments of Cooperatives (one in the Ministry of Labour and the other in the Ministry of Agriculture) into one department, now located in the Ministry of Agriculture.

Actual and potential growth of genuine cooperatives

Three main factors drive the growth of registered cooperatives in Enugu State – (a) external credit or state aid, (b) politics, and (c) genuine problem solving cooperation.

Unfortunately, neither of the first two categories could lead to sustainable cooperative development. Too much reliance on state financial assistance could make cooperatives vulnerable and hence subject to state manipulation. Porvali (1993) reported that the reasons for poorly developed cooperative savings and credit activity in most states of Nigeria can at least be partly linked to the initial motives behind the formation of cooperatives. The primary motive to cooperate has been and still is the promise of cheap credit from external sources. On the other hand, cooperatives formed as a result of politics lack the requisite motivation and hence fizzle out with time. For instance, one of our respondents reported that some local government functionaries were recently directed to register cooperative societies in their wards. They of course complied with the directive, but most of the cooperatives registered in this way died prematurely.

The third category has all the ingredients for sustainable and vibrant cooperative development. Such cooperatives are not only founded on a commonly felt need with a common bond and motivation but also tend to be largely self-sustaining and hence largely away from the prying eyes of the state. For instance, Lions Micro-credit Society, University of Nigeria, Nsukka that started in 2001 with a membership of five people now has a total of 122 members. The interesting thing about this society is that it operates in all respects as a cooperative society but has refused to register with government to avoid interference in its affairs. Registered cooperatives in this category tend to stand the test of time paticularly well. For instance, Nguru Nsukka Farmers Multipurpose Cooperative Society that was inaugurated in 1970 is still intact. Despite its present travails, Uzondu Cooperative Society also belongs to this category. Most active primary agricultural cooperatives operate simple savings schemes and issue loans from accumulated funds to member farmers for personal needs and production purposes (Porvali 1993).

Donors: a tricky role

All the people interviewed during the course of this research indicate that there is only one donor to the cooperatives in Enugu State at the moment – the government. We interpret this to mean that all other donors (foreign or local) to the cooperatives go through the government. The donors' financial support comes mainly through the National Agricultural and Cooperative Bank and the assistance is channeled directly to the cooperative societies. Other types of assistance include general training through seminars, workshops, government cooperative experts in the field, and technical/managerial assistance especially to cooperative federations (both at the secondary and apex levels) and the Cooperative College. The importance of this donor support, especially in finance, cannot be overemphasized. For instance, most societies can only embark on capital intensive projects with donor assistance.

The problem in this regard is that loan recovery is very low, especially with the "political" cooperatives, which spring up primarily to collect such loans. This is because many of such cooperatives die even before the loan matures for recovery. Porvali (1993) also reported a low percentage of loan recovery by cooperative financial institutions in Nigeria. In addition, there is the problem of donors (i.e. government) not recognizing that cooperatives are to be initiated and owned by their members. Such an arrangement is not compatible with the transition of cooperatives to the private sector.

However, cooperatives essentially concern self-help response by members to their own self-perceived needs. In order to be sustainable therefore, the organizations must reflect and respond to the needs of their members. Their operations must be commensurate with the ability of members to manage, control and finance the business. Action from any source that obstructs the process of self-help, self-administration and self-direction is inimical to genuine cooperative development and acts as a constraint upon it (Hussi et al.,1993).

Institutional dependence on the state apparatus

The feeling of the membership of primary societies towards the government Cooperative Department is mixed. Very many members describe the activities of the Cooperative Department as supportive, as well as facilitative: supportive through tax exemptions, subsidies, grants and membership education: facilitative because they assist them in obtaining loans from other agencies of government like the Agricultural and Cooperative Bank through their certificate of recognition.

However, some others see the bureaucracy and interference associated with the relationship between the Cooperative Department and the cooperatives as a burden to cooperative development. Because the secondary cooperatives and the state apex body are managed by civil servants from the Cooperative Department, many members of primary societies look on them as arms of government, even though these bodies are supposed to be set up, and run, completely by primary societies themselves. Similarly, the state Cooperative College is completely a branch of the Department of Cooperatives both in staffing and finance.

Employment effect: only estimates but hopeful

There is hardly any systematically compiled information available on the employment impact of cooperatives in Enugu State. Available information shows that, at the moment, there are no workers' cooperatives in the state. Estimates from the Enugu State Department of Cooperatives put the number of self-employed people who would not be able to continue their activities without cooperatives – mostly members of primary societies – at about 80,000. Similarly, there are about 80 people employed by the government's Cooperative Department. This number includes those working at the state Cooperative College, the state cooperative federation and secondary societies, because, as noted earlier, staff of the Cooperative Department is just posted to these agencies.

The spillover effect of the cooperative sector on the employment market is much diffused and difficult to quantify with any degree of certainty. In a state whose cooperative sector is dominated by the Farmers' Multipurpose Cooperative Society, one would expect that the impact of cooperatives on the agricultural market (which is controlled by private traders) would be obvious, so that one could easily hazard a guess as to the number of people that are indirectly employed by the cooperatives in this regard. Unfortunately, this is not the case. Back in 1993 Porvali reported that cooperatives in Nigeria have a negligible role in agricultural markets. This may be because these cooperatives are very small in size, lack working capital, have poor business and management acumen and are unincorporated.

However, the direction of the direct and spillover impact of cooperatives on the employment market is positive and improving, particularly since the year 2000. According to an official of the Cooperative Department in Enugu State, there are recent instances where cooperatives have successfully established small-scale industries, hospitals, health care centres, food processing plants and poultry farms. Okonkwo (1989) made similar observations regarding the impact of women's cooperatives during the Better Life for Rural Women Programme in Nigeria. Moreover, the Uzondu cooperatives at Nsukka, Enugu State, have some landed properties on which a hospital and a petrol filling station are set up. These two establishments employ about 30 people.

Given that it is difficult to discuss accurately (because of lack of relevant information) the employment estimates for registered cooperatives, it is even more difficult to talk about estimates for unregistered cooperative (pre-coop and non-coop) societies. However, their impact on the employment market is positive. For instance, the Nkpunano Awareness Union, Nsukka, has a lot of plantation projects in which they hire lots of labourers to perform one farm operation or the other, in addition to fully engaging their members.

As noted earlier, because of the size of most primary cooperatives, both in terms of membership and financial status, they generally do not engage any workers outside their membership. Their affairs are often managed by elected officers and volunteers from among the membership.

However, we have noted before that the number of cooperatives and thus also the membership is on the rise. This also means that more and more people rely on their cooperative for their income and employment.

But still, agricultural input and product distribution could be better coordinated and organized with much price stability if cooperatives were to be adequately mobilized for the sector. In 1993, Porvali noted that Nigerian cooperatives have an extensive network of unions and primary societies through which a large number of people can be reached. At the moment, pockets of scarcity exist along with pockets of abundance with regard to agricultural product and input marketing, because of inefficient distribution. Efficient marketing stimulates production with a lot of positive chain effects on employment, starting from production through distribution and processing to manufacturing.

The small size of cooperatives, the poor state of rural infrastructure, lack of access to good market information and enough investment capital, inability to recruit permanent career management staff and continued government interference in the management of cooperatives may militate against the full realization of the potential of cooperatives to create employment.

Although there are quite a number of unregistered "cooperative" societies, their activities go almost unnoticed. However, their employment potential is high. Most of them are financially independent and have a more committed and cohesive membership. Hence, within the limits of their resources, they tend to do better than registered cooperatives. An example is the Lions Micro-credit Society, University of Nigeria, Nsukka, mentioned above.

The role of cooperatives in poverty reduction

Legally, there is no discrimination in terms of who (poor or rich, man or woman) qualifies for membership of cooperative societies. The only pre-condition in this regard is that all members must reside within the society's area of operation. But in many places, there are women only cooperative societies, which are designed to address the peculiar problems of women in society. For instance, the University Women Cooperative Society sometimes embarks on public enlightenment campaigns regarding the equality of men and women in society. They also occasionally give scholarships to deserving children from poor homes. Ijere (1991) noted that there are instances when cooperatives exclusively for women are more desirable. This is to enable the women to learn self-government and self-management in addition to helping them solve their peculiar socio-economic problems. The main objective of the Better Life for Rural Women Programme, launched by Nigeria's first lady in 1987, was to better the living standard of rural women through the formation of cooperative societies (Okonkwo 1989).

Farm households are among the poorest segments of society (World Bank, 2000). The predominance of the Farmers' Multipurpose Cooperative Society in Enugu State as noted before suggests the presence of cooperatives in the poorest areas of society. Cooperatives are also present in many urban slums in the country. And there is evidence that cooperatives can lift people out of poverty in Nigeria. For instance, the earlier mentioned Lions Micro-credit Society, University of Nigeria, Nsukka, mobilizes savings from its members and advances loans at a very low interest rate of 5% to the very poor people in society or among its group for the purpose of poverty alleviation. The beneficiaries of such funds often start businesses like petty trading or pay their children's school fees with them. Nguru Nsukka Farmers' Multipurpose Cooperative Society also does similar things among its members. Government loans to cooperatives also attract low interest rates because they are considered as a tool for poverty alleviation. Okonkwo (1989) reported that cooperative societies of the Better Life Programme have led to a remarkable economic and social revolution in the lives of Nigerian rural women. They have not only enhanced the scale of their farming activities, but also diversified their income base through the setting up of small-scale industries like ceramics, textiles and bakeries.

In recognition of the crucial role that cooperatives can play in poverty reduction, the Cooperative Department was made a major player in the newly

(2004) created Ministry of Human Development and Poverty Reduction in Enugu State. The cooperative movement in the state and particularly the Cooperative Department now see themselves as the vanguard for poverty reduction. This has been very effective because the membership of cooperative societies have been fully mobilized and sensitized for this role. Very often, seminars and workshops are organized for cooperatives in this regard.

Cooperatives re-enforce traditional social protection systems

In general, there is no established formal system of social security for the membership of cooperatives in Nigeria. What exists is the traditional social security prevalent in most rural African communities with some re-enforcement. We use the word re-enforcement because in the case of cooperatives, the extent of social protection is usually spelt out in their constitution, whereas in typical African rural communities, the system is conventional. In addition, the cooperatives are a much tighter community with stronger bonds than the traditional societies. This enables the cooperatives to act faster and in a more coordinated manner.

In the traditional social protection institutions, members do not make regular (monthly or annual) contributions towards it; rather, they levy each other as the situation arises. That is, if a misfortune befalls a member, all members contribute in cash or kind to assist the individual overcome the misfortune. The misfortune could be fire, flood, plague, death, serious ill-health or robbery. Cooperatives adopt these kinds of traditional protection systems and strengthen them. Affiliation, contribution and coverage then are automatic (i.e. as soon as you become a member of the cooperative).

How can government-dependent federations and apex bodies represent the movement?

Most of the people interviewed during the course of this research indicate that communication between the apex body in Enugu State and the primary societies is open, accessible and democratic, with the apex representing the wishes and aspirations from the bottom. However, a few members of primary societies still see the cooperative federation as an agent of government and therefore representing the wishes and aspirations of the government.

Information from the cooperative federation shows that it has a special unit with qualified personnel in charge of projecting the wishes of cooperatives as well as lobbying government on their behalf. But given that the cooperative federation is staffed with employees of government as noted before, the effectiveness of this aspect of their function is open to question. Can the government lobby itself on behalf of cooperatives? Available information shows that the cooperative federation has never spoken out for, or adequately represented, any group.

Conclusion

Just as the Nigerian economy is dominated by agriculture, cooperatives in Enugu State are predominantly agricultural. The membership is also dominated by rural smallholder farmers. The influence of government on cooperative management and education is still largely in place. Hence, a mixture of state aid, politics and genuine problem-solving cooperation drives the number of registered cooperatives in the country. At the primary society level, there is not much integration in reality. While cooperatives have in general made appreciable impact on employment and poverty reduction, they have not done much to improve voice and representation for the poor. It is believed that cooperatives can indeed be the engine of economic growth and development if government can free up its management and allow it to evolve on its own. This is because cooperatives essentially concern self-help responses by members to their own self-perceived needs. Action from any source that obstructs such processes of self-help, self-administration and self-direction is inimical to genuine cooperative development and acts as a constraint upon it. This was the conclusion of the World Bank study (Hussi et al., 1993). This is still the conclusion ten years later. Nigeria has not followed the path many other countries have followed with regard to cooperative development.

Sources

This article is based on a series of interviews, carried out during the autumn of 2005. The author wishes to thank Mr. Omeje and Mr. Anwuta, Department of Cooperatives, Enugu State; Mr F.S. Ezemah, Cooperative Federation of Enugu State; Mr. Umerah, Enugu State Cooperative College; Mr. Ominyi and Dr. Obayi, Uzondu Cooperatives, Nsukka; Mr. Fidelis Eze, Leader of (1) Nguru Nsukka Farmers' Multipurpose Cooperative Society, (2) Modern Farmers' Multipurpose Cooperative Society, Nsukka, and (3) Pigree Farmers' Cooperative Society; Amagu Omo, Umulokpe Farmers' Multipurpose Cooperative Society; Mr. F.U. Agbo, Lions Micro-credit Society, University of Nigeria, Nsukka.

Bibliography

- Adeyemo R. (2004), 'Self-Help Farmer Cooperatives' Management of Natural Resources for Sustainable Development in Southwest Nigeria', *Journal of rural cooperation*, 32(1), pp. 3-18.

- Central Bank of Nigeria (2003), 'Annual Reports and Statement Accounts. CBN, Abuja, Federal Government of Nigeria (1993)', *Nigerian Cooperative Societies Decree n° 90 of 1993*, Federal Government of Nigeria, Abuja.

- Hussi P. et al. (1993), *The Development of Cooperatives and other Rural Organizations*, The World Bank, Washington, D.C.

- Ijere M. O. (1991), *Women in Nigerian Cooperatives*, Acena Publishers, Enugu, Nigeria.

- Okonkwo N. P. (1989), *Better Life for Rural Women Cooperatives*, Cooperative Publishers, Enugu, Nigeria.

- Porvali H. (1993), *Nigeria: Review of Agricultural Cooperatives and Other Farmer Organization*, World Bank, Washington D.C.

- Puri S. S. (1979), *Ends and Means of Cooperative Development*, National Cooperative Union of India, New Delhi.

- UNDP (2004), *Nigeria Development Profile*, March, UNDP.

- USAID (undated), *SO13: Increased use of Social Sector Services*, USAID, Nigeria Mission, Abuja.

- World Bank (2000), *Can Africa Claim the 21st Century?* The World Bank, Washington.

Chapter Eight – Bad Memories, Good Prospects: Cooperatives in Niger

by Sanda Maman Sani[1]

Introduction

Cooperatives have existed for over 40 years in Niger. They have evolved in an economic and socio-political context in which at times they managed to receive some praise, although, in recent years, they have often been on the receiving end of fairly sharp criticism. The advent of the new developments triggered by the adoption of structural adjustment programmes, which has resulted in the liberalization of the economy, practically requires that the Nigerien cooperative movement makes some adaptations. Its legal, economic, administrative and institutional environment will have to be overhauled if this adaptation is to take place and the movement is to develop harmoniously. While in the past cooperative creation and operation could be sponsored by the public authorities, the same is not true now as the socio-economic and political environment has radically changed.

In this article, we argue that the Nigerien policy on cooperatives will need further – and rather drastic – revision, not only due to this new context of structural adjustment, democracy, freedom of association and enterprise, but also the imperative for economic and social development in an extremely poor country.

The extent of the cooperative movement in Niger

The legal framework pertaining to cooperatives institutionally and structurally provides for a dual cooperative sector. Two pieces of legislation cover the two separate segments of the sector. One law promulgated in November 1996

---

[1] Mr. Maman-Sani Sanda studied sociology at EHESS (Paris) and worked as a research fellow in IRD (Montpellier, France). Since the 1990s he has been based in Niamey as a consultant, carrying out training, studies and evaluation in the domain of rural development for agencies like DANIDA, SIDA, UNDP and the World Bank as well as the French, Dutch and Belgian Cooperations.

lays down the rules on rural cooperatives whilst another law (likewise promulgated in November 1996) regards credit and savings mutual societies and cooperatives. Alongside these two separate sub-sectors, there are also organizations with no legal basis which are difficult to oversee and monitor but – within a social economy tradition – have a prominent role in society and the local economy.

The first law regulates cooperatives in the fields of agriculture, stock breeding, forestry, crafts, fisheries and other sub-sectors of the rural economy. Their numbers are not known accurately, but as of 30 November 2003, over 11,351 cooperative organizations had been registered as well as 224 unions and 31 federations. National, regional and trans-regional cooperative networks are now starting to emerge and represent a relatively large number of grassroots organizations. Examples of such networks include the Jaraka Federation, the Mooriben Federation, the Niya Federation of Market Gardener Cooperatives and the Federation of Rice-growing Cooperatives, among many others.

To get an idea of the extent of these federations, we could cite the example of Mooriben which represents 15 unions, 413 groupings and 19,112 members. The rice-growers federation has 20,937 individual members while the craft workers' federation accounts for 301 grassroots organizations and 45,778 members.

In some cases the structuring of the movement is local or regional. For instance, the cooperative support service centre of the city of Zinder brings together an inter-bank organization (OIB), a union of women's credit groups (UGFC), a union of cooperative pharmaceutical warehouses (UDPC) and other 220 grassroots organizations. Their outreach is 16,940 members. We should also not overlook the restructuring of a number of old unions into a national confederation called CONACOOP representing eight regional federations, 115 unions and intermediate federations, 2,391 cooperatives and groupings, with some 210,000 members.

Credit and savings institutions (which may be either mutual societies or cooperatives) are supervised by the Ministry of Economic and Financial Affairs. They are subject to the second law of 1996 mentioned above. On 15 September 2003 there were 120 recognized credit and savings banks. The only recognized network of savings and credit unions, the *Mouvement des Caisses Populaires d'Epargne et de Crédit* (MCPEC), represents about 30% of all operating savings and credit unions in the country. These organizations seem to be somewhat better monitored and supervised bearing in mind the delicate nature of their task, the quality of their management and in particular the extent of the resources mobilized to support them.

As already pointed out, many other organizations exist that do not have a clear-cut legal base. They operate as *de facto* organizations, but knowingly or unknowingly follow standard cooperative principles. They are active in various economic and social areas. Among them are youth and female producers' associations as well as processing, trading or organized rotating savings groups ("tontines"). Rural wood markets and the water point management committees can also be seen as organizations of this type. They are fairly large in number and their social utility is on a par with that of the formally established organizations.

The shaky background of the Nigerien cooperative movement

As early as 1947, the French colonial rulers established a legal framework in order to recognize existing para-cooperatives on the territory of present-day Niger. These included the Greniers Villageois (GV – Village Granaries) during the 1930s, and the Sociétés Indigènes de Prévoyance (SIP – Native Provident Societies) and Sociétés Mutualistes de Production Rurale (SMPR – Mutual Rural Production Societies) in the 1940s and 1950s. These organizations, however, did not gain real momentum because they were not suited to the Nigerien socio-cultural context and were run in an authoritarian and bureaucratic way. Moreover, they lacked voluntary and genuine participation by the people.

In the fifties, another series of colonial decrees helped to set up more cooperatives such as the builders' cooperative and the transporters' cooperative in Niamey, and in rural areas, the Toukounous stockbreeding cooperative, the Kollo agricultural cooperative and the Mirriah market gardening cooperative. Following independence, only the Kollo and Mirriah cooperatives survived.

Gradually, the Nigerien cooperative movement took shape. The three major landmarks were first, the creation in 1962 of the Union Nigérienne de Crédit et de Coopération, a national apex body; second, the withdrawal of the state following the introduction of structural adjustment programmes at the beginning of the 1980s; and third the Sovereign National Conference held in 1991.

The creation of the UNCC in 1962 certainly marked the start of genuine cooperative action in Niger. As a financially independent administrative service set up to translate state policy on cooperation into practice, the UNCC's purpose was threefold: to develop the spirit of mutualism and cooperation in rural areas; to offer rural cooperatives help to facilitate and coordinate their action; and to encourage the creation of multipurpose cooperatives able to provide all the services needed for technical, economic and social development, taking traditional social organization as a basis.

This mission was to be achieved primarily by creating and supervising cooperatives and providing education and training for cooperative members. When it was first set up in 1963, the UNCC started to establish mutual societies and cooperatives. For four years, these mutual societies and cooperatives were set up using the conventional French system of individual membership and payment of shares. This system quickly showed its limits, as only the better-off farmers could pay their shares. They corrupted the system and used the cooperatives for speculative purposes. Non-member farmers' output was bought by members and registered as theirs in order to get the related premiums. The cooperative thus became the prerogative of a few individuals, which ran counter to the aim of reaching as many rural people as possible. This approach was called into question in 1968, when shares were abolished and the principle of collective membership of villages organized into mutual groups was introduced. It was on this basis that the UNCC continued to launch cooperatives. It tackled different domains in successive stages: first in groundnut, cotton and rice areas (between 1968 and 1973) and further on throughout the seventies in cereal growing areas. With the advent of development projects, cooperatives became more widespread. In 1983, a genuine National Cooperative Union (UNC – Union Nationale des Coopératives) was created to replace the dissolved UNCC.

At that time, the cooperative fabric included 12,056 rural organizations of a cooperative and mutual nature, including 10,628 GMVS (Village Mutual Groups), 1,167 cooperatives, 213 local cooperative unions (ULC), 40 sub-regional cooperative unions (USRC), seven regional cooperative unions (URC) and, as said, the national cooperative union (UNC).

With structural adjustment (1984-1990) came the ideas of self-management and self-supervision of cooperatives. The national cooperative union (UNC) had its own technical personnel, which promoted cooperatives within development projects. Consequently, the number of registered cooperatives increased to 13,585 in 1989. In general, during this period state services were more or less absent, including supervision and training. Meanwhile, and often at the instigation of foreign NGOs, other organizational models made an appearance in the form of savings and credit groups and other mutual societies.

The Sovereign National Conference held in 1991 was a major turning point in the history of the country and the cooperative movement. It drew up a diagnosis and formulated recommendations with regard to the promotional strategy of the cooperative sector. The main idea was to deregulate and stimulate producers' structures and associations, by affirming freedom of association and support for a whole range of producers' organizations. This dynamism would in 1996 lead to another legislative initiative on rural cooperatives, which was to restore individual membership and the payment of shares and to lift the requirement for cooperatives to be structured in line with administrative divisions.

As a result of these changes, the UNC set in motion a restructuring process which led, in 1997, to a network of 869 cooperatives and 48 unions with 93,975 members. These structures were however dissolved on 11 December 1997 by a decree tabled by the Ministry responsible for supervising cooperatives. This decree, which also set up a commission to oversee the liquidation of union assets, was only partially applied as a result of the wave of protests to which it led in political circles and in national civil society. It was against this backdrop that yet another decree (in the year 2000) was enacted, authorizing the UNC and its branches to perform their activities again.

One could euphemistically say that the government's treatment of the cooperative movement was a back and forth process. Successive regimes dealt with cooperatives by decrees. But with policy implementation lacking, cooperatives were subjected to the oscillation of day-to-day Nigerien politics. It seems questionable whether this could inspire much of people's confidence in cooperatives.

Weaknesses inside cooperatives

The perception of the failure of cooperative organizations in Niger at the beginning of the 1990s led many rural development activists to prefer different types of organization, in particular development associations and NGOs. There is little doubt at present that the spirit of commitment and voluntary work (to help others or to defend a cause), which is the foundation of any association, requires capacities on the part of members that many Nigerien associations lack. In practice, to rally the resources for their policy, Nigerien development associations have only two options: either they extend their membership base and bring in more local capital, or they forge partnerships with international agencies. For many, attracting international donor money is the prime reason for their existence. To offset too much dependency on donor money and agendas several development associations in the rural sector are again looking at the cooperative form of resource mobilization. This is illustrated by some cases we studied such as the Niya market gardeners' federation and the Tahoua husbandry producers' union.

Our field research uncovered severe shortcomings within Nigerien cooperatives. Most prominent is the lack of management skills, particularly book keeping and account skills. It is not rare that cash books are replaced by notebooks held at the treasurer's home. Many cooperatives lack an accounting plan or do not even have a bank account or a safe. Many of the federations and unions use management tools suggested or imposed on them by their donor. These are often designed for small grassroots organizations, yet they apply them in large cooperatives. When the donor changes, the management system also changes.

Training for the management of cooperatives in Niger is extremely poor. During the field research, not a single manager could be identified who had attended two or more training sessions on (cooperative) organizational development, management and business. However, even the ones who had received some "how to ..." introductory lessons stressed that training on these subjects was badly needed. A glance through the existing training curricula made clear that the content was invariably the same whatever the type and level of the cooperatives visited. The situation can partly be attributed to the absence of specialized technical and professional skills in the trainers concerned. Training sessions are often given by trainers with few or no teaching skills or any real knowledge of cooperative theory and practice.

Other than that, internal and external communication in the cooperatives under review proved to be very inadequate. None of them had an operational communication plan. Only Mooriben was cognisant of the fact that this issue was a major problem that needed to be tackled. Many a Nigerien cooperative operates in a permanent atmosphere of conflict and disputes. This is not the least the case in the profitable ones. Very few are thinking about reliable procedures in which internal disputes can be managed. This of course affects their capacity to retain members. Even successful cooperatives live with the permanent risk of losing embittered members and sudden collapse. The Nigerien cooperative sector is not imbued with a culture of enterprise. Many cooperatives are solely oriented towards the acquisition of (donor-) projects and the collection of member fees. Very little attention goes to the generation of surplus for the members and the enterprise through a profitable undertaking.

The role of the state: hollow directorates and confusing legislation

The state and other promoters of the cooperative sector have followed a laissez-faire approach. This approach cannot be called pro-active, as it is based on encouragement and raising people's awareness, rather than systematic or material support. Cooperatives also seem to be seen as the preserve of the rural sector, with the result that cooperatives have not been set up in other sectors that are otherwise very complementary, such as consumption, processing (industry), transport, insurance or banking.

Over the years several directorates and departments have been responsible for the promotion and supervision of the cooperative sector. It started with the UNCC (Nigerien Credit and Cooperation Union) which was in charge of this portfolio from 1962 to 1984 and followed by the DFAC (Directorate for Cooperative Training and Action) in 1985. Subsequently, from 1986 to 1989 cooperative development became the preserve of the SAAC (Cooperative Action Support Service) within the Agricultural Production Directorate. This was replaced by the DPC (Cooperative Promotion Directorate) in 1990; the CAAC (Cooperative Action Support Unit) in 1991; and the DPOR/GER (Directorate for the Promotion of Rural Organizations and Management of Rural Areas) from 1992 to 1997. The DAC/POR (Directorate for Cooperative Action and Promotion of Rural Organizations) took responsibility for cooperative policy and implementation in February 1997. In addition to this, and following the enactment of the decree on savings and credit mutual societies and cooperatives in 1996, a monitoring unit for decentralized financial services (CSSFD) was set up at the Ministry of Economic and Financial Affairs.

Apart from the UNCC that has developed a system of supervision and methods of promotion of cooperatives, and recently the DAC/POR and the new CSSFD, the other structures were little more than token bodies lacking skilled human resources as well as working methods. Often, cooperative policy making was restricted to the drafting of a chapter on cooperatives in the economic and social development plans, the formulation of cooperative policy and guideline documents as well as many workshops and national forums on rural development.

We have already mentioned the utterly confusing avalanche of laws and regulations that has affected the cooperative scene throughout the years. The 1962 laws, for instance, did not target cooperatives as in practice they only foresaw the creation of state services to promote cooperation. Niger's real legislation on cooperatives came no earlier than 1978, setting out statutes for rural bodies of a cooperative and mutual nature. Since then, laws have been repeatedly promulgated to restrain or restrict cooperatives' activities, membership and competence. The 1996 decree has so far brought some stability in cooperative policy.

Supervision and support structures: still at square one

In its time, the UNCC developed a network to promote, supervise and control all levels of the cooperative sector, including primary cooperatives. However, the personnel of this network lacked technical skills and was not able to bring alive a viable cooperative scene. Subsequently, the promotion and supervision of cooperatives were stepped up through major projects. These made it possible to carry out a large number of training programmes and to develop income-generating cooperative activities. Among the latter were grain banks, cooperative shops, village mills, cooperative pharmacies, cooperatives involved in sheep and cattle fattening and credit unions. Apart from the AHA (Hydro-Agricultural Planning) cooperatives which benefited from relatively efficient supervision, all these efforts produced disappointing results. Most cooperatives that were established proved to be deficient in terms of ownership and a genuine dynamic of cooperation.

The involvement of NGOs as an alternative to cooperative promotion and supervision led to a proliferation of organizations which complicated the monitoring and legal scrutiny of cooperatives by the competent state services.

Despite its importance, cooperative action in Niger has never been the subject of genuine research. The few studies that have been produced have been ancillary to project evaluations or project design, very often by consultants with limited knowledge of the cooperative peculiarities. New policy lines and proposals have rarely taken account of technical concerns, successful national experiences, and even less of rural people's perception of the socio-economic utility of organizations. This has resulted in a Niger that serves as testing ground for all types of rural organizations, where the focus is on new ideas, which systematically replace existing experiments with no concern to build on prior experience.

Development partners interested in cooperative development in Niger are chiefly multilateral cooperation agencies (for instance, the World Bank and the European Development Fund), government agencies (like the French, Swiss, Italian and Canadian cooperation agencies), international NGOs (for instance Green Africa, the Canadian Centre for International Research and Cooperation (CECI-Niger)), and the cooperative movements of the northern countries. NGO financing mainly comes through support structures temporarily put in place, while some bilateral agencies (for instance the Canadian and Luxembourg cooperation agencies) work directly with cooperative structures. This flow of money often requires financial audits. Internal auditing organs within cooperatives are poorly organized and in all cases are technically not up to the requirements of their task. To prove that they are reliably run, cooperatives have to call on the services of qualified auditors or set up appropriate facilities for this purpose. This observation though, brings us back to the internal weaknesses of the sector, a topic we have already extensively dealt with.

Even in an unfavourable environment, one finds examples of good practice: MOORIBEN

The federation of unions of rural groups called "Mooriben" proves that even in an unfavourable environment, it is possible to stir up "good vibes" that root the spirit of cooperativism. Ownership and local embedding stand out as the key factors for this success story. Mooriben was among the very first rural organizations to be set up on the initiative of farmers themselves outside the state-controlled cooperative system. The name "Mooriben" is a slogan chosen by the federation's founders to express, in a single word, their expectations of this organization. In Djerma-Sonrai, Mooriben means "poverty is ended". The federation was, therefore, established with a view to fighting poverty, ignorance and their consequences. From 1988, following exchanges with the NAAM movements of Burkina Faso and Six "S" International, the first groups were set up in the western part of the country.

According to its statutes, Mooriben's objectives are the promotion of rural enterprises and the organization of economic, social, educational and cultural activities for members. Members of the Mooriben Federation are exclusively unions of groups. At present, the Federation has 15 unions and 413 groups, representing 19,112 members, 10,561 of whom, i.e. over 50%, are women. Mooriben's activities include institutional and management capacity building, support for production and income-generating activities, improvement of women's economic and decision-making capacity and development of multipurpose partnerships.

Mooriben and its unions have made a significant impact indeed. The grain banks and shops set up by Mooriben in this region have changed practices substantially, with the storage and use of fertilizers to manage crises and improve production. Before, farmers consumed or sold the whole of their harvest and accrued debts to traders before the next harvest. This dependence on traders has declined sharply since the creation of the grain banks. The existence of Mooriben shops, together with an understanding of technical information and backup for leaders and overseers, has made farmers much more willing to trust inputs, especially plant health products. Farmers are able to make informed choices between the various inputs in order to improve productivity. In terms of food security, the grain banks made it possible to cover the food needs of 24,941 people during two months of famine in 2005, i.e. 37% of the needs of the total population of the villages concerned in that period.

Mooriben's success lies in the fact that it is so well rooted locally and owned by farmers. This ownership has been helped by the way in which groups and unions are set up: through their own dynamics. Mooriben does not, for instance, play any part in setting up groups and unions but simply leads the organizational framework. Considerable effort has been made to mobilize internal funding for the Federation. In the unions and groups, a very high percentage of activities are self-financed through collective fields and the revenue from credit activities.

An evaluation has shown that Mooriben's success is very much due to the local rooting, the quality and the range of services and the partnership with decentralized governmental structures (i.e. mayors and decentralized services of ministries). A crucial element is the sharing of a common vision and the spirit of belonging to the same extended family based on solidarity and mutual aid. This internal cohesion is shaped by the transparent way in which business is managed by the Federation, the unions and the groups, and the various training schemes on running associations. Mooriben's package of services includes training (in running associations and in technical skills), grain banks, shops, credit lines and community radio stations. Each element of this package of services meets a specific need; the synergy between all the elements of the package nevertheless helps to promote development and improve farmers' living conditions. In particular during periods of food crisis, the neighbourhood services put into practice by local leaders have played an important role. Cooperation links between the ministerial decentralized structures and Mooriben are good at all levels. By way of example, Mooriben was one of the three civil society organizations to which the Ministry of Agriculture turned for the distribution of seed in order to manage food crises. Mooriben and these services are now working together on a more regular basis to draw up sectoral policy, including the agricultural input policy which is currently being drawn up.

Some conclusions

Despite the major efforts made since independence, there is all the doubt that cooperatives of the desired type, i.e. self-supporting, dynamic and independent economic enterprises, have emerged in Niger. The use of cooperatives by the state and other promoters as instruments to achieve their own development objectives has meant that the Nigerien cooperative movement has been shaped largely from outside and has not, therefore, been able to build on a genuinely popular base. The many reforms, very often initiated without any real justification or technical preparation, as regimes or political systems have changed, reflect a political perception of the concept of cooperative action which is not keeping the values and principles of cooperation.

The very poor technical and institutional capacity of cooperatives; the difficulty of controlling the agents of cooperative development and ensuring that cooperatives are monitored and supervised; and the lack of statistics on cooperatives and their contribution to the national economy reflect the failure of the cooperative promotion strategies that have been used. The lack of cooperative training for both cooperative members and staff; the lack of education in the midst of illiteracy among cooperative members; the lack of financial resources and problems of accessing credit; the poor understanding of legislation which in itself is often defunct, all show that the cooperative movement has evolved into an institutional, legal, technical and socio-cultural environment running counter to its development.

Nevertheless, it has also been shown (e.g. in the case of Mooriben) that cooperatives can win the "hearts and minds" of the Nigerien population as long as some preconditions are carefully observed: a genuine, locally rooted solidarity, a wide range of services and a positive partnership with decentralized governmental structures.

Sources

This article is based on a series of documents and interviews, carried out during October and November 2005. The author wishes to thank Daouda SG (Acopec), Zakari Oumarou, El Hadj Moussa Mohamadou and Boucabar Bouzou (FUCAP-Tahoua), Azori Amoumoun, Rhissa Mohamed, Acho Mohamed and Ahamed Oha (UCMA-Agadez), Kader Hado, Ibrahim Ihossey, Adam Efangal and Efal Ahalhass (UCMT), Issa Adam and Zakori Idrissa (Centre de Services, Zinder), Alfari Seydou, Idrissa Hassane, Sanoussi Hassane and Illiassou Dandakoye (Mooriben), and Doulla Hassane and Samba Ly (DAC/POR, Niamey).

Acronyms and abbreviations

AHA	Aménagement Hydro-Agricole (Hydro-Agricultural Development)
CAAC:	Cellule d'Appui à l'Action Cooperative (Cooperative Action Support Unit)
CONACOOP	Confédération Nationale des Coopératives (National Cooperative Confederation)
CMO/P/COOP	Comité National de Mise en Oeuvre et de Suivi / Politiques Coopératives (National Implementation and Monitoring Committee / Cooperative Policies)
DFAC:	Direction de la Formation et de l'Action Cooperative (Directorate for Cooperative Training and Action)
DAC/POR:	Direction de l'Action Coopérative et de la Promotion des Organisations Rurales (Directorate for Cooperative Action and Promotion of Rural Organizations)

DFS:	Decentralised Financial System
DPC:	Direction de la Promotion Coopérative (Directorate for Cooperative Promotion)
DPOR/GER:	Direction de la Promotion des Organisations Rurales et de la Gestion de l'Espace Rural (Directorate for the Promotion of Rural Organizations and Management of the Rural Area)
GMV:	Groupement Mutualiste Villageois (Village Mutual Group)
HIPC:	Heavily Indebted Poor Country
MAG-EL:	Ministère de l'Agriculture et de l'Elevage (Ministry of Agriculture and Stockbreeding)
MDA:	Ministère du Développement Agricole (Ministry of Agricultural Development)
MDR:	Ministère du Développement Rural (Ministry of Rural Development)
MEF/P:	Ministère de l'Economie, des Finances et du Plan (Ministry of Economic and Financial Affairs and Planning)
MCPEC:	Mouvement des Caisses Populaires d'Epargne et de Crédit (Popular Credit and Savings Banks Movement)
ONAHA:	Office National des Aménagements Hydro-Agricoles (National Office for Hydro-Agricultural Development)
OIB:	Organisation Inter Banques (Inter-bank Organization)
ONASO/P/COOP:	Observatoire National de Suivi et d'Orientation / Politique Coop (National Guidance and Monitoring Observatory / Cooperative Policy)
OP:	Organisation Paysanne (Farmers' Organization)
ORASO/P-COOP:	Observatoires Régionaux d'Action et de Suivi / Politique Coop (National Action and Monitoring Observatories / Cooperative Policy)

PRN:	Presidency of the Republic of Niger
RDS:	Rural Development Strategy
RVA:	Regroupement des Villages Animés (Village Group)
SAAC:	Service d'Appui à l'Action Coopérative (Cooperative Action Support Service)
SIP:	Société Indigène de Prévoyance (Native Provident Society)
SMDR:	Société Mutuelle de Développement Rural (Mutual Rural Development Society)
SMPR:	Société Mutuelle de Promotion Rurale (Mutual Rural Promotion Society)
UNCC:	Union Nigérienne de Crédit et de Coopération (Nigerien Credit and Cooperation Union)
UNC:	Union Nationale de Coopératives (National Cooperative Union)
ULC:	Union Locale de Coopératives (Local Cooperative Union)
USRC:	Union Sous-Régionale de Coopératives (Sub-Regional Cooperative Union)
URC:	Union Régionale de Coopératives (Regional Cooperative Union)
UGFC:	Union des Groupements Feminins de Crédit (Union of Women's Credit Groups)
UDPC:	Union des Dépôts Pharmaceutiques Coopératifs (Union of Cooperative Pharmaceutical Warehouses)

Bibliography

- Abdou Acharou Souleymane (2003), *Etude diagnostic des ONG et Associations nigériennes par rapport à leurs capacités organisationnelles, opérationnelles et d'implication dans les domaines des problématiques environnementales et du développement durable au Niger Niamey*, Conseil National de l'Environnement pour un Développement Durable (CNEDD) & Coopération Italienne.

- BOAD (2002), *Diagnostic institutionnel et organisationnel de la Plate forme paysanne du Niger et des organisations membres*, Projet d'utilisation des fonds Suisses/Banque Ouest Africaine de Développement (BOAD).

- Boukari Y. (2002), *Les organisations paysannes nigériennes en mouvement. Diagnostic participatif rapide de 20 organisations paysannes, Cadre pour l'Action et la Solidarité des Producteurs Agricoles du Niger (CASPANI)*, Projet de Renforcement des Organisations Professionnelles Agropastorales du Niger (PROPAN), Niamey: Coopération française.

- FIDA (2003), *Actualisation du diagnostic des Systèmes Financiers Décentralisés candidats aux contrats plans avec le Programme de Développement des Services Financiers Ruraux: Diagnostic des coopératives et mutuelles d'épargne et de crédit et propositions d'appuis, Niamey: Programme de développement des Services Financiers Ruraux (PDSFR)*, Fonds International pour le Développement Agricole (FIDA).

- Floridi M. & Maman L. T. (2005), *Etude de faisabilité pour un Programme d'appui aux acteurs non étatiques au Niger*, Profil et diagnostic des capacités des acteurs non étatiques, Niamey: Délégation de l'union Européenne au Niger.

- Mahamadou S. (s.d.), *Diagnostic des capacités des organisations professionnelles agricoles et propositions d'actions de renforcement des capacités*, Projet de Renforcement des Organisations Professionnelles Agropastorales (PROPAN), Niamey.

- McKeon N. (2003), *Mission de capitalisation 'Programme de Renforcement Institutionnel du Réseau des Organisations de base et des plates formes des Organisations paysannes dans 4 pays du Sahe'*, Niamey, Programme de Coopération FAO/Gouvernement de la République Italienne.

- Raguzzoni K. (2004), *Définition de la plateforme de négociation et de la stratégie de la participation des organisations de la société civile dans le cadre de la consultation sectorielle sur l'environnement et la lutte contre la désertification*, Niamey, Conseil National de l'Environnement pour un Développement Durable (CNEDD) & Coopération Italienne.

- SNV (2001), *Etude de faisabilité pour la création d'un centre d'appui conseil pour le renforcement des capacités des organisations intermédiaires*, Niamey, SNV-Niger.

Chapter Nine – The Egyptian Cooperative Movement: Between State and Market

by Mohamed H. Abdel Aal[1]

Introduction

The cooperative movement in Egypt is one of the oldest in the developing countries. A swift review of the cooperative movement shows emerging popular initiatives when Omar Lotfi established the first cooperative in 1909. The cooperatives, especially the agricultural ones, were used as parastatal instruments during the 1960s and 1970s for implementing the country's development policies. This period was marked by over-promotion by the state. Soon after, a slow transition to a more liberal economy following the adoption of Structural Adjustment Programmes (SAPs) saw cooperatives fall steadily into a state of neglect (Aal & Hassan, 1998: 279).

The revitalization process of cooperatives in developing countries including Egypt should take into consideration some important elements, including government's promotion and support, the levels of citizens' awareness about the socio-economic rewards of cooperation, and the nature of the power structures especially in the rural areas.

This study aims at analyzing the peculiar development path and state of affairs of the Egyptian cooperative movement. For this research we used a number of methodologies including review of literature and in-depth interviews with leaders of apex and affiliated cooperative federations. Also, an interview schedule was drafted, in Arabic, to guide interviews with leaders and administrators of primary cooperatives. The primary cooperatives were selected from several parts of Egypt including lower, middle and upper Egypt regions. This was done to reflect the different levels of poverty in the country.

---

[1] Mohamed Abdel Aal received his PhD in agricultural extension at Cairo University in 1980. He is currently a Professor and Vice Dean for Community Service and Environment Development at Cairo University and Research Professor at SRC. He has been a consultant for, among others, the Netherlands Development Agency, DANIDA, the Canadian International Development Agency, and FAO. His main research interests are in the organization and management of agricultural services, and in rural development.

Also the levels of performance and types of the cooperatives were considered when selecting the cooperatives in each region. The total number interviewed is 23 cooperatives covering agricultural, production, consumer, fishery and housing primary societies.

A widespread and highly structured movement

The apex body of cooperative structure in Egypt is the General Cooperative Union (GCU). The structure involves the membership of five main federations which are; Agriculture, Fishery, Housing, Consumer and Production. Table 9.1 illustrates the structure of each affiliated federation and the corresponding numbers of societies at different levels.

Agricultural cooperatives: the backbone of the sector

As is evident from Table 9.1, the agricultural cooperatives form the largest segment of the sector. All agricultural cooperatives in Egypt are organized within the structure of the Central Agricultural Cooperative Union (CACU). It involves over 5,000 primary multipurpose cooperatives divided into 4,263 credit cooperatives. This number almost equals the number of villages in the valley and delta. There are also over 600 cooperatives that were formed in areas where farmers benefited from the land reform laws of 1952, in addition to 571 cooperatives formed in reclaimed areas in the desert. The primary cooperatives provide multiple agricultural services to farmers from provision of agricultural inputs to mechanization and marketing services. The structure involves also about 700 village level specialized cooperatives. These cooperatives operate on the basis of a commodity. Some of the cooperatives are specialized in field crops, vegetables or fruits, and others are specialized in animal production, dairy products or provide marketing facilities and services.

The number of members of agricultural cooperatives exceeds 4 million and their volume of business is about 25 billion Egyptian pounds. However, the recent economic changes in the structure of the economy and the withdrawal of the state from supporting the cooperative sector have greatly affected the volume and quality of primary agricultural cooperatives.

Table 9.1: Structure of cooperation federations and numbers of societies

Type of Federation and structures	No. units
Agricultural Cooperation Federation:	
- Primary Multipurpose Societies – Credit	4 263
- Primary Multipurpose Societies – Land Reform	687
- Primary Multipurpose Societies – Land Reclamation	571
- Specialized Regional Cooperatives – Credit	70
- Specialized Village Cooperatives	732
- General Society	11
Total No. of Societies	6 334
Volume of Business (L.E. Billion)	25
Number of Members (Million)	> 4
Fishery Cooperation Federation:	
- Primary Societies	82
- Fishery Societies	8
- General Societies	1
Total No. of Societies	91
Volume of Business (L.E. Billion)	> 1
Number of Members	89 713
Housing Cooperation Federation	
- Primary Societies	1 969
- Federation Societies	11
- Joint Societies	7
Total No. of Societies	1 978
Volume of Business (L.E. Billion)	8
Number of Members (Million)	2
Consumer Cooperation Federation	
- Primary Societies	4 300
- Regional Federations	20
Total No. of Societies	4 320
Volume of Business (L.E. Billion)	10
Number of Members (Million)	4
Production Cooperation Federation (PCF)	
- Primary Societies	466
- General Societies	13
- Federation Societies	3
Total No. of Societies	482
Volume of Business (L.E. Billion)	10
Number of Members	58 184

Source: Information data on the General Cooperative Union, General Cooperative Union of Egypt, 2005a, pp: 4-5.

Fishery cooperatives

The structure of the fishery cooperative sector includes 91 cooperative societies, with about 90,000 members, who own 26,699 motor and sailing fishing boats. The fishery cooperatives account for around 90% of national fish production which is worth over L.E.1 billion annually.

Consumer cooperatives

The consumer cooperatives form the second largest cooperative sector. The number of primary societies is over 4,000. Most of the primary societies exist in urban or semi-urban areas. The structure of the Consumer Cooperative Union consists of the primary consumer cooperatives at the local level, the regional cooperative consumer unions at regional level and the general consumer cooperative at national level. According to the 2005 figures, the number of consumer cooperatives reached 4,005 societies with 5.1 million members, L.E.10.5 million of capital, and L.E.17.2 million in reserves. L.E.700 million in sales were recorded. The activities of the consumer cooperatives are expanding, especially because of the growing demand for goods and services.

Production cooperatives

The production cooperatives represent the "workers-owned" type of cooperatives. There are over 400 primary societies. Despite the small number of societies and members, the production cooperatives are operating an L.E.10 billion business. Currently the sector involves cooperative societies engaged in a wide range of production and crafts activities including: garments, photography and printing, customs services, carpets and rugs, shoes and leather products, passenger and cargo services, transport as well as furniture and carpentry.

Housing cooperatives

The housing cooperatives involve about 2,000 primary societies. Most primary housing cooperatives are urban based and are formed to serve the housing needs of a specific segment of the population. The volume of business reaches 8 billion Egyptian pounds.

During the last decade, as shown in Table 9.2 below, the total number of cooperatives decreased from 15,055 to 13,162. Yet, the number of members has not run in parallel and has only slightly decreased from 10.287 to 10.148 million. The volume of business has also decreased from L.E.42,474 to 36,000 million The major decrease in the number of cooperatives is demonstrated in the consumer cooperative societies. On the contrary, both the housing and agricultural cooperatives are gaining ground with their numbers increasing from 1,660 to 1,987 societies, and from 5,502 to 6,598 societies respectively.

Table 9.2: Number of cooperative societies, members and volume of business

Cooperation sector	1996		2005	
	No. of societies	No. of members (1000)	No. of societies	No. of members societies
Agriculture	5 502	3 530	6 598	4 000
Fishery	95	90	90	90
Housing	1 660	1 500	1 987	2 000
Consumer	7 334	5 100	4 005	4 000
Production	464	67	482	58
Total	15 055	10 287	13 162	10 148

Source: GCU 2005a.

GCU: the apex body of a unified sector

The membership of the board of directors of GCU consists of 26 members including three representatives for each of the five affiliated federations. In addition, six cooperative experts are appointed by the prime minister. The number of administrative staff of GCU is ten employees. However, a mark of the apex body in Egypt was the presence of a generation which dominated the cooperative movement for a long period of time. The ex-president of the GCU presided over the union for a period of approximately 20 years. In the last few years, the GCU board of directors witnessed an important change whereby 14 members of the board were replaced including the president.

The mandate of the GCU, according to the law of 1984, includes:

- Setting, in collaboration with the concerned ministries, the general policies for the cooperative sector

- Planning and coordination of the activities of all the sectors of the cooperative movement

- Conducting studies and research and compiling statistics related to cooperation
- Promoting cooperation by using all available media and methods
- Providing technical assistance and legal advice to the affiliated unions
- Promoting cooperative education and preparation of cooperative leaders
- Representing the cooperative sector nationally and internationally

The GCU holds an annual general conference during which the issues directed from the affiliated central unions are studied.

The involvement of GCU in providing technical assistance and training is limited to sporadic seminars. This is mainly due to the lack of finance. This in turn is related directly to the disinclination of affiliated federations to pay their financial contributions to the apex body.

Since the implementation of the Economic Reform and Structural Adjustment Programme the cooperative movement is almost absent from the political arena. State reliance on the private sector to shoulder the development activities has weakened the cooperatives' political presence in the country. Currently connections by the cooperative movement with members of the People's Assembly, the "Shura" council (senate), and other officials and decision makers are only ad hoc and personal.

Different laws and regulations

The current Egyptian constitution of 1971 contains clear statements which emphasize and endorse the cooperative sector in three articles. Article 26 states: "The law guarantees both small farmers and craftsmen 80% representation on the boards of directors in agricultural and industrial [productive] cooperative societies". Secondly article 28 provides the following: "The state endorses all types of cooperative establishments and encourages craftsmen industries in a way that secures production development and income increase. The state also supports agricultural cooperative societies in line with recent scientific principles". Finally article 29 states: "Ownership is subject to peoples' control and protected by the state; ownership includes three types: public ownership, cooperative ownership and private ownership" (Rashad, 2000).

The historical development of the movement, the diversity of sectors' activities and the multiplicity of supervising bodies led to the fact that there are several dispersed laws affecting the functioning of cooperatives[2]. According to the cooperative laws, the supervision of cooperatives is dispersed among several government administrative bodies located in a number of ministries including Agriculture, Housing, Social Affairs and Local Development.

According to recommendation No.193 the term *"cooperative"* means *"an autonomous association of persons united voluntarily to meet their common economic, social and cultural needs and aspirations through a jointly owned and democratically controlled enterprise"* The degree of compliance of the definitions of a cooperative in Egypt with recommendation 193, varies from one sector of cooperation to the other.

The Agricultural Cooperation Law No.122, 1980, article 1, defines a cooperative as:

> *"Every group formed willingly from natural or incorporeal persons who are engaged in different areas of agricultural work, in a way not contradicting internationally agreed upon principles of cooperation".*

According to article 1 of the Fishery Cooperatives law No.123/1983, fishery cooperatives are:

> *"socio-economic units which aim at developing and improving Fishery in its diversified areas, and provide different services to the members, and participate in the social development of their area to raise the level of living of the members and others, socially and economically within the general framework of the state policy, in a way not contradicting the internationally agreed upon principles".*

According to article 2 of the Consumer Cooperatives law No.109/1975, consumer cooperatives are:

> *"democratic and popular organizations composed of consumers of services and commodities, which aim at meeting the socio-economic requirements of their members through developing direct relationships between producers and consumers".*

According to article 2 of the Housing Cooperatives law no.14, 1981, housing

---

[2] There are seven laws for cooperatives, which indicate definition and activities of the concerned cooperative sector. These laws are: (1) General Cooperative Union Law (Apex) No. 28/1984, (2) Agricultural Cooperation Law No. 122/1980 (3) Fishery Cooperatives Law No. 123/1983 (4) Consumer Cooperation Law No. 109/1975 (5) Productive Cooperation Law No. 110/1975, (6) Housing Cooperation Law No. 14/1981, and (7) Educational Cooperation Law No. 1/1990.

cooperatives are:

"democratic, popular organizations which aim at providing housing for their members, and the required services needed for integrating the housing environment, in addition to providing the property with maintenance and care".

Supervision or suffocation?

Each central cooperative federation is under the supervision of a certain ministry. The agricultural and fishery cooperatives have been under several ministries. In 1960 they came under the permanent supervision of the Ministry of Agriculture. Production cooperation started under the supervision of the Ministry of Social Affairs. It moved to the Ministry of Industry and then finally the Ministry of Local Development in 1973 where it remains today. Housing cooperatives started and remain under the supervision of the Ministry of Housing. Consumer cooperatives are supervised by the Ministry of Supply.

In accordance with the different cooperative laws, the minister of each concerned ministry is in charge of enforcing the pertaining law. This includes administrative and financial inspection, review of records, monitoring boards of directors, managers, and employees. In addition the Central Authority for Auditing is in charge of inspecting the financial records of all the societies including GCU, the central federations and the regional level unions (El-Chazli Fawzi, 1993).

The relationship between the different segments of the state apparatus and the cooperative movement is rather tense and not improving. Although there is no explicit negative governmental position towards cooperatives, as is the case with the public sector, cooperative leadership does not feel at ease with the attitude of many officials. In the past, government dominance and control were accepted because they also involved support, provision of facilities, services and privileges to the cooperative movement. Yet, now, the governmental form of support has gone but the submission of cooperatives to government agencies remains. In some cases, the extreme hegemony of the administrative body is brutally maintained. They can block, dissolve or obstruct the activities of any cooperatives whenever they like. At times, this has a suffocating effect on the cooperatives concerned and the movement as a whole. In addition, many administrative bodies are engaged in unhealthy "corrupted" relations with cooperatives.

The registration of new cooperatives is facing a great deal of complication from the administrative bodies. The establishing of a new agricultural credit cooperative is almost impossible because officials feel that there should be only one such society in each Egyptian village. It is also hard to establish a new land reclamation cooperative due to tedious and cumbersome procedures.

It is however felt by many cooperative leaders that liberating the agricultural cooperative movement would unleash its ability to compete with the private sector.

The new cooperation legislation:

The cooperative movement in Egypt has been struggling for years to get legislative approval on a new unified law for cooperatives. The General Cooperative Union drafted a proposal of law and submitted it to the people's assembly (Egyptian Parliament) for discussion and approval.

The leaders of the cooperative movement are of the view that the current cooperative laws are not compatible with the socio-economic and political changes which have occurred in the last two decades. The proposed cooperation law aims at achieving legislation that secures: a) the autonomy of the cooperative movement, b) a coherent structure that emphasizes the economic identity of cooperatives as non-governmental organizations, and c) the international principles of cooperation (GCU, 2005).

The leaders of the cooperative movement emphasize that the vibrancy of the movement requires a new law to unleash its potential. However, changing the law is not an end in itself. What is needed is an overall correction and genuine change in the cooperative environment.

Cooperative development strategy

In 2005, the General Cooperative Union of Egypt issued an important document entitled *The Strategy of Cooperation in Egypt until 2020, and the role of the movement in modernizing Egypt* (GCU, 2005). The document detailed the importance of the cooperative movement to the Egyptian economy and society. It also discussed the main features of cooperation strategy until 2020 and the requirements for achieving such a strategy.

The strategy is based on the principles of the international cooperative movement. The strategy outlines a number of future actions in both the economic and social sectors, as well as in relation to capacity building. It also deals with the challenges and obstacles facing the cooperative movement. The document ends with detailing the economic and social objectives, as well as the potential and challenges for each of the five affiliated federations.

The strategy proposed by the GCU is broken down as follows:

1. Acquiring recognition by the state, along with its executive bodies, of the importance of cooperation in the national economy

2. Issuing cooperative legislation compatible with the socio-economic changes resulting from the economic reform policies. This legislation should be based on a number of principles such as the autonomy of the cooperatives, the equality of the cooperative, private and public sectors, the acknowledgement of the leading role of the General Cooperative Union (also in supervising, controlling, and monitoring), and a reduced role for governmental bodies

3. Unifying and simplifying the cooperative structure

4. Establishing a cooperative academy to encompass all the existing cooperative training institutes.

5. Allowing autonomy of cooperative finance (amongst others through the establishment of a cooperative bank or a central cooperative fund).

6. Involving the cooperative sector in policy-making bodies.

Foundation and registration of cooperatives

In Egypt, the registration of a cooperative is a rigorous process that may deter many from taking the initiative to form a cooperative. The registration of a cooperative requires the submission of several documents and going through several steps. Taking the registration of an agricultural cooperative as an example the foundation contract submitted must include the date and place of editing the contract. It also must have the name of the society, the area of service, type, and purposes of the society. The next facet the contract must include is the value of the paid capital. After this it must contain the names of founders, their residential areas, occupations or professions, and finally a bank certificate showing the deposit of the society's paid capital must be present.

Vibrancy and sustainability of cooperatives:

Position and scale

The vertical integration of different levels of cooperative organizations is demonstrated through the formulation of the General Cooperative Union of Egypt (GCU), the apex of the cooperation structure. This union was established by law in 1984 and its board of directors is composed of the presidents and three members of each cooperative union, as well as six members appointed by the Prime Minister from persons having considerable experience within the area of cooperation. This is a clear indication of the articulation of the cooperative sector with the State apparatus and the political regime.

Box 9.1: A productive cooperative triggered by an inspiring leader

The Village Markets Productive Cooperative Society is located in a rural area, Menshat Kasseb village, 50 km south of Cairo. The society was established in 1998 as an initiative by Dr. Mahmoud Sherif, Ex-Minister of Local Development, and presently the head of the General Union of Non-Governmental Organizations. The initiative was a response to the need felt to solve the marketing problems faced by young farmers especially. The main goal of the society is to provide technical assistance to its members as well as the means of transport to ship the produce to the nearby urban centres.

The government granted the society L.E.300,000 from the Local Development Fund. The loan was used by the society to establish greenhouses to provide a number of outlets for displaying and selling farmers' produce in some parts of Giza Region.

The cooperative employs 25 persons (16 males, and nine females). The society offers sufficiently attractive working conditions, including modern communication facilities such as five telephone lines and a fax machine.

Of the 145 farmer members 60 are females. The society is aiming to increase the number of members/beneficiaries of the society to about 4,000. Members' fees are set at L.E.25 annually (around $5). The society provides non-economic services, including training courses for the members and their families, leisure time activities, home economics activities for female members, health care, and awareness-raising

---

workshops in areas of members' rights and responsibilities. The society also provides special assistance to small and poor farmers, through annual financial donations and subsidized transport to market.

In 2005 the society's turnover was about L.E.5 million, which allows the society to cover the overhead, administrative and managerial costs.

The society also provides a good example of horizontal integration and partnership with organizations in the region, as it partners a local NGO in a project for orphans' care, a religious society in holding extension seminars and meetings for members and beneficiaries, and another NGO in the area of exporting horticultural crops.

The scale of operations within the cooperation sector varies significantly. According to the 2005 figures, the agricultural cooperative sector did business of approximately L.E.25 billion. In contrast the fishery cooperatives only realized L.E.1 billion. Meanwhile the scale of operations in both consumer and production cooperatives is nearly L.E.10 billion. The impressive figures for the agricultural cooperatives could be attributed to both the relatively large number of agricultural cooperative societies (6,334) and the fact that almost the entire agricultural sector depends on the cooperatives which exist in all Egyptian villages.

Human resources

The managerial and accounting skills available in most cooperatives interviewed are reported as satisfactory. Cooperatives sometimes employ university graduates trained in commerce and cooperative topics in the fields of administration, accounting and public relations. They also employ commerce and agricultural high school graduates. In addition, all central cooperative unions regularly organize training courses for the staff of the affiliated cooperative societies on different managerial and accounting topics. Most of the cooperatives interviewed indicated that their staff received training on management and accounting topics. It is worth mentioning that almost all the interviewed agricultural "parastatal" cooperatives reported that their employees did not receive any training at all in recent years.

Quite a number of staff, but also directors and members of cooperatives are trained by one of the three specialized cooperative training institutes. The High Institute for Cooperative and Administrative Studies in Cairo has a roll of no fewer than 40,000 students. The High Institute for Agricultural Cooperation (Shubra El_khiama) caters for 20,000 students and the High Institute for Cooperation and Agricultural Extension (Assuit) for 10,000 students.

In addition academic courses and training on cooperation are also offered in most commerce and agricultural colleges.

Market oriented character of cooperative activities

The market competitiveness among the primary cooperatives in our sample is moderate. The agricultural cooperatives are trying hard to keep a foothold in the market since they started facing fierce competition from the private sector. Their competitiveness is likely to come from their capital and management skills. However, a number of studies (Aal & Hassan, 1998:289; El-Zoghby et al., 1995: 25-28) confirm that the majority of agricultural cooperatives' members and clients still have confidence in and preference for cooperatives due to their proximity, quality assurance and better prices than the private sector.

The agricultural cooperative societies established after the Economic Reform and Structural Adjustment Policies (ERSAP) are showing comparatively better market performances. They closely monitor the prices in the local markets and provide their members and clients with goods and services at competitive prices. These more recently established cooperatives do not face as much control by the Ministry of Agriculture as their older colleagues. The productive cooperative societies are even more oriented to the market. They provide a wide variety of goods and services with different levels of quality and prices for an expansive market. For most of the producer cooperatives in our sample the issue of competitiveness did not pose a threat or burden.

Limited financial participation by members

The financial participation of members in most cooperative societies is limited to the annual membership fees. In 1961 membership of farmers in agricultural cooperative societies became compulsory. Annual fees were automatically deducted from farmers' transactions with the cooperative. All in all this represented a meagre financial contribution. In addition to the membership fees cooperatives used to charge extra fees on fertilizers and seeds distributed to farmers. After the promulgation of law no. 96 of 1992 which aimed at amending the relationship between the landlord and the tenants of agricultural land, the membership map in agricultural cooperatives changed dramatically because a considerable number of tenants were evicted. This had a very negative effect on the turnover and the income of the cooperatives. In addition increased competition by the private sector forced agricultural cooperatives to reduce fees levied on agricultural inputs.

The financial situation of new agricultural cooperative societies (formed after ERSAP) is comparatively better. The director of one cooperative interviewed reported that members pay about L.E.25 (<$5.0) as an annual fee, and they also receive voluntary financial as well as in-kind contributions.

Few facilities and security

It was revealed from in-depth interviews that primary agricultural cooperatives lack the basic communication facilities such as telephone lines. In contrast, the housing and consumer cooperatives have telephones and sometimes a fax machine.

Security measures against robbery and theft are lacking in most agricultural and fishery cooperatives, and in some cases are limited to a night guard. Again in contrast, the majority of the production cooperatives have a wide range of security and safety measures including trained and armed security personnel and insurance policies against robbery, theft, fire and other hazards.

Vertical and horizontal integration among cooperatives

Compared to many other African countries, the Egyptian movement is known to have many vertical and horizontal linkages. An example of vertical integration is the attempt by the GCU to contract with farmers at "Al Wadi Al Gadid" Region for the marketing of their dates among local cooperatives all over the country. An example of horizontal integration is given by the consumer cooperative federation which is contracting with some land reform cooperatives for delivering rice to be sold in primary consumer cooperatives.

However, integration and cooperation between cooperatives happen on a case by case basis. Further integration is hampered by the lack of coordination between GCU and some federations. Several federations do not regularly pay their contributions to the GCU. This creates financial headaches for the GCU leadership but, in addition, weakens the authority of the apex body tremendously.

Relation with donors: through government

In Egypt, cooperatives societies and unions have no direct relations with the donor community. The administrative bodies monopolize and jealously guard this relationship. During the interviews with apex leaders, they expressed dissatisfaction with the allocation of donor funds earmarked for the cooperative movement. For example: an Italian donor provided funds to upgrade consumer cooperatives. This was done through the Ministry of Supply. However the funds were diverted for refurbishing the state-owned consumer shops. Furthermore, attempts by the GCU and some cooperative federations to have cooperative development included in some international cooperation programmes have been frustrated.

As a consequence most cooperatives work without any external support, loans or grants, be it from donors or from the government. Only a few production cooperatives were able to get loans from certain government agencies or were offered marketing outlets in urban centres by local authorities.

Employment estimates in the cooperative sector:

The total number of members in all the cooperatives of Egypt is over 10 million. The distribution of members in the main five federations is shown in Table 9.3 below. It does not seem imprudent to assume that most of these members rely heavily on their cooperative for either their employment or for a substantial part of the income they generate through self-employment.

Table 9.3: Total number of cooperative members in Egypt

Federation	Number of members (Thousand)	%
Consumer	4 000	39.4
Production	58	0.6
Agricultural	4 000	39.4
Housing	2 000	19.7
Fishery	90	0.8
Total	10 148	100

Source: GCU 2005a unpublished data (21:5-7).

The total number of staff in all cooperatives is about 9,500. Most cooperatives only employ a few staff but some do employ a significant number of people. Each of the consumer cooperative societies established for government employees employs between 20 and 30 workers. A number of worker-owned cooperatives also have a large staff and create new jobs at a rapid rate. The cooperative society for the workers in Misr Spinning and Weaving Company, El Mehala El Kobra City, for example, created about 1,000 new employment opportunities during 2000-2005. The state owned "Cooperation House for Printing and Publishing" which is the main publishing house for cooperative newspapers, magazines and books is one of the biggest employers in the sector. It has about 1,500 staff on its payroll.

As has been indicated the cooperative movement in Egypt has very ambitious plans in terms of expansion and the creation of employment. The cooperative federations and the General Cooperative Union want to create about 710,000 jobs over the next 15 years. The following table sets out these plans for the different sub-sectors of the movement.

Table 9.4: Expected work opportunities in the cooperative sector

Cooperative sector	Expected work opportunities	%
Consumer	20 000	2.8
Agricultural	500 000	70.4
Production	100 000	14.1
Housing	15 000	2.1
Fishery	75 000	10.6
Total	710 000	100.0

Source: GCU 2005a data.

The development plan of the Consumer Cooperative Federation foresees the merger of some of the cooperative societies and dissolution of the inefficient ones. This will reduce the number from the current 4,500 to about 1,000 societies. The plan aims to create new positions in each cooperative society including: three positions for computer and accounting, three for sales, and three for marketing and supervision. This alone would create approximately 9,000 jobs. The plan also includes new projects for the packaging of goods as well as the establishment of new consumer cooperative societies in new communities.

The Federation of Housing Cooperatives aims to establish 200 societies in the new communities. Each of these could employ ten university graduates.

The Fishery Cooperative Federation presently involves 95 societies and more than 5,000 fishing boats. The plan of the federation is to upgrade, modernize and mechanize these boats. This would create between 10 and 20 jobs for each boat.

Cooperative leaders interviewed hastened to add that these ambitious employment plans are facing several obstacles. Above all is the enduring intervention of governmental bodies. In addition, cooperative transactions are subjected to the rules of the new tax law which will make cooperatives less competitive. Cooperatives have also lost their long-established privileges related to public auctions and tenders.

Cooperative business for poverty reduction and social protection

Cooperatives operate mainly in areas where poverty prevails. In their membership policy as well as in their day-to-day operations they show concern for the poorer strata in society. The housing cooperatives might be an exception as they target a population that is economically more capable. Officials in these cooperatives confirmed that the members from poorer social groups do not exceed 25%.

Box 9.2: The cooperative society of the workers in Egypt's company for spinning and weaving, El-Mehala Al-kubra

This cooperative society was established in 1934. It currently owns 40 consumer and services branches and has a membership of about 38,950. The cooperative has an impressive number of assets.

- Five bakeries to provide members with bread.

- 28 vehicles, including trucks, pick-ups and private cars to facilitate service provision.

- 20 buses and micro-buses for transporting members' sons and daughters to schools and colleges and for recreational tours.

- A "society-owned" summer resort in Raas El-Barr includes 125 residential units.

In addition, the cooperative also gives financial support to members and their families who face medical expenses. And, in the tradition of consumer cooperatives, it pays the members a bonus on their purchases as an application of the cooperative principle of "cost-based selling".

It has to be noted though that poverty reduction and targeting the poor as such are not on the agenda of most cooperatives. Their aim is to enhance the welfare and purchasing power of all the members (poor and not so poor) through their main economic activities. The same can be said for their contribution to the extension of social protection mechanisms. Cooperatives do reduce the risks faced by their members and as such give them a certain security and protection. But they do not deliberately target their poorer members for this.

Another reason why combating poverty is not a clear and separate component of cooperative programmes is that the cooperative movement is not invited to participate in state initiatives in this field. The state opted to combat poverty through encouraging individual small businesses rather than collective cooperative projects.

Limited Voice and Representation

The cooperative movement – according to GCU leaders is weak in lobbying politicians and legislators. It does not have many political advocates for the issues of concern to the movement. As a consequence quite a number of policy measures are taken that harm the movement. This was the case with the new law taxing cooperative transactions. In addition the movement leadership sees a need to activate the media with regard to promoting cooperative interests. The GCU therefore plans to use all available media, and especially the newspapers, and not to limit itself any more to the cooperative press.

Conclusion

The transition from a situation where the state promoted and protected the cooperative sector to one where the state opts for a market led economy and neglects cooperative interests has been and is still very painful for the sector. The cooperative movement in Egypt is struggling to survive. Notwithstanding their free market discourse, state agencies still heavily intervene in the activities of cooperatives. This paralyzes the movement and keeps it from responding to economic changes. This is particularly so for the agricultural cooperatives. Still, there are numerous examples both in the agricultural and other cooperative sectors that prove that cooperatives can effectively compete with other players in the market. Cooperatives have a lot of growth potential and can significantly contribute to creation of employment. This requires an uncompromising policy reform and the transformation of cooperatives from components of the public domain to private economic enterprises with full and unrestricted freedom to operate. A new legal framework is, therefore, needed that at the local level allow individuals to create and run their cooperatives without too many administrative burdens and at the national level permits the GCU to take autonomous leadership of the entire movement.

List of Acronyms

GCU	General Cooperative Union
HCC	Housing and Construction Cooperative
HCCU	Housing and Construction Cooperative Union
ESDF	Egyptian Social Fund for Development
PCF	Production Cooperation Federation
PBDAC	Principal Bank for Development and Agricultural Credit
L.E.	Egyptian Pound ($ 1=L.E. 5.7, 1 Euro= L.E. 6.9)

Bibliography

- Aal A. & Hassan M. (1998), 'Farmers and Cooperatives in the Era of Structural Adjustment', in: N. S. Hopkins & K. Westergaard (Eds.), *Direction of change in Rural Egypt*, The American University in Cairo Press.

- *Agricultural cooperation Law*, No. 122, 1980.

- Arab Cooperation Federation, (2000), *Consumer cooperatives and their role in the development of Pan-Arab Trade*, Kuwait, 13-17 February (In Arabic).

- Birchall J. (2004), *Cooperatives and the Millennium Goals*, ILO, Geneva.

- The Central Administration for Public Mobilization and Statistics (1974), *Statistical Year Book 1974*.

- The Central Administration for Public Mobilization and Statistics (1979), *Statistical Year Book 1979*.

- The Central Administration for Public Mobilization and Statistics (1982), *Statistical Year Book 1982*.

- The Central Administration for Public Mobilization and Statistics (1994), *Statistical Year Book 1994*.

- The Central Consumer Cooperative Federation (1975), 'Law of *Consumer cooperation*', n° 109/1975.

- Central Consumer Cooperative Union of Egypt, (1975), 'Consumer Cooperation Law', n° 109/1975, *Consumer Cooperation*.

- Central Housing Cooperative Union of Egypt (1981), 'Housing Cooperation Law ', n° 14/1981, *Housing Cooperation*.

- Cooperative Union for Fishery Cooperatives (1993), '1-Law', n° 123/1983, *Fishery cooperatives*, '2- Law' n° 124/1983, *Fishing, organizing fish farms*.

- El-Chazli Fawzi (1993), *Cooperative Organizations at International and Arabic Levels* (in Arabic), Cooperation Book Series, Cooperation House for Printing and Publishing, Cairo.

- General Cooperative Union of Egypt (2005), Information data on the General Cooperative Union.

- General Cooperative Union of Egypt (2005), *The Strategy of Cooperation in Egypt until 2020, and the role of the movement in the modernization of Egypt*.

- http://0www.eiu.com.lib.aucegypt.edu/index.asp?layout=displayIssue Article&issue.

- http://dwvdata.worldbank.org/external/CPProfile.asp?PTYPE=CP&C CODE=EGY.

- Khalid Y. (1993), *The Role of Cooperatives within the Contemporary Socio-economic Changes* (in Arabic), Cooperation Book Series, Cooperation House for Printing and Publishing, Cairo.

- Mahmoud S. A. (1993), *Agricultural and Cooperative Policy within Economic Liberalization* (in Arabic), Cooperation Book Series, Cooperation House for Printing and Publishing, Cairo.

- Murad A. (1996), *Cooperative Movement in Egypt, The Dilemma and the Way Out* (in Arabic), Cooperation Book Series, Cooperation House for Printing and Publishing, Cairo.

- National Planning Institute (2001), 'Horizons and Future of Agricultural Cooperatives', *Planning and Development Issues Series*.

- Rashad M. (1994), *Cooperative Solution – The Right Way* (in Arabic), Cooperation Book Series, Cooperation House for Printing and Publishing, Cairo.

- Rashad M. (1997), *Lights on Agricultural and Cooperative Development* (in Arabic), Agricultural and Cooperation.

- Rashad M. (1998), *Agricultural and Cooperation Media* (in Arabic), Cooperation Book Series, Cooperation House for Printing and Publishing, Cairo.

- Rashad, M. (1998), *Cooperative Egypt, and Future Challenges*, (in Arabic), Cooperation Book Series, Cooperation House for Printing and Publishing, Cairo.

- Rashad M. (2000), *Cooperative System and the Third Direction* (in Arabic), Cooperation Book Series, Cooperation House for Printing and Publishing, Cairo.

- Rashad M. (2002), *Cooperative and Agricultural Sector-Contemporary Challenges* (in Arabic), Cooperation Book Series, Cooperation House for Printing and Publishing, Cairo.

- World Bank (1993), *The Development of Cooperative and other Rural Organizations*.

- Zoghby E., El-Din S., Mohamed A. & Kader A. (1995), *Institutional Changes Required for Rural Community Development in Egypt-Final Report*, Academy of Scientific Research and Technology.

List of Persons Interviewed

Dr. Ahmed Abdel-Zaher Osman, President of the GCU.

Dr. Medhat Ayoub, General Manager of the GCU.

Dr. Mahmoud Mansour, Vice-President of the General Cooperative Union.

Mr. Yehya Abu Zaid, Head of Board of Directors, Village Markets Society (production).

Mr. Gaber Abdel Aal, Head of Board of Directors, Barnacht Agricultural Credit Cooperative.

Mr. Samir Abu Bakr, Manager, Mit Rahina Agricultural Cooperative.

Mr. Mohamed Azaz, Head of Board of Directors, Carpet & Rugs productive society.

Mr. Samy M. Hakim, General Manager, Cargo transport cooperative society.

Mr. Sayeed, Administrative staff, "Ofok Horizon" Housing Cooperative Society.

Mr. Mohamed, Cooperative Society for Construction and Housing.

Mrs. Hekma Hussien Aly, Financial Manager, Housewives Cooperative Society.

Mr. Sabry Abdul Hakim Ismaiel, Manager, Mansafis Agricultural (Credit) Cooperative.

Mr. Gamal M. Aly, Manager, Hawasliya Agricultural (Land Reform) Cooperative.

Mr. Hussien Abdul Karim, Manager, Sahala Agricultural (Credit) Cooperative.

Mr. Hassan M. Hassan, Manager, Bee Breeder Productive Cooperative Society.

Mr. Maher Samoul Hana, Vice-President, Productive Cooperative for Poultry Development.

Mr. Yossif Maximus, Board Member, Veterinary Productive Cooperative Society for Service and Development.

Dr. Alla Eldin Taha, Manager, Veterinary Productive Cooperative Society for Service and Development.

Mr. Ahmed Sedik, Advisor to the GTZ Project for Cooperative Development.

Mr. Wagdy Bahr, Director of Foreign Relations Department, The Central Agricultural Cooperation Federation.

Mr. Mohamed Al-Saeed Abdul Rahman, Head of Board of Directors, The Agricultural Credit Cooperative Society – Mit Ali Village.

Mr. Ibrahim Abdul Halim, Head of Board of Directors, The Agricultural Credit Cooperative Society – Mit Al Haloug Village.

Dr. Mohamed I. Zean El Din, Member of Board of Directors, The Housing Cooperative Society for Employees of Mansoura University.

Mr. Sami S. Khalifa, General Manager, The Animal Wealth Cooperative
   Society, Mansoura, Dakahliya.
Osama Galal, Member of Board of Directors, The Fishery Cooperative
   Society, Nasayma village, Matariay, Dakahliya.
Manoud Abdel Moniem, Member of Board of Directors, Consumer
   Cooperative Society for Employees of Mansoura University.

List of Primary Cooperatives Sampled

I) Cooperatives selected for interviews in Lower Egypt "Delta" –
   Dakahliya Region:
1) The Agricultural Credit Cooperative Society – Mit Ali village
2) The Agricultural Credit Cooperative Society – Mit Al Haloug village
3) The Agricultural Credit Cooperative Society
4) The Housing Cooperative Society for Employees of Mansoura University
5) The Animal Wealth Cooperative Society, Mansoura, Dakahliya
6) The Fishery Cooperative Society, Nassayma village, Dakahliya
7) The Consumer Cooperative Society for Employees of Mansoura
   University
II) Cooperatives selected for interviews in Middle Egypt-Giza Region:
8) The Markets of Productive Village Cooperative Society
9) The Agricultural Cooperative Society – Barnacht village
10) The Agricultural Cooperative Society – Mit Rahina village
11) The Cooperative Productive Society for Carpets and Rugs
12) The Cooperative Productive Society for Cargo Transport
13) The Cooperative Society for Construction and Housing
14) The "Ofok *Horizon*" Housing Cooperative Society
15) The Production Cooperative Society for Housewives, Giza city, Giza
III) Cooperatives selected for interviews in Upper Egypt-Minia Region:
16) The Agricultural Credit Cooperative, Mansafis
17) The Agricultural Land Reform Cooperative, Hawasliya
18) The Agricultural Land Reform Cooperative, Al Matahra Al Qiblia
19) The Agricultural Credit Cooperative, Al Sahala
20) Veterinary Productive Cooperative Society for Service and Development
21) Productive Cooperative for Poultry Development
22) Bee Breeder Productive Cooperative Society
23) The Cooperative Society for Construction and Housing for Minia City
   People, Minia

Chapter Ten – Surviving on the Islands: Cooperatives in Cape Verde

by João Gomes Mendonça[1]

Introduction

The present-day cooperative movement in Cape Verde emerged only after independence in 1975. For a long time, it has been the subject of policy efforts to promote participatory development in order to empower the local populations to improve their living conditions. Such participation can best occur in people's organizations like cooperatives. At this moment, however, Cape Verdean legislation on cooperatives falls short of providing the required support to promote and develop the cooperative sector.

This paper attempts to explain this severe shortfall in politics and the effect it has had on the strengths and weaknesses of cooperatives in terms of dynamism, sustainability, scope, scale and the support mechanisms available to them. Data for this study were gathered through documents, interviews and three case studies. The first case study is Adalgiza Moniz. It is a successful consumer cooperative, founded in 1983 and based in a working-class district of Praia City (the country's capital). It is affiliated to the Praia Union which is in turn a member of Fenacoop. It has 250 members: 200 women and 50 men. Sales in 2004 totalled €400,000. It runs several vocational training schemes for its members, employs five full-time staff and has an efficient accounting system. The second case study that is also affiliated to Fenacoop is the São Domingos consumer cooperative with 300 members, most of them female. Sales in 2004 totalled €326,486. Its accounting is handled by Fenacoop. It has six permanent staff of its own. Finally, there is Trabalho e Progresso, a carpentry and joinery cooperative, which was formed in 1975 just a few months after the country became independent. It has 14 members, all of them employed in the cooperative. At the time of writing, this

---

[1] João G. Mendonça has a Master's degree in languages (University of Lomé). He developed a career in the leadership of the cooperative movement of Cape Verde. Specialized in subjects related to social economy and cooperatives, he has worked as a private consultant the ICA, UNDP and other agencies since 2002.

cooperative was clearly in trouble due to problems of internal organization, leadership, competition and conflicting personal interests of its members. So we have three cases, all of them based in or about the Praia urban perimeter but quite different in terms of performance and sustainability.

The rise and fall of Cape Verdean cooperatives: a short history

In the past, Cape Verdean cooperatives played an important part in supplying staple commodities such as rice, maize, milk, sugar, oil and soap to the poorest rural populations, replacing the main distribution agency, **A Central das Cooperativas**[2], which had existed prior to national independence. Other cooperatives came to be organized around activities in the sectors of light manufacturing/crafts and small businesses, fishing, agriculture, forestry and stock breeding, housing, savings and credit[3] plus a rare service cooperative. These are detailed in Table 10.1.

The period from 1993 to the present is critical for cooperatives in Cape Verde. Democracy has been introduced and the principles of the market economy have been adopted, yet the state has not put in place any policy to support cooperatives through this transition period.

Of the 183 cooperatives formerly making up the cooperative sector, which are registered and legally recognised by the appropriate authorities, only 85 seem to be active. The largest group (50) is formed by grassroots consumer cooperatives affiliated to an umbrella organisation called Fenacoop[4] (National Federation of Consumer Cooperatives), which consists of four cooperative unions, namely: Unicoop-Praia, Unicoop-Fogo, Unicoop-Santo Antão and Unicoop-Maio.

---

[2] The aim of this Central, formed on 1 August 1975, was to provide support for cooperatives and its work focused on supply, transportation, and technical and financial assistance. In order to fund its work the Central operated a bakery. The status of this body was ambiguous and it was not equipped to foster the development of an autonomous cooperative movement.
[3] Savings banks and credit institutions are associations of persons designed to promote mutual assistance by saving money which is then lent out to their members. The current position of micro-finance in Cape Verde is that there are two institutions: Citi Habitat and Fami Picos. The latter was formed in 2000 when three of the 15 mutual societies that already existed on Santiago Island merged. Because the country still has no relevant legislation, Fami Picos is registered as an association and reckoned to be one of Cape Verde's providers of micro-finance.
[4] Formed in 1991, Fenacoop is headquartered in Praia, the national capital. It supplies and gives administrative support to cooperatives in all the islands through the cooperative unions (Unicoops). It was given legal recognition in the *Official Gazette of Cape Verde*, No. 31, of 3 August 1991.

Table 10.1: Cooperatives in Cape Verde by branch of activity

Branch of activity	1975 – 1992		1993 – 2005		Structural integration	
	Formal organizations	No. of members	Formal organizations	No. of members	2nd degree	3rd degree
Consumption	124	19 520	50	4 000	4	1
Small-scale fisheries	4	36	8	60	1*	
Light manu¬factur¬ing/ crafts & small businesses	14	104	10	50		
Agriculture, forestry & stock breeding	22	284	2**	18**		
Housing/Construction	6	138	10***	60***		
Credit	12	870	4	2 000		
Services	1	60	1	6		
TOTAL	183	21 012	85	6 194	4+1*	1

Source: INC/DEPC and Fórum Cooperativo – Cape Verde.
* This Union is not yet operational for the reasons given later on in this chapter.
** These cooperatives are failing. Problem factors: lack of water, no access to credit.
*** The members of these cooperatives took bank loans to build their homes and are still repaying the bank. But they are not engaged in any cooperative activity.

According to Fenacoop's articles of association, its main objectives are as follows:

• to manage purchasing operations, import goods and distribute them to the unions and grassroots cooperatives;

• to supply inputs to agricultural production and stock breeding cooperatives and help them market their products;

• to provide technical assistance to the unions and cooperatives; and

• to coordinate and implement training measures.

The total number of members for the consumption sector, which is the largest, is 4,000. The other sectors have a membership of 2,194. This gives the cooperative sector a total membership of 6,194, or a penetration rate of 1.4%. Prior to 1990, this rate was 6.6%. Then, there used to be other branches of cooperative activity too, such as light manufacturing, small-scale fishing, agriculture, forestry, stock breeding and housing. Today, these cooperatives have all but collapsed, or they are on the brink of bankruptcy. The only exception to this trend of cooperative development is the credit unions sector, which is on the rise again.

The reasons for this decline are multiple. Cape Verdeans tended to be too much dependent on donors. They had difficulties in access to credit, given the lack of any proper system of loans following the abolition of the FAC and INC. Furthermore, they were not helped by a weak support structure at state level (inadequate human, financial and material resources) and by the total absence of any national policy on cooperative development appropriate to the current socio-economic context.

Who they are and how they operate

The members of Cape Verdean cooperatives are for the most part civil servants and thus lower middle-class as well as farmers, stock breeders, and small traders. Women make up a high proportion of the membership, but – due to their lack of formal schooling – are seldom appointed to posts as directors or officers.

Cooperatives also have another category of members, namely workers deployed under certain labour-intensive infrastructure programmes (FAIMO). These are unskilled people whom the state regards as a vulnerable group because of their minimal social security entitlements. They are given employment on farms or on public infrastructure projects like water and soil conservation, construction work or road maintenance. For obvious reasons, they are mainly members of consumer cooperatives.

Cape Verdean cooperatives are usually organized and structured around a general meeting, which is the supreme body of the cooperative, bringing together all its members. The general meeting is held at least once a year, when, amongst other things, it conducts a review of the past year's activities, elects the members of the cooperative's management bodies and approves the budget for the following year. However, not all cooperatives abide by these principles laid down in their articles of association. For example the Trabalho e Progresso cooperative founded in 1975 has not held a general meeting since 1995.

Box 10.1: Dynamics of UNICOOP – Fogo

The Union of Consumer Cooperatives for Fogo Island (Unicoop–Fogo) was formed in 1987. Seven grassroots cooperatives are members of the Union. Its chief activity is the sale of food and other staples, agricultural production factors and building materials to the population of the 37,000 inhabitants of this small island.

Its management bodies, which work well, are the general meeting, the board of directors and the audit committee. Under the articles of association officers are elected for a three-year term. The Union is governed by direct democracy, and every member has the right to vote.

Of the 404 members, 344 are active. 64% of cooperative members have been members for more than ten years. Over half of the members are forty years old or above. One quarter is illiterate. Total indirect beneficiaries are estimated at over 2,300. The cooperative, which has 16 sale outlets island-wide, employs 58 people of whom 15 are members. But also on average 40 seasonal workers are engaged per month, mainly for loading and unloading merchandise.

The yearly turnover realized by the cooperative is about 2.8 million euro. Since 1987 Unicoop – Fogo has paid a dividend to its members based on the year-end results (surplus). For example: a dividend of €8,978 for the year 2004 was distributed amongst seven grassroots cooperatives which are members of the Union. This dividend is 30% of the reserved surplus. The remaining 70% was channelled into education, training and investment. The cooperative also accepts that members buy on credit.

Members do not only get special prices in the shops, Unicoop-Fogo also gets involved in quite a number of welfare activities. The huts of exceptionally poor members have been repaired, their medical consultations are also paid for and medicines are bought. Payment of school fees for members' children is made annually. Every member is also entitled to a death grant of €137.

Unfortunately, the property of the Union was seized by the state years ago; a matter that has not been settled.

The board of directors of a cooperative usually comprises five people. If a cooperative has fewer than 15 members, they could limit themselves to a chairman. All cooperatives usually elect an audit committee but in practice, this body is not operational in most of them. Of the three cooperatives under review in this study, only two had a functioning audit committee. This has to do with a gross underestimation of the importance of auditing the activities, as well as with audit committee members lacking the necessary skills and abilities. Moreover, in most of the cases very close family or neighbourly ties prevent an objective scrutiny of the administrative and financial measures taken by the cooperative's bodies.

Only two of the three cooperatives studied pay out a year-end dividend to their members. These dividends are converted into goods which are distributed to each member. The value varies from €6 to €7 per member depending on the cooperative's results for the year. The São Domingos cooperative occasionally has trouble paying out dividends because its members buy goods on credit and the value of these debts cancels out any dividend.

From constitution to naught: cooperatives and the law

The Republic of Cape Verde's first Constitution was approved during the ninth parliamentary session of the First Legislature on 5 September 1980. Article 11 of this basic law recognized three forms of property: state, private and cooperative. It said that cooperative property, organized on the basis of free consent, referred to land and farming activity, the production of consumer goods, craft and small business activity and other activities stipulated by the law.

Later, the National Institute of Cooperatives (INC) was established by Decree as an autonomous agency of the state, governed by pubic law. Its mission was to promote cooperativism by implementing government policy and studying, disseminating and popularizing cooperativism. The INC was also to organize and coordinate support for cooperatives in the areas of technical and financial assistance and vocational training.

This favourable legal environment was, however, radically revised by a Decree-Law in 1990. This decree very much reflected the spirit of structural adjustment, which had become more prevalent and "fashionable" by that time. The 1992 Constitution of the Republic continued to make express mention of cooperatives, but at the same time placed them within the private sector. It defined the private sector to consist "of the means of production whose property and management belong to individuals or private organizations, including cooperatives". In 1994, a Decree-Law abolished the Cooperatives Support Fund (FAC), replacing it with the Rural Credit Bank (CCR) whose purpose was to grant loans to cooperatives, except consumer cooperatives. But for technical and political reasons, this institution did not last long. Three years later, another Decree-Law abolished the INC, replacing it with the Ministry of Environment and Agriculture's General Directorate for Rural Development and Promotion of Cooperatives, whose purpose was to promote cooperativism.

The 1999 revision of the Constitution then removed all references to the cooperative sector, mentioning only the public and private sectors as economic actors. Subsequently, yet another Decree tacitly repealed the *diploma* (public document) approving the General Rules on Cooperatives. Since then, the cooperative sector has been governed by the Commercial Code which does not distinguish cooperatives from any other type of private enterprise. Thus, by 1999, the cooperative movement, left to its own devices, was clearly running out of steam.

It must be pointed out, however, that Structural Adjustment Programmes (SAPs) have had no direct effect on cooperative development in Cape Verde, cooperatives being to some extent immune from the demands of the International Monetary Fund. The sector went through these wilderness years not because of SAPs but the total disengagement of the Cape Verdean government. And, while in these years a number of cooperative structures were disappearing, other similar organizations such as community development associations, community enterprises and economic interest groups emerged.

Realizing this, more than half of the country's existing cooperatives were prompted to examine the crises the Cape Verdean cooperative movement was experiencing at a workshop held in Praia City in August 1999. This meeting led to the creation of a Fórum Cooperativo which received a mandate from the Cape Verde Prime Minister in January 2002 to work together in partnership with the Government (Ministry of Employment and Solidarity) and with civil society. This Forum's aim was to revitalize and consolidate the movement on the basis of projects selected by Fórum Cooperativo and approved by the Government. The Fórum Cooperativo's project for a national policy on cooperative development dates back to 2003. This has not as yet had an impact in terms of legislation. The Ministry of Employment and Solidarity gives Fórum Cooperativo a small subsidy (€707 per month) to cover its operating costs. The state also pays the salaries of three civil servants working for the Forum. In addition, it meets the costs which the Forum incurs when negotiating funding for its projects.

Cooperatives used to be registered with the National Institute of Cooperatives (INC) at no cost to them. INC had legalized a total of 294 cooperatives for all the branches between 1978 and the beginning of April 1999. Since then this function has been transferred to the Government Notary's Office, which makes the process of securing legal recognition for cooperatives pretty unwieldy. In order to perform well in this task, this Office has neither enough qualified personnel, nor a set of transparent rules and regulations on the subject. Moreover, the registration (and recognition) process now costs each cooperative €454, and each cooperative must produce a bank statement showing that its registered capital is at least one-third paid up, that is to say, to a value of €605. This is just one of the factors which complicate things further. Only through the *Official Gazette* could it be worked out how many cooperatives the Notary's Office has recognized, because it does not liaise at all with Fórum Cooperativo.

Disarray and rejuvenation

Cooperativism was understood by the élites of Cape Verde not in terms of economic and social effectiveness but rather as the logical consequence of a dominant ideology whose ultimate expression was the one-party state. This vision, which ended with the birth of the 2nd Republic in 1991, was, however, not shared by many. Most of the country's traders, for example, viewed cooperatives as an instrument created to work against them. It had never occurred to anyone that the creation of a cooperative enterprise could be above all a conscious choice and even an act of responsible citizenship.

The 2nd Republic in 1991 brought new reforms aimed at creating a political and institutional framework that would favour private sector development. This was pursued through the adoption of a series of policy measures, focused upon encouragement of foreign investment, promotion of exports, liberalization of trade and labour markets, privatization of public enterprises and tax reform. These reforms heralded a new chapter in the history of the Cape Verdean cooperative movement: an end to state paternalism and a new governmental attitude to cooperatives as a component of the private sector. In practice, the state's disengagement became apparent, primarily in the weakening and subsequent abolition of two instruments of support for the cooperative movement, namely the INC and FAC, followed by the "usurping"[5] of resources generated by the cooperative movement[6]. Cooperatives have fallen into obscurity, losing the high profile and social importance they had worked hard to achieve.

As far as the structure of the cooperative movement is concerned, the first

[5] Jacinto Santos, in: *O Cooperativismo em Cabo Verde: relato de um percurso*, Democracia, Sistemas Eleitorais e Economia Social/Assembleia Nacional de Cabo Verde, October 2002.
[6] At the 6th ICA Africa Regional Assembly held in Praia in July 2004, the Prime Minister of Cape Verde, Dr. José Maria Neves, announced in his opening address that his Government would be giving the cooperative movement back its "confiscated assets". This decision was upheld by the Council of Ministers in December 2005.

experiences of integrating cooperatives were obtained in the consumption/distribution sector where cooperative unions (2nd degree) and a national federation of consumer cooperatives (3rd degree) were created. The latter now has an annual turnover of € 22,670. Cooperative unions are presently in place in the form of the Unicoops for Santo Antão, Fogo, Maio and Praia. Through this system of vertical integration the cooperatives seek not only economies of scale but also more professional management. Encouraged by the obvious advantages of integration, the fishing cooperatives on Santiago Island also showed an interest in forming a union for their industry. However, the financial difficulties which the grassroots cooperatives encountered meant that the project never got off the ground. In addition, as we pointed out earlier, the procedures for having cooperatives or unions registered and legally recognized proved to be too cumbersome.

Even with a cooperative sector in disarray, the cooperative spirit is still very much alive through the social economy, of which cooperatives along with mutual societies and associations are an integral part. Whilst their operations are consistent with the universal principles of cooperativism, social economy initiatives do not call themselves cooperatives, but rather associations. In this way they avoid the controversial cooperative identity. "Cooperatives have been a failure … as an instrument of socioeconomic development" is the continuing verdict of many political leaders and writers. This poor image of cooperatives which has lodged in people's minds continues to worry potential associations that could perfectly well choose the cooperative formula as a way of participating in society and working for the sustainable development of their members and the environment of which they are a part.

Despite this reluctance, initiatives such as fair trade, micro-finance or micro-insurance may give rise to new cooperatives and a further boost to existing ones. At the moment, in Cape Verde, an accelerated wave of new mutual-type organizations is discernible, along with community associations with cooperative-style socioeconomic objectives, common-interest groups based on cooperative principles and values, etc. Table 10.2 below shows the current state of these informal associations.

Self-help or self-promotion groups cannot be seen as an obstacle to potential cooperative growth. On the contrary, there are good reasons to believe they are genuinely intested in adopting a sustainable legal form that respects their ownership roots and their social goals. These groups are concerned only with satisfying their members' aspirations in respect of health (health mutual), education (saving through a *tontine* to pay children's school fees), improving or building their own homes (*tontine, djunta mon*[7]) or, when a member dies, paying his or her funeral expenses. What is needed is a political consensus, underscored by the state apparatus, the existing cooperatives and civil society organizations that these groups (could) belong to the cooperative movement and (should) be legally recognized as doing so.

Table 10.2: The current state of informal organizations

Type of organizations	No. of organizations	No. of members
Savings and credit mutuals	32	3 850
Health mutuals	4	1 210
Cooperative-style community associations	65	2 562
Economic interest groups	no figures available	no figures available

Sources: Fórum Cooperativo, NGO Platform in Cape Verde and OASIS (Organisation of Associations on the Island of Santiago), 2005.

Donors and support from above: crucial but hesitant

The Cape Verdean economy is predominantly a service economy (trade, transport and public services). In 2002 services accounted for about 71.6% of GDP compared with 17.2% for industry in the same year. Agriculture (based on subsistence farming) and fishing accounted for just 11.2% of GDP in the same year.

But the economy remains heavily dependent on foreign aid and remittances back to the country from expatriate Cape Verdeans. State development aid, which represented as much as 24.1% in 1998 and 23.3% in 1999, dwindled to a mere 13.5% of GDP in 2001. Remittances from expatriate Cape Verdeans were almost 10% of national GDP in 2001. State development aid and these remittances compensate for the non-existence of household savings in Cape Verde and help to encourage investment.

In a similar way, the cooperative sector depended and still depends on overseas aid. Between 1980 and 1990 Cape Verdean cooperatives enjoyed an unprecedented state of economic health, thanks to foreign assistance. The penetration rate of the sector at the end of that decade was as high as 6%. In those years cooperatives mobilized, on average, more than € 350,000

---

[7] Secular practice of helping one another with the building of huts or in agricultural work (labour).

through international cooperation and support from a variety of organiszations such as FAO, HIVOS (Netherlands), ICCO (Netherlands), Oxfam, Solidarité Socialiste (Belgium), Association Cap-Vert Genève (Switzerland), Danida (Danish cooperation), Konrad-Adenauer-Stiftung (Germany), OCPLP, ICA, USAID and ILO.

After 1992 the state's abrupt disengagement from the cooperative sphere (making no preparation for the transition to allow cooperative members to take over), together with the seizure of all assets which international organizations had donated to the cooperative movement as well as the promotion, for political reasons, of community-based associations as an alternative to the cooperative model, disgusted most international donors to the point that they stopped funding cooperatives. Still, a number of national and international partners expressed interest in backing Cape Verde in its efforts to secure greater autonomy and viability for cooperatives and associations and to revise the country's policy and legislation on cooperatives. These partners were the UNDP, ILO-CoopReform, the European Union, ACDI/VOCA and the ADF.

Nowadays, the cooperative sector has lost almost all the donors listed above except for the ICA, ADF and ILO (STEP programme). Some get support from the Cape Verdean NGO Platform and through the National Poverty Reduction Programme (NPRP). There are only a few isolated cases where cooperatives manage to secure financial and technical assistance from national and foreign NGOs. Assistance is usually financial (institutional support, working capital, specific production projects, etc) and focuses on training the executive staff of cooperatives in organization, management and accounting.

Not only are the donors hesitant when it comes to supporting Cape Verde's cooperatives, the government is not too keen either. The only support structure for cooperatives and mutuals is the Fórum Cooperativo. Cape Verde does not have any cooperative college or training establishments either. Still, there are umbrella bodies – the Unicoops – and (currently just one) federative body – Fenacoop – that provide support to the grassroots cooperatives. However, the consumer cooperatives studied for this report do not think much of the services they receive from their umbrella organizations or from Fenacoop. They argue that these bodies give priority to commercial activities, in other words making money, whilst forgetting the social and training aspects. In this way they do not respect the law on cooperatives which requires them to invest in member education and training.

Weak significance in terms of employment

Generally speaking the low rate of job creation in Cape Verde is due to the fact that the economy is poorly diversified and that the growth sectors in the country tend to be highly capital-intensive. As a result, the pace of job creation is slower than the growth of available labour. In the cooperative sector, consumer cooperatives have the highest proportion of workers who are non-members. ICA figures from 1995 indicate that the cooperative sector represented 209 self-employed persons, 306 salaried people and a further 87 people qualified as "induced employment".

Experts we interviewed confirmed that since 1995 the trend in employment creation by legally recognized cooperatives has shown a cautious but steady rise. Economic interest groups (EIGs), involved for example in mechanical joinery, sewing and dressmaking, have a certain employment impact too but data on this are not available. An important employment effect is also generated by the 60 plus community development associations or "community enterprises" that have emerged since the 1990s. They are particularly prominent in rural municipalities where they pursue activities related to the construction of community or family cisterns, dykes or dams (water or soil conservation), tree planting or local road building. For this they are contracted by the relevant ministries, namely the Ministry of Agriculture and the Ministry for Infrastructure and Transport, which for that matter receive financial support from the United States. Unlike employment in cooperatives, employment here is seasonal or occasional. It all depends on how many contracts the association secures, how much work they entail and, consequently, how long the work lasts. Even so, these associations are believed to have more than 2,000 people working for them on a regular basis.

The employment by Cape Verdean cooperatives is also poor in terms of quality of work. In this cooperatives do not differ from other enterprises in the country. There is no job security. Job training, insurance and social benefits are completely absent and wages are at the low end.

Poverty reduction and social protection: whose task is it?

At the present time poverty in Cape Verde continues to increase, as a result of the overall weak performance of the country's economy. Particulary vulnerable are female heads of family, young people and the rural population. These are people whose standard of living is low. It is estimated that 37% of the population live on less than a dollar a day.

At national level there is a programme to reduce poverty and social exclusion targeting a more or less homogeneous group. It focuses on building social infrastructure rather than supporting and promoting alternative employment in a way which directly helps to boost personal incomes. The programme also provides micro-credit and encourages self-help and income-generating initiatives. Some claim, however, that this programme makes the situation of poor people worse, since gains on productivity are transferred to the lending institutions, which charge interest rates as high as 36%.

Cooperatives in Cape Verde do not play a major role in reducing poverty. First of all, poverty in Cape Verde is a rural phenomenon, with 70% of the poor living in the countryside. Most remaining cooperatives are based in or around the towns. Secondly, different stakeholders have different priorities when it comes to the exact mission of cooperatives. Cooperative leaders are concerned mostly with the business aspect. Members may favour a more interventionist role for the cooperative in solving their daily problems. Then again, this is much less the members' attitude in the consumer cooperatives we studied. The Forum Cooperativo has not had any involvement in national and international poverty reduction programmes for the last 15 years.

When it comes to extension of social protection mechanisms, the prospects for a significant role for cooperatives do somehow look better. Self-help or *djunta mon* has been and continues to be a feature of popular life, especially in rural areas, where it applies in farming and community work, meeting the costs of everyday consumption or family burials.

There is no system of social protection specifically for cooperatives, though a couple of cooperatives such as Simplicidade and Don Bosco are members of the state-run scheme operated by the National Social Insurance Institute (*INPS*).

Recently Government has shown interest in new social protection instruments, drawing on the work of community-based associations and international organizations such as the ILO (STEP programme), World Bank and WHO. This is also the result of promotional and advocacy work by Fórum Cooperativo. Since 2002, Fórum Cooperativo has spearheaded the growth of mutual society networks in the fields of health and social protection, targeting the same group as the cooperatives. Today, about 2,000 families have been brought into this system, and the aim is to cover 10,000 families by the end of 2008.

This task might be made easier if the cooperatives could work as partners in the system, building through their membership a system of social security and benefits in rural areas that would act as an alternative to the classic social security scheme operated by the state, which covers only 25% of the country's population, mostly located in the towns.

Conclusion: the first steps on a long way ahead

As in many developing countries, the cooperative sector in Cape Verde has been hard hit by post-colonial strategies. Many cooperatives (200 or so) have not survived. Those that have are just clinging on, failing, or are close to bankruptcy. Cooperatives are no longer valued as they were in the 1980s. The name "cooperative" seems to have lost its *raison d'être*. There are a number of reasons for this, amongst them the fact that no particular attention is paid to "selling" the cooperative idea, plus a lack of rigour and sometimes cases of mismanagement, which are not addressed adequately.

It will take, both at national and local levels, "champions" of the cooperative ideal to present good practice of cooperative zeal and to educate and train people and popularize the cooperative ethic. Promotional efforts must include the following essential measures:

- Training cooperative leaders on how to "sell" the cause (advocacy). The cooperative sector currently needs a positive face and protagonists who can help improve the image of cooperativism in Cape Verdean society.

- Devising a model for communication, among cooperatives and between cooperatives and civil society, to make optimum use of the results obtained and disseminate cooperative principles and values as effectively as possible. To that end, it is essential to equip cooperatives with the necessary resources and skills.

- Definition of a strategic vision for the sector, giving priority to the development of promotional partnerships – involvement of the organizations of civil society, notably trade unions, mutuals and grassroots community associations, is a further imperative given that these organizations do not liaise with each other at present.

The good news is that the first steps have been taken. Cooperative leaders and Fórum Cooperativo have begun a debate on how to resolve the many problems facing the cooperative movement, with a view to holding a national congress on cooperatives at which the various players could make a key contribution to finding solutions.

Sources

For this article, the author acknowledges valuable information from the following key informants: Manuel Moreira (Forum Cooperativo), Arlindo Silva, Armando Freire and Jose Luis Barbosa (Fenacoop), Teodora Neves (Simplicidade cooperative), Maria Celeste Pereira (Sao Domingos consumer cooperative), Eduardo Afonso Cardoso (Adalgiza Moniz cooperative), Joao Pedro Delgado and Advino Fonseca (Unicoop Fogo & Santo Antao), Francisco Tavares (INE), Jacinto Santos (INC), H. Lopes Vaz and Silvino Monteiro Barbosa (Trabalho e Progresso Joinery Cooperative).

Acronyms specific for this article

ACOPAM	Organizational and Cooperative Support to Grassroots Initiatives
ADF	African Development Foundation
CCR	Rural Credit Bank
DECRP	Growth and Poverty Reduction Strategy Paper (GPRSP)
DEPC	Department for Research and Cooperative Planning
DGP	General Directorate for Planning
EIG	Economic Interest Group
FAC	Cooperatives Support Fund
FENACOOP	National Federation of Consumer Cooperatives
IDRF	Survey of household expenditure and income (SHEI)
INC	National Institute of Cooperatives
INE	National Institute of Statistics
INPS	National Social Insurance Institute
NPRP	National Poverty Reduction Programme
OCPLP	Organization of Cooperatives from the Lusophone (Portuguese-speaking) Countries
Unicoop	Union of Consumer Cooperatives

Bibliography

- *Análise das despesas directas dos agregados familiares com a saúde: Relatório preliminar*, 2001-2002, IDRF.

- Assembleia Nacional de Cabo Verde (2002), *Democracia, Sistemas Eleitorais e Economia Social:* parliamentary forum held in Praia on 15 & 16 April 2002. ANCV, Praia.

- Birchall J. (2003), R*ediscovering the cooperative advantage: Poverty reduction through self-help*, ILO, Geneva.

- Birchall J. (2004), *Cooperatives and the Millennium Development Goals*, ILO, Geneva.

- Develtere P. (1998), *L'économie sociale et développement: les coopératives, mutuelles et associations dans les pays en développement*, De Boeck University, Brussells/Paris.

- Develtere P. (2002), *L'économie sociale et la coopération au développement: Quo Vadis?* Paper given at the colloquium on 'Economie Sociale et Développement Local' as part of the 'Quinzièmes Entretiens' held at the Centre Jacques Cartier, Grenoble, 9-11 December 2002.

- DGP (2004), *Documento de estratégia de crescimento e de redução da pobreza (PRSP)*, Cape Verde, September 2004.

- DGP (2005), *Objectivos do Milénio para o Desenvolvimento em Cabo Verde: Relatório 2004: uma avaliação dos esforços realizados*, Praia.

- FENACOOP (2001-2004), *Relatórios financeiros e de actividades da Fenacoop*, Cape Verde.

- Fórum Cooperativo (2005), *Broad Lines of the Action Plan 2005-2007: Promotion of Health Mutuals in Santiago Island**, (*Translation: Portuguese title not given).

- ILO (no date), *Cooperating out of poverty: the global cooperative campaign against poverty*, ILO, Geneva.

- ILO (2000), 'Sub-Regional Office for Central Africa', *13th Panafrican Conference on Cooperatives*, Yaoundé, 24-28 July 2000.

- INE (2001-2002), *Demographic and Socioeconomic Characteristics*, IDRF, Cape Verde.

- INE (2001-2002), *O Perfil da Pobreza em Cabo Verde*, IDRF.

- Ministry of Employment and Solidarity, General Directorate for Social Solidarity (2005), *Estratégia de Protecção Social em Cabo Verde*.

- Schwettmann J. (1997), *Cooperatives and employment in Africa*, ILO, Geneva.

- UNDP (2001), *Project to Revitalise the Cooperative Movement in Cape Verde*, Praia, 2001.

- UNDP (2004), *National human development report: Cape Verde*.

- UNDP (2005), *National human development report: Cape Verde*.

Chapter Eleven – Jump-Starting the Rwandan Cooperative Movement

by Jean Damascène Nyamwasa[1]

Introduction: a blending of traditional and modern forms of cooperation

The Rwandan cooperative movement is part of a vast voluntary sector that exists in both town and country. Its roots lie in the history of development cooperation and in the evolution of the country's political, social and economic life. The cooperative movement and the voluntary associations are so closely bound, even to the point of occasional confusion that it becomes impossible to speak of the former without reference to the latter.

As elsewhere in Africa, the cooperative spirit is related to a community spirit, though not in the sense of a formally organized community (Ntavyohanyuma & Yakunda, 1992: 7). The largely rural population of Rwanda has long organized itself by means of social structures based on solidarity with a view to ensuring mutual protection, managing conflicts and providing mutual assistance. This is reflected in time-honoured collective practices that are predominantly social in purpose, such as informal neighbourhood ambulance services and assistance to anyone who is building a house.

The first collective practices relating to production primarily involved calling on neighbours' assistance to cultivate a field (*ubudehe*). This practice, organized on an ad hoc basis and unpaid, developed into the formation of mutual-aid associations known as "tontines" (*ibimina*). These *ibimina* appeared in several forms: labour pools, produce pools and, finally, the modern form of financial tontine. Until then, communal management had not yet been introduced. Associations had no common assets in the economic

---

[1] Jean Damascène Nyamwasa has a degree in agricultural engineering obtained from the National University of Rwanda in 1987. He has spent most of his career in the cooperative movement, working in the Ministry responsible for cooperatives and then in IWACU, an NGO dedicated to research and training in the sphere of cooperatives. Since 1997, he has been a rural development consultant.

sense of the term.

As in the rest of Africa, the modern cooperative movement was introduced by the colonial power. It is very much based on the concept of common assets in the economic sense. In order to introduce the cooperative system, the colonizers taught indigenous producers a set of administrative rules known as universal cooperative principles. During the colonial era in Rwanda, cooperatives were chiefly organized around export commodities, such as coffee and tea, and mining activity. On gaining independence in 1962, Rwanda had eight licensed cooperatives with a total of 22,475 registered members (Ntavyohanyuma & Yakunda, 1992).

After independence, the development of rural areas through the cooperative movement became a declared aim in many developing countries, including Rwanda. The Government, through its administrative structures and development projects, adopted a highly vigorous and interventionist approach to cooperatives, which led to the creation of associations and cooperatives which sometimes had no real involvement on the part of their members.

As the 1980s dawned, this approach was pursued through the NGOs, whose particular contributions were the provision of services on demand and special emphasis on the training of leaders among the peasant population. The incentives to form cooperatives led to the formation of several grassroots cooperatives, which were structured in their turn into joint bodies at the level of the communes and sometimes into cooperative unions.

These somewhat artificial regional, and sometimes even national, structures did not stand the test of time, and several of the joint bodies and cooperative unions were quite quickly bankrupted. Agricultural producers began to voice criticism of the cooperative system. Their participation in formal cooperatives began to dwindle, but at the same time smaller parallel associations managed to survive. These groups featured a combination of the modern cooperative model and traditional forms of mutual assistance. Some of them revised the system for the management of collective land. Others managed to develop credit services for their members through a system of tontine funds, mutual-aid funds for members in difficulties because of illness or funeral expenses, for example, and mutual lending of labour at times of peak farming activity.

Following the war and genocide of 1994, the humanitarian aid provided by the NGOs promoted the recovery of the associations and cooperatives, which

– like all the country's institutions – had experienced the devastating impact of those events. At the same time, however, humanitarian aid tended to revive a sense of financial dependence.

During the subsequent period, the cooperative movement has taken firm shape and consolidated its position in certain key areas of the economy, the existence of external support having invariably served as a springboard. Cooperatives in some profitable segments of the economy, however, soon underwent a change of mentality, and the aim of attracting subsidies gave way to that of promoting common economic interests through the supply of inputs, common management of production infrastructure and negotiation of remunerative prices for the sale of products. This applied especially to the rice, tea and coffee associations and cooperatives. The savings and credit businesses also underwent this development.

The present picture of the Rwandan cooperative movement is therefore a blend of modern cooperative structures and traditional forms of mutual aid within the community. The cooperatives are dominated by economic interests and the mutual-aid groups by social interests, and it is always difficult to strike a balance between the two. This explains the durability of the small associations, whose social viability enables them to survive in spite of their limited economic viability. It also explains the disappearance of large cooperatives and their joint bodies, whose lack of economic viability has led directly to bankruptcy.

The research conducted for this report relied chiefly on existing documentation relating to the cooperative movement and on interviews with people working in various relevant bodies: research centres, public institutions, NGOs and the cooperative organizations themselves. Two case studies conducted at the Union of Rwandan Rice Producers' Cooperatives (Uncorirwa) and the Union of People's Banks of Rwanda (UBPR) serve to substantiate and illustrate the ideas expounded in the report.

This study begins with a presentation of the main characteristics of the cooperative movement in Rwanda, goes on to examine the role of government in the structuring of cooperatives, their growth potential, the institutional and financial framework and the impact of the cooperatives on job creation, poverty reduction and social protection. Lastly, the study deals with matters relating to the way in which cooperatives express themselves and represent their interest.

Characteristic features of the Rwandan cooperative movement

The Rwandan movement is characterized by the predominance of informal groupings, the importance of savings and credit cooperatives, the disappearance of multifunctional cooperatives and joint cooperative bodies covering particular geographical areas and a tendency for cooperatives to be grouped on the basis of product categories.

Predominance of groups with a cooperative purpose

The cooperative movement is largely dominated by informal groups with a cooperative purpose, in other words entities that do not yet meet all the requirements for recognition as cooperative societies.[2]

In fact, the Cooperatives Act of 1988 sought to legalize a host of groups that already existed but had no legal personality. It was hoped that these groups would be able to develop gradually into a more structured cooperative form. The transitional period prescribed by the law is four years, with the possibility of a single two-year extension. These groups rarely satisfy the requirements for recognition as cooperatives within this time limit, however, and tend to remain indefinitely as informal groups.

An exhaustive inventory drawn up in the province of Ruhengeri (one of the eleven provinces)[3] in 2003 showed that, of 4,869 recorded organizations, a total of 3,895, i.e. more than 80%, were production organizations, operating in fields such as crop farming, livestock husbandry and manual crafts and trades. These organizations had 231,456 members, which corresponds to 48.6% of the province's adult population (Care International, 2003). While the survey covered all associations, it is noticeable that most of them engage in economic activity. This means that 3,895 associations may be regarded as cooperatives or as groups with a cooperative purpose within the meaning of Article 53 of the 1988 Act. Nevertheless, their role remains ambiguous in the sense that they often combine the functions of the three types of social economy organization – mutual societies, cooperatives and associations – defined by Develtere (1998).

In fact, the inventory revealed that most of the groups combined two or three activities, mainly crop farming, animal husbandry and savings and credit. It is

---

[2] Article 53 of The Cooperatives Act (Law No 31/1988 of 12 October 1988 on the organization of cooperative societies).
[3] With effect from January 2006, the number of provinces was reduced from eleven to four plus the city of Kigali.

also common to find groups with a small mutual-benefit fund to help members in difficulties arising, for example, from illness or responsibility for funeral expenses or to help with the cost of certain celebrations, such as marriages. In terms of the definitions presented by Develtere (1998), their functions can be classed as those of cooperatives (producing goods and services for sale; contributions and shareholdings returnable in the event of withdrawal; members' rebate) but also as those of mutual-benefit societies (loans and non-repayable grants available to members; periodic contributions to the mutual-benefit fund) or of associations, in the case of bodies defending the interests of producers of a particular commodity.

As a group evolves, one of these functions will plainly develop more quickly and will come to determine whether the group will ultimately be definable as a cooperative, an association or a mutual society. Unfortunately, the great majority of these groups hardly evolve at all.

Although the available statistics relate to only one province, there is good reason to suppose that similar situations exist in the other provinces. The voluntary sector remains a characteristic feature of the socio-economic life of Rwanda.

The importance of savings and credit cooperatives in Rwanda

The Care International study in Ruhengeri province shows that savings and credit services are often linked with other activities of the groups. This tendency is not only observable in rural areas but also manifests itself in the urban context in workers' cooperatives in the formal and informal sectors.

The presence in the field of several institutions engaged in credit provision, often anarchically managed, prompted the National Bank of Rwanda to issue two instructions: one in 2002 relating to the regulation of micro-financing activities and another in 2003 on the regulation of savings and credit cooperatives.

Of the 228 micro-finance institutions registered by the National Bank on February 2006, 211 were cooperatives. These cooperative savings and credit societies have a wide clientele among both the urban and rural population. The largest of them, the Union of People's Banks (*Union des Banques Populaires*) had 149 local branches in 2004 with 398,799 shareholders, which corresponds to 12% of the adult population.

How can this proliferation of micro-finance institutions, including savings and credit cooperatives, be explained? Three hypotheses can be advanced:

- The demand was created by the suspension of the NGOs' credit activities during the national emergency that followed the genocide of 1994. In fact, the instruction issued by the National Bank in 2002 suspended the provision of credit by NGOs and sponsors of development projects. The NGOs and project sponsors then used existing micro-finance institutions or helped to create new ones in order to have partner bodies through which they could resume their credit activities.

- The demand for loans in rural areas is high, given the high level of poverty resulting from structural factors and from the aftermath of the genocide (60% of the Rwandan population live below the poverty line).

- Donors have been providing generous funding for the micro-finance institutions. Apart from the People's Banks and some other savings and credit cooperatives, most of the micro-finance institutions were created with the support of external donors.

Disappearance of multifunctional cooperatives and cooperative unions

In most cases, cooperatives and similar groups operate in isolation. The study conducted by Care International in 2003 showed that the level of structural organization at the regional and national levels is still very low among the cooperative bodies that operate in Ruhengeri province. The same situation is observable in the other provinces.

Most of the joint bodies ("intergroupements"), cooperative unions and commercial cooperatives that were formed in the period from the 1970s to the 1990s have ceased to exist because of either mismanagement or a lack of interest among their members. This happened to the silo cooperatives, which operated storage facilities and of which there were 69 in 1990, and to the commercial cooperatives, also known as multifunctional cooperatives, 490 of which were operational in 1990. (Ntavyohanyuma & Yakunda, 1992).

The main reason for their bankruptcy is a lack of shared interest. The commercial cooperatives, whether in the form of storage facilities or retail outlets,[4] were created as part of a government initiative designed to make staple goods available to the population by creating stores of foodstuffs, manufactured products and household appliances. The members had nothing

---

[4] The terms "commercial cooperatives" and "multifunctional cooperatives" are used here to designate the societies that are also called consumer cooperatives.

in common other than living in the geographical area covered by the project.

In the case of the joint bodies, some disappeared, while others were restructured. The latter were restructured on the basis of what Hussi et al. (1993) call the three fundamental conditions for the development of a group: (a) the members must have a genuine need to band together; (b) the group must be based on members' participation and contributions; (c) the group must be economically viable and competitive and provide financial returns for its members.

Trend towards vertical structuring by product category

The structuring of cooperatives on the basis of viable agricultural products offers hope of a brighter future. The greatest potential lies in the markets for rice, tea, coffee, wheat, potatoes, cassava and maize.

The case of the rice producers' cooperatives is the most illustrative. Rice growers have established a three-tiered structure: producers have formed themselves into grassroots cooperatives, these cooperatives are formed into cooperative unions, and the unions have created a national federation.[5] The success of the rice growers' cooperatives is attributable to encouragement from the Government, which has begun a programme of swamp reclamation, but the main reason for their success has been the profitability of the crop.

Tea growing is another example. A national federation, Ferwathé, exists and is responsible for all tea producers who belong to cooperatives.

Coffee producers have yet to achieve this degree of organization. Whereas it is estimated that there are more than 450,000 coffee growers throughout the country, there are only 93 cooperatives with 36,265 members. A federative structure has not yet been formed.

In the potato, wheat, maize and cassava markets, a structuring process has begun to gather momentum. At the present time, however, associations with cooperative features remain the predominant form of organization, and their economic functions are not yet very developed.

In other areas of activity, such as crafts, housing, fishing and livestock husbandry, some voluntary associations and cooperatives do exist, but they still tend to be very loosely structured.

---

[5] There is still terminological confusion here, since the term "cooperative union" is used to designate both provincial and national bodies.

Seeking a role for the state

A political framework that encourages, does not over-regulate but provides little guidance

Cooperative activity in Rwanda began with the promulgation by the colonial power, the Kingdom of Belgium, of the decree of August 1949, followed by that of March 1956. Although Rwanda achieved independence in 1962, an appropriate legal basis for cooperation was not created until November 1966. That instrument was gradually amended to establish greater clarity. In 1988, the Cooperatives Act[6] perfected the law of 1966 and closed some of the gaps in its coverage (Ntavyohanyuma & Yakunda, 1992).

These two laws are fairly liberal. The 1988 Act even recognizes the existence of groups that have not yet fulfilled the conditions for registration as cooperatives.

Since Rwanda obtained its independence, its Government has always pursued a policy of promoting the formation of associations. The NGOs have followed suit since the 1980s. The result has been the creation of fragile voluntary groups and cooperatives designed to secure attractive government grants or funding provided through development projects. The Government, working through cooperative officers in the communes and prefectures and the leaders of the cooperative movement, should actually ensure that the structures within that movement adhere to cooperative principles. This function, however, has not been performed for several reasons, namely the very limited budget of the competent government ministry, unskilled staff who receive little training and the use of cooperatives for political rather than economic ends.

The process of obtaining legal personality is painfully slow. Procedures are centralized by the ministry. Nor is it particularly clear to small groups what benefit they can derive from legal personality. In spite of the absence of statistical data, it is now estimated that there are 370 registered cooperatives, which is insignificant when compared with the thousands of groups with a cooperative purpose that exist in every province.

Government awareness of the potential of cooperatives

After the war and genocide of 1994, responsibility for cooperatives kept shifting. As a result of the portfolio being passed from the Ministry of Youth

---

[6] Law No 31/1988 of 12 October 1988 on the organization of cooperative societies.

to the Ministry of Commerce to the Ministry of Social Affairs, relevant statistics have been lost.

Communal and provincial cooperative offices were abolished. Nevertheless, by setting up a task force at the meeting of the Council of Ministers on 29 July 2005, the Government sought to signal its ambition to make the cooperatives an instrument of poverty reduction in both rural and urban areas.

The mission of the task force is: (a) to draft a suitable political and legal framework for the promotion of cooperatives; (b) to analyse the current situation in the cooperative sector; (c) to pave the way for the establishment of a national committee for the regulation of cooperatives. According to the chairman of the task force, the new approach limits the role of the state to regulation, registration, monitoring and conflict settlement.

The dynamics of the cooperative movement

The dynamism of the cooperative sector in Rwanda can be analysed by means of a close examination of its role in those areas of the economy where cooperatives are most firmly structured, namely in rice growing, tea planting, coffee growing and the realm of savings and credit. Among the indicators of dynamism are the total number of members, the share of the market commanded by cooperatives and the ability of cooperative structures to fund their own activities.

Rice growers' cooperatives – a growth area

Rice growers' cooperatives control almost all rice production. In 2004, the paddy fields worked by the 40,148 members of rice growers' cooperatives covered a total area of 7,198 hectares with a yield of 32,000 tonnes of paddy rice. This output is equivalent to 20,800 tonnes of white rice, or 35% of the national demand for rice.[7]

The services provided by cooperatives to their members comprise technical support to growers, maintenance of agricultural water infrastructure, provision of input loans and marketing of produce.

Producers generally take part in the work of their cooperatives by buying a stake for 1,000 to 2,000 Rwandese francs (RWF) per member. Each producer also pays an annual levy of RWF 150 to 250 per are (100 square metres). The

---

[7] The national demand for white rice is estimated by the National Bank at 60,000 tonnes per annum.

primary cooperatives live chiefly from these levies. The annual membership fee payable to Ucorirwa, the national union of rice growers, is RWF 200,000 per cooperative.

Tea planters' cooperatives and privatization

In 2004, the cooperatives belonging to the federation of Rwandan tea planters (Ferwathé) had a total membership of 30,097 producers working a total of 8,868 ha out of a total of 12,869, in other words 69% of the total surface area of all tea plantations. The cooperatives' total production in 2003 amounted to 47,480,680 kg of green tea, equivalent to 10,551,262 kg of dried tea. This compares with a total national production volume of 13,922,827 kg, which means that the cooperatives are responsible for 76% of national output.

The services provided by the cooperatives to their members comprise the negotiation of prices for green tea with the Government, the establishment of nurseries for the rehabilitation and extension of plantations, the organization of work on track maintenance, agricultural supervision and the harvesting of green leaves and their sale to processing plants. Contributions to Ferwathé are calculated on the basis of RWF 0.40 per kilogram of green leaves. The primary cooperatives earn their income from members' shares, which vary between RWF 1,000 and RWF 8,000, and from supervision fees and track-maintenance levies paid by members; these charges amount to between RWF 5 and RWF 8 per kg of green tea.

The process of privatising tea-processing plants began in 1998. The Government agreed to award 10% of shares in these plants automatically to cooperatives. For additional shares they have to compete with the private sector. The privatization of two plants (Mulindi and Pfunda) out of a total of eight has been completed. Cooperatives hold 45% of the shares in the Mulundi plant.

Coffee growers' cooperatives: a cautious start

In 2004, the number of coffee producers was estimated at 450,000. There are now 93 cooperatives and cooperative-type groups with 36,265 members, which amounts to 8% of all producers.

Out of a total of 18 washing stations, 11 belong to cooperatives. Apart from the cooperatives that operate these washing stations, few of the groups of coffee producers are particularly dynamic. Nevertheless, some cooperatives have tried to market parchment coffee produced by members, but administrative problems have thwarted all but a few.

Savings and credit cooperatives make their mark in micro-finance

The network of People's Banks, created in 1975, is the oldest savings and credit cooperative and the largest in terms of geographical coverage, value of deposits and volume of loans. From 2001 to 2004, the number of local branches rose from 146 to 149, and the number of shareholders increased from 259,394 to 398,799; the value of deposits rose from RWF 14,334,380,000 to RWF 23,401,306,519. Most members are farmers (43% in 2004, compared with 31% who were wage-earners). The growth of the People's Banks can be attributed to their broad geographical coverage, which makes them accessible to the rural population. It is also worth noting that NGOs and sponsors of agricultural projects are becoming aware of the popularity of these banks and are channelling their credit funds through them.

There are other savings and credit cooperatives, most of which have been newly created. In February 2006, a total of 211 savings and credit cooperatives were registered by the National Bank as micro-finance institutions.

Preference for vertical structures

Vertical structuring by crop category

As we have already noted, the cooperative movement is structured on the basis of product categories for several reasons: (a) direct economic interest: where a crop was profitable, producers recognized the benefit to be gained from forming an association to look after marketing; (b) need to access production factors: collective management of infrastructure, requiring farmers to belong to a cooperative in order to grow a particular crop and in order to obtain inputs in advance and pay for them from sales revenue; (c) solidarity in dealing with a common business partner – normally a processing plant – in order to secure remunerative prices.

The vertical structure of the rice growers' cooperative system extends from grassroots to the national level. The same type of structure has been created by tea planters. As far as coffee growers are concerned, the establishment of cooperative unions and a coffee growers' federation seems premature, given the weak state of the grassroots cooperatives at the present time. Nevertheless, the rapid development of the cooperatives that operate washing stations may speed up the process.

The specific structure of the savings and credit cooperatives

Since the National Bank began to take an interest in savings and credit cooperatives, the development of their structure has advanced more rapidly to satisfy the Bank's requirements. Significant improvements were suddenly observable as cooperatives began to produce annual accounts, to reform their governing bodies and to appoint supervisory boards and permanent staff to ensure that their operations were properly managed.

In some cases, cooperatives had to form area associations in order to create the minimum financial base they needed to satisfy all the requirements of the National Bank. Cooperative unions were therefore hastily formed. Most registered savings and credit cooperatives formed themselves into such federations, the Union of People's Banks being the largest with 149 member banks. The idea of creating a cooperative bank uniting all the savings and credit cooperatives has been mooted but has yet to reach maturity.

A movement with growth potential

Key sectors for the consolidation of the cooperative movement

Cash crops and the savings and credit sector are the areas of activity in which the growth potential of the cooperative movement is greatest.

Cash crops

Rice growing is expanding rapidly as a result of the programme of swamp reclamation. Another reason for this rapid expansion is the profitability of rice crops. The Rwandan Government has ambitious plans to increase the area of land suitable for rice production from 8,000 ha to 12,000 ha by the end of 2009, which represents a 50% increase over a four-year period. The expansion of the rice-growing area will automatically lead to the birth of new cooperatives. The management of common infrastructure, such as irrigation channels and drying terraces, the preparation of plant nurseries and the provision of agricultural inputs are generally carried out on a collective basis, and cooperatives are the best way of ensuring that these things are done properly. Projections suggest an increase of some 22,500 in the number of cooperative members by the end of 2009.

There are real growth prospects for the coffee producers' cooperatives in the realm of washing stations. In 2005, 22 out of 46 stations were operated by cooperatives. Projections lead us to believe that the cooperatives could command 30% of the coffee-washing market in 2008.

In the tea trade, the number of cooperatives will not increase significantly. The total area under cultivation, however, may increase as a result of plantation expansion. It is the Government's aim to facilitate the planting, by 2008, of 3,000 ha for tea production managed by cooperatives, which would bring in 12,000 new producers.

Cooperative structures are developing for other agricultural products. The key factor in this structuring process is often the existence of a processing plant for agricultural products. In practice, once producers start to negotiate individually with the owners of these plants, they realize that they have little bargaining power and tend to organize themselves into associations.

Savings and credit

The growth of savings and credit cooperatives has been a phenomenon of recent years. Even though joint-stock companies have begun to develop an interest in micro-finance, the bulk of the market is occupied by the cooperatives. Of the 228 registered institutions, 211 are cooperative in form, and the other 17 are joint-stock companies.

The following table shows the evolution of the main characteristics of the network:

Table 11.1: Main characteristics of the network of people's banks

Characteristics	2000	2001	2002	2003	2004
Number of local banks	145	146	148	148	149
Number of shareholders	229 453	259 394	319 042	356 407	398 799
Deposits total (billions RWF)	11.13	14.00	16.58	18.87	23.41
Loans outstanding (billions RWF)	4.64	4.12	6.48	11.97	19.60
Number of loanees	44 739	43 156	49 940	56 564	68 368
Net results (millions)	-1 062[8]	293	571	541	846

Source : Union des Banques Populaires.

---

[8] Losses as a result of the tragic 1994 events which led to important provisions for possible claims.

The network of the Banques Populaires does cover a large geographical area. However, an increase is expected in the number of members of savings and credit cooperatives organized around segments of the agricultural market at the prompting of producers' cooperatives and labour unions. The main umbrella organisation of Rwandan trade unions, Cestrar, with the support of the International Labour Office (ILO), has initiated a project entitled *Syndicoop*, which helps workers to organize themselves into cooperatives and to launch income-generating projects. Similar projects for the organization of the informal sector are implemented by the Young Christian Workers (JOC).

The integration of voluntary associations in the cooperative movement

In the preceding chapters, we have seen that the Rwandan landscape is dominated by voluntary associations, many of which may be described as "pre-cooperative" in form. The economic functions of these associations are slow to develop, and their predominantly social characteristics continue to hinder the emergence of specialized and economic activities. We have also seen that the greatest growth potential for cooperative development lies in cash crops and in savings and credit institutions. This means that associations which opt for specialization in one of these fields are more likely to develop into cooperatives.

On the other hand, it should be noted that a major change has occurred in the voluntary sector as a result of the Government's institutionalization of the mutual health funds ("mutuelles de santé") throughout the country. The outcome of this move is that some mutualist functions performed by voluntary associations are set to be taken over by the mutual health funds.

It may be concluded that, in the long term, the current voluntary associations will either cease to exist or will restructure themselves into economically viable cooperatives for producers of a particular cash crop or local branches of a savings and credit cooperative. The extent and pace of this development will depend in part on the substance of the new Cooperatives Act that is currently being drafted.

Who's funding cooperative development?

The lack of institutional donors

The cooperative movement no longer has any providers of institutional funds, a role that was formerly played by NGOs dedicated to the organization of cooperatives, such as the IWACU a training and research centre for cooperatives or the Gitamara service centre for cooperatives. These two NGOs now live primarily from implementation contracts awarded in the framework of rural development projects, which limits their scope for initiatives in the cooperative domain. For this reason, there is not much research into cooperatives and the cooperative movement.

At the present time, external funding of cooperatives takes two forms: funds are either disbursed directly to the cooperative unions or are paid indirectly through NGOs and development projects. The aim of direct funding of cooperative unions is normally to enhance their capabilities, whereas funding through projects and NGOs focuses more on the promotion of a particular area of economic activity, cooperatives being perceived as a means to that end.

Among the financial partners identified are Minagri/RSSP, the Embassy of Canada, the Embassy of the Netherlands, the Dutch Agriterra Foundation, the Belgian NGO Solidarité Socialiste, ACDI-VOCA, the WOCCU, the Stabex Fund of the European Union, the International Fund for Agricultural Development (IFAD) and the USAID project Partnership for Enhancing Agriculture in Rwanda through Linkages (PEARL).

At the political level, the Government encourages south-south cooperation. This is the framework within which it called in 14 Kenyan experts in 2005 to assist in the formulation of a policy and law on cooperatives and in the restructuring of the savings and credit cooperative sector.

The case for direct funding of cooperative umbrella organizations

There is currently little tangible support for efforts to enhance the capabilities of cooperatives. It is observable that some piecemeal interventions are being made with very limited resources by NGOs and in the framework of projects. The only systematic involvement is that of the WOCCU, which has enabled the People's Banks to improve their credit management.

The NGOs that were specifically involved in organizational tasks no longer have the means to continue this work in the absence of institutional funding. The fact is, however, that a resurgence of the cooperative movement will depend on the provision of medium-term and long-term direct assistance to the unions and federations of cooperatives. In the areas of activity where these umbrella bodies do not exist, the ideal would be to channel funding through the specialized NGOs and the trade unions and producer syndicates.

Landlocked and isolated

The present institutional framework of the cooperative movement is marked by a "hands-off" approach, in that the law provides sufficient freedom, but the movement receives little active assistance.

In the eyes of the cooperatives, the Government is very remote and out of touch with their problems. They have no one on the ground to help them when they run into difficulties. In the districts, it is very often the case that the person who is supposed to be specifically responsible for overseeing the cooperatives has not yet been recruited.

As far as the savings and credit cooperatives are concerned, the National Bank is more active in enforcing the prudential rules of savings and credit management. The cooperative banks complain that the ministry responsible for cooperatives does not help them enough to meet the standards imposed by the National Bank.

The services provided by the federations and unions of cooperatives are fairly well appreciated by the member cooperatives. The problem is that a lack of resources makes it impossible for these umbrella organizations to satisfy all of their members' demands. The member cooperatives, for their part, are not prepared to increase their annual contributions.

For want of a sound national structure, no national cooperative organization is a member of the International Cooperative Alliance (ICA). This has tended to keep the Rwandan cooperative movement isolated. Only the Union of People's Banks maintains an international link through its cooperation with the World Council of Credit Unions (WOCCU).

The significant impact of the cooperative movement

Cooperatives do create and maintain jobs and income: even more in the future

In the absence of statistics, it is not easy to assess the role of cooperatives in the creation of employment. It is, however, possible to distinguish between two types of job: salaried employment created by the cooperatives and jobs created by the work that their members perform.

As far as the impact on salaried employment is concerned, this is still minimal, because most cooperatives are small businesses. But some do employ quite a number of people. The People's Banks, for example, employ almost 600 staff, the UCT 150, Ucorirwa 50 and Ferwathé 32.

In estimating the volume of hired labour, we must also take the use of temporary workers into account. Two cases will illustrate the scale of this phenomenon, namely the tea and rice cooperatives. Among the tea planters' cooperatives, more than 80% of the people who harvest tea are temporary workers; their contribution is roughly equivalent to that of nearly 4,476 permanent employees,[9] injecting almost RWF 418,953,053 into the national economy in 2004.

In the domain of rice production, the Coproriz-Mirayi cooperative in Butari estimates that producers with more than 20 ares of land will automatically use wage-earning employees, because family labour is no longer sufficient to deal with an area of that size. The same cooperative estimates that family members account for half of the labour force, while the other half are hired workers.[10]

The second form of job creation, and by far the most significant, is the fact that the cooperative keeps its members engaged in an economic activity which could well be unprofitable if the cooperative did not exist.

The prospects of job creation by cooperatives are linked to the growth of the cooperative movement. The economic activities in which the future of the cooperative movement seems brightest are most likely to yield new jobs. These are rice cultivation, with 22,500 new rice growers forecast for 2009, and tea planting, with a projected increase of 12,000 producers by 2008. A less optimistic forecast for the coffee trade puts the number of members of coffee producers' cooperatives at 36,265 by 2008.

Cooperatives will also be major employers in the realm of savings and credit. In fact, there will be a need for more and more qualified staff if the cooperative banks are to meet the requirements laid down by the National Bank.

Despite the potential for job growth in the cooperatives, there are three obstacles to its full exploitation, to do with management skills, technical skills and the socio-economic context.

---

[9] Our calculations are based on a daily picking capacity of 30 kg of green tea per person and a five-day week. The pickers are paid an average of RWF 12 per kilogram of green tea.
[10] The Coproriz-Mirayi cooperative in Butare province has 1,517 members who work a total of 610 ha, of which 320 ha is properly reclaimed land. This represents an average of 40 ares per family. The first 20 ares can be worked by family members and the rest with the aid of hired labour.

As far as *management skills* are concerned, it is observable that cooperative leaders still have limited knowledge of management practices, that there is not a clear division between the roles of elected and executive bodies, that budgetary constraints compel cooperatives to employ low-skilled staff, that some cooperatives have rather sketchy business plans and that duplication of tasks occurs between grassroots cooperatives and cooperative unions.

Among the *technical problems* are the low production capacities of producer units, failure to bring costs under control and the use of outdated production technology.

With regard to the *socio-economic environment*, the main problem is that some cooperative groups, especially in the towns, develop in the informal sector with all that this entails in terms of red tape and job instability and with little hope of ultimately attaining "formal" status.

Cooperatives' contribution to poverty reduction

Several authors have tried to analyse the impact of the cooperatives on the reduction of poverty, particularly through their involvement in the Government's Poverty Reduction Strategy Programme (PRSP) and the pursuit of the Millennium Goals. The general finding is that cooperatives are rarely involved in the preparation of measures but do nevertheless make a tangible contribution (Birchall, 2003).

The evaluation report for the first poverty-reduction programme (PRSP1) shows that the involvement of cooperatives in the drafting and implementation of the programme was minimal. The main mouthpieces of civil society were certainly invited to the discussions, but the role played by cooperatives in civil society continues to be underestimated.

In the wider context, the social role played in Rwanda by cooperatives and by groups with a cooperative purpose is undeniable. They are an instrument that enables poor people to subsist in a situation in which the means of production are scarce and incomes are low. They do this by creating mutual-assistance mechanisms, granting small revolving credits and establishing support funds to provide assistance in the event of sickness or death.

The cooperatives also play an important economic role in rural areas as a source of income for their members. The income they generate, however, is still too low to lift their members out of poverty. An analysis of monetary flows in the domains of tea and rice production supports this assertion.

In the tea trade, a total production volume of 43,640,943 kg of green tea in 2004 meant an injection of RWF 2,400,251,865 into 30,097 households, which comes to an annual average of RWF 79,750 per family. In order to earn more than one US dollar a day,[11] a producer would need 75 ares of plantation. In fact, the average area is only 29 ares per family.

The most revealing case is that of rice cultivation, which provided 40,148 rice growers with an aggregate income of RWF 5,120,000,000 in 2004. This makes an average income of RWF 127,528 for the year for each cooperative member, which boils down to a daily income of RWF 345, in other words $0.60 a day.

Our analysis of the figures that are available for these two crops leads us to conclude that their contribution to poverty reduction is limited, since in each case producers earn an average of less than one US dollar a day, which is the poverty line defined by the United Nations Development Programme (UNDP). Nevertheless, two other salient points must be considered: (a) rice growing and tea planting are not the only activities that generate income for the producer; (b) plots of land are not all of equal size, and some producers' holdings are above the average and comprise more than one plot of paddy field or tea plantation, which puts some producers' incomes well above the average.

In conclusion, cooperatives will remain a weapon in the fight against poverty once they are organized around a profitable area of economic activity. In the Rwandan context, however, where agricultural holdings are small, only a small percentage of producers can emerge from poverty and develop.

Cooperatives as an instrument for social protection

As the previous chapters have shown, cooperatives perform both social and economic functions. Although these two functions may sometimes come into conflict, they form the very foundation of the cooperative philosophy, and each function is at the service of the other.

Two examples of the role played by cooperatives in the provision of social protection seem important to us. First, cooperatives play a part in safeguarding jobs, particularly in the informal economy. The fact that they pool their efforts provides workers in the informal sector with greater bargaining power in relation to the administration with regard to taxes, workplace conditions and the relaxation of certain repressive measures

---

[11] One US dollar corresponds to RWF 562.50 at the average exchange rate for 2004.

targeted at the informal economy. The second example is the role played by cooperatives in helping members to pay their annual contributions to the mutual health fund. A member requests a loan from his or her cooperative in order to pay the annual health-insurance contribution. The member is then immediately entitled to benefit from the services of the mutual fund while gradually repaying the loan to the cooperative.

Cooperatives as a channel of communication

Limited lobbying power and little collaboration with the farmers' movement

The clout of the cooperative movement as a lobby generally depends on its level of organization at the regional and national levels. In fact, it is the unions and federations of cooperatives that engage in lobbying. In Rwanda, since the cooperatives are not well structured at these higher levels, they do not feature prominently as a lobby.

We should nevertheless cite the case of the Tea Planters' Federation, which was able to negotiate with the Rwandan Government an increase in producer prices for green leaves from RWF 45 per kg in 2003 to RWF 55-57 per kg in 2004. Ferwathé, however, does not carry sufficient weight in the present process of privatizing the tea-manufacturing plants. The Union of Rice Growers has also supported its member cooperatives in their bid for a remunerative price for paddy rice, securing increases from RWF 60 per kg in 1995 to RWF 160 per kg in 2005. The lobbying activities of Ucorirwa with regard to government privatization of the country's rice-processing plants have yet to bear fruit.

Collaboration between the agricultural cooperatives and the two main farmers' unions, Imbaraga and Ingabo, is still in its infancy.

Creation of mouthpieces for individual and multiple areas of economic activity

Two developments seem likely to occur in the realm of lobbying. The first is the structuring of the agricultural cooperatives by product category, which will be reinforced by the emergence of national federations for producers of coffee, cassava, fruit, wheat, pyrethrum and maize. These federations will add to the existing bodies for tea and rice producers.

The second development is consultation among all players in the same area of activity: cooperatives, industrialists and trade unions. It seems likely that the link between the cooperatives and trade unions will be stronger, because they often face the same problems. In this context, the Rwandan Federation of the Private Sector (FRSP) is prepared to welcome cooperatives into its various chambers, according to their sphere of activity: the chamber of agriculture, the chamber of financial services or the chamber of crafts and trades.

Conclusion

The cooperative movement in Rwanda is highly complex, and its dynamism varies from one area of economic activity to another. The most dynamic cooperatives are connected with the most marketable cash crops, namely rice and tea. Prospects are also favourable for cooperatives in the production of other cash crops, particularly coffee, potatoes, cassava, wheat and maize. The savings and credit business in rural areas and informal savings and credit services in urban areas are also dominated by cooperative banks with considerable growth potential. In other sectors such as crafts, commerce and housing, the cooperative movement has not yet developed. The voluntary associations that currently dominate these areas are developing slowly into formal cooperative structures and constitute a valuable breeding ground for the cooperative movement.

The following is a résumé of the many challenges facing the cooperative movement, presented by means of a summary review of the opportunities available to the movement, the risks confronting it and its strengths and weaknesses.

The main opportunities derive from the commitment of the Government of Rwanda to adopt a policy and legal framework through which it can support the cooperative movement and from the modernization drive within the segments of the agricultural sector in which cooperatives abound, as reflected in the establishment of food-processing plants and the privatization of state-owned plants.

The main risks are those that could ensue from any government attempt to push for rapid progress by adopting an excessively interventionist policy in which cooperatives were regarded as an instrument of poverty reduction. Similarly, the cooperative members themselves, by trying to engage as quickly as possible with the Government and donors, might rush into the establishment of regional and national structures without waiting until the primary cooperatives were sufficiently mature, thereby creating elephants with fragile feet.

The main strengths of the cooperatives are the enthusiasm of the low-income population, especially in rural areas and in the informal urban economy, and their increasing awareness that solidarity offers the only hope of progress. This explains the multitude of cooperatives and associations with cooperative aims that exist in town and country alike.

The main weaknesses are the misconception that cooperatives are a means of accessing support from the Government, donors and NGOs rather than a mechanism designed to improve members' living conditions by pooling their human, technical and financial resources, the low levels of training among members, which hinder their participation in the management of their venture, the low participation rate among the poorest sections of the population, people with disabilities and young people, the minimal involvement of women in decision-making, the lack of umbrella organizations at the regional and national levels and insufficient collaboration between the cooperative movement and the trade union movement.

Sources

The author wishes to thank the following persons for providing him with useful information: Adrien Omar (CFRC-IWACU), Bernard Itangishaka (Union of People's Banks), Claude Hategekimana and Innocent Bazimenyera (Ferwathé), Damien Mugabo (Minicom), Djalia Mutumyinka and Zacharie Manirarora (OCIR), Emmanuel Mutsinzi (UCT), Emmanuel Simpunga and Eric Manzi (Cestrar), Janvier Ngabonziza.

(Catholic Young Workers' Association in the Archdiocese of Kigali), Jonas Habamenshi (Ucorirwa), Kévin Kavugizo Shyamba (BNR), Laurien Jyambere (CSC), Rémy (UCT, Transactions Department) and a group of farmers from the Coproriz Rice Growers' Cooperative.

Acronyms

BNR:	Banque Nationale du Rwanda
Cestrar:	Centrale des Syndicats des Travailleurs du Rwanda (Trade Union Confederation of Rwanda)
Coproriz:	Coopérative de Production Rizicole (Rice Producers' Cooperative)
CSC:	Centre de Services aux Coopératives (Cooperative Service Centre)
Ferwathé:	Fédération Rwandaise des Théiculteurs (Rwandan Tea Producers' Federation)
FRSP:	Fédération Rwandaise du Secteur Privé (Rwandan Federation of the Private Sector)
Imbaraga:	Syndicat des Agriculteurs et des Eleveurs du Rwanda (Rwandan Farmers' Union)
Ingabo:	Syndicat des Agriculteurs et des Eleveurs de Gitarama (Gitamara Farmers' Union)
JOC:	Jeunesse Ouvrière Catholique (Young Christian Workers)
Minagri:	Ministère de l'Agriculture et de l'Elevage (Ministry of Agriculture and Animal Resources)
Minicom:	Ministère du Commerce et des Coopératives (Ministry of Commerce, Industry, Investment Promotion, Tourism and Cooperatives)
OCIR:	Office des Cultures Industrielles du Rwanda (government department responsible for cash crops)
PIFA:	Programme d'Investissement dans les Filières Agricoles (Agricultural Investment Programme)
RSSP:	Rural Sector Support Project
RWF:	Rwandese francs (€ 1 = approx. RWF 655)
UBPR:	Union des Banques Populaires du Rwanda (Union of Rwandan People's Banks)
Ucoribu:	Union des Coopératives Rizicoles de Butare (Union of Rice Producers' Cooperatives in Butare)
Ucorirwa:	Union des Coopératives Rizicoles du Rwanda (Union of Rwandan Rice Producers' Cooperatives)
UCT:	Union des Caisses de Solidarité des Travailleurs (Union of Workers' Savings and Credit Banks)

Bibliography

- Banque Nationale du Rwanda (BNR) (1999), Loi numéro 08/99 du 18 Juin 1999 portant réglementation des Banques et autres Etablissements Financiers (law governing the regulation of banks and other financial institutions), Kigali.

- BNR (2002), Instruction n° 06/2002 de la Banque Nationale du Rwanda relative à la réglementation des activités de microfinance (instruction regarding microfinancing), Kigali.

- BNR (2003), Instruction n° 05/2003 de la Banque Nationale du Rwanda relative à la réglementation des Sociétés Coopératives d'Epargne et de Crédit (instruction on the regulation of savings and credit cooperatives) (2003), Kigali.

- Birchall J. (2003), Cooperatives and the Millenium Development Goals, ILO, Geneva.

- Birchall J. (2003), Rediscovering the cooperative advantage, ILO, Geneva.

- Care International (2003), Inventaire et Analyse des Capacités des Organisations et Institutions de la Société Civile dans la province de Ruhengeri, Kigali.

- Develtere P. (1998), Economie Sociale et Développement. Les coopératives, mutuelles et associations dans les pays en développement, De Boeck University, Brussels.

- Hussi P. et al. (1993), The development of cooperative and other rural organisations. The role of the World Bank, The World Bank, Washington DC.

- Minicom (2005), Draft of the National Policy on Promotion of Cooperatives, Kigali.

- Ministry of Commerce, Industry, Investment Promotion, Tourism and Cooperatives (Minicom) (2005), Draft of the Law organising cooperatives, Kigali.

- Ndamage G. (2003), Rapport de recherche sur l'Informel au Rwanda sous l'égide de Syndicoop, Kigali.

- Ntavyohanyuma P. & Yakunda L. (1992), Cours de Formation Coopérative, Centre IWACU, Kigali.

- Overseas Development Institute (ODI) and Institute of Development Studies (IDS) (2006), Independent Evaluation of Rwanda's Poverty Reduction Strategy 2002-2005 (PRSP1), Final report dated 20 February 2006.

- Ucorirwa (2004), Etude diagnostique des coopératives et associations rizicoles, Kigali.

- Union des Banques Populaires (2003), Rapport annuel 2002, Kigali.

- Union des Banques Populaires (2004), Rapport annuel 2003, Kigali.

- Union des Banques Populaires (2005), Rapport annuel 2004, Kigali.

- World Council of Credit Unions (WOCCU) (2002), 'Rwanda Credit Unions Member and Non-Member Survey 2002', Research Monograph Series, n° 20, Madison, Wisconsin.

Chapter Twelve –
Cooperatives in South Africa:
A Movement (Re-Emerging)

by Jan Theron[1]

Introduction

At the time of writing this contribution, the cooperative movement in South Africa itself is in a period of transition. On the one hand there are what I have characterized as the established cooperatives. These are the historically white-owned cooperatives, which are mainly involved in agricultural marketing and agro-processing, including wine. On the other hand there is the emergent cooperative movement. This comprises for the most part cooperatives established in the 1990s and subsequently.

There are undoubtedly lessons to be learned from the established cooperatives. However in some cases their members still comprise in the main those who have benefited from decades of assistance given to agricultural cooperatives. Even where there have been significant changes in membership since the advent of the post-apartheid era, it is unclear to what extent the traditions associated with a cooperative movement that served to bolster white privilege have changed.[2] It is also unclear as yet how these cooperatives will react to the introduction of the new Act. I have therefore not looked for a case study from amongst their number.

Yet it is difficult to select a useful or representative case study from amongst the emergent cooperatives. Firstly, the emergent cooperatives are mostly

---

[1] Jan Theron studied law and went to work for the democratic trade union movement that emerged in South Africa in the 1980s. He was the general secretary of what is now the Food and Allied Workers Union from 1976 until 1989. He is now a practising attorney and co-ordinator of the Labour and Enterprise project, based in the Faculty of Law of the University of Cape Town.
[2] IEMAS Cooperative Ltd is an example of a cooperative whose membership has changed significantly. Founded in 1937 to provide financial services to a white working class constituency, it now boasts 125,000 members, the majority of whom are black. It also provides services that are targeted at a black constituency. See www.iemas.co.za. However it is questionable whether the management and control of the cooperative reflect the transformation of its membership. In the case of agricultural cooperatives, the potential for transformation has also been constrained by the relatively slow pace of land reform.

small, primary cooperatives. Secondly it is an extremely diverse movement, both in terms of where they are located, the sectors in which cooperatives are operating, and in terms of the different kinds of cooperatives.

Compounding the foregoing problem is the fact that the legislative framework in terms of which cooperatives operate is also in transition. In 2002 it was decided to transfer cooperatives to the Department of Trade and Industry (DTI). However the physical transfer only took full effect in 2005. DTI in the meantime established a Cooperative Development Unit and adopted a Cooperative Development Policy. However many aspects of this policy have still to be implemented. A new Cooperatives Act was adopted in 2005, yet cooperatives are still being registered in terms of the 1981 Act ("the old Act"), because the new Act has still to be promulgated.[3]

For practical reasons, the case studies had to be selected from the region where the writer is based. Given the problem of finding representative case studies, it was decided to draw on an earlier study based on case studies of thirteen cooperatives in the Western Cape (Labour and Enterprise Project, 2003). The ones selected were thought the most interesting or most substantial of these cooperatives, with the object of establishing what had happened to them in the intervening two years. This would be an indication of the state of the movement. Two of the cooperatives selected were located in the town of Paarl, 80 kilometres from Cape Town. One was a workers' cooperative manufacturing woven goods (the weaving cooperative). It was still going, but its membership had dropped from ten to eight. The other was a workers' cooperative involved in clearing alien vegetation, called Masibambane 2000. Although it was the only cooperative from this sample listed in the telephone directory, the number was not working. With difficulty we eventually located its secretary, only to find out the cooperative had recently closed down.

Three cooperatives were in the Cape Town area. They comprised a trading cooperative marketing arts and craft, a cooperative of crèches and day care centres (the care cooperative), and a workers cooperative of information technology specialists (the IT cooperative). The IT cooperative had started with eleven members. Now there were only four, and it appeared the cooperative was hardly operational. The care cooperative was still operating, but had lost three of its fifteen members, and was struggling. The art and craft cooperative had survived the departure of its most successful member, to set up his own shop, and had increased its membership from 23 to 31 members. The sixth cooperative followed up on was involved in the manufacture and

---

[3] The Cooperatives Act 14 of 2005. It was assented to on 18 August 2005.

marketing of rooibos tea grown by small farmers in Niewoudtville, four hours drive from Cape Town.[4]

The rooibos tea cooperative is an unusually successful enterprise, having regard both to the growth of its membership, the increase in its turnover and the surpluses it has generated. For this paper, the rooibos tea cooperative and the cooperative that failed, Masibambane, provided the most useful case studies. However, where appropriate we will refer to other examples as well.

A marked growth of the sector

Although it was not underpinned by any formal policy, the focus of the old Act was mainly on agricultural cooperatives. Agricultural cooperatives are comprehensively defined in that law, and any cooperative that does not qualify in terms of this definition is regarded as a trading cooperative. Consequently there are cooperatives involved in agriculture in the broad sense but that for one or other reason have not been regarded as covered by the definition. This is the case with the rooibos tea cooperative.

At the advent of South Africa's first democratically elected government in 1994 there were 256 agricultural cooperatives and 213 trading cooperatives registered.[5] However, whereas many of the agricultural cooperatives were substantial enterprises in terms of assets and turnover, this was not true of trading cooperatives. Just over half of the trading cooperatives were described as home industries. Other forms of trading cooperative included general dealers, fishing cooperatives, buying associations and garages (petrol service stations).

Ten years later, as a result of the registration of new cooperatives, the numbers in both categories had swollen. The most up-to-date list of registered cooperatives available is dated 31 July 2004 ("the July 2004 list"). It comprises 307 agricultural cooperatives and 2,150 trading cooperatives.[6] This represents an increase of over 400%. However, this list is already hopelessly out of date.

---

[4] Strictly speaking Niewoudtville is just outside the boundary of the Western Cape, and falls under the Northern Cape.
[5] Statistics on coops compiled by the Registrar of Cooperatives for the period 1992-1995, submitted to the Cooperative Policy Task Team, 1997. The statistics show a steady decline in the number of agricultural cooperatives that continued until 1995. There was a corresponding decline in the number of trading cooperatives until 1994, with comparatively few applications for registration. However in 1995 there was an increase of some four-fold in this number.
[6] This is a list of registered cooperatives provided by the office of the Registrar. However the office spokesperson readily conceded that the list was not accurate, in that there are numerous omissions. It is also probable that there are numerous cooperatives that are defunct on this list.

Whether because of the transfer to DTI, or efforts by DTI and provincial governments to actively promote cooperatives, or as a consequence of the unemployment situation or other factors, there has been a marked increase in applications for the registration of cooperatives. Recent figures for cooperatives registered give some indication of this. During the period 1 April to 31 August 2005, 708 new cooperatives were registered. There are now altogether 5,024 cooperatives registered as at 31 August 2005.[7] Within a year, in other words, the number of registered cooperatives has nearly doubled.

The July 2004 list is nevertheless useful. Firstly, it gives a better indication as to the sector in which cooperatives are operating than the broad categories of agriculture and trading. In the case of agriculture it distinguishes between the different sub-sectors of agriculture.[8] These include activities ancillary to agriculture, such as packaging, cold-storage, financial services provided to agriculture, and the provision of agricultural equipment. In the case of trading cooperatives, the following kinds of cooperative are listed: transport cooperatives, providing taxi and other services to commuters; retail or consumer cooperatives, ranging from cooperative shops to bulk-buying schemes; financial services, including savings and credit cooperatives (SACCOs), insurance cooperatives and so-called village banks; cooperatives providing community or social services, including housing cooperatives, medical cooperatives (apparently composed of medical practitioners), training cooperatives, and social cooperatives; cooperatives involved in construction, from brick-making to (presumably) the actual construction of buildings; and fishing cooperatives.[9] Quite a number of cooperatives are categorized as general. Many are still categorized as engaged in home industries.

Secondly, the July 2004 list indicates in which of South Africa's nine provinces the exponential growth in new cooperatives has taken place. Most of these new cooperatives are categorized as trading cooperatives, and the provincial distribution of trading cooperatives is set out in the figure below.[10] This shows

---

[7] Figures provided by the Office of the Registrar of Cooperatives.
[8] Forestry and secondary agriculture, including wine manufacture, fall within the scope of agriculture. A further peculiarity as to the categorization of agricultural cooperatives has already been noted: for reasons that are not apparent, some emergent cooperatives have been registered as agricultural cooperatives whilst others have been registered as trading cooperatives.
[9] It is however known that the fishing cooperative is a form that has been abused by sharp operators who register cooperatives in the hope that it will improve their prospects of obtaining a quota from government to do so.
[10] The provincial distribution is quite different as between trading and agricultural cooperatives, because of the preponderance of established cooperatives, whose members are commercial farmers, in agriculture. For example the greatest number of agricultural cooperatives was in the Western Cape (86, or 28 per cent of the total), largely because of a strong presence in fruit packing and wine making.

that two provinces, Kwa-Zulu Natal and Eastern Cape, together account for 68% of trading cooperatives. Kwa-Zulu Natal is the most populous province and Eastern Cape the second poorest.[11]

Figure 12.1: Breakdown per province of trading cooperatives as at July 2004

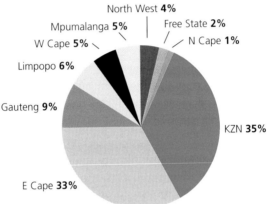

North West **4%**

Mpumalanga **5%**

Free State **2%**

W Cape **5%**

N Cape **1%**

Limpopo **6%**

Gauteng **9%**

KZN **35%**

E Cape **33%**

The new Act does not limit the number and variety of different kinds of cooperatives. This means a cooperative will be free to define itself as it chooses.[12] However there are specific provisions applicable to workers', housing, financial services and agricultural cooperatives.[13] Although very few cooperatives currently style themselves as workers' cooperatives, many would doubtless be categorized as such in terms of the specific provisions applicable to this form of cooperative. Undoubtedly a large number of these workers' cooperatives are also involved in agriculture, and it remains to be seen how these will be categorized.[14]

---

[11] The growth of cooperatives in Kwa-Zulu Natal may be attributable in part to a provincial policy in which ten per cent of procurement is allocated to cooperatives. There is also a bank established, the Tyala Bank, which provides funding to cooperatives. See in general the discussion on the role of government below.

[12] However the following kinds of cooperative are defined in terms of the Act: housing cooperative, workers' cooperative, social cooperative, agricultural cooperative, burial cooperative, financial services cooperative, consumer cooperative, marketing and supply cooperative and service cooperative. Certain of these different kinds of cooperatives were inserted late in the process of drafting the legislation, and certain definitions do not appear to be well-considered eg a social cooperative.

[13] See Parts 1-4, Schedule 1, Act of 2005.

[14] The July 2004 list indicates the number of so-called trading cooperatives engaged in some form of agriculture is as high as forty per cent. Most of these are likely to be workers' cooperatives. If the number of trading cooperatives engaged in agriculture is combined with those formally registered as agricultural cooperatives, 47.5 per cent of registered cooperatives as at this date are involved in the agricultural sector, broadly defined. This finding is consistent with other studies suggesting about half of all cooperatives are involved in agricultural activities (BMR review, 2005).

The Registrar's office does produce data regarding the overall financial position of the registered cooperatives, based on an analysis of the annual financial statements cooperatives are required to submit to the Registrar. However these data are aggregated for agricultural cooperatives as a whole and the different sub-sectors in agriculture, and for trading cooperatives as a whole, and "buying aids". Evidently the latter category includes certain established consumer cooperatives, since a large proportion of the assets of trading cooperatives are accounted for in this category. The same data contain figures of the active and non-active membership of cooperatives. However this information is evidently not reliable, since most trading cooperatives do not submit returns.[15] Presumably cooperatives that do not submit membership returns also do not submit audited financial statements. Evidently the capacity of the Registrar's office to tell us anything more about the character of the emergent cooperative movement is limited.

The sections of the cooperative movement about which such information is available are those that have formed secondary cooperatives. There are 28 savings and credit cooperatives, for example, affiliated to the secondary cooperative SACCOL. This constitutes a substantial and stable presence in the financial services sector, with 12,000 members and assets of R43 million. On the other hand nine of their members are considered inactive (SACCOL, 2004). The financial services sector also includes the so-called village banks, most of which have failed, and burial societies. A secondary cooperative has recently been established for burial societies, which are discussed below.

Housing cooperatives represent another section of the movement which has formed a secondary cooperative.[16] A recent study of housing cooperatives identified 21 cooperatives that could properly be described as providing housing services to their members, located mainly in the urban centres of Gauteng, Kwa-Zulu Natal and Western Cape provinces (Stewart and Associates, 2005). Although the number of persons housed by these cooperatives is relatively small in relation to the need for housing, particularly in the informal settlements that have mushroomed around every urban centre in the country, organizations operating along cooperative lines are also being used to assist people to build their own houses.[17]

The secondary cooperatives mentioned above are currently affiliated to an

---

[15] Figures produced by the Registrar's office in 2001 indicate the active membership of all trading cooperatives was an incredible 225,300. However the registrar's office assures me that this figure was not correct, and that the current active membership of trading cooperatives is only 3,751.
[16] SA Housing Cooperative Association (SAHCA).
[17] The best known such organisation is the Homeless People's Federation which together with an NGO, People's Dialogue, constitutes the Homeless People's Alliance.

apex body, the National Cooperative Alliance of SA (NCASA). However an apex body should ideally be comprised exclusively of secondary or higher forms of cooperatives. The bulk of NCASA's membership is primary cooperatives. NCASA claims to have 575 primary cooperatives affiliated to it.

The survivalist character of many young cooperatives

All indications are that the primary cooperatives that make up the emergent movement are all small primary cooperatives with few if any assets. It is, for example, a requirement of both the old and new Act that cooperatives have a registered office, and provide the Registrar with a physical address and their contact details.[18] The legislation is not prescriptive as regards what contact details are provided, and it is certainly not a requirement that cooperatives have a telephone to be registered. It is nevertheless indicative of the level of development of the emergent cooperatives that, gauging from the July 2004 list, a high proportion of registered cooperatives have provided only a cellular telephone number. Further, some 49.6% of trading cooperatives appear to have no telephone number at all. The costs of telecommunications are often cited as an obstacle to the development of small business in South Africa. The same would obviously apply to cooperatives.

It is probable that a cooperative that cannot be contacted by telephone has very limited prospects of expanding its operation, and is survivalist in character. A recent review of cooperatives in four predominantly rural provinces (Free State, Limpopo, Northern Cape and North West) undertaken for DTI[19] confirms that this is the case.

52% of groups surveyed were in the 10-49 member size category, and the average number of members per cooperative was 15.58. About half the cooperatives had a turnover of less than R10, 001 per annum, and 30.2% had had no income at all (BMR, 2005). A similar profile emerges from an earlier series of studies on worker cooperatives commissioned by the Department of Labour, and covering Kwa-Zulu Natal (Makho, 2003), the Eastern Cape and Western Cape (Labour and Enterprise Project, 2003). For example the average membership for the Western Cape, a more urbanized province, was 13.76.

In the absence of any official statistics on membership, the above studies provide the best available indication regarding the total membership of

---

[18] In this regard, it is significant that a large proportion of cooperatives in the July 2004 list provide only a post box number, as opposed to a physical address.
[19] It is unclear why these provinces were selected.

cooperatives. Assuming an average of 15 members per registered cooperative, a reasonable estimate of the total membership would be in the region of 75,000. It is of course not possible to analyse the make-up of its membership by race, gender, occupational status or the like. However a national study of 654 cooperatives found that two-thirds of the members of the typical cooperative (according to the median membership) were women (NCASA, 2001). It would also be safe to assume that apart from the established cooperatives, the membership of the emergent cooperatives is overwhelmingly black in the generic sense, including so-called coloureds and Africans, and poor.

A new role for government in the making

The role of government in relation to cooperative development is or should be to create an enabling legislative and policy environment, and to facilitate an appropriate institutional framework, which is discussed below. As regards the legislative environment in South Africa, cooperatives have been regulated by a single Act since 1922. This will still be so in terms of the new Cooperatives Act, although it is contemplated that financial cooperatives will also have to register in terms of separate legislation.[20] The new Act was drafted in consultation with the International Labour Organization, and can be regarded as conforming to ILO Recommendation 193.

Soon after the transfer of the administration of cooperatives to DTI, DTI began a process of consultation regarding the adoption of a cooperative development policy. The latest draft of this policy distinguishes between the established and emerging cooperatives, focussing on the latter. It emphasizes the role cooperatives can play in bridging the divide between the formal and informal economy, and in creating employment for disadvantaged groups such as women and youth. It also spells out a role for government in supporting cooperatives.[21] This is primarily to create a favourable legal, economic, administrative and institutional environment for cooperatives.[22]

Amongst the measures envisaged to promote cooperatives are access to the same tax incentives as are available to micro, small and medium enterprises, which are currently being revised, and access to preferential procurement

---

[20] The National Treasury plans to introduce a Cooperative Banks Bill in 2006. It is envisaged that a financial cooperative will have to comply with certain provisions of the Cooperatives Act as well as this new law.
[21] A Cooperative Development Policy for South Africa ("the Policy"), June 2004.
[22] Paragraph 10.1, the Policy.

policies.[23] Government is also committed to promoting cooperatives, specifically workers' cooperatives and consumer cooperatives, in terms of its integrated manufacturing strategy, and in terms of local economic development strategies.[24] The establishment of a Cooperative Development Fund for "technical assistance and capacity building" is also envisaged.

The rapid growth in the number of registered cooperatives, and the increase in the number of applications for registration in recent months[25], is an indication that the message that government will support cooperatives is getting across. However the capacity of the DTI's Cooperative Development Unit to implement effective support measures is clearly limited. Currently there are only nine persons employed by this office with three positions remaining to be filled. A further twelve persons are employed in the Registrar's office. There are also competing priorities, particularly given the direction so-called black economic empowerment has taken.[26] Indeed there is a view that government's commitment to cooperative development amounts to little more than a sop, to appease left-wing critics of government economic policies.

At least since 1994 and notwithstanding the comparatively onerous requirements of the 1981 Act, the registrar's office has adopted a permissive attitude towards the registration of cooperatives. As a result it is relatively easy and comparatively cheap to register a cooperative.[27] No doubt this has also contributed to the exponential increase in registered cooperatives. However this increase can only be viewed as a positive development if a significant proportion of newly registered primary cooperatives become sustainable enterprises, and are able to establish viable secondary cooperatives. Clearly this represents a major challenge.

Given the geographical extent of South Africa, provincial government, as well as local government, clearly has a key role in meeting this challenge. In all the provinces persons have been designated to promote cooperative development. However in some instances this is the same office that is responsible for small business development.[28] The danger in such a setup is that, whether deliberately or not, cooperatives are marginalized or

---

[23] Paragraphs 10.3.6 and 10.3.7.
[24] Paragraphs 16 (c) and (d), Policy.
[25] Since the physical transfer of the Registrar's office to DTI.
[26] Black economic empowerment refers to policies to redress a situation in which control of the economy is predominantly in white hands. Although government has adopted a policy that empowerment should be broad based, this is arguably a belated response to the transfer of wealth to a select few, politically well-connected, black individuals.
[27] The current cost of registering a cooperative is 224 Rands, the rough equivalent of 36 US dollars.
[28] This is the case in the Western Cape, for example.

undermined in favour of conventional business forms.

The case of Masibambane 2000 illustrates this danger. This cooperative was established in response to the opportunities created by the government's premier public works programme, clearing alien vegetation.[29] A public works programme lends itself to the cooperative form, as its participants are by definition all persons in need. However, the agency implementing this programme, itself a part of government, was not happy to work with the cooperative, with three teams of 25 members, each having an elected team leader. The model it wished to promote was that of the so-called "emergent contractor", in which this contractor "employed" the rest of the team. It also wanted to give other "emergent contractors" a chance. It was thus evident from the outset that it would be extremely difficult to sustain a cooperative in these circumstances. It was probably only due to political pressure from the apex body and the determination of its leadership that it survived as long as it did.

The example of the Rooibos Tea Cooperative

Rooibos is a plant that grows naturally in a dry, mountainous region north of Cape Town. The fourteen persons that decided to form the rooibos tea cooperative were all small farmers, some of whom owned small tracts of land, individually or as a group, and some of whom rented land. This was in 2000, after a representative of an environmental NGO introduced them to a proponent of organic tea farming.

Their original object in forming a cooperative was an extremely limited one. It was to establish a facility to process each member's tea, so that it could be delivered to a company marketing rooibos tea. This company was formerly a cooperative, but had converted to a company, and some of the small farmers were contractually bound to deliver all their produce to it. However, there was unhappiness with the price it paid. It soon became apparent that the cooperative could get a much better price by marketing their tea through an agent, under a fair trade label and as organically produced.

During the first year of its operation the cooperative leased a centrally located facility to produce the tea, some of which was then marketed through an agent. So successful was this that the following year all the members were marketing their tea through the cooperative, and the cooperative realized a substantial surplus. The cooperative's constitution stipulates that the board

---

[29] The programme is known as the Working for Water Programme.

may retain a portion of any surplus for reserves and that the balance is available for distribution to members as a bonus. However, only 70% of any such amount may be distributed as a bonus calculated in accordance with the patronage proportion.[30] The remaining 30% "must be used to further the objects of the cooperative of enabling its members to develop sustainable economic activity. This may be done by supplementing any bonus payable to members who, in the opinion of the board, have been most disadvantaged because of their race, and/or because they are women, or by sponsoring a training or development programme to assist such members".

The principle of retaining 30% of the amount available for distribution to benefit the less advantaged members of the cooperative is well accepted by the members. It has enabled the proportion of women members to increase significantly. Two of the fourteen founding members were women. There are now thirty-six members, of whom twelve are women. At the same time the cooperative has sponsored a number of training and development programmes, which has included topics ranging from financial management to global climate change, an issue of direct relevance to the sustainable cultivation of the tea.

"It gives me a headache to see how rapidly the co-op has grown ...", the treasurer of the board commented. "I am not capable enough ... we are board members but we are also farmers." The R100 entrance fees contributed by each member gave an initial capital of R1,400 in 2001. At the end of 2004 the cooperative had a turnover of R1.25m and assets of R896,708, including a truck to deliver the tea, a welding machine and a tractor used in the production of tea.

In fact the greatest threat to the future of the cooperative could be ascribed to its financial success. A member in financial need began to agitate for the payment of bonuses that, on the advice of the auditors, had been retained in reserve accounts. It was a demand that could easily have precipitated the dissolution of the cooperative. Instead, by a process of deliberation and debate we shall consider further below, members ultimately came to a solid understanding that their cooperative was not for the short-term gain of the members for the time being. Undoubtedly it is an understanding that will stand the cooperative in good stead now that it has employed its own marketing manager, as well as administrator.

---

[30] The patronage proportion is calculated in accordance with the volume of business a member does with the cooperative. However, in a context in which there is unequal access to land, and the title to land is often held by a male, a principle which might otherwise seem fair may reinforce existing inequalities.

The employment of a manager marks a new stage in the development of the cooperative. It is also a stage less successful cooperatives are often unable to arrive at on their own. In the case of the weaving cooperative, a manager who is able to find markets for their rugs is critical for their viability. In this instance the cooperative is part of a cluster of cooperative and self-help groups which share the services of a manager and administrator.

Elements in favour of a vibrant cooperative sector and movement

By 2004 the rooibos tea cooperative had realised that it could do far better for itself by dispensing with the agent who marketed its produce, and dealing directly with the buyers. However this required that they obtain the requisite certification from the Fair Trade Labelling Organisation (FLO), which is a relatively sophisticated process. One of the potential benefits of the cooperative form is that collectively producers are able to engage in such a process, as well as to achieve vertical integration of the different units making up the enterprise, by means of pooling equipment and collectivizing the costs of seasonal labour.

At the same time and apparently without any prompting by outside organizations or individuals, the members have realized that cooperation extends to assisting others to form cooperatives, and cooperating with other cooperatives. Wupperthal is an area to the South where rooibos tea is grown by a far greater number of small farmers, almost all of whom rent the land they utilize from the Moravian Church. With the assistance of the cooperative, these Wupperthal small farmers are now in the process of forming themselves into a cooperative, and are also marketing their tea under the FLO label. The basis for a secondary cooperative being formed, to represent both communities of small growers, is readily apparent.

As already indicated, however, there is very little new growth at the secondary level. In the Free State, Limpopo, Northern Cape and North West provinces fewer than ten per cent of the cooperatives surveyed were members of secondary cooperatives, and none were affiliated at a tertiary level (BMR, 2005).

Realizing the potential of the cooperative sector

The exponential growth in the number of registered cooperatives could not be explained unless a significant proportion of them were previously informally constituted. A recent study commissioned by DTI in four predominantly rural provinces (Free State, Limpopo, Northern Cape and North West) sought to identify not only registered cooperatives, but what it termed pre-cooperatives, using the offices of the local authority or municipality to locate them. It found that 63% of the groups located were pre-cooperatives. It concluded there was a "vast potential for an increase in cooperatives in these provinces and probably in other provinces as well" (BMR, 2005). In the case of Limpopo, South Africa's poorest province, the number of registered cooperatives represents only some 25% of the groups identified in this study.

Burial societies provide another indication for the potential of cooperatives. It has been estimated that 29% of South African adults, representing almost 8 million people, are members of burial societies, and that they contribute some 10 billion Rands to these societies. Burial societies are not cooperatives. However they subscribe to cooperative principles and can become formally constituted as cooperatives. With this in mind, SAFOBS has recruited 199 societies with 20,210 members (SAFOBS, 2005). The social benefits of such a development are that it would facilitate the formalization and regulation of such societies, in the interests of the members. For the legislation that is supposed to regulate such societies is ineffective.[31]

Transport is also a sector in which the cooperative form has obvious potential for growth. Here too there would be enormous social benefits. Cooperatives could contribute to eliminating the phenomenon of taxi violence, stoked by taxi bosses competing for business. Cooperatives could also alleviate some of the problems associated with the increased utilization of owner-drivers, who as individuals are powerless vis-à-vis the large companies that give them work. The July 2004 list indicates there are some 78 registered cooperatives that provide taxi or other transport services. This represents a fraction of the potential of cooperatives in the sector. At the same time it underscores the need for cooperatives to form secondary cooperatives if the movement is to fulfil its potential.

A variety of different strategies have been adopted to develop cooperatives. In Gauteng, South Africa's most urbanized province, the Cooperative Policy and Advice Centre (COPAC) has piloted two projects that may provide useful

---

[31] The Friendly Societies Act, No 25 of 1956.

lessons for cooperatives in an urban environment. One is a cooperative established to manage an eco-village where a number of cooperative based projects are located, including organic farming, waste recycling, eco-building and paper-making. The other is the establishment of a sustainable local manufacturing hive in conjunction with the Ekurhuleni municipality.[32]

The precious but delicate role of donors

The role of donors in relation to the cooperative movement is a delicate one. On the one hand it is difficult to conceive of the emergent primary cooperatives becoming sustainable, and forming viable secondary cooperatives, without donor support. On the other hand reliance on donor funding can encourage a top-down approach to organization, which is ultimately ineffective.

It is not clear whether donors themselves always appreciate this dilemma, although those associated with the international cooperative movement probably do. In the case of the German federation DGRV, for example, support is channelled through a registered cooperative based in Pretoria. This provides a variety of services to its members, which are cooperatives and self-help groups, including advice and counselling, training, financial services and bulk buying of consumables such as maize meal as well as commodities such as fertilizer, seed, cement and the like.[33]

Housing cooperatives have benefited from technical and financial assistance from the international cooperative movement and agencies associated with it, including Rooftops Canada, the Cooperative Housing Association and the Norwegian Federation of Housing Associations. They have also been funded by the Norwegian and South African governments. In the case of SACCOL, it has received funding from a variety of sources, including the international cooperative movement (the Swedish Cooperative Centre, the Irish League of Credit Unions Foundation) and sources such as USAID and Ford Foundation (Mhembere and Masunda, 2005). It has nevertheless achieved a degree of self-sufficiency. It appears that funding is now primarily to finance its expansion and stabilization.

NCASA has for the past three years received funding from DTI, but there is currently an impasse over the renewal of this funding. It would appear that

---

[32] In terms of the concept document for this project, the concept of sustainable local manufacturing is premised on a critique of mass production. It is manufacturing for local or community need, utilizing appropriate technologies and as far as possible, local resources.
[33] www.yebocoop.co.za

this impasse relates to its lack of progress in becoming self-sufficient, using funds generated from its own members. All forms of external funding tend to undermine cooperative autonomy and particularly so when the funder is the government. On the other hand it is difficult to see how the dissolution of an apex body at this point will help meet the challenges the establishment of the movement faces.

In the case of the rooibos tea cooperative, it received a fairly modest grant towards establishing the production facility at its inception. Recently it received a small grant from the Global Environment Facility, for amongst other things a project to enhance soil conservation, and a mentor farmer project to advise small farmers about how to cultivate in a sustainable way. Aside from these grants, the only assistance it has received is the social premium charged by the fair trade organizations.[34]

Masibambane 2000, by way of contrast, received no assistance from donors whatever. The fate of this cooperative also illustrates why the role of donors should not be discussed only with reference to those donors who fund cooperative development, but also with reference to those who actively propagate other models, even in circumstances in which the cooperative form is indicated, and to those who determine what can be described as "donor fashions". Thus even though it was a government agency that was responsible for implementing the programme to clear alien vegetation, the funds it utilized were from donors, and the policy it adopted towards cooperatives was almost certainly driven by the donors' preference for funding a programme to create emergent contractors.

Need for an institutional framework

Sometimes cooperatives can flourish with a minimum of institutional support. The arts and craft cooperative is a case in point. The members are from diverse backgrounds, ranging from shack-dwellers to residents of the middle-class suburbs. All that unites them is their ability to produce a saleable product, and a wish to have access to Cape Town's premier tourist site. The cooperative form ideally suits this limited purpose, and it appears they have no contact with a broader cooperative movement. Contact with the Registrar of Cooperatives in such an instance is confined to the submission of annual returns.

---

[34] The social premium is a charge on sales by the fair trade marketing organization that is refunded to the cooperative, and is to be used exclusively for developmental purposes. It does not form part of the revenue of the cooperative for the purposes of determining whether there has been a surplus, and may not be distributed to the members.

On the other hand this cooperative has probably not developed its full potential because of its institutional isolation. A vibrant movement cannot develop without supportive institutions and an enabling environment. It remains to be seen what role provincial government, or local government, will play in this regard. There is also provision in the new Act for a Cooperative Advisory Board, composed of representatives of government, the cooperative movement and civil society.[35] The establishment of this board would hopefully help focus the government's endeavours, as well as the orderly development of secondary cooperatives.

Without such development, and without effective regional or provincial structures, the apex body does not have the capacity to provide significant support to primary cooperatives. In the case of Masibambane 2000 this lack of institutional capacity was evident at many levels. But what is perhaps paramount is the lack of capacity to provide practical advice as to how to establish a viable enterprise, as well as the technical expertise any enterprise needs to be able to access. So for example the cooperative had to accept the services of a book-keeping agency, which manifestly did not understand the cooperative form, and which was perceived to be unsympathetic and untrustworthy.

The failure of Masibambane 2000 has also to be understood in a context in which extensive and continuous support was provided to the so-called emergent contractors. Thus team leaders of the cooperative were sent on training courses designed for emergent contractors. The effect of this training, and the financial incentives that were on offer for emergent contractors as opposed to team leaders, resulted in certain of the team leaders defecting and becoming emergent contractors. The cooperative was ultimately dissolved when the last of the team leaders to remain loyal to the cooperative found it was facing debts it could not pay.

In this regard it is significant that the development of the rooibos tea cooperative has taken place beyond the ken of the apex body, which would in any event not have had the resources to be of much practical assistance. On the other hand it would clearly not have taken place at all without a close relationship with the environmental NGO, from whose representatives it rents offices, and who have been a guiding presence throughout the trajectory of its development. For purists this may raise question about the autonomy of the cooperative. But the question of autonomy must also be located in a context in which cooperation is undervalued if not actively undermined. It is

---

[35] See Chapter 12 of Act 14 of 2005. The Board will be appointed only once the new Act is promulgated.

also unrealistic to expect a cooperative whose members have had little formal education to be sustainable without access to expertise such as the NGO provides in this case.

Employment estimate of the cooperative sector

There are no official data concerning employment by cooperatives. It is however clear that in any analysis of the impact cooperatives have on employment, or rather unemployment, it is necessary firstly to distinguish those whom the cooperative itself employs. Secondly, there is the employment provided to the members and by the members. Thirdly, there is the employment effect a cooperative has, by generating ancillary activities.

The employment of a manager and administrator by the rooibos tea cooperative exemplifies the first form of employment. Present indications are that most emergent cooperatives have not developed to this point, and it is only the larger established cooperatives which employ significant numbers, apart from management and administrative staff. Rather most employment is provided to the members only. (BMR, 2005). If the estimates of members suggested above are accepted, that would translate into employment (in the extended sense of the word) for some 75,000 persons.

This is a relatively small number in the context of the entire labour market. However it is employment at a low cost, and in areas where there is little alternative employment. In the case of the rooibos tea cooperative, the cooperative provides the members with employment, by ensuring they have a steady income. As one board member expressed it, it had "given us stability in terms of development". However as small farmers for the most part they do not employ others to assist them. This is not of course the case with the commercial farmers, who employ a workforce in the same way as any other farmer.

The rooibos tea cooperative provides three examples of an employment effect it has had. Firstly, it provides seasonal employment to a team of about nineteen during the harvest season. As required, the whole of this team could be deployed to one farm, or different teams to different farms. The net effect is more stable employment for the workers concerned, and almost certainly higher wages than workers would have earned if they had been employed by individual farmers. Secondly, the cooperative has an agreement with three local groups of women to buy cloth bags sewn by them, which are used to package the tea. Thirdly, yet another group of women were assisted in establishing a tourism project, which caters for what appears to be a steady stream of visitors to the cooperative. In an impoverished rural community where the prospects of formal employment are very limited, this represents a significant impact.

The employment effect Masibambane 2000 had was of a different kind. It provided employment to a larger number than the teams of workers employed by so-called emergent contractors, because it rotated job opportunities amongst its members with the object of ensuring the benefits were spread as widely as possible.

Employment potential and possible hindrances

To appreciate the employment potential of cooperatives one must first of all acknowledge the dramatic decline of formal employment opportunities in the South African economy over the past decade.[36] Two aspects of this development are of specific relevance to cooperatives. The first is that even in the most optimistic projections for economic growth there will be chronic high unemployment for the foreseeable future, leaving many with no alternative but to resort to self-help remedies.

The model of the rooibos tea cooperative is obviously relevant in this context, particularly since employment opportunities are more restricted in rural than urban areas. At the same time the relevance of this model presupposes a vigorous implementation of land reform programmes.

The second aspect of the decline of formal employment concerns the extent to which it is associated with an increased utilization of intermediaries such as contractors to supply a range of services. The failure of Masibambane is directly relevant in this context, for in theory a contractor is supposed to be independent. The declared object of the emergent contractor training was to enable these emergent contractors to become independent. But the undeclared object of utilizing this model was for the programme that devised it to avoid the legal obligations employing teams of workers would entail

---

[36] In a study conducted by the UNDP the figure for those in formal and informal employment are given as 67.5% and 32.5% of a total of 10,896,420 persons employed in 2002. The total of unemployed is given as 4,783,502, and the total of those unemployed plus those in informal employment significantly exceed the number in informal employment. This is compared to a situation in 1990, when the number in formal employment was 82.7% of the total employed compared with 19.2 in informal employment, and those in formal employment far exceeded the combined total of the informally employed and the unemployed. See UNDP Report, 2004, Table 3, 238-239.

(although they do require the contractors to comply with certain standards).

In precisely the same way, in the private sector, employers are externalizing jobs on a massive scale. Arguably this phenomenon offers scope for cooperatives providing the same services as are being provided through intermediaries such as contractors, which because they are cooperatives, they can do under less exploitative conditions, at the same cost. This argument is even more compelling when the services are being provided to a government ostensibly committed to cooperative development.

Cooperatives: a response to poverty and to the need for social protection

Over half the population of all provinces with the exception of the Western Cape and Gauteng are estimated to live in poverty, constituting between 45 and 55% of the population.[37] The poorest provinces are Limpopo and the Eastern Cape provinces, where on average three out of every four persons live in poverty. The increased prevalence of cooperatives in these two provinces, Limpopo and Eastern Cape, strongly suggests that the formation of cooperatives is a response to poverty.

The regional studies undertaken for the Department of Labour suggest that marginal and irregular though it may be, the cooperatives in question were often the sole source of income for an entire household (Labour and Enterprise Project, 2003). Moreover in the case of Masibambane 2000, even after it was compelled by the implementing agency to disband one of its teams, and a section of its membership had to face up to a month and a half without employment, there was a reserve fund to help tide them over.

In Kwa-Zulu-Natal, 70% of the members of thirty-two cooperatives interviewed had never been employed at all prior to joining the cooperative. A high proportion of these members were young people (Makho, 2003).

Compared with other African countries the South African government has a relatively developed system of social protection, with grants for the aged and young children. It includes provision for mitigating risks, such as a grant for disability cover and unemployment insurance. However there are major gaps in this system, particularly for those who have never entered the formal economy, or the self-employed, or those in informal employment.

---

[37] This is according to the Commission of Inquiry into a Comprehensive System of Social Security for South Africa, otherwise known as the Taylor Commission.

Savings is one strategy to mitigate risks, and is common to SACCOs, burial societies as well as a range of other schemes in the informal economy, commonly described as stokvels. Members contribute to a fund from which they can draw in order to access emergency loans, or in order to cope with contingencies affecting themselves or members of their household. In the case of SACCOs, at the more formal end of the spectrum, members are able to mitigate their own risk through life or credit insurance (Genesis, 2005).

SACCOL has been meeting with the other two secondary cooperatives, SAFOBS and SAHCA, to encourage their members to form SACCOs and this is obviously one way in which cooperatives not engaged in the financial services sector could enhance the social protection of their members. At the same time by forming secondary cooperatives they ought to be able to offer insurance and other services tailored to their members' needs, as the established agricultural cooperatives have done.

Improving voice and representation

As a membership-based form of organization cooperatives should of course operate democratically, enabling their members to voice their interests. But as with any membership-based organization, cooperatives are susceptible to manipulation by their leadership or by their management. Although there is a dearth of contemporary research on the established cooperatives, there is much anecdotal evidence that suggests that many cooperatives were beholden to their management. Indeed management was often the prime beneficiary of the conversion of cooperatives to companies.

In marked contrast to the old Act, the new Act places considerable emphasis on the control members should exercise over their cooperatives, and measures that should strengthen their voice in the cooperative. However even legislation underpinned by a well-drafted constitution is no guarantee that the members will have a strong voice. In the course of the deliberation and debate amongst the members of the rooibos tea cooperative over a demand that the reserves be distributed, it emerged that none of them had properly understood the purpose of the reserve accounts. This was because it had been their auditor's idea in the first place, and they had relied on the auditor to explain it. The important lesson learned was that board members themselves need to be able to motivate policy decisions, and explain matters relating to the finances of the cooperative. Voice means quite literally one's own voice, in terms the members understand.

There needs to be voice representation not just at a primary level. The undeveloped state of the emergent cooperative movement is such that there is no forum at a secondary or higher level to which members are able to affiliate. There is therefore no structure to mediate relations between the apex body, NCASA, and members on the ground. More practically, there is no body to give practical inputs and advice to the thousands of primary cooperatives as to how they can attain viability.

Conclusions

Cooperatives in South Africa are at a pivotal moment. The achievements of the established cooperatives provide a positive example of the economic viability of the cooperative form. But the economic and political context in which the established cooperatives emerged was significantly different. The established cooperatives also provide a negative model, insofar as they have failed to give their members adequate voice, and cannot be described as a vibrant movement.

The exponential growth of cooperatives currently taking place is a strong indication that it is feasible to establish a vibrant cooperative movement. However to do so it will first of all be necessary to transform what are essentially enterprises in the informal economy into formal enterprises. This in turn will not happen unless enough survivalist cooperatives become economically viable as are able to form a critical mass, around which a secondary movement can cohere.

The case of Masibambane 2000 suggests that economically viable cooperatives will not be established without measures targeted to actively promote the cooperative form, and without appropriate support. The case of the rooibos tea cooperative suggests that while support can take many forms, it should be at hand when it is needed. Undoubtedly the most serious constraint to the development of sustainable cooperatives is the failure to materialize of a secondary structure that can provide this kind of support.

The moment to develop such a structure is now. Yet unless a concerted effort is made to do so, and unless there is perceptible progress in doing so, the moment will be lost, and the possibility that a vibrant cooperative sector can open up will again recede.

Sources

This paper is based on a series of interviews, carried out during October and November, 2005. The author wishes to acknowledge valuable information from the following: Cooperative Development Unit, Department of Trade and Industry; Office of the Registrar of Cooperatives, Department of Trade and Industry; Lita Kutta, Enterprise Development Manager, Western Cape Provincial Government; Social Housing Foundation (www.shf.org.za); Dora Tamana Cooperative Centre; Tebogo Phadu, SA Federation of Burial Societies; David De Jongh, SACCOL; Sabelo Mamba, NCASA; Richard October, NCASA Western Cape; Vishwas Satgar, Cooperative Policy Advice Centre, Johannesburg; Nomsa Ndumuse, Masimbambane 2000 Cooperative; Titus Hendricks, Ikhwezi Centre, Mbekweni; Noel Oettle and Bettina, Environmental Monitoring Group; and Board members, Heiveld Cooperative Ltd, Nieuwoudtville.

Acronyms

DTI	Department of Trade and Industry
DGRV	Deutsche Genossenschafts- und Raiffeisenverband
NCASA	National Cooperative Association of SA
SACCOL	Savings and Credit Cooperatives League
SAFOBS	SA Federation of Burial Societies
SAHCA	SA Housing Cooperative Association

Bibliography

- Amin N. & Bernstein H. (1996), 'The role of agricultural cooperatives in agricultural and rural development', *Land and Agriculture Policy Centre policy paper* 32.

- Berold R. (1991), 'Cooperatives: The struggle to survive', *New Ground*, n°3, pp. 29-32.

- Bureau of Market Research – University of South Africa ('BMR') (2005), *Analytical review of cooperative aspects and environment in the following selected provinces: Free State, Limpopo, Northern Cape and North West*, Unpublished report commissioned by Department of Trade and Industry.

- ECI Africa (2003), *A review of the capacity, lessons learned and way forward for member-based financial institutions in South Africa*, Unpublished report commissioned by Finmark Trust.

- ECI Africa (2003), *Member based financial institutions: Design and feasibility of regulating and support structure*, Unpublished report commissioned by Finmark Trust for National Treasury.

- Genesis Analytics (2004), *Making insurance markets work for the poor in South Africa – Scoping study*, Unpublished report.

- Ignatius Mhembere & Lloyd Masunda (2005), *Assessment of the savings and credit cooperative rural expansion and capacity building project in the Eastern Cape Province of South Africa*, Unpublished report commissioned by Swedish Cooperative Centre.

- Jaffe G. (1991), 'Cooperative development in South Africa', *in South African Review*, Ed., pp. 364-377.

- Labour & Enterprise Project (2003), *Worker cooperatives in the Western Cape*, Unpublished report commissioned by Department of Labour.

- Makho Communications (2003), *Research on worker cooperatives: an avenue for job creation*, Unpublished report commissioned by Department of Labour.

- Mhembere I. & Masunda L. (2005), *Assessment of the savings and credit cooperative rural expansion and capacity building project in the Eastern Cape Province of South Africa*, Unpublished report commissioned by Swedish Cooperative Centre.

- National Cooperative Association of SA (2001), *Hope in action: Cooperatives in South Africa*, Unpublished report on the 2001 NCASA baseline study.

- Philip K. (2003), *Cooperatives in South Africa: Their role in job creation and poverty reduction*, Unpublished paper commissioned by the South African Foundation.

- Savings & Credit Cooperative League (2004), *General Manager Report*. Unpublished report to members of SACCOL.

- Social Housing Foundation (2005), *Emerging cooperative housing models in South Africa*.

- South African Federation of Burial Societies (SAFOBS) (2005), 2005 *Burial society survey report*.

- Stewart B., Associates & Masimanyane Management Consultancy (2005), *Report on the status and institutional development needs of the cooperative housing sector*, Unpublished report commissioned by Social Housing Foundation.

- Tamana D., Cooperative Centre and National Cooperative Association of SA (2003), *A survey of Eastern Cape cooperatives*, Unpublished report commissioned by Department of Labour.

- Thompson R. J. & Posel D. B. (2002), *The management of risk by burial societies in South Africa*, Actuarial Society of SA.

- Yebo Cooperative Ltd (2005), *Report*.

Chapter Thirteen – The Senegalese Cooperative Movement: Embedded in the Social Economy

by Dr. Abdou Salam Fall[1]

Introduction

In Senegal, cooperative movements formed part of a distinct social plan right from the beginning and were carried along by an ideological current that wanted to break away from the systems which had dominated the working classes. In order to fully understand the way in which cooperatives have developed in Senegal, we must go back to the 1960s, when there were two conflicting ideological tendencies among the ruling elites: on one side there was the "assimilationist" tendency, whose figurehead was Léopold Sédar Senghor, the first President of Senegal, who wanted to catch up with the West, and on the other side there was the "nationalist" tendency personified by Mamadou Dia, who was Prime Minister after independence, and who wanted to lay the foundations of a socialist State. The cooperative movement was an essential lever for this nationalist system that would benefit the working classes.

The nationalist tendency advocated self-managing socialism, which was to take off during this period, largely as a result of Mr Dia's strategic position. It was influenced by the planning philosophy of the communist countries, and included the option of getting groups of people to organize themselves and become part of a broader view of social transformation. In doing this, the cooperatives would be cutting the ground from under the feet of the traders,

---

[1] Dr Abdou Salam Fall is a sociologist, and a researcher at the Institut Fondamental d'Afrique Noire (IFAN) at Cheikh Anta Diop University (UCAD) in Dakar. He holds a Third-Cycle Doctorate in Urban Sociology from UCAD, and a Doctorate in Economic Sociology from the University of Amsterdam in the Netherlands. His research is concerned, in particular, with economic sociology (social networks, poverty, urban economy, domestic economy, negotiating public policies, rural development, and wealth creation) and the social anthropology of development (health sociology, social policies, migrations, organizational development, and the analysis and evaluation of development programmes).

who ultimately benefited most from the economic system because of their position as middlemen in the marketing chain for agricultural products. On the input side, the cooperatives had to guarantee that their members would be able to pool their resources in order to obtain the supplies they needed, while on the output side they had to gain a foothold in the commercial network without being dependent on the middlemen. The model was accompanied by rural education and public awareness projects, and by the mobilization of groups of people involved in the process of levelling structural inequalities. This model did not have the time to prove itself, and the elite who supported it developed an approach that focused more on anticipation than participation. The cooperative initiative came to be associated with the State which had conceived it. Those with government responsibility imposed the cooperative model rather than allowing it to grow naturally. During this initial period the cooperative movement suffered as a result of the lack of autonomy in the way it was founded, despite being firmly anchored, paradoxically, in an innovative social plan.

Following the departure of Dia after he was accused of plotting a coup in 1962, the cooperative system gradually ran out of steam, despite the success of certain programmes designed to accompany the cooperatives, such as rural education, and the creation of the Ecole Nationale d'Economie Appliquée (National School of Applied Economics – ENEA), which trained middle managers in this philosophy. The cooperative movement entered a second period, from 1960 to 1980, in which its activities were confined to the distribution of agricultural inputs and the involvement of groups of people in the marketing of groundnuts. It became less anchored in ideology, and the State distanced itself from the idea of a revolutionary upsurge in the cooperative movement. Nevertheless, thanks to its associative and entrepreneurial nature, it allowed workers and small farmers to organize themselves in order to cope with economic difficulties linked to the inadequate supply of inputs, the impossibility of producing goods and services under normal conditions, the failure to satisfy essential demands for foodstuffs and other consumables, members' lack of information and training owing to the absence of specific programmes and projects and the lack of efficient networks for marketing products in optimum market conditions.

It was against this background that, alongside the rural cooperatives which seemed doomed to decline, other cooperatives emerged during the 1970s within groups of workers in the towns. The creation of the Castors housing cooperative in Dakar was a symbol of this. In the same way, cooperatives in the form of buying syndicates were started by various trades unions and organized workers' groups. During the same period, other groups emerged, in particular the non-governmental organizations (NGOs). They replaced the cooperative philosophy with community development, where the emphasis was not on pooling resources but on philanthropic intervention in development instead. This community development paradigm was not separate from the cooperative paradigm: it was a re-reading of it. The two could be superimposed on one another in order to supplement each other.

We now come to the third distinctive period in the recent history of the cooperatives, when they enjoyed a revival. The economic crisis in Senegal, culminating in the adoption of Structural Adjustment Plans – SAPs in the 1990s, triggered a revival in the cooperative movement, which was seen as a solution within the reach of those who were the victims of increasing vulnerability, in particular lack of job security, flimsy social insurance cover, and the possibility of further economic crises. The SAPs represented a new deal, because the cooperatives, which were most highly developed in rural areas, now became the self-help tool of the urban middle classes. We must not forget that the crisis of the 1990s made the middle classes much more vulnerable.

This growth in the cooperative movement occurred during the period from 1990 to 2000, which coincided with periods of decline for State-promoted housing associations: Société Immobilière du Cap Vert, (Cape Verde Property Association – SICAP), Habitation à Loyer Modéré (Low Rent Housing – HLM), Habitat Moderne (Modern Housing – HAMO). It should also be noted that most social housing programmes conducted by the national associations were only for employees in the public and private sectors. In the 1980s the provision of housing by public housing associations became expensive and very selective, leaving the working classes with only two options: self-build or cooperative organizations. The fact that the State made plots of land available to organized groups, and the success of the first cooperatives, strengthened the mutualist movement, which had achieved an excellent reputation in the housing sector, particularly in towns that were still under construction where public associations had failed to meet the demand for housing.

In other areas too, particularly as regards access to funding, the banks had proved unable to help the people involved in these projects. People therefore revived such common practices as "tontine" agreements, and various mutualist-type financial arrangements. Craft industries, fishing, forestry, and tourist promotion offices in the tourism and heritage management sector were other areas in which the cooperative system was rapidly revived, in some cases retaining the name, though it was beginning to sound rather old-fashioned. One might wonder, therefore, whether the sectoral approach and the absence of any dialogue with the social movements that were characteristic of this cooperative revival were in themselves the principal constraints on its capacity to develop, along with other sectors of the social economy, into an alternative solution, given the failure of development policies.

This paper focuses on the cooperative movement in Senegal in general, and housing cooperatives in particular, in order to measure their potential for generating employment and growth. The theoretical framework for it is based on the analysis by Norbert Elias (1987), who developed the idea of "self-restraint imposed by social constraint". The cooperatives involved in this "forced saving" (Kane, 2000) combine the following features:

- economic thinking, because of the efficiency it aims for;

- the adoption of a political stance owing to its organizational independence and the fact that it provides an alternative solution, given the shortcomings of government policies; and

- social thinking, due to its confidence-building effect as much as to the class solidarity on which it is based.

Cooperative movements are defined in the broad sense as any practices followed by people who join forces to fulfil a common need (ad hoc or long-term) in accordance with mutualist or solidarity-based procedures combining the need for economic integration with the social objective of this common enterprise.

In this contribution we first deal with the structure of the cooperatives, the accent on their institutional framework and their relationship with the State. Next, we look at the cooperatives and their financing problems. Further on we examine the impacts and constraints on the cooperatives, and in particular the ways in which they relate to the reduction of poverty, social protection and potential employment and growth generation. Finally, the paper places the cooperatives in their historical context in Senegal and examines the conditions for their sustainable growth. Some sections of this paper will focus upon the housing cooperatives in particular.

Cooperatives in Senegal: their presence, dynamics, sectoral organization, support and sustainability

The Senegalese Cooperative Plan

"Through its instructive action, cooperation educates man without uprooting him, by giving him a taste for personal initiative and a sense of responsibility, while at the same time reinforcing within him a sense of solidarity. It teaches black peasant farmers how to discover their human personality without running the risk of uprooting them." Mamadou Dia, quoted by Keita, 1975).

That was how, in the 1960s, at the start of independence, the Prime Minister Mamadou Dia defined, amongst other things, the Senegalese cooperative movement and its ideological implications. Originally, this movement, as conceived by ideologists such as Dia, drew its doctrine from three complementary sources:

- its community dimension in Senegalese society;
- its place in the worldwide organization of cooperation; and
- its connection with African socialism.

It seems that the precursors of cooperatives in Senegal had had the important ideological idea of giving a philosophical framework to cooperative action. Thus, in 1962, in order to provide a framework for cooperative action, Circular 032 established the overall strategy for turning such action into a movement and determining how it should act. That circular set out three major movements which corresponded to the three phases of the process, as listed below:

- the education phase, corresponding to the gaining of independence, a phase which was to be as short as possible;
- the generalization phase, which was longer and an important time when political awareness was gained and the Senegalese economy recovered; and
- the profitability phase, which was to be the point when the movement became mature.

Table 13.1: Structure of the Senegalese cooperatives

Name	Number	Members	Comments
Union Nationale des Coopératives d'Habitat (National Union of Housing Cooperatives)	606	150 000	+ CFA 15 billion in savings in the country's various financial institutions
Rural cooperatives	4 500 village sections and 359 rural communities	1 500 000	11 regional unions, 94 local unions, 33 'département' unions and one national union (UNCAAPS)
Union Nationale des Coopératives Artisanales, d'Art, de Productions et de Service (National Union of Craft, Art, Production and Service Cooperatives)	125	133 210	10 regional unions and one national union
Union Nationale Coopérative des Exploitants Forestiers (UNCEFS) (National Cooperative Union of Forestry Producers)	89	27 225	10 regional unions
Union Nationale des Coopératives des Eleveurs (National Union of Livestock Farmers' Cooperatives)	165	16 250	9 regional unions and one national union
Association des Unions Maraîchères des Niayes (AUMN) (Association of Market Gardeners' Unions of Niayes)	16	13 200	
Union Nationales des Femmes Co-opératrices du Sénégal (UNFCS) (National Union of Cooperating Women of Senegal)	10	15 800	10 regions, experience in health insurance, mutual health insurance companies, savings and credit
Réseau des Organisations Paysannes et Pastorales (RESOPP) (Network of Small Farmers' and Pasture Organizations)	6	15 600	Network of 6 multisectoral cooperatives in 3 regions, with 4 other cooperatives in preparation
Union Nationale Coopérative de Consommation (National Consumers' Cooperative Union)	122	12 800	Turnover of over XOF 4 billion. A regional union.
PAMECAS (credit mobilization)	1	150 000	43 funds
Crédit Mutuel Sénégal (CMS) (Senegal Mutual Credit)	1	203 000	83 funds
ACEP	1	48 000	33 funds

Source: BS/OAP, Senegal Ministry of Agriculture, 2006.

The cooperatives: structure and organization

The cooperatives were formed in the 1960s, following Senegal's independence. Today, they have three million (3,000,000) members and cover an extremely broad range of sectors. The summary in Table 13.1 shows the different types of cooperatives and the degree to which they are representative.

The table is not exhaustive: it should be noted that, in addition to the types of cooperatives listed above, there are other associative bodies which operate in accordance with the same cooperative principles. This demonstrates the broad extent of the movement, which takes the form of increasingly structured networks.

The diversity of cooperatives in Senegal: two examples of Senegalese cooperation

Example 1: Conseil National de Concertation et de Coopération des Ruraux (National Consultation and Cooperation Council for Rural People – CNCR)

As the Table 13.1 shows, the cooperative movement in Senegal is currently being reformed and expanded in the form of networks in both the urban and rural environments. Thus, we have the Conseil National de Concertation et de Coopération des Ruraux (CNCR), which is one of the spearheads of the Senegalese small farmers' cooperative movement. Created in 1997, the CNCR brings together the principal small farmers' and producers' federations of Senegal, and organizes consultation and cooperation between them. For that reason it is now a privileged partner in relations with government bodies, international organizations and other actors involved in development.

The purpose of the CNCR is to help to develop agriculture based on small farmers, so as to ensure the sustainable socio-economic promotion of family farms. In order to do this, the CNCR aims, in particular:

* to promote consultation and cooperation among its members, and to encourage partnerships between its members on the one hand and the State and other public and private partners on the other; and

* to encourage the strengthening and expansion of the Réseau des Organisations paysannes et Producteurs Agricoles de l'Afrique de l'Ouest (Network of West African Small Farmers' and Agricultural Producers' Organizations – ROPPA).

There is great diversity between the members of the Federations and Unions, as is shown in the following list:

Fédération des ONG du Sénégal (Senegal Federation of NGOs – FONGS);

Fédération Nationale des GIE de Pêcheurs du Sénégal (Senegal National Federation of Fisheries Economic Interest Groups [EIGs] of Senegal – FENAGIE/Pêche);

Fédération Nationale des GIE des Horticulteurs (National Federation of Horticultural EIGs of Senegal – FNGIE/H);

Fédération Nationale des GIE des Eleveurs (National Federation of Livestock Farmers' EIGs – FNGIEE);

Union Nationale des Coopératives Agricoles du Sénégal (Senegal National Union of Agricultural Cooperatives – UNCAS);

Union Nationale des Coopératives d'Exploitants Forestiers du Sénégal (National Union of Forestry Cooperatives of Senegal – UNCEFS);

Fédération Nationale des Groupements de Promotion Féminine du Sénégal (Senegal National Federation of Women's Promotion Groups – FNGPF);

Fédération des Périmètres Autogérés (Federation of Self-Managed Perimeter Areas – FPA) of the Senegal River valley;

Association pour le Développement de Namarel et villages environnants (Association for the Development of Namarel and neighbouring villages – ADENA);

Fédération des Producteurs de Coton (Cotton Producers' Federation – FNPC);

Union Nationale des Producteurs Maraîchers du Sénégal (Senegal National Union of Market Garden Producers – UNPM);

Fédération Nationale des Producteurs Maraîchers de la zone des Niayes (National Federation of Market Garden Producers of the Niayes Area – FPMN);

Fédération des Producteurs du Bassin de l'Anambé (Federation of Producers of the Anambé Basin – FEPROBA);

Union Nationale des Apiculteurs du Sénégal (Senegal National Federation of Beekeepers – UNAS);

Collectif National des Pêcheurs Artisanaux du Sénégal (Senegal National Collective of Small-scale Fisheries – CNPS);

Association Nationale pour la Promotion de l'Elevage du Sénégal (Senegal National Association for the Promotion of Livestock Farming – ANAPES);

Directoire National des Femmes en Elevage du Sénégal (Senegal National Directory of Women in Livestock Farming – DINFELS);

Fédération des Aviculteurs de la Filière Avicole (Federation of Poultry Farmers in the Poultry Industry – FAFA);

Regroupement des Professionnels de l'Horticulture Ornementale
  (Ornamental Horticulture Professionals' Group – REPROH);
Cadre de Concertation des Producteurs d'Arachide (Groundnut Producers'
  Consultation Framework – CCPA).

For the CNCR, the principles and actions of cooperation are based on four dimensions which structure its intervention. These are as follows:

- recognition of the State's authority in defining agricultural policies;

- acceptance of the integrity and autonomy of its member federations;

- recognition of the existence of other players in the rural development arena; and

- acceptance, by people in rural areas, of their destiny.

Example 2: Fédération Nationale des GIE d'Eleveurs – National Federation of Livestock Farmers' Economic Interest Groups – FNGIEE

Another characteristic feature of the Senegalese cooperative movement is the case of the Federations of Economic Interest Groups (EIGs). This type of association operates like a cooperative even though it is not governed by the same legal and regulatory framework. The FNGIEE was created in 1989. Its aim is to contribute fully towards removing constraints of any kind which are a burden on its members in particular and on the livestock-farming sector in general.

The FNGIEE has 12,800 EIGs spread throughout the country, with 992,000 individual members, of whom one third are women. With regard to the structure of the Federation, there is a General Assembly consisting of delegates from the regional federations (10 delegates per region), which meets once a year. The General Assembly defines policy, examines various reports by the Management Committee, decides on the admission of new members and adopts the draft budgets. The Management Committee consists of 53 members of the General Assembly, and is responsible for implementing the policies defined by the General Assembly. It meets once a quarter. Within the Management Committee there is an elected Executive Bureau which is responsible, at the national level, for coordinating all the activities of the Federation. The Executive Bureau meets once a month. In addition, there are also three technical committees which support the Management Committee in drawing up, implementing and monitoring programmes. These are: the Finance and Public Relations Committee, the

Training and Research Action and Development Committee, and the Social, Cultural and Sports Committee.

The limitations of an approach via cooperative networks

These two examples illustrate to some extent the maturity of the Senegalese cooperative movement, the fine detail of its organization and the extent to which it is representative of its sociological base. These assets are derived from the history of the Senegalese associative movement in general, with its fifty years of experience, taking forms as varied as the "navetaan" movement (football), associations of people originating from the same district or village cooperatives. The Senegalese cooperative movement should, therefore, be regarded as an extension of the associative movement which as a whole has become more valuable over the years.

In addition, being organized in the form of a network provides a high level of flexibility in the coordination and enlargement of the social base of the movement. The Senegalese cooperative movement has succeeded in carving out for itself a national dimension which makes it a political force that the political authorities can negotiate with. As a result of becoming so large and being structurally reorganized into networks, the movement has succeeded, in those sectors where it has taken action, in creating a powerful social movement.

However, it should be noted that even these advantages cannot hide serious problems in the movement. Precisely because it has taken the form of networks, the movement has serious organizational limitations in the quality and abilities of its managers in particular. When it comes to the actual hands-on running of the cooperatives, the managers are not prepared to get to grips with the management tasks that are needed in order to turn the cooperatives into a network. Operation is, therefore, dependent on proactive militants who are often out of step with the development requirements and risks involved in the cooperative movement. Admittedly, some organizations have made an effort, particularly the CNCR, which has acquired technical managers to advise it on its overall strategy. However, internal operational constraints have reduced the strategic effectiveness of their advice. The social profile of the members in general reveals low levels of training.

In addition to these structural and organizational problems in the cooperative movement, there have been other more general constraints relating to the economic crisis, which has badly affected those sectors where the cooperative movement is generally most active (housing, small-scale farming etc.). We are, in fact, a long way away from the 1960s and 1970s, when the State of Senegal pursued a very strong proactive policy with regard to the social economy in general and cooperatives in particular, especially in the housing sector. Thus the adoption of the structural adjustment programmes (SAPs) of the 1980s and 1990s forced the Senegalese Government to accept the idea of less State involvement, which had repercussions on the organization of the cooperative sector.

This political readjustment, through the SAPs, of the Government's attitude towards the cooperative movement in general and the housing cooperatives in particular can also be explained by an analysis of the process of urbanization in Senegal and its effect on the emergence of cooperatives, including in particular the appearance on the scene of new private-sector property developers.

Cooperatives and the urbanization process in Senegal

Senegal is among the countries of West and Central Africa that are experiencing an inversion of demographic trends, to the advantage of the urban centres. By 2020 the ratio of city dwellers to people living in the countryside will be about 60/40, completely reversing the current situation in the space of the next fifteen years. There are a number of factors which account for this (Fall, 2005a).

From independence until the beginning of the 1990s, the demographic structure was top-heavy, centred on Dakar, which accommodates half of all city dwellers and one in five Senegalese. In addition, there was also a slight growth in shanty towns, followed by the rapid proliferation of slums in working-class districts and in the suburbs. There was growth in those districts consisting of better-class housing inhabited by the middle classes and the better-off, thanks to mass-produced and self-build housing.

The years between 1990 and 2005 saw the development of multipolarity in urban growth, including in particular the emergence of large secondary holy cities such as Touba, the population of which passed the one million mark in 2004 and Medina Gounas in the south-east. There will be a certain amount of rivalry between these new towns and the cities, owing, in particular, to the considerable investment being made by international migrants (from the United States and European countries such as Italy, Spain, France and Belgium as well as from other African countries). This last group, owing to their interest in permanent housing, will stimulate unprecedented urban expansion. Then there is the town of Richard Toll, where the sugar-cane processing industry has become a major source of employment, in a valley of the Senegal River currently under development, leading to new expansion in the form of major urban centres around St Louis, the capital of the northern region.

Elsewhere Mboro, in the Thiès région, is benefiting from the arrival of Industries Chimiques du Sénégal (Senegal Chemical Industries – ICS) which is an important source of new jobs. These economic opportunities have stimulated growth in this area, which has seen an influx of thousands of workers setting up homes in the vicinity of the factory.

In general, Senegalese urban architecture is set to undergo radical change in the form of major investment programmes in planned building projects which are replacing anarchic, informal housing, for example in Thiès, Dakar, Touba, Kebemer, the planned new town of Diamniadio and the improvement zones in various cities. In urban areas, the socio-economic composition of each district is more or less homogenous, giving certain suburban areas an air of being second-best, so that some social groups feel excluded from the advantages of living in the city.

One of the most striking phenomena today is that urban and rural areas are not as different as they might seem. Despite the poor infrastructure (roads, equipment, small and medium-sized industries), there are both material connections and various kinds of flows in both directions. There are more hybridization factors than major differences. Such hybridizations act as bridges reflecting reciprocal influences and continuities. The unemployed in the cities are not migrants from rural areas. Nor do socially excluded people in urban areas originate only from among rural people living in the towns. Cities generate their own excluded. The proportion of urban growth attributable to migrants is relatively small compared with the effects of natural growth in the populations of the towns. Of the migrants in large cities such as Dakar, most come from small towns and secondary towns. The myth of cities thrown into confusion by a migrant culture which is at odds with the city dwellers' civilizing values is fading, giving way to a structure of inequality which is based on access to resources and power within the city itself.

This background of profound change in the Senegalese urban structure makes it easier for us to understand the process by which the cooperative movement emerged in Senegal and the various ups and downs which it has experienced.

The emergence of private property investment by migrants

In Senegal there are, broadly speaking, three forms of housing cooperative: public, private and informal. Table 13.2 below attempts to make this distinction.

Table 13.2: The three types of housing cooperative in Senegal

Type	%	People involved
Public	50	Public servants working for the same department or body, e.g. teachers' union
Private	44.5	Employees of the State-supported private sector
Informal	5.5	Represented in particular by women

Property investment has played a role in cushioning the effects of the urban crisis, with international migrants and traders some of the more dynamic players. There are various issues at stake here with regard to private property investment by migrants, which is becoming increasingly important in a situation where the State cannot possibly satisfy the housing demand (Tall, 2000; Fall, 2003,). These issues are often the result of a combination of several factors. First, being a home-owner is of symbolic and practical importance, particularly in a property market where it is becoming increasingly expensive to rent. Second, investments are secure – and profitable if property is rented out. Third, administrative formalities are limited (important for migrants with a low level of education). Finally, property investment management has been made easier.

The profits from property investment are reinvested in other sectors such as, in particular, family maintenance. In Senegal investing in property is one of the prevailing trends among migrants, but unfortunately various technical, organisational and social obstacles have emerged here. Many migrants fail to take professional advice, they are unable to master technical and administrative procedures and lack institutional support and supervisory structures in relation to property investment. They also face organizational obstacles regarding partnership arrangements and obtaining additional financing, particularly when the level of investment is high. In addition, the involvement of family and (religious) brotherhoods as investment managers often causes trouble.

However, it should be noted that property investment is the result of individual initiatives, despite the existence of translocally based mutualist movements.

The emergence of private property developers, administrative delays and the inefficiency of the cooperative movement

Although the associative movement really took off in the 1970s and 1980s, thanks to the support and supervision of the State via its various social housing policies, the years between 1990 and 2000 saw the emergence of private developers, who pushed up selling prices and developed a profit-making approach. By way of example, we need only look at the regular applications for the reclassification of social housing, the ceiling for which is to be raised from CFA 20 million to CFA 30 million. Table 13.3 below shows the major trends in this new development.

Table 13.3: Selling prices for different types of houses

Type	Selling price	Tax collected by the State	%
Economy (4 rooms)	10 840 000	1 904 651	18%
Medium quality (4 rooms)	13 646 099	2 333 105	17%
Good quality (5 rooms)	26 475 598	9 468 100	36%
Luxury (4 rooms)	36 849 894	12 680 842	29%

These new trends have greatly disrupted the cooperatives and, more generally, the Government's policy of promoting access to planned housing. There are various examples of how certain policies initiated by the State have failed to deliver, including those listed below.

SNHLM and SICAP, the natural source for civil servants looking for housing, are at breaking point because of the prices being asked, which are much more than the civil servants can afford. The HAMO company has disappeared. SIPRES prices are out of reach for the middle classes. BHS, too, turns down most of the applications it receives because of "insufficient earning".

The cooperatives have been affected by this situation. In July 1995, only 30 cooperatives had been able to complete a collective project. At present, the cooperatives are supposed to have a hundred thousand (100,000) members, with savings of CFA 9 billion in various banks. Unfortunately they have managed to complete fewer than 100 collective projects. This poor performance is linked to a combination of factors, including the lengthy procedures involved. For example, Table 13.4 below gives a summary of the authorizations and formalities required for organizing a building project.

Table 13.4: Summary table showing administrative delays

Action required	Time needed
Identification of the site	1 month
Zoning certificate	1 month
Authorization of transaction	1 month
Preliminary draft of architect's plans	2 months
Preliminary construction agreement	2 months
Building permit	6 months
Plan of utilities networks	2 months
Implementation dossier	2 months
Reinforced concrete plans	1 month
Calls for tender	2 months
Approval of property programme	2 months
Approval of network plans by utilities companies	2 months
Award of contracts	1 month
Notice of start of building	1 month
Total before work begins:	26 months
Duration of work	14 months
Record of completion	3 months
Land registry office	plots of land
Sones	connection to mains water
Senelec	connection to mains electricity
TP Cape Verde	roads
Onas	connection to sanitation facilities
Zoning conformity certificate	1 month
Authorizations to split up plots	2 months
Authorizations of transactions with purchasers	6 months
Creation of individual title documents	6 months
Ten-year exemption for land with buildings	2 months
Total after construction work	20 months

There are thus twenty (20) months of administrative formalities after work has ended.

This means that a minimum of sixty months, i.e. five years, is needed to complete a housing construction project.

In addition to these administrative difficulties there are others, equally significant. Cooperative investors, which generally have low levels of savings, face difficulties in obtaining credit, with the banks charging high interest rates. The costs of acquiring building plots and connecting them to utilities networks are increasing. And, supervision of the management leading the associative movement is limited.

The role of the government in supervising the cooperatives

Since independence, the State of Senegal has been involved in the development of the cooperative movement as a means of educating the people. Thus, under the institutional system, the government plays the role of trustee, drafting legislative and regulatory texts, monitoring their application, settling and managing disputes, approving cooperative structures and implementing legislative and regulatory reforms (Sylla, 2006).

In order to achieve its cooperative objectives, the State introduced a proactive policy of promoting social housing for the benefit of the disadvantaged classes in particular. In order to do this, a number of financial, technical and spatial instruments were set up as follows:

- financial: the creation of a suitable financing structure, the Banque de l'Habitat du Sénégal (Senegal Housing Bank – BHS);

- technical: the setting up of the Bureau du Projet d'Assistance aux Collectivités pour l'Habitat Social (Bureau of Assistance to Communities for Social Housing – BAHSO); and

- spatial: the creation of the Zone d'Action Concertée (Concerted Action Zone – ZAC).

In addition to these facilitation structures a fund was also set up with the support of the World Bank to facilitate cooperatives' access to land.

A legislative and regulatory arsenal – example of the housing cooperatives

The housing laws of Senegal are hybrid in nature, having been derived from two sources: common (or customary) law and statute law. This situation is accentuated by the preponderance of unauthorized housing development in the cities of the country. Housing policy has passed through several stages.

As far as cooperatives are concerned, Senegal has capitalized on its long experience, particularly regarding housing cooperatives. That experience dates back to before independence in the 1960s, when there were self-build associations like the Castors in Dakar. Admittedly, this movement did not really take off during the first decade of independence.

Against this background, in the 1960s and 1970s a number of laws and regulations were adopted by the Government concerning State land, compulsory purchase for public use, architectural policy and the right of appropriation, which is another way in which the State can acquire land. In addition to these laws and regulations, the Zoning Code was revised, a Building Code was drawn up and a law on joint ownership was adopted in the 1980s.

In the 1970s there were accompanying measures provided by the State, including the creation of SICAP and later of the Office des Habitations à Loyer Modéré (Low Rent Housing Office – OHLM). These were two major strategic tools in the government's policy of providing social housing. The policy of access to planned housing made sizeable individual projects possible, with a cost to income ratio which was particularly advantageous to beneficiaries, i.e. CFA 7,000 to 8,000 per month compared with wages of around CFA 35,000 to 40,000. However, this success story was to be brought to a halt by a combination of two factors: the oil crisis of 1973 and the years of drought. As the crisis continued, the middle classes gradually started to resort to the housing cooperatives as a collective way to create housing.

To back up this new movement, the State established a general legislative and regulatory framework which defined cooperatives and their unions as groups of natural or legal persons of a particular type, based on the principles of union, solidarity and mutual assistance, whose members have voluntarily come together in order to achieve a common economic and social goal, by forming an enterprise which is managed democratically to their common advantage and at their common risk, and in the operation of which they actively participate.

The creation of instruments for promoting planned housing

In 1979, anxious to cushion the shocks resulting from the crises referred to earlier, the State of Senegal decided to set up the Banque de l'Habitat du Sénégal (Senegal Housing Bank – BHS), which would have greater powers than the Fonds d'Amélioration de l'Habitat et de l'Urbanisme (Housing and Zoning Improvement Fund – FAHU) created in 1976. In order to overcome the lack of experience, as well as problems to do with the management of the cooperative movement, the State of Senegal decided to set up the Bureau d'Assistance aux Collectivités pour l'Habitat Social (Bureau of Assistance to Communities for Social Housing – BAHSO) in 1986. The aim of BAHSO is to provide administrative and technical supervision for the cooperative movement.

> **Box 13.1: The Bureau of Assistance to Communities for Social Housing – (BAHSO), an example of an instrument for supervising and facilitating access to planned housing**
>
> Senegal has a population of 8 million with 40% living in urban areas. Due to the high population growth, the housing programmes initiated by real estate companies in most parts of Senegal did not succeed in meeting the demand for housing and land. This situation was worsened by the 1994 economic crisis that put access to shelter and land out of reach for most low-income households. This situation heralded the construction of temporary housing units on government or privately owned land.
>
> The BAHSO was established in 1986 within the Ministry of Town Planning and Housing in partnership with UNHABITAT and German Technical Cooperation (GTZ). BAHSO's mission is to assist the cooperative societies in the implementation of their building programmes related to accessing serviced parcels of land, housing and infrastructure. BAHSO operates on a national scale handling administrative and financial processes for purchase of land and houses, training and supervising cooperative members in building construction and ensuring popularization of new building technologies. Within the framework of a partnership between the State, donors, civic/social partners and the different actors, BAHSO has a specific approach ranging from the setting up of cooperatives, mobilization of savings, participatory design of construction-related operations to delivery of houses. From 1986 to 1994, BAHSO operated mainly in the Dakar region and expanded its activities to other interior regions of Senegal through the "Women and Housing" Programme sponsored by UNHABITAT

in 1995. Currently, BAHSO supervises over 350 housing cooperatives through Senegal's ten regions. These cooperatives have over 40,000 members and aggregate savings of about 10.6 million US dollars deposited in various banks.

BAHSO's support is based on a free and voluntary affiliation of cooperative members. In this regard, BAHSO has played a part in the construction of over 3,000 houses and acquisition of 4,500 serviced plots. The initiative is being replicated in Mali.

Other housing programmes were to emerge in 1981 and 1988, with the setting up of the HAMO property association and the Société d'Aménagement des Terrains Urbains (Urban Land Development Association – SCAT-URBAM) respectively. The State of Senegal supplied accompanying measures by providing plots of land connected to sanitation facilities by the Société Nationale des Habitations à Loyer Modéré, a support office for self-help organizations, trials using local materials, a working capital fund for social housing and a relative reduction in tax.

These incentive measures on the part of the State of Senegal substantially strengthened the associative movement, which had combined to form the Union Nationale des Coopératives d'Habitat (National Union of Housing Cooperatives), consisting of four regional unions:

- the Dakar Regional Union (more than 350 cooperatives);
- the Thiès Regional Union (45 cooperatives);
- the Louga Regional Union (50 cooperatives); and
- the St Louis Cooperative Union (32 cooperatives).

It also includes 25 cooperatives which belong to the "Femme et Habitat" (Women and Housing) network. This association was created in 1997 with the support of UNHABITAT.

Box 13.2: The experience of the Building and Housing Cooperative of the Workers of Taïba, Senegal (CCHTT)[2].

Taïba Housing Cooperative, located at Mboro, 90 km from Dakar commenced with a jump-start. After its first ordinary general meeting it had 231 members. At the beginning members contributed CFA 2,500 (approx. US$ 5) per month to a working capital fund and a monthly fee of

---

[2] Interview arranged with the help of Mr. Ibrahima Ndour, Chairman of the CCTHH, President of the Conférence Panafricaine des Coopératives (Panafrican Cooperative Conference).

at least CFA 10,000 (approx. US$ 20). It had exceeded the needs expressed collectively and individually. The collective needs were concentrated on the towns providing accommodation for workers, such as Mboro, Tivaoune and Dakar. As for individual needs, demand was mainly centred in those three towns as well, although it should be noted that members also wanted to build in the town or village where they were born. During the first five years, the investment part of the working capital fund enabled funding to be provided, without interest, for those who were close to retirement age, for projects not exceeding CFA 2 million (approx. US$ 4,000). Collective programmes were arranged for Mboro-Tivaoune-Dakar. In Dakar, for example, this working capital fund enabled 23 building plots to be acquired without interest in a "medium quality" housing area.

In addition, one of the special features of the CCHHT is the fact that, following the collapse of Senegal Chemical Industries (ICS), the first collective project in Mboro and Tivaoune, the cooperative arranged to purchase work using qualified workers which it was able to find in its vicinity or from among its own ranks. From that moment onwards, a collective ambition of "self-empowerment" was born. People could now build for themselves, so that they were no longer at the mercy of dubious entrepreneurs. The CCHHT signed confidential contracts directly with all the beneficiaries of the building that it was able to identify. It was also able to obtain equipment, and purchased a cement-mixer lorry. In order to do this, the CCHHT created an Economic Interest Group (EIG) which was later turned into a public limited company. From then on, the cooperative became the successful bidder for the contract. Now it is the only cooperative in Senegal which really builds for itself and its prices defy all competition: CFA 3,800,000 (US$ 7,600) for a house, while others are around CFA 8,000,000 (approx. US$ 16,000).

The CCHTT also introduced a system of internal insurance which made it possible to cover four deaths, where the dependants remained the owners without further formalities. As far as job creation is concerned, the CCHTT now employs, on a full-time basis, an advanced construction engineer and technician, a secretary, a driver and two caretakers. On a temporary basis it employs, for three quarters of the year, five foremen (two labourers per foreman), three masons, one form setter, one electrician and one painter. Finally, in the period from 1995 to 2006, the CCHTT succeeded in raising CFA 800,000,000 (US$ 1,600,000).

The dynamism and sustainability of cooperatives

If we compare social inclusion processes in Senegal, we can see that scope for access to employment is provided chiefly through the networks of the religious brotherhoods, which offer more opportunities to the poorer middle classes.

Recourse to and dynamism of social networks

If we look specifically at access to housing, political connections are undoubtedly the most successful kind of network. This situation shows their continuing role as vertical levers in the process of accessing housing, whereas in other areas it is horizontal solidarity which is more significant. The housing cooperatives have introduced a new dimension into an environment in which one would expect to see intervention, either on the part of the authorities or on the part of private developers. Such intervention tends to exclude certain non-earning categories.

The types of changes which cooperatives bring to housing management reveal that such vertical mechanisms are gradually consolidating horizontal connections between groups of actors who have similar living and working conditions. Housing cooperatives are the lever by which earning and non-earning categories achieve inclusion in an environment whose assets lie in the informal economy.

Another innovation is to discourage informality and give preference to legal procedures to provide access to housing. Obviously the cooperatives do not have this subversive role, because they help to perpetuate the uniform nature of the districts in which they operate, or at least their "specialization" according to the socio-economic groups which go to make them up. In other words, the cooperatives place actors or members in districts which are homogenous from the point of view of their socio-economic configuration. This type of partitioning according to socio-economic groups does not facilitate social mobility and contributes to the process of relegation which characterizes the structure of urbanization in Senegal.

In the case of religious towns such as Touba or Medina Gounas it is horizontal (associative) solidarities which have made it possible for groups of people, together with the State, to coproduce such towns. In the urban centres it is family solidarities which, through self-build projects, have created housing. The State has concentrated its intervention on roads and utilities infrastructures, whereas housing is the business of family groups, which do not really qualify as mutualist or cooperative organizations. The increasing use of cooperatives could boost spending on the construction of towns and the management of housing.

This shows, therefore, that emerging solidarities not only extend beyond relationships between members of the same cooperative, but also take the form of encouraging people to invest in the housing sector, because they can have individual ownership, and also because housing is a sign of belonging to a symbolic "space".

Housing cooperatives and residential strategies

Residential strategies are one of the most obvious ways of coping with crises. They take different forms. In some mainly middle-class districts (Parcelles, Grand Dakar, Ouakam), many people rent out their houses and actually live elsewhere. Generally, this strategy is based on the profits that can be made from letting out one's house in order to be able to manage one's household budget. Households avoid "decohabitation", with young men living with their parents for as long as possible. Some owners, in addition to renting out part of the house, offer services to their tenants (meals, washing etc.) in an effort to diversify their household income (Fall, 2005a).

Other people rent out land without buildings, allowing third parties to set up home there. In such cases the houses built are generally makeshift (Cité Baraque – shanty towns). This is not the same as selling land in areas where property rents are high and then acquiring another house for one's own accommodation in less expensive suburbs. In other cases, part of the house is sold. This involves splitting one plot of land into two parts, and also generates income from the part which is sold.

Another alternative is to rent accommodation in less expensive districts. In fact, because of land speculation, people have to retreat to the outskirts (Thiaroye, Pikine, etc.) in order to pay less. There are also cases in which people are all crammed into a single room, and share the cost of the rent. Those who are employed as caretakers, and also the holy men known as "marabouts", often live temporarily in houses which have been abandoned or which are in the process of being built. In other circumstances, people squat, thereby gaining at least breathing space before the inevitable eviction process follows its course.

One of the main problems in the suburbs of the town of Guédiawaye is illegal occupation of land and the lack of any allocation of plots. This is made worse by the fact that the suburban districts are situated in catchment basins, low-lying areas into which surface water drains from all the surrounding districts. Given the frequency of flooding, the defenceless residents have no alternative but to bank up the yards of the houses and the roads. This makes it possible to make the walls of the houses higher. The material used for these embankments varies, depending on what each resident can afford.

Another strategy is to leave the house during the flood season and return to it six months later when the water has gone down. During this time, people rent somewhere and live in reduced circumstances. This forces people to develop different ways of managing the family's living area. It explains why the street is essentially the "living room" of men both old and young, who can be found there from morning till night.

However, in the mornings, until around midday or 2 p.m., they can sleep because the bedrooms are free. At night they all go to bed late. Those who are lucky enough to have a bedroom to themselves will find it invaded by the others, who will become permanent squatters in their homes. This is particularly true in the case of adolescents. The older men remain in the town square, which becomes their meeting place and the place where they socialize. At night living rooms become bedrooms. This explains why there are so many mattresses and sleeping mats to be found in the yards during the day. The living space is thus broken up, there is no privacy indoors, and the accommodation is compromised or at best confined. Coverings for walls – or for what serve as walls – like those for floors, are makeshift or cobbled together. Equipment is inadequate and facilities have the air of being temporary. There seems to be unprecedented pollution in an environment where poor living conditions are widespread.

How the housing cooperatives are funded

Various institutions support the housing cooperatives. These include NGOs such as Habitat for Humanity, which supports the ICS cooperatives. Apart from institutional, technical and financial support from the State, the cooperatives receive very little support from donors, and largely rely on the support of their members. The majority of the latter, given their history and sociological structure, are middle-class or working-class people who find it hard to afford their membership contributions.

They therefore often seek credit from banks, in particular from the BHS, at the preferential rate of 8%. They can also obtain credit from the Direction de la Monnaie et du Crédit (Money and Credit Directorate – DMC), a process which involves benefits such as no interest and loans repayable over 48 months for amounts not exceeding CFA 2 million.

Funding generally faces serious problems as regards access to bank credit, the limited saving potential of members owing to their socio-economic profile, and the cooperatives' lack of ingenuity in canvassing donors and potential financial partners. Then there is also the fact that production costs are high and beyond the reach of the members.

Cooperatives, poverty reduction and social protection

Poverty and strategic readjustments

The adjustments that have been made in housing provide evidence of how the poor are trying to safeguard areas in which they still have freedom of action. However, they also demonstrate how such people's freedom of choice has been taken away. As Sen accurately defined it in his analysis (1992), poverty is the loss of "freedom of choice". The circuitous manoeuvres attempted by urban actors in an attempt to recover their basic right to housing reveal what Bartoli (1999) refers to as material wretchedness which of course prevents a person from achieving, for himself and his family, a life which is fully human, though this is only one facet of exclusion among many others.

Poverty is structured on the basis of major inequalities, while the strategies adopted by the poor tend to consist of patching things up rather than finding more long-term solutions. The initiators of housing policies are not thinking ahead when they carry out schemes to make new housing areas viable, and those areas gradually become transformed into districts where housing is informal, where space is occupied in a piecemeal fashion, and where equipment is improvised or non-existent. This does not take account of the analysis by Favreau and Frechette (1996), who demonstrate – rightly – that urban poverty is first and foremost a matter of district, where macro-economic factors come together with more specifically local factors to structure or destructure environments.

The poor have not yet attacked public or private urban policies, but when they form networks to give a political perspective to their current "every man for himself" strategies, there is a risk that reactions will become revolts in an effort to drive new, more democratic dynamics in local development planning and management.

Even the ZAC (Concerted Improvement Zone) scheme, which was designed to provide sustainable solutions, did not see its first housing projects completed until more than ten years later, for only about ten cooperatives.

The cooperatives' function in cushioning against the effects of crises

Cooperatives allow their members to gain access to planned housing, to have a place to live which is regarded as a factor of success and security in the face of spiralling property prices, to combat unplanned housing, with all its problems of public health, overcrowding, insecurity etc., to carry out urban reclassification and to relocate people to other sites, ensuring better cohesion in the urban structure.

However, apart from these important achievements, the economic role of cooperatives in the fight against poverty is difficult to measure in terms of economic impact. The cooperatives have major weaknesses when it comes to keeping statistics, and studies of this kind are extremely rare or even non-existent. It should also be noted that, at a more general level, there is a lack of any strategic vision on the part of the State as regards its cooperative policy. It is surprising to note, for example, that there is no such vision at the heart of the Poverty Reduction Strategy Paper (PRSP), which is the State of Senegal's economic reference framework for the coming years. Admittedly, new laws are being developed to give cooperatives a more helpful legal and regulatory framework, but these laws do not appear to form part of a globally coherent political vision.

Recently, we have seen the emergence of alliances specifically intended to combat poverty. Cooperatives do play a leading role in this. This is the case, for example, with the Réseau Sénégalais de Formation et de Renforcement des Capacités des Coopératives et Associations par l'Entreprenariat Coopératif (Senegalese Network for Training and Strengthening the Capacities of Cooperatives and Associations by Cooperative Entrepreneurship) FORCE-LCP-ILO. This network consists of four large leading cooperatives, four groups of affiliated trades unions, three civil society associations, the State, represented by the Ministry of Agriculture and Water Resources' office for monitoring self-help organizations, and the ILO.

Box 13.3: Cooperatives and women's strategies – The example of Enda Rup

This programme forms part of the implementation of the National Housing Plan, particularly the application of Chapter 7 of Agenda 21 and the Guiding Principles of Habitat International Coalition.

The programme began with a pilot project, the Women's Housing Cooperative of Grand Yoff, a working-class district in the inner suburbs of Dakar. The families who had set up home there were tenants and had no legal status. The district had a high rate of population growth and a lack of housing. At the beginning of an Enda project for a savings and credit bank set up with a group of women from the district, concern arose over their housing conditions. A large part of the women's savings was set aside for the purpose of obtaining suitable housing. This women's group from Grand Yoff had over 20,000 members.

With the support of Enda, which acted as negotiator with the government authorities, they obtained 1.5 ha of land situated in another district in the suburbs of Dakar. This was State-owned land in a Concerted Improvement Zone (ZAC). It was divided into 70 plots. This ZAC was divided up into several areas belonging to fourteen cooperatives from various places. In order to reach that stage, the women had previously, and with the help of Enda Rup and Graf, formed themselves into a cooperative so that their application would have legal status. It was the first housing cooperative formed by women originating from the disadvantaged classes. The Dakar Region has at least 400 housing cooperatives. They have formed themselves into a regional union of housing cooperatives in order to assert themselves and carry greater weight (the amount of capital saved by members for housing purposes is over CFA 7 billion), and to act as an interface between the cooperatives and the authorities. The Grand Yoff women's cooperative is a member of this regional union. In the case of this particular ZAC, the regional union is trying to harmonize its overall development by the fourteen member cooperatives concerned. On the basis of a survey, selection criteria have been established, and about 70 women have been selected to move into the ZAC. However, there is a long waiting list of women requiring housing.

An Enda inter-team structure has been set up in order to coordinate all the planned activities. This unit provides assistance regarding technical aspects, social mobilization, profitability studies and training courses.

Cooperatives and social protection

Social protection can be seen in terms of a number of different aspects, the most constructive of which are those centred on ideas of solidarity. For example, there are vertical solidarity-based systems in which stronger members carry poorer ones when it comes to establishing the share capital of the cooperative. Moreover, those who pay their statutory contributions regularly are the first to be rewarded in terms of access to housing.

Although the overwhelming majority of cooperatives do not have a social protection policy, others, by contrast, have done their utmost to develop one. For example, the ICS cooperatives set up an internal insurance scheme in order to ensure that retired members would be guaranteed housing.

Such forms of internal solidarity are found elsewhere too. BAHSO, for example, set up a working capital fund to help certain members of the cooperatives, in order to avoid delay in the procedures for granting land, servicing it and gaining access to housing. The fund is thus compensatory, and enables the cooperative to cope with emergencies and unforeseen difficulties.

Potential for employment generation and possible constraints

In Senegal, the vast majority of cooperatives, especially housing cooperatives, do not have an employment policy. As a general rule, it is the chairman and permanent members who take on the responsibility of ensuring that the cooperative operates effectively.

The cooperative movement occupies an important place in the Senegalese economy. As far as turnover is concerned, we can measure its economic impact and, incidentally, its importance in combating poverty. Several billion CFA francs are generated annually in a wide range of activities, such as the marketing of groundnuts, arable products, vegetables, fruit and livestock products. For example, the housing cooperatives have deposited CFA 15 billion in various banks within the country. As for the consumer cooperatives, they have a turnover of more than CFA 3 billion. Along the same lines, the recently created Union Nationale des Femmes Coopératrices (National Union of Cooperating Women) has more than 25,000 members and carries out several socio-economic activities on a broad social scale in order to combat poverty and underemployment.

In addition, and indirectly, cooperatives contribute towards combating unemployment and underemployment. A developer or businessman who is engaged in building housing uses a sizeable number of workers. If we look, for example, at the case of the housing cooperatives, we can estimate that each cooperative may potentially employ three to five permanent staff and between 15 and 20 temporary staff, in other words it can create 18 to 25 jobs. If we look at the 606 housing cooperatives which form the Union Nationale des Coopératives d'Habitat (National Union of Housing Cooperatives – UNCH), then potentially the Union is capable of employing over 15,000 people annually, not to mention its savings that are estimated at CFA 15 billion (Source: IFAN estimate, 2006).

As we have seen, the cooperative movement emerged as a result of the Senegalese State's proactive policy in supporting it with legislation and regulations. Today, it has to be admitted that the objectives assigned to the cooperative movement are far from having been achieved, owing to the various constraints which hamper it.

- *Constraints relating to land*
  One of the constraints is still to do with State-owned land, which should have been able to be reclassified and redistributed to individuals and to collective programmes (cooperatives). At present, for example, property developers are no longer given preferential treatment. Housing cooperatives are experiencing enormous difficulties in gaining access to land, because there are no reserves of land available, accessible and connected to the utilities networks. As a result, cooperatives are obliged to acquire inaccessible land and to take on the servicing costs, which pushes up the cost of the housing they provide.

- *Constraints relating to town planning and unregulated occupation*
  Despite the efforts made by the authorities in favour of towns, in the form of the Urban Planning Framework Plan, it is evident that these have not been followed up with the implementation of a consistent policy of urban development, hence the proliferation of shanty towns and of vulnerable and improvised housing.

- *Constraints relating to the funding of urban planning operations*
  In 1976, the State of Senegal created an instrument for funding urban planning operations, in the form of a Housing and Zoning Improvement Fund (FAHU). Unfortunately, this fund is no longer supported today, owing to financial constraints and changes in the policy of the Government, which prefers to intervene via the consolidated investment

budget. This means that only nominal sums are allocated to pay for operational urban planning, and general studies of town planning and housing.

- *Constraints relating to the financing of cooperatives*
  In order to facilitate access to the houses that were built, the State set up the Senegal Housing Bank (BHS), which specialized in collecting savings and funding social housing. Because of administrative delays within BHS, housing cooperatives can no longer easily obtain the necessary funds.

- *Tax constraints*
  The State of Senegal has introduced practical tax provisions to facilitate access to housing for the disadvantaged classes. Taxes are reduced to a third for developers who concentrate on the development of social housing and a ten-year exemption for buildings used for residential purposes is applied.

  However, despite these tax incentives, there are still substantial problems owing to the various dues and taxes which affect the cost of housing. Many building materials are taxed at 20%.

- *Constraints relating to the production of building materials*
  Housing cooperatives face setbacks when importing building materials (fibrocement sheets, terracotta tiles etc.). Overall, the state is willing to use various measures to encourage planned social housing for the benefit of the disadvantaged classes. However, its policy is often inconsistent. Demand is becoming ever greater, against a background of growing difficulties in gaining access to social housing.

Conclusion

Following independence in 1960, African countries still had some way to go before reaching equitable development. Despite their youth and the crushing weight of Western colonialism, some services were free. Some countries, influenced by the countries of the East, believed that priority should be given to planned development. In Tanzania, Senegal, Mali and Benin, to quote just a few examples, forms of mutualization and cooperatives emerged, encouraged by the national authorities. The latter became interventionist and were handicapped by poor infrastructure and equipment, and there were difficulties with access to services, though to a less worrying extent than in the last three decades, which were marked by the adoption of structural adjustment programmes.

The desire to tackle the roots of the inequalities became evident among a section of the independent elites. One example here was the self-managing socialism model of, amongst others, Mamadou Dia, the Prime Minister of Senegal at the beginning of the 1960s, who endeavoured to lay the foundations for this movement among small farmers (Favreau and Fall, 2005). Rural education was used to promote democratic planning, hand in hand with similar measures on the part of central government. Production cooperatives took over responsibility for the marketing of products. They had their deposit funds, which financed their equipment requirements by means of a participative approach. They also had support at various stages from local investment funds. Rural communities were envisaged along the lines of the China-inspired model of people's communes. The cooperative movement would give rise to development cooperatives. As Mr Dia put it so passionately, "That was the touchstone of my policy, my objective: that the introduction of such a system would put an end to the trading economy ... That being so, the whole of our agricultural economy was socialized, not in the State sense, but in the self-managing sense" (1985: 120).

Dia was thus also attacking various players in the trading economy who grew rich under such a system. The working classes did not design this model, which benefited them almost without their knowledge. Everything worked as if Dia, in his position as Prime Minister and with the support of severe but bold intellectuals, was the only one who knew and did what was in the interests of the peasant-farming working classes. Self-managing socialism did not succeed in becoming established, but the model continued to be influential, despite the imprisonment of the Prime Minister by President Senghor. It took a firm hold among the farmers' organizations and NGO initiatives, which rapidly changed from emergency measures during the droughts of 1972 and 1973 and the cycle of desertification which followed, into what could be described as grassroots community development measures.

The generation that included Mamadou Dia, Père Lebret, Abdoulaye Ly, Joseph Ki-Zerbo, Cheikh Anta Diop and other leading figures in endogenous development was highly influential in assuming organic intellectual positions for the benefit of the working classes, but unfortunately this was precisely what was most sorely missed in the periods which followed in Africa. The universities distanced themselves from the social movements, with no one willing to systematize knowledge originating from the working classes.

Cooperatives in Senegal have a history, right from the beginning, of taking on this theoretical framework which was to determine their policies and development as well as their vicissitudes (African systems of socialism, mutualism, and cooperation). Today, this movement is taking off again, despite weaknesses relating to the overall legal and economic framework in which it is evolving. From the start it assumed the position of a response to the crisis which burdens the underprivileged. A typical feature of Senegalese cooperatives is the diversity of their forms of association and the representativeness of their sociological base and of the sectors in which they are active (small farming, livestock farming, fishing, forestry, housing, savings and credit, etc.).

In order to consolidate this social representativeness, the cooperatives are increasingly organizing themselves in the form of networks. This new institutional configuration could give the cooperative movement a new dimension and a place as a political player in the economic system of Senegal.

However, structural limitations and the level of technical and administrative skills of its management are greatly reducing its influence. In effect, the movement is searching for itself, and is having difficulty in establishing institutional sustainability, which clashes with its organizational framework. The institutional operation of the cooperatives reveals substantial managerial problems. This is partly the result of the increasingly diminished role of the State in supervising the cooperative movement, despite the legislative arsenal which it has at its disposal. In fact, cooperatives are increasingly facing the emergence of private developers, who are better organized and who are developing more structured capacities for mobilizing funds. In addition, there is also the Senegalese bank-finance context, which offers very few opportunities to the traditional cooperative movement.

There is very little institutional support from donors. The cooperatives fight on alone through their members, who bear the financing costs on their own. This is due to the lack of any strategic vision on the part of the State of Senegal as to the role of the cooperative movement in the country's overall economic system, as can be seen in the major strategic plans for economic development, particularly in the Ninth Plan.

Although the housing cooperatives create jobs, mainly during their house-building cycle, they were intended essentially to provide solidarity-based access to housing. Other forms of mutualization and solidarity-based financing have a greater effect in terms of generating employment, in particular their impact on the creation of micro-enterprises. Cooperatives and solidarity-based financing have very high development potential because of the size of the social groups involved in the efficient mobilization of local savings. This potential is all the more substantial in the light of the failure of government policies in various sectors such as housing, credit, savings and entrepreneurship.

The potential of cooperatives to generate growth is bound to increase, owing to the fact that the horizontal solidarities which constitute their "niche" are being accentuated by the inadequacy of public and private policies. In effect, the current crisis has caused the disappearance of vertical solutions within Senegalese society, forcing social players, whatever their socio-economic group, to join together with their peers in greater solidarity. Cooperatives, then, remain one of the forms of horizontal solidarity at the heart of social dynamics in both rural and urban areas of Senegal. Their power to integrate is based on the fact that they go beyond the social obligations of traditional reciprocity, which are tending to fade away, and take the form of new contractual relationships between players who share similar socio-economic conditions.

However, if the cooperative movement is to assert itself and provide a long-term solution, it is essential that it should network with other social movements in order to develop from a default response into a response which is at home in various social groups, and a response in which policies are produced jointly with a civil society of which they are a part, with a State which gives more impetus to its policies, and with a private sector which is more attentive to the alliances and development conditions within societies. In other words, having regained its autonomy and liberty, the cooperative movement now needs to become part of an alternative social plan and, as a consequence, regain the political planning and active citizenship which distinguish it from a random response to a failure in public policy. In this way, its potential for generating both growth and employment will be even stronger, reflecting the success of a distributive society.

Acronyms and abbreviations

BAHSO:	Bureau du Projet d'Assistance aux Collectivités pour l'Habitat Social (Bureau of Assistance to Communities for Social Housing)
BHS:	Banque de l'Habitat du Sénégal (Senegal Housing Bank)
CGI:	Code Général des Impôts (General Tax Code)
CNCR:	Conseil National de Concertation et de Coopération des Ruraux (National Consultation and Cooperation Council for Rural People)
DH:	Direction de l'Habitat (Housing Division)
DMC:	Direction de la Monnaie et du Crédit (Money and Credit Division)
DPS:	Direction de la Prévision et de la Statistique (Forecasting and Statistics Division)
EIG:	Economic Interest Group
FAHU:	Fonds pour l'Amélioration de l'Habitat et de l'Urbanisme (Housing and Zoning Improvement Fund)
FENAGIE-Pêche:	Fédération Nationale des Groupements d'Intérêt Economique de Pêcheurs (National Federation of Fisheries EIGs of Senegal)
FENOFOR:	Fédération Nationale des Organismes d'Exploitants Forestiers (National Federation of Forestry Producers' Organizations)
FEPROBA:	Fédération des Producteurs du Bassin de l'Anambé (Federation of Producers of the Anambé Basin)
FNGIE/H:	Fédération Nationale des Groupements d'Intérêt Economique Horticole du Sénégal (National Federation of Horticultural EIGs of Senegal)
FNPC:	Fédération Nationale des Producteurs Cotonniers (National Federation of Cotton Producers)
ICS:	Industries Chimiques du Sénégal (Senegal Chemical Industries)
IFAN:	Institut Fondamental d'Afrique Noire (Black Africa Foundation)
MUH:	Ministère de l'Urbanisme et de l'Habitat (Ministry of Urban Planning and Housing)
OHADA:	Organisation pour l'Harmonisation du Droit des Affaires (Organization for the Harmonization of Business Laws)

OHLM:	Office des Habitations à Loyer Modéré (Low Rent Housing Office)
PDU:	Plan Directeur d'Urbanisme (Urban Planning Framework Plan)
SCAT –URBAM:	Société d'Aménagement des Terrains Urbains (Urban Land Development Association)
SICAP:	Société immobilière du Cap Vert (Cape Verde Property Association)
SNHLM:	Société Nationale des Habitations à Loyer Modéré (National Society of Low-Rent Housing)
UCAD:	Université Cheikh Anta Diop de Dakar
UCH:	Union des Coopératives d'Habitat (Housing Cooperatives Union)
UNACOIS:	Union Nationale des Commerçants et Industriels du Sénégal (National Union of Merchants and Industrialists of Senegal)
UNCAS:	Union Nationale des Coopératives Agricoles du Sénégal (National Union of Agricultural Cooperatives of Senegal)
UNCES:	Union Nationale des Coopératives d'Eleveurs du Sénégal (National Union of Cooperatives of Stockbreeders of Senegal)
UNDP:	United Nations Development Programme
UPT:	Unité de Planification Technique (Technical Planning Unit)
ZAC:	Zone d'Action Concertée (Concerted Action Zone)

Bibliography

- Bartoli H. (1999), *Repenser le developpment, en finir avec la pauvrete*, Unesco/Economica, Paris

- Desroche H. (1964), *Coopération et développement: mouvement coopératif et stratégie de développement*, Paris, PUF.

- Dia M. (1952), 'Contribution à l'étude du mouvement coopératif en Afrique Noire?', *Présence Africaine*, 3rd edition, Paris.

- Dia M. (1985), *Mémoires d'un militant du tiers-Monde. Si mémoire ne ment …*, PULISUD, Paris.

- Elias N. (1987), *La société des individus, Editions Fayard*, 1991, p. 301 French translation of Die Gesellschaft der Individuen, Suhrkamp Verlag.

- Fall A. S. (1995), 'Relations à distance des migrants et réseaux d'insertion à Dakar', in Antoine Ph. (ed.); Diop, A. B. (ed.) *La ville à guichets fermés?*, Itinéraires, réseaux et insertion urbaine, IFAN; ORSTOM, Dakar/Paris, 1995, pp. 257-275.

- Fall A. S. (2003), *Enjeux et défis de la migration internationale de travail ouest-africaine*, ILO.

- Fall A. S. (2004), *L'économie domestique en Afrique de l'Ouest*, (eds), (in coll. with O. S. Sy), Editions du CODESRIA, p. 335.

- Fall A. S. (2005a), *Bricoler pour survivre. Perceptions de la pauvreté dans l'agglomération urbaine de Dakar*, Amsterdam, Bureau Grafische Producties, University of Amsterdam, p. 245.

- Fall A. S. (2005b), *Urbain-Rural. L'hybridation en marche*, (eds) in coll. with Cheikh Guèye, Editions Enda, p. 478.

- Fall A. S., alii (1995), *Les familles dakaroises face à la crise*, IFAN; ORSTOM; CEPED, Dakar/PARIS, 1995, p. 209.

- Favreau L. & Fall A. S. (2005), 'L'Etat social dans une perspective Nord Sud. Essai d'analyse politique', *Colloque international du Réseau de Création de Richesse en Contexte de Précarité*, (CRCP), Québec.

- Favreau L. & Frechette L. (1996), 'Pauvreté urbaine et exclusion sociale: pistes de renouvellement du travail social auprès des personnes et des communautés locales en difficulté', *Cahier du Centre d'étude et de recherche en intervention sociale* (CERIS), Université du Québec en Outaouais, Série Recherche No. 5, p. 28.

- Institut Fondamental d'Afrique Noire Cheikh Anta Diop (2003), 'Figures politiques du Sénégal: Abdoulaye Ly et Mamadou Dia', *Notes Africaines*, n° 205, IFAN Major Conference Series. Université Cheikh Anta Diop, Dakar.

- Kane A., (2000) *Les caméléons de la finance populaire au Sénégal et dans la diaspora. Dynamique des tontines et des caisses villageoises entre Thilogne, Dakar et la France*, Thesis for Doctorate in Social Sciences, University of Amsterdam, p. 318.

- Keita A. B. (1975), *Le cancer du mouvement coopératif*, ENA, Dakar.

- Republic of Senegal (2001), *Lettre de politique de développement du secteur de l'habitat*.

- Republic of Senegal (BAHSO), *Guide pratique des coopératives d'habitat du Sénégal*.

- Sen A. K. (1992), *Inequality Reexamined*, Oxford: Clarendon.

- Sylla Y. (2006), *Note technique sur les enjeux sociaux et économiques des coopératives d'habitat au Sénégal*, Document multigraphié, BS/OAP, Ministry of Agriculture, Senegal.

- Tall S. M. (1998), 'Un instrument financier pour les commerçants et émigrés mourides de l'axe Dakar-New York: Kara International Exchange', L. Harding, L. Mairfaing & M. Sow (eds), *Les opérateurs économiques et l'Etat au Sénégal*. Hamburg, LIT 73-90.

- Tall S. M. (2000), *Les investissements immobiliers à Dakar des émigrés sénégalais*, Geography Thesis, Université Louis Pasteur, Strasbourg, France, p. 553.

- Union Régionale des coopératives d'habitat de Dakar (1999), *Restricted Interministerial Council held on 10 November 1999*.

Chapter Fourteen – The Invisible, but Resilient African Cooperatives: Some Concluding Remarks

by Fredrick Wanyama

Being the least developed continent on the globe, the development agenda in Africa is still very high. In the recent past, underdevelopment on the continent was partly attributed to state-led and highly centralized approaches that characterized development efforts up to the 1980s. It is for this reason that the triumph of neo-liberalism in the early 1990s was followed by the "rolling back" of the state from the development process in favour of the market and voluntary initiatives. Since the latter initiatives properly find expression in people's organizations, many development researchers and practitioners have since argued for a greater role of the said organizations in the fight against poverty. The various types of people's organizations that have been proposed to spearhead the development process may be classified into three broad categories of non-governmental organizations (NGOs), community-based organizations (CBOs) and cooperatives[1]. The latter organizations, by virtue of their nature of combining business ventures with social virtues, are increasingly being presented as a pre-condition for a successful drive against poverty and exclusion in Africa and other parts of the world[2].

Nevertheless, a survey of the literature on people's organizations and

---

[1] See, for example, Uphoff N. (1993), 'Grassroots Organizations and NGOs in Rural Development: Opportunities with Diminishing States and Expanding Markets', *World Development*, vol. 21, n° 4, pp. 607-622; Holmen H. & Jirstrom M. (1994), 'Old Wine in New Bottles? Local Organization as Panacea for Sustainable Development,' in H. Holmen & M. Jirstrom (eds.), *Ground Level Development: NGOs, Cooperatives and Local Organizations in the Third World*, Lund University Press, Lund; Michael, Sarah (2004), *Undermining Development: The Absence of Power Among Local NGOs in Africa*, Oxford: James Currey and Bloomington & Indianapolis: Indiana University Press.

[2] Birchall J. (2004), *Cooperatives and the Millennium Development Goals*, ILO, Geneva; Birchall J. (2003), *Rediscovering the Cooperative Advantage: Poverty Reduction through Self-help*, ILO, Geneva.

development in African from the late 1980s reveals a proliferation of studies on NGOs and, to some extent, CBOs while cooperatives have recorded very little interest or attention among researchers and scholars. It is not easy to explain this bias, but perhaps one reason that could account for this neglect of the cooperative sector, as has been argued in this book, is that in many countries, cooperatives more or less served the interests of the state than the ordinary members and the general public. In some countries, particularly the Anglophone ones, cooperatives originated from government policy and directives rather than people's common interests and own motivation. These institutions were subsequently engulfed into state politics as politicians either took, or influenced, their leadership. By serving as instruments for implementing government socio-economic policies, the failures of state policies found expression in the cooperative movement. To the extent that neo-liberals faulted the state for the development crisis in Africa by the end of the 1980s, cooperatives could not have got any other verdict. Reports on the failure of cooperatives, just like the state, to meet their expectations abound in the literature. The 1993 World Bank studies[3], for example, grudgingly acknowledged the potential role that cooperatives could play in the development process, but only if they were restructured and disentangled from the state and run on business principles in line with the market economy. The implication, therefore, was that as long as cooperatives operated under the wings of the government, there was little to learn about their contribution to development; and hence the apparent lack of interest in researching them.

With the liberalization of the economy in most African countries through the adoption of Structural Adjustment Programmes (SAPs) in the early 1990s, cooperatives were arguably afforded more room to run their affairs following the "retrenchment" of the state from the development scene. The previous perception that cooperatives were largely a "state writ large" could no longer hold. Yet the interest to research African cooperatives seems not to have been rekindled as evidenced by the little literature that has been generated since the early 1990s. One hardly comes across comprehensive accounts that inform the current status and functioning of the cooperative movement in any country on the continent. Indeed, the continuing debate on cooperatives as the preferred form of organization for alleviating poverty is based on expectations as defined in the principles of cooperatives rather than the

---

[3] Hussi P., Murphy J., Lindberg O. and Brenneman L. (1993), *The Development of Cooperatives and Other Rural Organizations: The Role of the World Bank*, The World Bank, Washington, D.C.; Porvali H. ed. (1993), *The Development Of Cooperatives*, Agriculture and Rural Development Series No. 8, The World Bank, Washington, D.C.

empirical functioning of these organizations in Africa. In short, the dearth of up-to-date literature that conveys the status of African cooperatives since the liberalization measures of the early 1990s is quite conspicuous.

It is in this regard that this study has made a difference. Despite the waning interest in cooperatives by donors, who now increasingly prefer the market; and the withdrawal of the state from the affairs of cooperatives relative to the past, it is evident in this book that cooperatives have not withered away; the cooperative sector is still alive in Africa and continues to play an important role in the economy. In some countries, the membership and number of cooperatives have significantly increased in the era of economic liberalization following the revitalization of the previously underperforming cooperatives and the emergence of new ones. It is estimated that seven per cent of the African population reportedly belongs to a cooperative, but some countries like Egypt, Senegal, Ghana, Kenya and Rwanda report a higher penetration rate of over ten per cent. Our data indicate that there are about 150,000 cooperative organizations in the countries under review. Among these are both large and small cooperatives; the former are mainly found in "traditional" cooperative sectors like credit and agriculture while the latter are organized around the relatively new cooperative ventures like handicraft, distribution, manufacturing and social services. For instance, one of the largest cooperatives in Africa in terms of membership is Harambee Savings and Credit Cooperative Society in Kenya with 84,920 members, but Mwalimu Savings and Credit Cooperative Society in the same country, with a membership of 44,400, probably has one of the highest annual turnover of Kshs. 711,562,812 (US$. 98,828,816). Small cooperatives can also be viable. A good example is the Rooibos Tea Cooperative in South Africa that has only 36 members, but with an annual turnover of 1,250,000 South African Rands (US$. 198,413).

This era of "cooperative freedom" has also witnessed a renewal in the integration of the sector as the previously state-imposed and non-viable federations as well as apex bodies have been rendered redundant and alternative voluntary, autonomous, strategic and more viable consensual cooperative networks are being formed. Such networks are emerging in response to members' needs in the unfolding new socio-economic environment rather than public policy demands as was the case in the past. Indeed, the emerging networks are increasingly eroding the unified cooperative model that was very common in the Anglophone countries. There are indications that the sector is drifting towards the Francophone-oriented social economy model that blends cooperatives and other group-based organizations like CBOs along socio economic motives. In line with the cooperative principles, this tendency seems to be realigning cooperatives away from being used as instruments of the state and towards their ideal form of being autonomous group-based democratically controlled enterprises. Indeed, there is a momentum towards the renaissance of cooperatives in Africa.

Nevertheless, we note that the liberalization of the economy and the subsequent government withdrawal from the management of cooperatives also triggered some negative consequences in the development of cooperatives in some countries. The cases of Cape Verde and Uganda show the collapse of many cooperatives to the extent that the sector is "starting again". In other countries, like Ghana and Kenya, governments had to step in to re-orient cooperatives to work in a liberalized environment in order to prevent the possible collapse of some cooperatives. It should, however, be emphasized that such negative consequences seem to have occurred not primarily because liberalization is bad for cooperatives, but largely due to the poor or lack of adequate preparation of the sector, which had been handed a monopoly status by the state over the years, for the challenging competition in the market economy. This is evidenced by the fact that those cooperatives that have adapted to the new environment have come out stronger than they were before the liberalization of the sector.

The loss of the monopoly status, coupled with the business-oriented demands of the market, is increasingly seeing cooperatives redesign their activities competitively. For instance, though agricultural activities remain predominant, those that are no longer profitable (like cotton and pyrethrum in Kenya) are being abandoned in favour of others (like dairy and savings and credit in the same country) that are more viable on the market. This partly explains, for example, why the continent is witnessing substantial growth of cooperatives in the financial sector. The main reason is the high demand for financial services on the market and the profit that results from such transactions. Savings and credit cooperatives are now financially stronger than the agricultural cooperatives despite the fact that the latter are slightly more than the former in some countries. Furthermore, some cooperatives are steadily shifting from being unifunctional to take on other activities as demanded by the members as well as the market. For instance, hitherto agricultural cooperatives are diversifying their activities by also venturing in the fields of savings and credit as is the case in Ghana, Egypt and Kenya. To this end, cooperative ventures in Africa are increasingly becoming market-driven and responsive to changing circumstances.

Whereas past studies correctly indicated that excessive donor funding of activities that had been imposed on cooperatives had significantly contributed to the poor performance of these organizations, the evidence in this study is that successful cooperatives on the continent have enjoyed some structured collaboration and partnership with external actors. Such partners have collaborated with cooperatives in the provision of low-interest credit for capital-intensive investments; marketing of cooperative produce, particularly through fair trade arrangements; facilitating the creation of suitable legal and policy environment for cooperative enterprises; and facilitating educational and training programmes in cooperatives, among others. It is thus apparent that donor support to cooperatives is not necessarily negative, particularly when cooperators are involved in making the decision on what kind of support they require before it is provided. Indeed, the evidence from some countries suggests that lack of such structured support had adversely affected cooperative enterprises; for such support enables cooperatives to effectively compete with private enterprises that are financially stronger in the market. The success of African cooperatives, therefore, requires both local and international networking to provide supplementary support services that would enable them to even out with the relatively stronger private competitors. It should, however, be emphasized that the emerging trend in the relationship between cooperatives and donors is characterized by consultation between the partners rather than one partner imposing the decision on the other as was the case in the past.

We have also learned from this study that the success of cooperative enterprises in Africa can significantly contribute to poverty alleviation in a number of ways. For instance, it has been demonstrated that cooperatives create employment and income-earning opportunities that enable members to pay school fees, build houses, invest in business and farming, and meet other family expenses. They also create solidarity mechanisms to re-enforce the traditional social security system, which is largely undeveloped, by setting up schemes to cater for expenses related to education, illness, death and other unexpected socio-economic problems. And by integrating the poor and the relatively well-off in the same income-generating opportunities, cooperatives also make a contribution to the reduction of exclusion and inequality.

On the whole, this study has succeeded in unveiling the African cooperative sector since the liberalization of the economy in the early 1990s. The main motivation here was to show the state of affairs of the cooperative sector in Africa in this period by indicating the presence and growth of cooperatives as well as their contribution to employment creation, social protection, voice and representation and poverty reduction. It is apparent that the cooperative sector is present, but somehow silent and, to a certain extent, timid due to the absence of vertical structures to articulate its interests and show what it is doing. Perhaps it is this lack of a voice that has seen governments, donors and even researchers by-pass the sector; thereby denying it the very much needed visibility on the development scene.

To the extent that African cooperatives survived the onslaught of the state when they were made dependent agents or clients of the former up to the early 1990s and subsequently found their way into the market following the liberalization of the economy, these organizations can be said to be silent and invisible, but quite resilient in their endeavour to improve the wellbeing of their members. We hope that this study rekindles the interest in investing in, as well as researching, African cooperatives and makes a case for the visibility of the cooperative movement on the continent.